Archaeology and the Social History of Ships

Underwater archaeology deals with shipwrecks and submerged settlements, and its finds are recovered by divers rather than diggers. But this is by no means a marginal branch of archaeology. Studying maritime history, analysing changes in shipbuilding, navigation and shipboard life, reconstructing the infrastructure of overseas commerce, underwater archaeologists provide important fresh perspectives on the cultures that produced the ships and sailors. Drawing on detailed and recent case studies, Richard Gould provides an up-to-date review of the field, and a clear exposition of new developments in undersea technologies. He also argues for the careful management of underwater cultural resources.

RICHARD A. GOULD is Professor of Anthropology at Brown University. He is the author or editor of ten books, including *Living Archaeology*, published by Cambridge University Press in 1980, and *Shipwreck Anthropology* (1983). The common theme of his research is a broad anthropological interest in the relationship between material culture and human behaviour. His original interest, ethnoarchaeology, led him to research among Tolowa Indian communities in North West California, the Ngatatjara Aborigines in Australia's Western Desert, and farmers in Finnish Lapland. He became involved in underwater archaeology fifteen years ago, and he has done fieldwork in Bermuda and Florida, and published widely in this area.

Archaeology and the Social History of Ships

Richard A. Gould

CAMBRIDGE
UNIVERSITY PRESS

PUBLISHED BY THE PRESS SYNDICATE OF THE UNIVERSITY OF CAMBRIDGE
The Pitt Building, Trumpington Street, Cambridge, United Kingdom

CAMBRIDGE UNIVERSITY PRESS
The Edinburgh Building, Cambridge CB2 2RU, UK http://www.cup.cam.ac.uk
40 West 20th Street, New York, NY 10011–4211, USA http://www.cup.org
10 Stamford Road, Oakleigh, Melbourne 3166, Australia

First published 2000

Printed in the United Kingdom at the University Press, Cambridge

Typeset in QuarkXpress Bembo [WV]

A catalogue record for this book is available from the British Library

ISBN 0 521 56103 5 hardback
ISBN 0 521 56789 0 paperback

Contents

Figures

Tables

Acknowledgements

As a relative newcomer to the field of underwater archaeology, I benefited more than usual from the help and advice of friends and colleagues as I labored on this book. Sometimes the learning experience was exhilarating, at other times it was humbling. Researching and writing this book was a voyage of sorts. First I had to get my "sea legs" and acclimatize myself to unfamiliar surroundings. In my previous academic existence I was a land archaeologist and ethnoarchaeologist. I had never been a sport diver, and, indeed, the idea of becoming one had never crossed my mind until I met Keith Muckelroy in Cambridge in 1977. We were both writing books for Cambridge University Press at that time and shared the same editor, so we wound up conversing in the waiting room (and later in the pub) more than once. It was Keith, more than anyone else, who planted the idea in my mind that underwater archaeology had scholarly legitimacy beyond the arcane details of nautical history and technology. A student of a leading pioneer of analytical and anthropological approaches to archaeology, David Clarke, he led the way in this direction with his *Maritime Archaeology* (1978). Twenty years later, Keith's intellectual influence on my book will be apparent to anyone familiar with his work, and I am grateful for the stimulation and encouragement he provided at the beginning of this voyage.

Several institutions have played a key role in aiding and supporting the efforts leading to this book. Special thanks go to the Western Australian Museum, both in Perth and at the Maritime Museum in Fremantle. Graeme Henderson, Jeremy Green, Charlie Dortch, and Mike McCarthy were unstinting in their advice and support and communicated a sense of direction and purpose for their discipline that is seldom found. This same sense of purpose was echoed by Ian MacLeod, Myra Stanbury, Pat Baker (whose "photo tips" were invaluable), and everyone else on the staff of the Western Australian Maritime Museum.

The same can be said for the Submerged Cultural Resources Unit of the U.S. National Park Service in Santa Fe. Dan Lenihan and Larry Murphy, in particular, coached me in the skills of underwater site recording and imparted a high level of professionalism while doing so. It was always a pleasure as well as a learning experience to work with the SCRU team. Their support for our research in the Dry Tortugas from 1989 to 1997 deserves special mention. I also wish to acknowledge the generous advice and support of the Bermuda Maritime Museum, most notably that of Edward Harris and his able staff, especially Steve and Catherine Hoyt. Special thanks go, too, to Jack Arnell and to the late Rowan Sturdy and Douglas Little. And, of course, none of our work in Bermuda from 1987 to 1992 would have been possible without the generous aid and support of Earthwatch and the splendid volunteers they recruited for our field projects. Certain volunteers stand out, and special mention here goes to Eugene T. Rowe and William May, who aided in the fieldwork in Bermuda and in the Dry Tortugas and also coached me in various "unsolved mysteries of the Bermuda Triangle" such as Brownie's Third Lung, underwater photography, and small-boat handling. My wife, Elizabeth, deserves special thanks, too, for her editorial expertise and assistance but, above all, for her endless patience throughout this long process.

Many individuals also contributed scholarly advice and expertise along the way. I have learned much from my students and former students, and particularly I want to acknowledge and thank Donna Souza, Brenda Lanzendorf, Rebecca Upton, Steve Lubkemann, Cathie Hall, and David Conlin. Other scholars also offered useful suggestions in general discussions or on various drafts of the manuscript. In particular, I wish to thank James Bellingham, J. Richard Steffey, Rodger Smith, Ben Finney, Nan Godet, Patrick McCoy, Nicholas Rodger, Daniel Martinez, James Delgado, Stuart Frank, Christian Ahlström, Patrick Malone, Jim Smailes, Iain Stuart, Michael Schiffer, David Lyon, Colin Martin, Fred Lipke, Ross Holloway, Ray Sutcliffe, and Fred Walker for their advice. I remain responsible, however, for any conclusions or interpretations presented in this book. Unless specifically stated otherwise, all photographs in this book are mine.

Richard A. Gould
Brown University
Providence, RI

Introduction: Underwater Archaeology as Historical Science

Underwater archaeology has evolved rapidly in recent years with the advent of new technologies in marine science and exploration – innovations that have enhanced diving capabilities and enabled researchers to dive and work underwater without the need for heavy suits and surface-supplied air, improved technologies for exploring the underwater environment, including magnetometry, underwater photography, depth-finding equipment, and the sophisticated application of acoustics and computers, and new small submersibles, remotely operated vehicles, and autonomous underwater vehicles for deepwater exploration and survey.

All of these technologies provide opportunities for improved scientific research in the underwater world, and sciences like oceanography, marine biology, and geology have clearly benefited from them. But what about archaeology? What kind of science is underwater archaeology, and what have these new technologies enabled it to accomplish? Problems still remain for underwater archaeology, however, in achieving the credibility accorded to land archaeology. Although as the pioneer underwater archaeologist George Bass argued thirty years ago, it is easier to train an archaeologist to record and excavate sites underwater than it is to train a diver to become a good underwater archaeologist (Bass, 1966: 19), underwater archaeology is still viewed by some land archaeologists as a less scholarly or scientific discipline than their own.

Archaeologists and others have tended to consider the underwater world a chaotic mix of disassociated and dissolved features lost to human view for all time. Wave action, currents, silting, deterioration due to the action of marine organisms, and other little-understood factors have been assumed to make the study of shipwrecks impossible or impractical. Until the appearance of sophisticated diving apparatus and electronic devices for locating and identifying submerged remains after World War II, approaches to recovering shipwrecks and other submerged cultural remains were characterized by relatively crude methods such as bucket dredging, grappling with hooks, claws, or nets, blasting, and pumping, all of which only created a chaos of their own by jumbling, fragmenting, and homogenizing site materials. Treasure hunters, who have a vested interest in persuading the public to let them salvage valuables from submerged shipwrecks and other sites, have fostered this "chaos theory" for their own purposes and often contributed to or created underwater chaos themselves by planting materials from other sources or by blasting shipwreck sites in search of marketable items.

Thanks, however, to work by competent maritime and underwater archaeologists and practitioners of several branches of marine science, the view of the underwater world as chaotic is no longer tenable. The challenge to underwater archaeology today is the application of scientific methods to the archaeological record in an effort to construct a picture of the human past that is not distorted by intervening natural processes and human activities. Underwater environments afford us unique opportunities for studying past human behavior, sometimes preserving complex associations of cultural remains better than they can be preserved on land. Many important issues in human prehistory may ultimately be resolved by archaeology conducted underwater.

The archaeological study of shipwrecks requires approaches common to the natural, social, and historical sciences. Most shipwreck and maritime archaeological research so far has employed scientific techniques but not social-scientific hypotheses. Historical archaeologists in both land and underwater contexts have tended to prefer descriptive, particularistic approaches that focus upon the singular characteristics of the period and place they study. This historical–particularist perspective, though legitimate, is inadequate to the task of interpreting archaeological results. Underwater archaeology must become a historical science in which hypothesis testing and historical particularism are complementary.

This complementarity of social-scientific generalization and historical particularism has the potential to move underwater archaeology toward more credible reconstructions of the human past. Controlled use of archaeological evidence according to scientifically acceptable standards has always been the hallmark of good archaeological science. The time has come for underwater archaeologists to make greater use of archaeological science to build more believable ideas about past human behavior in relation to a maritime environment. Hypotheses drawn from in-depth studies of shipping today can be tested against the evidence of ancient wrecks to produce a picture that goes beyond their immediate circumstances to include the social conditions that surrounded them. For example, accounts such as that of the wreck of the *Marine Electric* can provide insight into the contexts of wrecks of earlier times.

The *Marine Electric* was lost in a storm thirty miles off the Virginia coast on 12 February 1983, and had it not been for some unusual investigative reporting (Frump and Dwyer, 1983), its loss might have gone unnoticed. The *Marine Electric* was built in 1945 as a tanker for use in World War II and had been in commercial service ever since. It was an example of a standardized type known as the T-2, and, like the Liberty ships and other standardized types constructed in large numbers for wartime use, it had become increasingly hard to maintain as it aged. It was one of six such ships, all more than thirty-five years old, operated by Marine Transport Lines (MTL), a respected bulk-carrier operator with large fleets of more modern and better-maintained ships.

Like the other T-2s in MTL's fleet, the *Marine Electric* had been "jumboized" − that is, modified and enlarged for bulk cargoes (Fig. 1a–b).

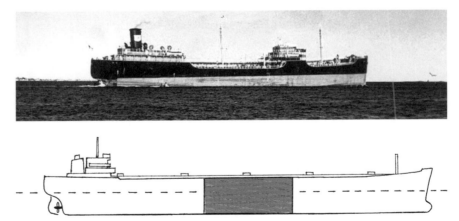

Fig 1a. Unmodified T-2 tanker leaving Boston Harbor, 1958. 1b. Generalized view of "jumboized" version of a T-2, similar to the *Marine Electric*. Shaded area shows increase of capacity by removing the forward island and stretching the hull.

Thirty-eight years old in the bow and stern, it was younger in the middle, where an extra section had been inserted. Although corrosion and wear had been noted repeatedly, especially in the hatches and parts of the outer hull, little had been done to correct them. Various temporary fixes employing epoxy, coffee-can lids, and duct tape were recorded within the two years preceding the ship's loss, but no definitive repairs were made. On its final voyage, the ship was transporting coal from Norfolk, Virginia, to Somerset, Massachusetts, when it was overtaken by a severe winter storm. It deviated from its normal route to assist a fishing boat and then turned back toward its original course in 6-meter waves. Although the wind had subsided and the *Marine Electric* had seen worse conditions, it began to settle by the bow, with waves coming over the deck onto the hatches and up to the foot of the bridge. In less than two hours the ship sank, with the loss of thirty-one of its thirty-four crew members. Although the shipowners claimed that the *Marine Electric* struck the seabed in shallow water, causing the hull to split, the survivors insisted that the ship was in at least 33.5 meters of water – a view later supported by the findings of the U.S. Coast Guard. Divers who examined the wreck later found a gap in the hull 11 meters long and 2.1 meters wide extending from port to starboard at a point about 12.2 meters behind the bow. The ship's operational and maintenance history indicated that this gap probably resulted from a small hole in the hull that had widened during the storm.

Whatever the proximate causes of the ship's loss, the question remains why a thirty-eight-year-old ship with a poor maintenance record was allowed to continue operating at sea, especially by a large shipping firm that sailed other, more modern vessels. Similar questions were raised by the author, Noël Mostert (1974), in his account of supertankers built for use during the Arab oil embargo.

Ship losses like this can often be linked to the employment of flags of convenience, whereby ships are registered outside their countries of origin to avoid the strict rules of manning, safety, and maintenance that those countries apply. Countries like Liberia and Panama, whose own merchant marine fleets are insignificant, offer safe havens for marginal shipping operators who wish to continue to use overage ships. But this was not the case for the *Marine Electric*. This ship was U.S.-registered and was expected to conform to U.S. standards. Then, as now, the United States requires that cargoes transported between U.S. ports be moved on ships built and registered in the United States and manned by Americans. The old, convert-ed T-2 ships were retained to meet these requirements. Thus they became part of what is known as the "cargo-preference" trade. MTL's aging T-2s were a second-class fleet retained specifically to garner profits in a protected trade reserved for U.S. vessels. Some of these old ships were also used for other cargo-preference trading, such as the U.S. Food for Peace shipments of grain to Haifa. Survivors of the *Marine Electric* reported how they dreaded such oceanic voyages in the ship and tried to take their vacations when such voyages were scheduled.

Most of the press reports about the loss of the *Marine Electric* focused on the proximate causes of the sinking and the ordeals of the survivors. A historical-scientific perspective requires a broader view of such a loss. By viewing it as the result of a cultural process – that is, as the product of the social institutions that produced it – the investigative reporters called attention to the socioeconomic and legal factors that ultimately caused the disaster – social institutions of long-standing that motivated shipowners to push their ships beyond their intended use-lives. One of the goals of underwater archaeology in the study of shipwrecks is to identify convinc-ing linkages between the physical associations represented by the wreck and social institutions such as those converging in the wreck of the *Marine Electric*. Risk-taking and loss are not merely events in the chronicle of mar-itime history but the products of sociocultural processes that need to be identified and explained.

Processes comparable to those affecting the *Marine Electric* certainly operated in the past, and underwater archaeology affords us direct access to materials that can be evaluated in relation to historical documents to provide explanations that extend beyond the proximate causes of the wreck. The archaeology of the wreck of the sixteenth-century Spanish Armada transport *La Trinidad Valencera* is a particularly good example of how large-scale socioeconomic factors can be linked to the physical remains of a ship. *La Trinidad Valencera* was not a warship but an armed transport of Venetian origin. Along with numerous portable artifacts, por-tions of the ship's structure, including oak planks held together with iron fasteners, were recovered and documented by an archaeological team led by the maritime archaeologist Colin Martin. Iron fasteners were quicker and easier to attach than wooden ones, making it possible for unskilled workers to construct the ship's hull. Because of corrosion, however, the working life of iron fasteners was not long – generally ten years or less. Martin (1979: 34) linked the use of iron fasteners to mass production of merchant ships by the sixteenth-century Venetians at a time when their commerce was under competitive pressure and in decline.

Venetian merchant ships then were designed for relatively intensive but short use-lives, and the reliance upon iron fasteners is comparable to the modern practice of welding instead of riveting on supertankers (Mostert, 1974: 75–77) in the interest of rapid and cheap production for short-term but intensive use. Further study of *La Trinidad Valencera*'s structure revealed that the iron fasteners were arranged in straight lines along the wood planks instead of staggered in the manner favored by builders of most wooden ships. Again, it was probably easier and faster for untrained workers to attach fasteners in straight rows, but the effect was to weaken the ship's hull by making it easier for cracks in the wood planks to travel in a straight line. Such cracks can be expected to appear in wooden-hulled ships after a few years of service at sea because of the flexing of the ship's structure, and therefore Martin and his associates suggested that this short-cut was another indicator of expediency in the ship's construction. *La Trinidad Valencera* was requisitioned for service in the campaign of 1588 and was subsequently exposed to the hazards of English gunfire and heavy seas and weather in the North Atlantic off the coast of Ireland, where it was ill-equipped to survive. Thus its loss seems to have been probably the result of decisions made during construction in the socioeconomic context of sixteenth-century Venetian commerce combined with battle, wind, weather, and geography.

The lesson of these two cases for our purposes is that past social institutions and cultural processes can be compared with those of the present and therefore even extinct sociocultural systems can be identified and studied. This book is about underwater archaeology's contribution to this effort.

1 · Interpreting the Underwater Archaeological Record

For experienced divers, the underwater world is a familiar neighborhood, and its rewards and hazards are as open to human experience as any on land. Although strikingly different from the land environment, it is knowable in the same way. Underwater archaeology is just as amenable to scientific methods and its results are measurable by the same standards as archaeology on land. The issues with regard to acquiring knowledge of the human past through archaeology are equally relevant underwater and on land. Just as land archaeology has had to distance itself from its early connections with tomb-robbers and pothunters, underwater archaeology is progressively disengaging itself from its unfortunate association with treasure hunting. Increasingly, it is characterized by the use of controlled methods of data recovery and by analytical approaches to inferences about past human behavior based on those data.

History and Archaeological Science

Underwater archaeology encompasses a broad range of submerged cultural remains. As a historical science, it is structured by many of the same sorts of assumptions and general principles that guide paleontology, evolutionary biology, and geology. Underwater archaeologists, like their land counterparts, rely heavily upon scientific methods of dating as well as upon controlled laboratory methods for studying ancient diet, technology, and ecology. One of the major questions confronting underwater archaeologists today, however, is the extent to which archaeology should also be viewed as a social science. To what extent should underwater archaeologists apply and test ideas about the human past based on concepts of culture and society more commonly associated with social sciences than with history? This question is especially significant in the case of shipwrecks that are the products of historically documented situations in the past.

Not everyone agrees on the value of archaeology in studying the human past when documentary evidence is available, and there is even greater disagreement about the relevance of anthropologically based attempts at historical analysis. Some maritime historians and archaeologists argue that is not worthwhile to engage in the archaeology of shipwrecks or related materials later than the eighteenth century, when ships' plans, drawings, and other documents and general written accounts become plentiful for the first time (D. Lyon, personal communication; Muckelroy, 1980a: 10; see also Ballard, 1987: 138). This view categorically rejects the archaeological record as a primary and legitimate source of information about past human behavior whenever written documents are available. Archaeologists often counter that the historical record is inherently biased and incomplete – that it commonly concentrates on the activities of cultural elites and major events at the expense of the everyday behavior of ordinary people, (Glassie, 1966; Deetz, 1977). The rationale that archaeology serves to overcome elitist bias is fine as far as it goes, but it provides a timid and inadequate basis for archaeological scholarship because it assigns primacy to the historical record in setting the archaeological agenda.

A more extreme version of this argument points to the self-serving uses of written histories by various elites to justify their behavior and presents archaeology as a similar form of revisionism (Shanks and Tilley, 1988: 186–208; Trigger, 1990: 370–411). Some archaeologists have proposed that archaeological science has achieved dominance by suppressing or ignoring alternative views of the past. The victims of such dominance include women, various ethnic minorities, and other groups defined by religious beliefs, low economic or social status, and generally marginal relations to mainstream Western-oriented culture. Advocates of this view argue that every cultural, ethnic, or other special-interest group has a unique view of the past that must be understood and appreciated on its own terms and accepted as valid to the same degree as archaeological science. Seen from this point of view, archaeological science is hegemonic – an extension of Western cultural imperialism and should be relegated to the status of an ethnoscience – no better for understanding the human past than, say, Australian Aboriginal concepts of the "Dreamtime" or modern creationism.

A view that is more widely accepted is rooted in assumptions about the scientifically controlled study of the archaeological record as a valid and compelling source of information about the human past. The archaeological record is an assemblage of material associations that provides circumstantial evidence about past human activities. Like the written record, it is subject to bias, but this bias is mainly of a different order from the biases that affect historical or political interpretations in that it is physical rather than ideological. Archaeologists must first identify and control for the postdepositional factors that can alter the physical associations of archaeological materials. Focusing on those aspects of past human behavior that can be reliably inferred from the archaeological record once relevant postdepositional factors have been identified and controlled means that the results of archaeology and documentary history should be compared as alternative accounts based on different kinds of evidence and assumptions. Employed in this fashion, archaeology serves as a reality check on historically received information and ideas about the past.

Much of contemporary archaeological theory is aimed at recognizing postdepositional processes and measuring their relative effects on the archaeological record. In the case of shipwrecks and submerged terrestrial sites, postdepositional factors such as sedimentation, currents, corrosion, marine growth, and mechanical disturbances due to wave action, ice, earthquakes, and volcanic activity, among others, operate to alter the condition of the deposits. About the only factor of this kind that has been mentioned consistently by maritime archaeologists is the shipworm (or "gribble") *Teredo navalis* (Robinson, 1981: 12–14), which accounts for the rapid loss of wooden structures and artifacts exposed above the siltline in most saltwater environments. The study of these processes has not always been rigorous, and therefore there is often uncertainty about which material associations were products of human behavior and which due to processes of nature.

The archaeologist Michael Schiffer (1987), for example, distinguishes between the cultural system as it existed while the inhabitants were alive and functioning as a society and the archaeological record, which contains material remains of an extinct cultural system but exists in a domain governed by the laws of physics, chemistry, geology, and biology even when human activities were present. A comparable approach to underwater site formation processes can be found in the work of the maritime archaeologist Keith Muckelroy (1978), who distinguished between "extracting filters", which lead to the loss of materials, and "scrambling devices," which rearrange, mix, or alter them. Among his extracting filters were wrecking, salvage operations, and disintegration of perishable materials; He noted, for example, how elements of wood structure at a shipwreck site may simply float away after wrecking thus removing or "extracting" these items from the archaeological record. Scrambling devices were the disorganizing effects of wrecking and the subsequent rearrangement of materials resulting from seabed movement, currents, marine organisms, storms, and other factors. Interpreting the distribution of shipwreck remains requires attention to the differential effects of these filters and scramblers.

Discovery-Mode Archaeology

Underwater archaeologists, no less than their land counterparts, have a long history of using archaeology to confirm the historicity of documentary accounts and oral traditions. On land such efforts have been identified with archaeological research aimed at demonstrating the historical reality of the Homeric epics (Schliemann's studies of Troy), the historical validity of the Bible (the Garstang expeditions search in the 1930s for the walls of Old Testament Jericho and Glueck's search for King Solomon's mines), the discovery of the "lost city" of the Incas at Macchu Picchu (described by the explorer-archaeologist Hiram Bingham); and the tracing of ancient sea routes of human migration by the ancestors of the Polynesians as represented in oral traditions (especially the studies by the New Zealand anthropologist Peter Buck and the archaeologist Kenneth Emory). Strong elements of this orientation are present in underwater archaeology as well. This tradition of seeking to confirm past events contributes to one of archaeology's most common pitfalls – the *fallacy of affirming the consequent* assuming the very thing one is trying to find out. The difficulty here is that discoveries made without the benefit of an organized sampling approach tell us nothing about those parts of the region where nothing was discovered. The absence of finds elsewhere may simply mean that potential discoveries were overlooked. These kinds of ambiguities present acute practical difficulties for archaeologists engaged in aerial or underwater surveys, where cost can be an important consideration.

Discovery-mode archaeology has been a dominant feature of shipwreck studies, and it continues to make it hard to evaluate the significance of finds. Without appropriate controls, such discoveries may provide the public with dazzling spectacles but do little to advance our understanding of the past. Major historical events have produced celebrity shipwrecks that attract media attention like iron filings to a magnet. To varying degrees, however, these celebrity ships were atypical for their time and period and by focusing on them archaeologists risk presenting a distorted view of the past. In archaeology as in all historical and scientific scholarship, the first priority is to present as clear a picture as possible of the sociocultural processes that have produced the patterning observed in the archaeological record. Recently underwater archaeologists have been paying attention to more commonplace ships, often unidentified or anonymous, and to vernacular methods of building and operating ships, and in the process they are becoming increasingly concerned with the issue of sampling and the representativeness of their finds.

Whereas the results of search are difficult to evaluate in relation to the area or domain covered, survey involving probability-based sampling will produce results about the complete archaeological contents of the area or domain. Surveys vary according to local conditions, but they always involve a framework, such as parallel lanes or a grid, in which observations can be made while controlling for factors like visibility, vision (if human observers are used) or sensing parameters (if remote sensing is used), elevation, speed, and other key variables that affect survey coverage. The logic of survey observations is reminiscent of Sherlock Holmes's conclusion about the dog that didn't bark during the night in "Silver Blaze"; it was the anomalous silence of the dog that led to the solution of the mystery. Similarly, the archaeologist should be able to say that, given the known parameters of the factors controlled during a survey, it is probable that if nothing matching the profile of the materials being sought was sighted, *it is because it was not there*. This seemingly counterintuitive ability to state with some certainty that a given area covered was empty of the items being sought gives significance to the cases in which such items were found.

Events vs. Processes

Many archaeologists and historians expend a disproportionate amount of effort in chronicling events – identifying, dating, and arranging them in sequential order. Nowhere is this more apparent than in shipwreck studies. Maritime archaeologists are fond of referring to shipwrecks as "time capsules," by which they mean that the event of a vessel's loss encompasses a moment in time that produces a unit of contemporaneity in the archaeological record. The assumption is that all objects aboard the ship at the moment of its loss were deposited at the same time. Such moments in time offer opportunities for archaeological inference that are relatively rare and much sought after on land. The site of Pompeii is probably the best-known instance, and archaeologists sometimes refer to assumed units of contemporaneity preserved in the archaeological record as examples of the "Pompeii premise." Of course, Pompeii's fame arises largely from its uniqueness and the relative rarity of such occurrences on land. In general, the best opportunities for building inferences based on this assumption in land archaeology come from undisturbed tombs and burials.

More commonly, land archaeologists encounter stratified deposits which reflect varying degrees of mixing and alteration of materials due to the operation of postdepositional factors including later reoccupation or reuse of the site. Much of contemporary archaeological theory is aimed at recognizing and controlling for these postdepositional factors. Archaeologists who address this problem soon realize that what seem to be events in the archaeological record are actually processes that operate over time. However eager archaeologists may be to arrive at conclusions about past human behavior, they cannot expect these conclusions to be convincing unless they have first dealt effectively with the physical processes that affect the association, distribution, and condition of the materials that occur together in the ground or on the seabed.

For maritime archaeologists this problem is acute in areas where multiple shipwrecks occur. These localities were usually known hazards to navigation that either were unavoidable or offered advantages that made them attractive despite the risks. Such places included the rocky ledges of Yassi Ada off the Turkish coast, the reefs and shoals of Bermuda, the coral heads and sandy keys of the Dry Tortugas in Florida, and the turbulent waters of the capes along the east coast of North Carolina. It would be unwise to assume that shipwrecks found in such areas represent simple, Pompeii-like events. What is more likely is that such areas abound in "ship smears" – that is, localities where wreckage and debris fields from different wrecks overlap and materials deposited from strandings (where the vessel escaped wrecking only after jettisoning heavy items such as guns, cargo, or ballast) further complicate the picture. Such situations more closely resemble stratified or disturbed sites on land and require the same attention to postdepositional factors.

If archaeological events derived from assumptions about Pompeii-like or "time-capsule" associations are illusory, so, too, are historical events such as the wrecking, scuttling, and even construction of ships. Upon close examination, these so-called events prove to be embedded in ongoing processes linked to social, economic, and even symbolic activities. The drama of a shipwreck focuses attention on the event, but the conditions that produced the wreck and the consequences arising from it are as significant as the event itself. Dramatic moments at sea tend to attract attention from archaeologists at the expense of the sociocultural processes leading to the ship's loss or the effects of the loss on the sociocultural system to which the ship belonged.

Nothing illustrates this problem of how event-oriented studies can overlook the processes at work better than the case of the *Titanic*. It should be noted at the outset that no archaeology has been attempted so far on the wreck of the *Titanic*. The underwater photographs and videos produced by the oceanographer Robert Ballard and his colleagues, useful and dramatic as they are, are not maps or site plans; nor has there been any systematic attempt to record the site's physical associations. The wreck of the *Titanic*, along with other deeply submerged shipwrecks, continues to present a technical challenge to such studies. The usual historical accounts of the wreck of the *Titanic* tell the now-familiar story, emphasizing the celebrities on board at the time and the drama of the surrounding events. More thoughtful accounts, such as that of Wyn Craig Wade (1986), examine the testimony given at the inquest that followed the sinking and raise questions about the behavior of the captain, who continued to steam at high speed at night through an area known to contain icebergs. Did the presence of senior White Star Line officials on board and the publicity surrounding the ship's maiden voyage encourage such risk-taking? And what about the failure to equip the ship with enough lifeboats for all the passengers? Was this deficiency a reflection of post-Victorian overconfidence in engineering, especially with regard to the ship's compartmentalization and its image as unsinkable? The inquest was an important part of the sociocultural processes surrounding the wreck involving institutional elements such as the government, insurers, and the press, as well as the surviving members of the crew and passengers. These are examples of the sorts of issues that need to be considered whenever shipwrecks are examined.

The Pitfalls of Presentism

It is tempting to view the past as leading to some conclusion known to us in the present. Philosophers of science caution against this kind of reasoning, which creates a false sense of the inevitability of the outcome and omits or ignores developments that did not lead to it. This ex post facto history is, in fact, another example of the fallacy of affirming the consequent, and underwater archaeology has been strongly influenced by it.

One variant of ex post facto history presents the past as a series of stages leading to a final result. This approach, sometimes called *unilineal cultural evolution*, can be traced to the late-nineteenth-century writings of scholars such as Lewis Henry Morgan and E. B. Tylor and the more recent work of the anthropologist Leslie White and his students. Another variant is the idea of *cultural diffusion*. At its most extreme, this theory considered human beings essentially uninventive and capable of producing cultural traits only once; the traits were then spread through culture contact like ripples in a pond. These evolutionist and diffusionist theories each had chronological implications. In the case of evolutionism, it was generally assumed that more complex cultural institutions and technologies inevitably followed earlier, simpler stages; the occurrence of so-called simple or primitive cultural institutions in recent times was considered a *survival*. For diffusionists, the spread of cultural traits from one society to another was envisioned as having produced sequential layers of institutions and technologies that provide a picture of the history of each society; traits instead of cultural stages were viewed as the survivals in this case. Neither theory has survived the tests provided by controlled archaeological research.

The principal lesson that underwater archaeologists can learn from these early anthropological gropings at theory is that the present can never be safely used as a direct guide to the human past. Maritime historians and archaeologists continue to study the ship- and boat-building traditions of different cultures, often acquiring useful information but sometimes also perpetuating the notion that technologies observed in the present can be projected backward. The problem with this presentism is that it can blind us to past situations and behavior that have no extant counterpart.

Issues surrounding the initial arrival of human beings on the Australian continent illustrate this problem. Archaeological research in Australia and New Guinea has shown that the ancestors of the modern Australian Aborigines arrived over 30,000 years ago, with possible dates for prehistoric sites extending back as much as 55,000 years (Lourandos, 1997: 87–88). Although Australia, New Guinea, and Tasmania were connected until around 12,000 years ago, when world sea levels were much lower than they are today, no land bridge has existed between Southeast Asia and Australia for millions of years. Recent bathymetric data on changes in sea levels and consequent changes in land surfaces and shorelines in this region over the past 65,000 years (Butlin, 1993: 14–34) implies that the first migrants to Australia traveled out of sight of land in watercraft of some kind. Various alternative routes at different times have been considered (Birdsell, 1977; Butlin, 1993), with a strong argument in favor of early movement by sea from Timor to somewhere on Australia's northwest coast. No modern or historical Australian Aborigines have produced watercraft likely to have been capable of making a voyage of this kind. Experimental voyages and ethnohistory suggest that reed, bark, and log canoes similar to those of indigenous Aboriginal design were capable of voyages of 25 to 60 kilometers under ideal sea and weather conditions (Jones and Meehan, 1977; Rowland, 1995), but it remains to be seen if such canoes could account for this ancient migration. This conclusion is supported by a recent attempt at experimental voyaging from Timor to Australia (Bednarick, 1998).

Although preceded by shorter voyages within sight of land as far back as *Homo erectus* (*Science*, Vol. 279, 13 March 1998), the initial settlement of Australia reflects the earliest long-distance overwater voyage known. No direct evidence of it (such as canoe remains or likely arrival sites), however, has so far been found. We can assume that the watercraft that were used for this journey were not necesarily sophisticated in their design or construction, but they had to be sufficiently large and strong to transport a viable colonizing population and then return to communicate their discovery. Nothing produced by the ethnographic and historic Aborigines definitively meets these requirements. This highlights the dangers of presentism and can serve as a caution against the temptation to extrapolate human behavior from the ethnographic present directly to the ancient past.

Intuition and Science

Unexpected connections between seemingly unrelated phenomena sometimes point the way to conclusions about archaeological findings. The maritime archaeologist George Bass offers as an example the case of the so-called ox-hide ingots of copper found as cargoes in Bronze Age shipwrecks. The received wisdom at the time was that these four-handled ingots were made in the shape of prepared ox-hides. During a visit to a foundry in Philadelphia, Bass saw copper being cast in open molds, and the surfaces exposed to air exhibited the same rough surface texture as the Bronze Age ingots. Moreover, the molds included protrusions to make the ingots easier to lift and transport. Bass concluded that the ox-hide shape of the ancient ingots was intended to facilitate lifting and carrying them, and later he found ancient Egyptian tomb paintings showing ingots of this shape being carried.

Serendipitous connections of this kind should not be ignored or discouraged, but not everyone is able to make them. However useful, intuition cannot serve as a guide to the conduct of research in underwater archaeology. One of the benefits of a scientific, analytical approach is that it provides a framework for evaluating archaeological findings apart from subjective, intuitive judgments. Intuition should always be tested by good archaeological science.

Subjective judgments often enter into the interpretation of patterns in the archaeological record, where it may be assumed that a particular pattern is unique to a specific culture-historical tradition. This is in fact one of the most difficult propositions to demonstrate when dealing with past human behavior. Patterning in the archaeological record may sometimes have more to do with the laws of physics than with any cultural construction. The mid-nineteenth-century addition to warships of structures projecting below the waterline at their bows (Fig. 2a–b) illustrates this

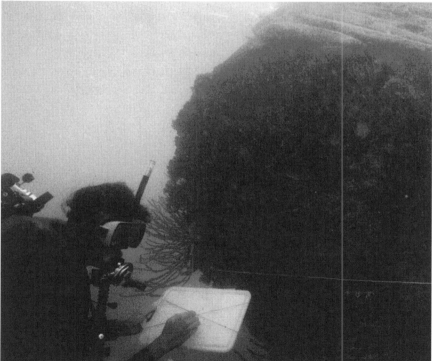

Fig 2a–b. Above- and below-water views of the ram bow on the wreck of *H.M.S. Vixen*, Bermuda.

problem. The original purpose of these structures was ramming opposing vessels during battles at sea, but their later examples were too lightly constructed to have served effectively as rams and were in fact attempts to lighten the ships' bows while under way. And, as Fred Walker, naval architect at the National Maritime Museum, Greenwich (U.K.), has pointed out (personal communication), mid- to late-twentieth-century commercial ship construction saw the widespread introduction of bulbous pointed bow extensions underwater that improved the efficiency and economy of ship movement. In short, it is possible that, on a purely trial-and-error basis, shipbuilders were realizing similar increases in efficiency as a by-product of the introduction of the ram bow. The widespread adoption of ram bows on warships during the second half of the nineteenth century may have had as much to do with these sorts of efficiencies as with a desire by the Admiralty to employ ramming tactics at sea. Before we attribute this innovation wholly to British naval tactical planning, we must be prepared to consider the more general possibility that ships built with this feature performed better with respect to speed, fuel economy, and structural integrity. The historically particular explanation in this case needs to be examined and tested against more general ones.

This cautionary review is not intended to discredit historical particularism as a general approach to archaeological materials. Not all underwater archaeologists will want to address broad social-scientific themes or to use statistically based analytical approaches to do so. But underwater archaeologists operating in a historical-particularist mode are obliged to take these kinds of critical considerations into account if they wish to see their conclusions about the human past taken seriously or widely accepted.

Materialism and Archaeological Interpretation

Archaeologists depend primarily for their inferences about past human behavior on material associations in the archaeological record. The materialist Marxist assumption that human behavior and history are structured primarily by the relations of production – that is, the technological and economic factors involved in the development of human institutions – coincides nicely with the remains found in the archaeological record. The biggest gaps in the record have to do with social and symbolic relations, which often either leave nothing behind or produce remains that are open to a variety of subjective interpretations. Marx's materialism – expressed in his monumental *Capital* (1867) – viewed changes in technology and economy as prime movers in history and coincides with the archaeologist's reliance upon material remains of past human behavior that reflect such changes. Through the work of V. Gordon Childe, this materialism became a major component of archaeological theory. The rise of economic archaeology in Europe and its extension to Australia and North America resulted directly from his efforts and those of his students for over three decades. The New Archaeology of the 1960s and 1970s also had strongly Marxist roots. Underwater archaeology offers new opportunities to examine the materialist assumptions. One example of these opportunities is the archaeological record from the Dry Tortugas, a collection of tiny sandbars and reefs lying between Florida and Cuba that is a classic example of a ship trap. At least 241 ship casualties occurred there from prior to 1800 (and probably as early as the sixteenth century) until 1969 (Murphy, 1993a). This figure suggests that ships approaching or transiting the Dry Tortugas were taking unusual risks, and documents indicate that the risks were recognized. Anecdotal information about storms in this area has been accumulating since Columbus's first voyage, and much information has been gathered more recently about weather, currents, shoals, and other elements of the local geography. Lighthouses were introduced as early as 1825, revealing an early awareness of the navigational hazards. From documents such as the letters that passed between the Tift brothers of Key West on 25 February 1860 concerning the brig *Wabash*, we can begin to understand the nature of this risk taking. Tift and Company had contracted with the U.S. War Department for the transport of bricks manufactured in Pensacola to Fort Jefferson in the Dry Tortugas and Fort Taylor in Key West, and the *Wabash* was one of its ships. It had recently been condemned by its insurers, but in their correspondence the Tift brothers agreed to continue to operate it in the Straits of Florida without insurance.

Shipwrecks documented so far in the Dry Tortugas for the period from about 1830 to 1910 contain evidence of risk taking and cost cutting that a materialist Marxist might expect to see. The Tift correspondence applied only to ships transporting construction materials to Fort Jefferson and Fort Taylor, but even if we did not have these documents we could tell from the archaeological remains of these wrecks that they were being pushed beyond their normal limits of use and were exposed to unusual hazards. They show physical signs of shortcuts in their operations and maintenance such as hull patches, deadeyes made of pinewood (an inferior material for this purpose but likely to be available during a voyage), and massive amounts of cement mastic to stop bilge leaks and fill in rotted or missing internal elements of the hull. The Dry Tortugas have proved to be a mother lode for the study of shipwrecks that can be used to test materialist–Marxist propositions about relationships between maritime technology and economy and the nature of commerce at sea during the late nineteenth century.

Stripped of the polemics that have sometimes accompanied attempts to discuss Marx as a social theorist, however, the materialist–Marxist view remains a useful explanatory approach, especially where capitalist economic relations are a dominant feature of historical traditions. This testing of the idea that material relations play a dominant role in human affairs has been one of the great, mainstream historical traditions of modern archaeology, and it is a process in which underwater archaeologists should participate.

2 · Underwater Archaeology: the State of the Art

Nearly all archaeological recording techniques represent trade-offs between the desire for precision and the practical limitations imposed by funding, time, logistics, and personnel. Underwater archaeology has available to it a wide array of tools ranging from the simple trowel to sophisticated remote-sensing devices like the magnetometer, side-scan sonar, and sub-bottom profiler, none of which were ever originally intended or designed specifically for archaeological use. As we review some of the methods of underwater archaeology, it will be important to keep in mind the minimalist principle of using the simplest tool or technique available for the task required. This does not mean taking shortcuts with controls needed to obtain convincing results, but it does warn against relying upon complex and often untried or experimental technologies when simpler or more reliable techniques are available to accomplish the same task. The reason for such caution is the destructiveness of archaeological excavation. Careless or inadequately controlled excavation will result in the permanent disruption of archaeological associations and the consequent loss of essential information about the site and how it was formed. The choice of archaeological techniques and controls to be employed at a particular site where excavation is deemed necessary is perhaps the most critical decision the archaeologist faces.

An example of what can happen in the absence of archaeological techniques and controls is the recovery of the USS *Cairo*, a Federal ironclad river gunboat that sank in 1862 near Vicksburg, Mississippi, after falling victim to a Confederate explosive mine during the Civil War. Nicknamed the "hardluck ironclad" by the historian Edwin Bearss (1980) because it was the first ship to be sunk by electrically activated mines (then called torpedoes) controlled from the shore, this ship proved an irresistible attraction for Civil War enthusiasts. Portable artifacts including swords, a revolver, blacksmith's tools, and medicine bottles were recovered from the wreck in 1959 by salvors. Attempts to lift the wreck in 1960 using salvage techniques with steel cables and a floating crane ripped the ship's pilot-house free and brought it to the surface, leaving the rest of the 53.6-meter-long vessel on the bottom. In 1965 a more ambitious attempt to raise the ship using four cranes in combination with two pontoons and seven thick cables resulted in severe damage to the ship's structure. The shipwreck was finally cut into three sections that were raised separately. Although much has been learned from the *Cairo* (McGrath, 1981), valuable information has been lost because of the uncontrolled removal of artifacts. This is especially unfortunate because the *Cairo* is the only example recovered so far of a casemated (embrasured) ironclad gunboat intended for river operations in the Civil War. It is also one of the relatively few early steamship wrecks from the period of the transition from sail to steam propulsion and from wood to iron construction. Nowadays the conduct of underwater archaeology is increasingly guided by approaches that are a far cry from those employed with the *Cairo*. In particular, *designed research* and *coordination of specialist skills* are gaining wider acceptance.

At the Western Australian Maritime Museum in Fremantle, underwater research has followed the general path established by pioneers such as George Bass and Colin Martin. The focus is on improving techniques for the excavation and recovery of ship remains and associated portable artifacts. Excavations by the archaeologists Jeremy Green and Michael McCarthy and their colleagues have been characterized by well-designed analytical approaches. These range from the use of historical sources in the Netherlands relating to Dutch East Indiamen wrecked along the Western Australian coast during the seventeenth century to the application of sophisticated conservation techniques (see Penderleith and Werner, 1971; Pearson, 1987; Hamilton, 1996) the remains of the *Xantho*, an iron steamship wrecked near Geraldton in 1872.

In a somewhat less traditional manner, the Submerged Cultural Resources Unit (SCRU) of the U.S. National Park Service, based in Santa Fe, New Mexico, has applied carefully designed research incorporating the use of specialist skills to the task of site preservation. Wildlife, both above and below water, coral reefs, historic and prehistoric structures, and basic environmental factors such as shoreline erosion and vegetation must always be considered. Nondestructive approaches place more emphasis on controlled use of regional sampling and in-situ recording than one finds in excavation-oriented archaeology. In most cases they involve leaving the wreck and its associated remains in place on the seabed as close as possible to the condition in which they were found, including replacing any items removed to the laboratory for recording and analysis.

The different approaches of these institutions are both acceptable options for underwater archaeological research, depending upon the circumstances. For example, the research on the *Xantho* led to the total recovery and conservation of the ship's engine in a location where treasure hunters and relic collectors were known to be active and no protective management was available. The engine itself was unique and significant in the engineering history of early steam and thus warranted special treatment. Prompt action was necessary to preserve it and analyze it for whatever information about steam technology and maritime social history it could yield. The nondestructive approach has worked well in the Dry Tortugas, where the Park Service can exercise its management options. One of these is facilitating public access to sites of cultural and/or historical significance. In the Dry Tortugas National Park, sport divers can visit shipwreck sites recorded and left intact on the seabed in underwater surveys. Selected shipwrecks are provided with moorings for dive boats. Divers can obtain a plastic card bearing a detailed site map and information about the wreck based on SCRU surveys and documentation to take underwater with them when they visit the site. No plaques or signs are present on the site but visitors are reminded of the park rules that forbid the removal of materials or damage to the wreck or the surrounding reef environment.

The first requirement in any archaeological research design is the framing of an organized set of expectations, or *hypotheses*, with specified *test implications*. For prehistoric or undocumented shipwrecks these expectations may be based on other archaeological findings, often resulting from land-based research. The idea that human beings arrived in Australia by watercraft of some kind during the Pleistocene is one such hypothesis. So far, no direct evidence in the form of ancient remains of watercraft or submerged sites of initial colonization has been found. The Australian coastline, however, contains many offshore islands that were part of the mainland during periods of lowered sea levels in the Pleistocene and have been cut off from the mainland for at least 12,000 years. Stratigraphic excavations at locations such as Hunter Island (Bowdler, 1984), Kangaroo Island (Lampert, 1981), and the Montebello Islands (Veth, 1993) have documented sites with evidence of sustained and intensive human occupation extending back as far as 27,000 years. Had no evidence of human occupation prior to about 12,000 years ago been found on these islands, the inferred presence of these early inhabitants over wide areas of now-submerged landscapes would have been effectively disproved. Further investigation, including the search for submerged rock-art sites and other inundated remains of these early colonists, is under way.

The testing process is no less important where historical documents are available. Written records provide a basis for constructing expectations that can direct archaeological investigations. Underwater archaeology provides circumstantial evidence in the form of material associations that can be evaluated in relation to historical accounts. The first step in any such evaluation is the recognition and control of postdepositional factors affecting site associations. Then historical documents can be used to frame expectations that can be evaluated archaeologically. One example of this approach is Colin Martin's (1972) analysis of the guns of the Spanish transport *El Gran Grifón*, sunk in 1588. Historians have questioned the competence of the Duke of Medina Sidonia, who was appointed on short notice to lead the Armada following the death of the admiral originally chosen to lead the assault, and some have blamed him for the Armada's defeat. Martin's analysis showed, however, that the types and disposition of guns aboard the wreck of *El Gran Grifón* were consistent with the defensive requirements of an armed transport as opposed to a first-class fighting ship. This demonstrated that Sidonia had behaved rationally and competently in distributing guns among the different Armada ships just before they departed – a point that historians relying upon documents alone had been unable to resolve.

In addition to emphasizing research design, underwater archaeologists are also increasingly called upon to act as coordinators for different kinds of specialized expertise at every stage of the research. This is a familiar role for land archaeologists, many of whom have effectively coordinated the efforts of zoologists, soil specialists, paleobotanists, and other skilled specialists at their sites with significant results. This coordination often extends beyond laboratory analysis after the excavation to include the use of specialists (e.g., conservators, metallurgists, ceramics experts) on-site and even in the research design phase.

Conservation

Most submerged materials are susceptible, to varying degrees and at varying rates, to deterioration, especially after exposure to air. For example, recent videotapes of timbers recovered from the freshwater crannogs of the Scottish lochs, which may date to the Bronze Age (Morrison, 1980), showed sections of the wood turning black and starting to deteriorate within a few seconds of their removal from the water. This demonstration highlighted the importance of having adequate conservation facilities close at hand whenever excavation of this kind takes place. Sometimes this treatment can be slow and costly. It has been almost forty years since the seventeenth-century wooden warship *Vasa* was recovered largely intact from the bottom of Stockholm Harbor, but conservation of its timbers is still in progress. Similar efforts are under way in Portsmouth, U.K., with the remains of the sixteenth-century English warship *Mary Rose*, requiring the construction of a special building to house the sprayers, support frames, and other devices. The conservation efforts associated with these wrecks are aimed at preservation for purposes of exhibition, and large numbers of visitors view these displays every year.

More than simply a way of preserving objects for storage or display, conservation of once-submerged materials is a research tool. An intriguing example of conservation serving the combined interests of research and preservation appears in a recent study (Carpenter and MacLeod, 1993) of iron cannons from the wreck of the Dutch East India Company armed merchant ship *Batavia*, sunk in 1629 in the Houtman Abrolhos. The cannons were treated at the Western Australian Maritime Museum using electrolysis in sodium hydroxide solutions (a technique that had previously been used to conserve the cannons from Captain Cook's *Endeavour*). Further conservation of cannons from other wrecks in Australian waters, some of which (like the armed whaler *Lively*, sunk in 1810) were studied in situ to determine the extent and depth of corrosion, resulted in data suggesting that the removal of chloride ions during the conservation process proceeded at constant rates that was linearly dependent upon the square root of the treatment time. This meant that as a plateau in the diffusion of chlorides was reached, it was time to change to a fresh solution of sodium hydroxide in the electrolytic bath. Conservation can be a lengthy process, requiring more than five years for the complete treatment of some guns and three or even four changes of the sodium hydroxide solution, but studies of the porosity of the corroded metal in each case and careful monitoring of the treatment rates for each gun in a total of twenty-six guns from ten wreck sites revealed a method for calculating the number of days it would take to reach the first and successive chloride plateaus in the electrolysis solutions. The formula, which calculated the rate of diffusion of chloride ions in each solution, was essentially reversed or "read back" to estimate the time elapsed since each cannon was exposed to the saltwater environment and the "corrosion clock" started. Further testing of this method is currently under way with a shipwreck in Scotland known to be from the Cromwellian era (MacLeod, personal communication). In this case, materials analysis in the laboratory for conservation purposes has provided a potential dating method for iron cannons and perhaps other robust objects of corroded iron from shipwrecks of unknown date.

The wreck of the *Xantho* affords us a close look at the relationship between archaeological recording and conservation. The *Xantho*, the first steamer to operate commercially along the coast of Western Australia (McCarthy, 1988), was originally constructed by Denny's of Dumbarton in 1848 as a paddle steamer. It was 32.2 meters long and operated commercially in British waters until 1871, when it was refitted as a screw steamer in Glasgow and subsequently sold to C. E. Broadhurst, a colonial entrepreneur from Western Australia. It was powered by a 60-horsepower horizontal engine similar to those produced after 1854–55 for Royal Navy gunboats, a type notable for its relatively small size (20-inch cylinder diameter and 13-inch stroke) and for being perhaps the first example of mass production in marine technology. As described in *The Engineer* for December 1897, the cylinders were comparable in size to those of the steam locomotives of that time and had a boiler pressure of 90 pounds per square inch – a major increase over earlier boilers.

Soon after the *Xantho*'s arrival in Western Australia, the ship succumbed to its advanced age and the stresses of the voyage. While steaming from

Port Gregory to Fremantle with the owner on board, it began to sink and was driven onto a sandbar about 91 meters offshore near Geraldton, where it settled in about 15 meters of water. Archaeological work at the *Xantho* site was begun by the staff of the Western Australian Maritime Museum in 1983, with major excavations and the raising of the engine in 1985. Throughout the initial predisturbance survey and excavation, conservation specialists from the museum dove on the wreck with the other archaeologists and collected data on such key variables as water temperature, salinity, pH, currents and wave action, dissolved oxygen content, marine concretions and other corrosion products, and seabed conditions (McCarthy, 1989a; MacLeod, et al., 1986).

The engine was found to be in better condition than other parts of the ship's structure and machinery. It was recovered by means of lifting bags in combination with an underwater sled pulled to shore with a bulldozer-drawn cable. Throughout the operation, controlled measurements were taken of the corrosion potential of both the engine and the remaining wreck. Once ashore, the heavily concreted engine was immediately covered with layers of wet burlap to prevent drying during its transport to the museum. Once there it was placed in a specially built steel treatment tank and the process of deconcretion was begun (Fig. 3). After only three months of treatment, a total of 1.8 tons of concretion had been removed, along with over 10 kilograms of chloride ions. The process of deconcretion continued without interruption until 1994, and the final cleaning and disassembly of the engine parts continues.

The principle governing this project is the idea of conservation and analysis as a continuation of the excavation process, and McCarthy's (1989b: 22) adoption of this approach revealed makeshift arrangements in the installation of the engine and propeller. The engine had been run in reverse during most of its colonial career, producing abnormal wear. It had no condenser and no bedplate, and the pumps could not be disconnected. A bronze valve, while well-cast and produced to contemporary standards, was found to have irregularly shaped flange holes – suggesting that expediency guided the construction of what might otherwise be regarded as one of the most advanced marine engines of its day. In short, the technology of the engine revealed through the analysis of its parts during the conservation program departed from expectations based solely on the documentary understanding of mid- to late-nineteenth-century marine steam

Fig. 3. Removal of the engine of *S.S. Xantho* from its conservation tank at the Western Australian Maritime Museum, Fremantle. Published with permission of the Western Australian Maritime Museum.

engineering and raised questions (now being explored in detail) about the social history of the use of the ship. Although conservation occurs after excavation, it needs to be considered from the beginning of the archaeological recording effort if results like these are to be achieved.

Survey

There are several kinds of underwater survey in archaeology. Each has its own role in the research program, and some are complete research programs in themselves. All underwater surveys depend upon spatial controls, and the conduct of underwater surveys in archaeology has been influenced by rapid advances in technology relating to such controls, especially in the use of electronic positioning, remote sensing, and remotely operated vehicles (ROVs). Acceptable archaeological practice nowadays places a premium on good research design in underwater survey, keeping in mind that such planning may be affected by improved technologies.

Regional Survey

Archaeologists have long employed two kinds of sampling approaches – random and stratified. Both are probability-based survey methods (Nance, 1983), and they are sometimes described as "siteless surveys" (Dunnell and Dancey, 1983) because they identify and record the distribution of observed cultural materials over landscapes without regard for a priori designations of particular localities as sites. The assumption here is that sites need to be identified by replicable scientific methods rather than assumed to be present beforehand.

Random sampling allows one to establish a sample which, on statistical grounds, can be considered representative of the area within which the distribution of items occurs. The size of the sample or, more correctly, the percentage of coverage needs to be established first. For example, an area of 100 square kilometers of seabed can be gridded into 1-kilometer squares. Depending upon time and resources available, local conditions affecting visibility, and the nature of the objects being sought (along with factors that might affect the conduct of the survey such as currents, depth, or wave action), a percentage of the total number of gridded squares will be surveyed completely to produce a representative sample of the occurrence of these materials in the entire area. If one wishes to survey 20 percent of the total area, 20 squares will be covered. The random selection of these squares can be as simple as drawing numbered squares from a hat. The distribution of cultural materials within the randomly selected samples of squares should be representative of the total gridded area and will produce patterning that can be compared with a null hypothesis; that is, the spatial patterning of the cultural materials should be significantly different statistically from a distribution produced by chance. Since nonrandom, patterned distributions of cultural materials can arise for reasons other than human activity, the possible factors producing such patterning need to be evaluated with regard to local conditions.

In 1991 a small-scale underwater survey and mapping project was carried out near the shore of Paget Island in Bermuda in conjunction with a larger research program by the Bermuda Maritime Museum at Fort Cunningham. This fort was strategically placed on Paget Island to defend The Narrows, an opening in Bermuda's fringing reef that is still the only passage for large ships. Fort Cunningham began in the 1820s as a small masonry fort but was expanded in the 1870s with the introduction of iron armor (it was the only ironclad fort built outside of England) and the largest guns ever installed in Bermuda. The earliest extant military camouflage in the world, modern gun batteries, an electrically activated minefield, and searchlight batteries were added during modifications that continued until the turn of the century. Throughout these phases of construction, a small cove close to Paget Island and immediately downslope from Fort Cunningham served as a dump for portable artifacts such as broken hardware, crockery, machinery, and a cannon. In the course of surveying and mapping this underwater locality, which covered a relatively small area with a maximum depth of 6 to 8 meters, we noted that small items such as broken pieces of glass and ceramics tended to occur in linear scatters or rows while larger items such as the cannon (Fig. 4, a typical cast iron, smoothbore gun of late- eighteenth- or early- nineteenth-century origin, probably a discard from the earliest phase of the fort) and pieces of machinery were more evenly distributed over the seabed, with a tendency for larger pieces to lie closer to shore (Gould, Harris, and Triggs, 1992).

Fig. 4. Archaeological recording at "One-Cannon Site," Fort Cunningham, Bermuda. Note that this work is being done by means of surface-supplied air rather than with SCUBA.

Although dives were conducted on relatively calm days whenever possible, strong easterly winds sometimes generated a powerful surge in this cove. The sandy bottom was easily moved by the surge, and bits of ceramics and glass were distributed and redistributed whenever one developed. Heavier items remained in place, although alternately covered and uncovered by loose sand. This sand movement scoured the exposed surfaces of these objects, keeping them relatively free of marine growth. Our underwater mapping and survey here revealed differential horizontal distributions of artifact materials according to their susceptibility to movement by the surge. Smaller and lighter pieces tended to be more mobile while larger and heavier (and/or more compact) items tended to conform to what Schiffer, Downing and McCarthy (1981) have termed the "at-rest effect" for such objects.

The debris at the bottom of the small cove at Paget Island contributed little to our understanding of the culture history of Fort Cunningham beyond a few historically identifiable relics. From collection within a 10 percent random sample of gridded squares we learned that these items were derived from all phases of the fort's history and even included more recent discards such as car batteries, forming a seabed surface deposit lacking any stratigraphic integrity. Smaller items, mainly of glass and ceramics but including iron nails and broken bits of iron and nonferrous metals, were continually being washed back into the cove and did not extend very far out onto the seabed beyond it. Many items were heavily abraded from this process of more or less constant redeposition in the loose, sandy substrate of the cove, further influencing the character of the archaeological record there.

Larger areas than this can also be surveyed, and in these cases it is often better to employ *stratified sampling*. This approach distinguishes subunits within the area being surveyed based on differences in terrain, ecology, or other factors that might affect one's ability to see and identify the intended items. For example, a heavily forested area within a larger region of open grassland or desert plains not only represents an ecologically significant subunit of the total area but also presents special difficulties with regard to the visibility of small objects of cultural origin on the surface. In such a case, the grid might be constructed differently, with smaller squares (keeping the percentage of coverage constant) to force closer observation. Or one could keep the grid size the same as for the grassland areas but increase the percentage of coverage – an approach known as *oversampling*. In either case, total observation and collection within each gridded square, arrived at randomly as before, are more intensive than in the overall survey in accordance with the terrain, ecology, or other characteristics of the subunit. Stratified samples represent different levels of random sampling nested within the larger survey area.

Stratified sampling can also be done according to the probability of occurrence of sites or objects in the survey unit. For example, if previous work had shown that sites were more likely to occur in forested areas than in grassland, one could oversample the forested unit by looking at, say, 30–35 percent of its area while sampling the grassland at a constant, say, 20–25 percent. Oversampling is a useful technique for finding more sites or objects in subunits of restricted size, especially when one also needs a larger sample of items from those subunits for comparative purposes later on. It can be difficult to make valid comparisons of the occurrence of items in comparable subunits in different areas, such as forested areas in different regions, if the sample sizes for these items are too small or too dissimilar. Oversampling is one way to solve this problem.

Parallel situations arise underwater. Surveying a coral reef covered with marine organisms and deep crevices calls for more intense scrutiny than open silt or gravel seabed, and some form of stratified sampling may be in order in such cases. Gridding is not always necessary for good sampling as long as comparable controls are used. In one of the best examples to date of a large-scale areal survey, the SCRU team embarked in 1990 on a total survey of the Dry Tortugas National Park. The survey was designed to cover 100 percent of the reef areas at a depth of 9.1 meters or less, with reduced percentages of coverage for deeper areas. Prior to embarking upon the survey, the team analyzed the database of recorded casualties, focusing on 215 relatively well-documented cases, and found that roughly 15 percent were schooners, 15 percent ships and brigs, about 10 percent barks, and 13 percent engine-powered vessels, the rest being specialized ships such as gunboats, tankers, and fishing boats. One hundred seventy-two of these vessels contained known cargoes, with lumber, agricultural products, cotton, and construction materials heading the list. Many of the vessels carrying construction materials were bound for Fort Jefferson, the largest of the postwar (of 1812) generation of forts built mainly along the Atlantic and Gulf coasts. Construction at Fort Jefferson began in the 1840s and ended in 1869, resulting in a massive but unfinished structure that covered the whole of Garden Key (Fig. 5) and, together with the much smaller Fort Taylor in Key West, contained approximately 14.5 million bricks. Fort Jefferson was like a magnet for shipwrecks during its construction. The highest frequency of casualties occurred during 1850–59, when deliveries of brick and other materials to Fort Jefferson were at their peak, but there were also wrecks of other vessels passing through the Florida Straits to Gulf ports or to overseas destinations.

Since the Park Service analysis, additional wrecks and losses have been noted in the U.S. Army Corps of Engineers records in the U.S. National Archives, but they have not yet been entered into the database. This is a regional rather than a site-specific approach to shipwreck studies, and was intended to provide an indication of the major trends and characteristics of ship losses within the roughly 259-square-kilometer area of the park where the survey was to be carried out. Loggerhead Reef and adjacent areas in the southwestern corner of the park headed the casualty list, and, not surprisingly, the team chose to begin the underwater survey there.

Fig. 5. Aerial view of Fort Jefferson, Dry Tortugas National Park, Florida.

A system of blocks containing parallel tracks or lanes with 30 meters or less between them, depending upon underwater visibility and terrain, was established. Surface positioning was established by means of a differential global positioning system (DGPS). Whereas GPS provides data accurate to about 30 meters, DGPS corrects GPS signals to achieve (under optimal conditions) surface accuracies of 2–3 meters, and submeter accuracy is anticipated as the system is improved. Geographical and archaeological data from the survey are being integrated, stored, and analyzed through the use of Geographic Information Systems (GIS) techniques (Murphy and Smith, 1995).

A small research boat trailed a magnetometer over the seabed along the tracks laid down in the survey plan. The magnetometer detects and measures subtle anomalies in the earth's lines of magnetic force that may result from ferrous metal objects such as ships' hulls and cannons and heavy concentrations of ceramics and bricks (Green, 1990: 40–47). The size of the "hit" generally reflects the magnitude of the magnetic anomaly and, hence, the size and concentration of the submerged materials causing it. One practical problem in the use of this technique is that certain highly magnetized objects (usually of modern origin, such as cars, refrigerators, electric motors, washing machines, and lawn mowers) can create disproportionately large magnetic anomalies. (The biggest anomaly by far in the survey along South Loggerhead Reef was produced by a wire milk crate.) Another subtlety in the use of magnetometers in underwater survey arises from the fact that the spatial orientation of the object relative to the sensor being trailed behind the boat can affect the magnitude of the anomaly. For example, a cannon sticking straight up from the seabed presents a smaller anomaly than the same object resting lengthwise on the surface of the seabed. Such differences were taken into account in planning the survey sampling strategy. Magnetometers are widely used in land archaeology, but what makes them especially useful in underwater research is their ability to detect ferrous objects that are heavily encrusted with marine growth or covered by shallow deposits of silt and might be hard to detect through visual inspection alone.

The track spacing of the survey plan was designed to provide sufficient overlap in the magnetometer's range of detection to ensure that minor deviations from the track by the survey boat did not result in gaps in the subsurface coverage. The lane spacing was planned to ensure, to a certain level of probability, that an object of specified dimensions and properties would be detected. This coverage was aided by the fact that normal depths in the areas of reefs and shoals are less than 9.1 meters, so there was little difference between the surface position of the boat and the subsurface position of the magnetometer sensor head trailing behind it. For accuracy's sake, however, it was important to calculate the difference between the position of the GPS antenna on the surface and the position of the magnetometer sensor. Even in areas of the park where depths reached 18.3 meters, surface and subsurface positioning were regarded as essentially identical, through for more accurate, submeter positioning or greater depths this can be a problem.

Promising magnetometer indications were inspected visually by divers throughout the survey. Wrecks were designated for documentation, which meant full-scale mapping and site recording. By 1997 the team had conducted the survey based on stratified sampling of slightly over 50 percent of the total park area at 9.1 meters or less of depth. Further surveys are to include, in order of priority, (1) 100 percent coverage of the park area at that depth, (2) areas seaward of and adjacent to the 9.1-meter depth contour, and (3) sampling outside the reef/shoal system. Since these are stratified sampling surveys, percentages of coverage will vary with the terrrain and other factors. The survey blocks are based on documentary studies that show the locations of historical ship casualties. When all areas with recorded casualties have been surveyed, new survey blocks will be laid around entrances to the main channels. The final phase of the plan calls for high-resolution surveys of anchorages. If for some reason (such as changes in political and budgetary priorities) the survey must be halted or suspended before completion, the results can be evaluated by regarding them as a controlled sampling of shipwrecks and other cultural materials throughout the park.

Shipwrecks recorded in detail so far include remains of a sixteenth-century ship of Iberian origin, probably Spanish; two wooden ships carrying cargoes of cement, paving stones, and other construction materials, probably intended for Fort Jefferson (one sunk between 1847 and 1855, the other probably lost in the late 1860s); a small screw-propeller steamer sunk at Bird Key sometime between 1857 and 1861 with a cargo of bricks intended for the fort; the *Killean*, a large three-masted iron sailing cargo ship built in Britain in 1875 and lost in 1907 on Loggerhead Reef; a large wooden sailing cargo ship of late-nineteenth-century origin at Pulaski Shoal; and a small cargo schooner of Italian origin sunk near Loggerhead Key in 1917. Also documented as a result of this survey is a massive debris field across one part of Loggerhead Reef containing the remains of multiple shipwrecks from different periods. These remains appear to overlap, creating mixed deposits, and the locality is referred to as the Nine-Cannon site. Only two of these wrecks were mentioned in the historical sources used by the Park Service to study ship casualties in the Dry Tortugas. The survey is therefore adding previously unknown shipwrecks to the inventory of known marine casualties. Survey and documentation of wrecks are continuing.

Areal surveys can be expected to produce probabilistic results expressed in one of two ways: (1) as a probability (stated in percentage terms) that all items of a particular kind were detected (with the assumption that lack of detection means the absence of those items) during complete coverage of the survey area or (2) as a percentage of the total survey area required to establish to a reasonable level of certainty that the materials observed in the sampled area are representative of the area being surveyed.

Site-Specific Survey

Predisturbance surveys, are efforts to record site features and distributions of portable artifacts on the seabed prior to excavation. This type of survey recognizes that archaeological excavation may obliterate physical associations on the surface and ensures that an accurate record is made of these associations beforehand. Site survey and recording can be accomplished in a variety of ways. These range from relatively simple but labor-intensive approaches such as baseline trilateration to electronic systems such as the Sonic High-Frequency Archaeological Ranging System (SHARPS) that can measure and record underwater positions quickly and accurately but require technical support.

Baseline trilateration is widely used in many areas and works best on more or less flat underwater terrain where the vertical relief of the shipwreck remains is not too great. The approach involves establishing a relatively level horizontal plane across which to measure. A baseline is then placed through or alongside the site, zig-zagging as needed to avoid jumping over obstacles (in order to avoid angular distortions in the horizontal measurements as a result of slanting either the baseline or the tape measure used to record trilateration points). The baseline (or each segment, if zigzags are required) is marked in units (for example, 1- or 2-meter lengths) with a special clip firmly attached to the baseline. These clips are numbered sequentially and left in place. This step is usually referred to as "setting the baseline." A baseline can be as short as 7.6 meters, as was the case for the "One-Cannon Site" at Paget Island, Bermuda, or as long as 683 meters at the "Nine-Cannon Site" on Loggerhead Reef in the Dry Tortugas, where multiple, branching baselines were used across over 319 meters of reef.

The next step involves attaching small, labeled clips (called trilateration clips) to important features or landmarks on the site on either or both sides of the baseline, making sure that they are placed with an unobstructed view of two baseline clips. Where the ship's hull remains are visible it often works best to mark points along the gunwales or the outer ends of the futtocks (relatively short lengths of curved wood joined to make up a full-length frame) first. This step can be called "clipping off" the site.

Finally, a three-person team of divers with a tape measure and a recording form records the position of each trilateration clip. One diver places one end of the tape on the trilateration clip and holds it there while a second diver runs out the tape to a baseline clip and a third diver reads off and records the distance between the two clips. Then the diver at the baseline clip swims to the next baseline clip and measures the distance from that to the trilateration clip (with the end of the tape still attached and held in place by the first diver) while the third diver records the second clip-to-clip measurement. These measurements work best if the triangle between the two baseline clips and the trilateration clip is either a right angle or an acute angle. Measurements based on angles exceeding 90 degrees tend to be inaccurate. With practice, these measurements can be accomplished by two divers.

With two measured distances from the trilateration clip to the two baseline clips and the distance between the baseline clips already known, it is a simple matter to plot the position of the trilateration clip (and its associated site feature) to scale by means of triangulation on a plan of the site. This approach can also be used to map debris fields and prehistoric habitation camps in submerged terrestrial sites. Each trilaterated point can be regarded as a kind of subdatum from which direct measurements can be taken to subsidiary features and loose items at the site.

Some remarkable work has been accomplished using this relatively simple approach. Perhaps the single most spectacular example is the trilateration plan (Fig. 6) of the wreck of the battleship USS *Arizona*, sunk during the Japanese attack on Pearl Harbor on 7 December 1941. This plan was produced in 1984 by volunteer U.S. Navy divers supervised by the SCRU team for the *Arizona* Memorial (Lenihan, 1989). Among other findings, it revealed that the battleship was blown up not by a Japanese bomb dropped down one of its funnels, as had been proposed by some observers, but by a massive explosion of ammunition and fuel set off by a bomb strike between the bow and the forward gun turret.

The SHARPS system is a more technology-intensive device that can be run by a small crew, usually consisting of one diver and a surface operator. It consists of multiple acoustical transponders arranged on the seabed at the site and connected by wires. The diver carries a probe attached by a wire to the operator's console on the surface platform. By placing the tip of the probe on an object within the field enclosed by the transponders and squeezing the trigger, the diver can send a sonic impulse that locates the object in relation to the transponders and instantly triangulates the position of the object on the screen of the operator's console, where it is also saved in the console's computerized memory. Numerous points can be accurately positioned in this way in the course of a single dive. The system generally requires technical support that is not always available in remote locations, however, and its use in underwater archaeology must still be considered somewhat experimental.

Once structural features and portable artifacts are plotted, the positions and distribution of these materials can be analyzed. Close distributional analysis of materials on the seabed works well when there has been minimal postdepositional disturbance and rearrangement. In such cases a visual inspection of the plotted data often reveals the essential patterning of the remains. For example, van Doorninck's (1967; Bass and van Doorninck, 1971) analysis of materials from a fourth-century ship at Yassi Ada, Turkey, resulted in the probable identification of the ship's galley. Stone slabs, probably used to line the hearth, were found in an area 3 meters forward of the stern that was free of stacked amphorae (the ship's cargo). An amphora was a large pottery jar with a narrow neck and two handler

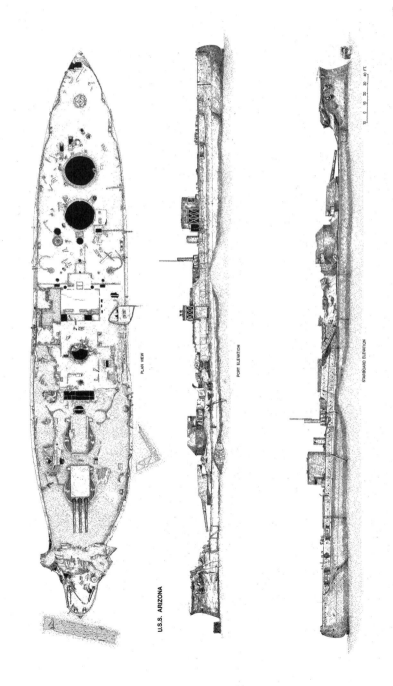

Fig. 6. Trilateration plan of *U.S.S. Arizona* wreck, Pearl Harbor, Hawaii, produced by the Submerged Cultural Resources Unit, National Park Service. This illustration demonstrates how effectively a relatively simple method like baseline trilateration can record large, complex sites. Published with permission of the National Park Service.

arranged vertically and opposite each other at the neck (Fig. 7). Below the neck the body of the jar expanded, though usually retaining a narrow shape that facilitated upright stacking alongside similar jars in the hold of a ship. Amphorae were packed closely together, often in layers, with brush or heather dunnage as protective padding. Similar distributions of tile fragments associated with cooking and iron bars – presumably from the hearth – and a relative absence of broken amphorae were recorded aft of frame 8 (as counted from the stern) on a seventh-century wreck at Yassi Ada (van Doorninck, 1967: 107–9), suggesting that this, too, was the ship's galley. Associated clay tiles in these parts of both wrecks suggested that both galleys had tiled roofs.

In cases where more severe postdepositional disturbance has occurred at a wreck site, close analysis, sometimes using statistical methods, may be the only effective way to build inferences about the ship and its loss. Muckelroy's analysis of the *Dartmouth* wreck is an example of this approach. The *Dartmouth* was an English warship wrecked in the Sound of Mull in 1690 after breaking loose from its moorings and drifting about 3 kilometers, finally grounding on gravel next to a small island (Martin, 1978). The ship settled on its starboard side and was rocked back and forth on its keel by wave action, which both wore away most of the hull and created a depression in the clays underlying the gravel. The ship's keel and

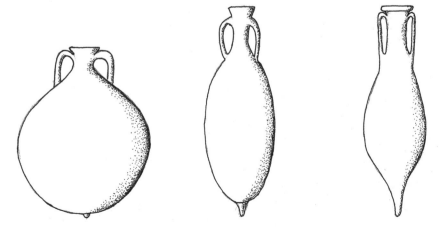

Fig. 7. "Tin cans of antiquity" – three Roman-era amphorae from the Port Vendres B shipwreck (after Parker, 1980).

deadwood (a structural element that connects and supports the keel and sternpost) and numerous portable objects settled into this depression, while the starboard planking settled into an adjacent, shallower depression.

The position of the deadwood indicated that the ship's stern was at the east end of the site. This interpretation was supported by the positions of portable artifacts that were viewed as indicators of bow and stern (Martin, 1978) on the basis of known arrangements aboard warships of that period, and three main areas of the *Dartmouth* site were identified: Area A (aft, including navigational instruments, surgical instruments, a flintlock pistol, balance weights, fine pewter tableware, fine ceramic tableware, and leaded mica for the stern windows), Area F (fore, including bosun's stores such as cordage, deadeyes, blocks, and loose sheaves and armory stores such as hand grenades, lead shot, and Highland musket shot), and Area S (starboard side, including lead scupper liners, bricks and tiles, coal and burned debris, animal bones, lead piping, and the ship's bell). The bottom topography and a line of cannons along the northern edge of the site indicated that the ship had rolled partway over onto its starboard side, causing the cannons to slide down from the upper deck to their location on the seabed.

Along with the indicator artifacts, there were also materials that were less easy to interpret. These included objects whose original locations in the ship were unclear and whose distribution on the seabed was scattered. These items were grouped into nine numbered classes: (1) pottery, (2) glass, (3) clay pipe bowls, (4) navigational instruments, (5) culinary utensils, (6) rigging fittings, (7) footwear, (8) personal possessions, and (9) lead patches. Classes 4 (navigational instruments) and 6 (rigging fittings) were included as controls, since these were already known to be associated with the stern and bow, respectively. Items belonging to these nine classes were plotted from the site map to calculate the arithmetic mean center (AMC) for the horizontal distribution of each class across the site (Muckelroy, 1978: 188–191). By plotting the AMC for each of these artifact classes in relation to its nearest neighbor, a pattern emerged that placed classes 4 and 6 at extreme opposite ends of the distribution, with the other classes clustering amidships in relative positions that may have approximated their original locations within the ship. These results were then compared with other expectations. For instance, leather footwear (7) and pottery (1) could reasonably be interpreted as more closely associated with the officers' quarters near the stern than with the seamen's berths near the bow. Other distributions, such as that of glass (2), were more problematical and will require further study.

The case of the *Dartmouth* shows how analysis can proceed beyond the more obvious distribution of structural remains and less mobile items such as cannons to a closer study of materials whose distribution must be understood statistically as a step toward making inferences about the relationship between seabed associations and spatial arrangments within the ship. Muckelroy's arithmetic-mean-center and nearest-neighbor analyses are useful approaches to the study of spatial distributions of materials on the seabed once their physical locations have been mapped and recorded.

Conventional survey and mapping techniques such as baseline trilateration work well at depths where human divers with scuba or surface-supplied air can operate safely and comfortably. But below about 12 meters many surface-supplied systems are difficult to use because the compressor on the surface may not be able to deliver usable air against the extra atmospheres of pressure at and below that depth. There are surface-supplied systems, however, that can be used to any depth that can be reached by scuba. Scuba works well to a depth of 58 meters, but prolonged bottom time below about 18 meters can require decompression. While it is possible to dive below the normal limits of scuba, the mixed-gas diving techniques with rebreathers that are required are logistically complex and physiologically demanding, making them impractical and even unsafe except for divers with advanced training and skills.

Remote-sensing surveys are an option for recording sites at depths below the maximum safe limits for scuba, although they can also be used in shallower waters. As underwater archaeologists develop a greater awareness of the need to identify and control for a wide range of natural factors that can affect the archaeological record, remote-sensing surveys can be expected to assume a larger role in their research designs. This process is being aided by new technologies that permit measurements of key environmental variables on the seabed and in the water column that affect the condition and characteristics of deeply submerged sites. The 1985 remote-sensing survey of the USS *Monitor* wreck site, at a depth of 67 meters off the coast of Cape Hatteras, North Carolina, is an example of a remote-sensing survey conducted as part of the preparation of a research design for further work. The *Monitor* was one of the best-known ships in American history as a result of its role in the Civil War in the first-ever combat encounter between ironclad vessels at the Battle of Hampton Roads, Virginia, on 9 March 1862. Its engagement with CSS *Virginia* (formerly *Merrimac*) was tactically inconclusive but effectively prevented the Confederate ironclad from breaking the Union blockade. On 31 December 1862 the *Monitor* sank off Cape Hatteras in rough seas while under tow (Fig. 8).

The shipwreck was located in the 1970s and was later designated as a marine sanctuary under the jurisdiction of the National Oceanic and Atmospheric Administration (NOAA). In the early 1980s it was photographed and visited several times in a project led by the underwater archaeologist Gordon Watts from East Carolina University, who recorded items of interest recovered from the wreck (Watts, 1985). These items included a lantern, which was the last thing seen of the *Monitor* when the ship sank, and the ship's anchor, a unique type invented by John Ericsson,

Fig. 8. Contemporary print depicting the loss of the *U.S.S. Monitor* off Cape Hatteras, North Carolina, on 31 December 1862. The proportions of the turret to the hull are inaccurate, but the picture shows the steamer *U.S.S. Rhode Island*, which had been towing the *Monitor*, rescuing the survivors. Published with permission of the John Hay Library, Brown University.

the ship's designer. Watts and his colleagues used mixed-gas scuba-diving techniques, operating from a mini-submersible called the Johnson Sea-Link. The Sea-Link has an air lock that allows a diver to exit and reenter it on the seabed. When it was used on the *Monitor*, its operator sat in the bubble-like cockpit watching the diver closely. These dives produced useful information about the wreck and recovered some important artifacts (now on display at the Mariner's Museum, Newport News, Virginia) but did not provide a complete picture of the site or its condition.

In 1985 NOAA embarked upon a major program to document the *Monitor* shipwreck site and to plan for its future management. The first steps in this program involved an inspection of historical archives pertaining to the *Monitor* (conducted by Ernest Peterkin) emphasizing the ship's engineering and construction history, and the development of a research design. A decision was made early in the planning phase to conduct an essentially nondestructive survey of the site without making any attempt to lift the wreck or its contents to the surface. It is important to regard this as the survey of a site and not simply the shipwreck, since it included the underwater terrain and debris field surrounding the wreck (Gould, 1988). NOAA did not want any doubts to arise later about the nature of the seabed surrounding the *Monitor* or the possibility of a debris scatter there. It was also important to establish the proximity of other wrecks in order to evaluate the possibility of mixed deposits.

Since the wreck site lay below a safe depth for conventional scuba diving, a remote-sensing survey was planned to measure the likely effects on the wreck of different conditions at the site and to consider ways to preserve it. The former U.S. Navy gunboat *Antelope*, renamed the *Anderson* and operated by the U.S. Environmental Protection Agency, was employed as the mother ship for a group of instrument arrays to be deployed over the site during the course of the survey. The ship was equipped with deck cranes and a laboratory that facilitated these efforts. Measurements were taken in a number of domains.

A sensitive fathometer measured the depth and contour of the seabed along each track. The seabed at and around the *Monitor* site consisted of a more or less level silt plain and from the start it was obvious that the condition of the wreck depended to a large extent on the lucky fact that it did not land upon the rocks when it sank.

Use of the magnetometer produced strong "hits" in the vicinity of the

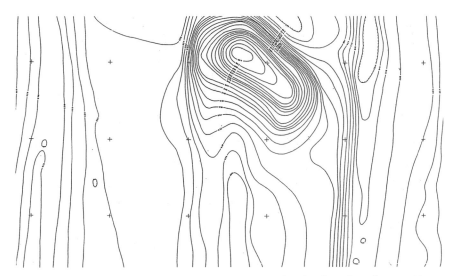

Fig. 9. Magnetic contour map of *U.S.S. Monitor* wreck. The shoe-shaped area with the narrowest contours is the site of the strongest magnetic anomaly, indicating the position of the wreck on the seabed. Published with permission of the National Oceanic and Atmospheric Administration (NOAA).

ship's iron hull that correlated with readings from the other survey instruments (Fig. 9).

Side-scan sonar was used to obtain images of the wreck. This device transmits acoustical signals at right angles to the path of the torpedo-shaped sensor as it is towed just above the seabed. These signals are reflected back from solid objects on the seabed, and the returns are received and processed electronically to produce ghostly images of the objects that seem almost photographic in a continuous readout as the sensor passes them. Side-scan sonar does not work well over rocky and irregular underwater topography, and here again it was fortunate that the ship came to rest on the only level silt plain in an otherwise rocky area of seabed. The images obtained showed the wreck resting upside down (something that had been known from earlier photographs of the site) with part of the circular gun turret projecting from under the side of the hull (Fig. 10).

A sub-bottom profiler was used to reveal possible layering and even objects under the seabed surface. It transmits low-frequency impulses

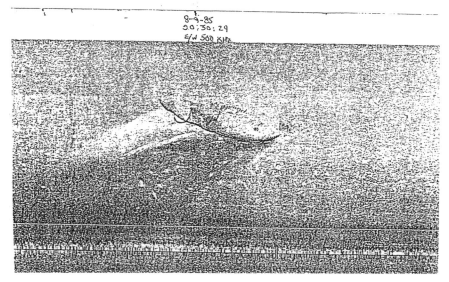

Fig. 10. Side-scan sonar image of *U.S.S. Monitor* wreck. The fuzziness is due mainly to the fact that this is an acoustical rather than a photographic image. Despite this, the outline of the armor belt along the hull and the turret resting partly underneath the hull are clearly visible, as is the scouring in the seabed leading away from the wreck. This image correlates exactly with the magnetic contour map in Fig. 8. Published with permission of NOAA.

downward into the seabed as it is towed slightly above the bottom, and these impulses are differentially reflected back and processed. The depth of signal penetration varies with the density of the bottom sediments and other conditions, and therefore the readouts require expert interpretation. The mother ship had to move faster through the water than the optimal speed for the sub-bottom profiler in order to maintain a straight survey track against surface currents, wind, and waves.

Temperature, salinity, and dissolved oxygen were measured using standard oceanographic instruments such as the bathythermograph and modern versions of the Nansen bottle. These measurements were necessary not only to record on-site conditions but also as controls for the use of the acoustical instruments, since the speed of sound through the water column is affected by the temperature and density of the water. For example, a thermocline, or layer of water of differing temperature (usually colder) from layers above it, can distort or reflect sound signals passing through the water column.

Long-term measurements of currents above the seabed and around the wreck site were taken using current meters placed on the seabed. These instruments are capable of recording and storing information for several months before the batteries and data tapes need replacement. The use of these current meters revealed the presence of a slow current across the seabed in a direction differing from the surface currents. The current meters were left in place at the site after the remote-sensing survey was completed to collect data for several years. They provided information about seasonal changes in the direction and intensity of this current and the likely effects of such changes on the site due to the movement of silt and the covering or uncovering of the ship's hull and associated material remains.

In addition to these measurements, a biological survey of the site was conducted later. It showed that the wreck acts as a sort of marine oasis in what is otherwise a biological desert. Marine organisms transported by subsurface currents through the water column tend to attach themselves to any sort of hard substrate they encounter. Some iron surfaces of the wreck are moderately covered with growths that have become established in this way and now support a community of fish, shrimp, and other associated creatures. The wreck is too deep for much sunlight to penetrate, but there is enough marine growth present to provide measurable protection against corrosion for certain parts of the wreck if left undisturbed. Corrosion has been slowed, too, by the fact that the wreck lies below the shallow-water, high-energy zone where oxygen circulates more freely.

The survey was conducted according to a creeping-line track plan, with 100-meter track spacing to provide adequate overlap for all the instrument sensors being towed. A creeping-line track is one that proceeds back and forth over the same terrain but moves sideways the same amount and in the same direction at the end of each track. This method produces a series of parallel lanes at whatever interval is required for adequate coverage. The essential element in such a survey plan is positioning. This survey used a commercially available microwave system called Mini-Ranger for surface positioning (the survey was conducted before GPS was available), using two shore-based transmitters operating on line-of-sight to the ship and producing electronic signals that were virtually instantaneous – that is, they traveled at the speed of light and could be processed into real-time position fixes more or less continuously throughout the survey. As long as shore stations are available within sight of the entire survey area, this is a good positioning system. For offshore use beyond sight of land, GPS and the older Loran-C systems are currently available. The main advantages of GPS over Loran-C are its greater positioning accuracy and its worldwide application (Gould, 1995). Using Mini-Ranger signals in 1985, the survey ship steered accurately enough along each of the survey lanes to ensure complete coverage by the instruments being towed.

Subsurface positioning was more difficult. Because of the depth of the *Monitor*, surface positions could not be used for underwater site recording. Electronic positioning systems such as Loran-C, GPS, or Mini-Ranger cannot be used underwater, and acoustical transmissions travel at the much slower speed of sound. Therefore, while position fixes on the surface of the ocean are real-time in nature and allow one to see exactly where one is at any given moment, underwater positioning involves delays. In other words, there is a measurable difference between surface and subsurface positioning that must be reconciled at some point to produce accurate results on the seabed. To resolve these differences, six aluminum stands were placed on the seabed, each containing a transponder. These stands were evenly placed on the seabed around the *Monitor* wreck (Fig. 11) and the transponders were turned on. Then a transducer was trailed behind the ship so as to pass through the array, acoustically interrogating the transponders in turn. The geometry of the responses enabled the survey team to pinpoint the position of each transponder and its stand on the seabed and then to correlate those positions with the surface lanes. The result was an electronic grid on the seabed that covered the *Monitor* site whenever it was turned on. This grid was accurately tied in to the surface positions established during the survey.

At the end of the 1985 remote-sensing survey the transponders were turned off and floated to the surface for collection. In 1987 another NOAA survey took place at the *Monitor* to begin recording the wreck itself. The first step was to relocate the site using electronic positioning on the surface. Then a sophisticated ROV called Deep Drone was deployed from the mother ship to place each transponder back in its stand on the seabed. Since the position of each stand was already known, it was simply a matter of turning on the transponders and using a transducer on Deep Drone to determine the ROV's exact underwater position within the electronic grid as it went about its tasks. In this phase of the project, the

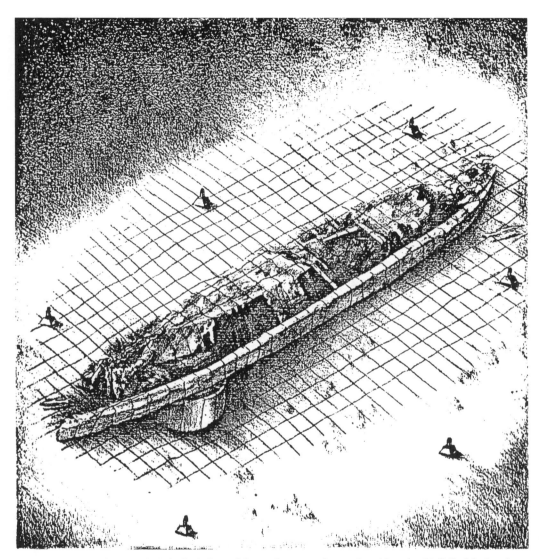

Fig. 11. Artist's depiction of the underwater electronic grid at the *U.S.S. Monitor* site, showing the six transponders in their stands on the seabed surrounding the wreck. Published with permission of NOAA.

ROV rather than the mother ship acted as a platform for various instrument arrays. These instruments included a computerized imaging system for making a three-dimensional map of the wreck (Stewart, 1991) and cameras for doing corrected photogrammetry. A photomosaic of the wreck was made in the 1970s, but because it was uncorrected for parallax distortion and underwater magnification effects it was not an archaeologically acceptable record of the site's physical associations. The cameras on board Deep Drone in 1987 provided a record of the site closer to current archaeological standards.

The remote-sensing survey of the *Monitor* site was one of the most ambitious efforts of its kind so far. What made it special was the way it served the needs of archaeological recording and preservation. In-situ recording by relatively nonintrusive methods also represented a departure from more usual approaches involving the excavation and recovery of material remains. The wreck site remains within the NOAA marine sanctuary off Cape Hatteras, and archaeological research there is continuing. Like the *Arizona*, the wreck of the *Monitor* constitutes a marine sanctuary in the strict sense of the word, namely, a holy place set aside as a memorial to members of the ship's company who went down with it. Therefore it seems appropriate to preserve it as long as possible. Such preservation also has the archaeological advantage of allowing for periodic restudy of the site as techniques of measurement and recording improve. The cost of the survey exceeded what is usually available for underwater archaeological research, and it is still largely the case that only government agencies can afford this approach. It does, however, point the way toward research designs that will be possible when the cost of these technologies comes down.

Meanwhile, underwater technology continues to improve in ways that may eventually be applicable to archaeology. The best examples right now of this kind of advanced technology are the autonomous underwater vehicles (AUVs) currently undergoing trials under the ice in polar waters. AUVs are self-contained units that can dive and navigate without the need for an umbilical line or tether from the mother ship. While simpler ones can be preprogrammed to navigate by means of known underwater landmarks (somewhat in the manner of a cruise missile en route to its target), more sophisticated ones such as Odyssey at the MIT Sea Grant Underwater Vehicles Laboratory and the Autonomous Benthic Explorer operated by the Woods Hole Oceanographic Institution have a form of on-board artificial intelligence that enables them to position themselves, navigate, and avoid obstacles, sometimes even when operating in unfamiliar areas. Trials so far with even the most complex AUVs are encouraging, and it is easy to visualize their future use as tools in systematic underwater archaeological surveys. As always, the key to their use will be well-designed surveys that can provide probabilistic coverage of an area in the manner already in use with simpler technologies.

Excavation

Excavation is often regarded as the quintessential activity in archaeological recording, but, as the Australian underwater archaeologist Jeremy Green points out, "excavation alone is not archaeology, but part of a process whereby information is obtained which allows archaeological interpretation" (Green, 1990: 124). We have already considered two important parts of the process Green is referring to, namely, conservation and survey. Excavation is as systematic and analytical as the rest of underwater archaeology (see Green, 1990).

Total Site Excavation

George Bass urged the total excavation of wreck sites (1983: 100), and with shipwrecks of limited size and essentially unknown characteristics this was a reasonable approach, especially when exploring shipwreck sites in a new region. However, archaeologists today increasingly favor limited-scale excavations based upon site-sampling strategies. Even large-scale land excavations today are expected to remove only a part of the site deposits, leaving an intact "witness column" or other unexcavated portion of the site for later stratigraphic inspection and possible further excavation. In the American Southwest, for example, unexcavated sites of ancient Pueblo origin at Wetherill Mesa were set aside during the 1960s as an archaeological preserve, with no excavations to be undertaken there for at least fifty years. This decision was based upon the expectation of technical improvements in archaeology that would make large-scale excavation unnecessary.

From a purely practical point of view, it is hard to justify total excavation except in cases of relatively small shipwreck sites such as those encountered by Bass and his associates from the Mediterranean region. The case of the Kyrenia ship, a fourth-century B.C. shipwreck off the coast of Cyprus excavated by M. L. Katzev, is an example of the utility of total excavation and recovery in situations of this kind (Swiny and Katzev, 1973; Katzev, 1974; Steffy, 1985). Underneath layers of portable artifacts, archaeologists found some of the ship's timbers, with the portside timbers surviving from the ship's centerline to a point above the turn of the hull. The starboard timbers survived only as a detached fragment of connected pieces. After the portable artifacts had been recovered, the timbers were lifted individually from the wreck. The entire craft was then reassembled on land following conservation and some reshaping of most of the timbers. More recently, Katzev and his colleagues have constructed and sailed a one-fifth-scale replica of the ship (Steffy, 1994: 42–59) and built a full-sized replica as well. In the process of hull reconstruction it became apparent that the ship's hull was slightly asymmetrical. It is hard to imagine that anything less than a complete excavation could have produced such detailed findings at this shipwreck site, since it was necessary to remove the cargo of amphorae and stones overlying the timbers before attempting to record the ship's remaining structure. The curvature of the hull and the ship's lines were, however, more clearly revealed during the process of in situ recording than in the later reconstruction based on timbers removed from the site.

The case of the Kyrenia ship generally supports Bass's views concerning total excavation. Steffy and his associates were able to identify internal details of the ship's construction that came to light only after conservation and during the process of reconstruction. Because it was small and was accessible to divers under relatively benign conditions, it was a good candidate for total excavation. Larger vessels and those wrecked in high-energy underwater environments or under other adverse diving conditions are more problematical. The knowledge gained from total excavation may not always justify the effort and expense.

The alternative to total site excavation is nondestructive recording, with most if not all materials left in place on the seabed. Nondestructive approaches have the advantage of being less labor-intensive and costly than excavation. Aside from techniques such as the use of sacrificial zinc anodes on iron or steel ship structures, little or no conservation of materials is required, because virtually nothing is permanently removed from the site. Nondestructive methods are a practical way to deal with large shipwrecks such as the Great Lakes steamer, wrecked at Isle Royale in Lake Superior the *Chester A. Congdon*, a 161-meter-long bulk carrier sunk in 1918,

(Lenihan, 1987), and the *Arizona* and the *Utah*, sunk at Pearl Harbor in 1941.

Some information cannot always be obtained by nondestructive methods. Excavation may be required at a later date, especially when key elements of ship structure are obscured or covered by other materials such as wreck debris or silt or when destruction is imminent. Meanwhile, nondestructive approaches present a challenge to archaeology to learn as much as possible about the shipwreck site by nonintrusive means before considering excavation. In some cases the amount of additional information to be gained from excavation is small. A well-designed program of nondestructive research will help to focus any later excavation.

Stratigraphy vs. Superposition

For land archaeologists stratigraphy and superposition are virtually indistinguishable. Stratified deposits indicative of sequential and/or prolonged human residence and activity at a site are encountered frequently, and their excavation is governed by the principle of superposition, modified by whatever postdepositional factors may apply. Underwater archaeologists who study shipwrecks more commonly encounter cases of superposition without stratigraphy. They have relatively few opportunities to excavate vertical cross-sections, except perhaps in thick mud. Sand and silt will seldom hold a sidewall, and, furthermore, shipwreck sites usually record single moments in time. Thus whatever stratigraphy is present may relate more to spatial relations or to the immediate chronology of the wrecking sequence than to long-term temporal changes. There is a kind of internal stratigraphy within some shipwreck sites that can provide information about the wrecking process and postdepositional effects on the wreck. Green (1990: 128–29) notes, for example, how the relative positioning of objects such as cannons on a wreck site can indicate whether the ship settled upright or on one side. Muckelroy (1978: 182–214) distinguished between shipwreck sites characterized by a continuous distribution of materials across the seabed and those in which the distribution was discontinuous. While this distinction is important, it fosters an essentially two-dimensional view of artifact scatters that is reflected in the analytical approaches Muckelroy used at the site of the Dutch East Indiaman *Kennemerland*, wrecked in 1664 near the Shetland Islands. What is needed is a framework for the spatial analysis of shipwreck materials that incorporates the principle of superposition and enables archaeologists to interpret physical associations on the seabed three-dimensionally.

The ship's remaining structure can serve as a basis for such a framework. Underwater archaeologists have sometimes noted that the frames and compartmentalization of a shipwreck can provide a kind of natural grid for recording physical associations. This basic idea can be proposed as a set of operating principles based on the degree of physical integrity of the material associations at the site. *Primary* associations are those represented by attached elements of ship's structure. For example, there is no doubt that the wooden futtocks, ceiling planks, and keel and keelson – elements that often are found directly attached to each other underneath the silt and ballast layers at shipwreck sites – represent a unit of contemporaneity in the archaeological record. The dating of the loss of the Bird Key wreck in the Dry Tortugas is an example of how primary associations based on attached elements of ship's structure can provide useful archaeological information. The Bird Key ship was an early screw-propeller-driven steamboat that was transporting a cargo of bricks when it was wrecked near Fort Jefferson (Fig. 12). The ship's hull was of composite (mixed

Fig. 12. Aerial view of Bird Key Wreck (arrow) in relation to Fort Jefferson, Dry Tortugas National Park, Florida.

iron-and-wood construction) and was hard-chined (angular instead of rounded and flat-bottomed, with no keel (Gould, 1995). The shape of the ship's propeller, with its flared blades and square blade-tips (Fig. 13), and the use of Muntz metal (a copper–zinc alloy introduced in England in the 1840s and in the United States in the 1850s as an alternative to higher-priced hull sheathing of pure copper [Flick, 1975]) pointed to a mid-nine-teenth-century date of origin for this ship.

Archaeological survey and mapping indicated that the ship had been damaged initially when it ran aground on Bird Key Bank. This ground-ing had torn off the stern deadwood section, including the propeller and propeller shaft. Later salvage attempts with dynamite and the removal of the ship's engine and machinery led to further damage, including break-age and detachment of iron frames, sponsons, and pieces of the ship's fire-box (Fig. 14). Finally, storms sweeping across Bird Key Bank, which is exposed and shallow, led to a further scattering of detached structural ele-ments and portable artifacts, forming a debris field that extended 256 meters north of the wreck.

Fig. 13. Four-bladed propeller on Bird Key Wreck, Dry Tortugas National Park, Florida.

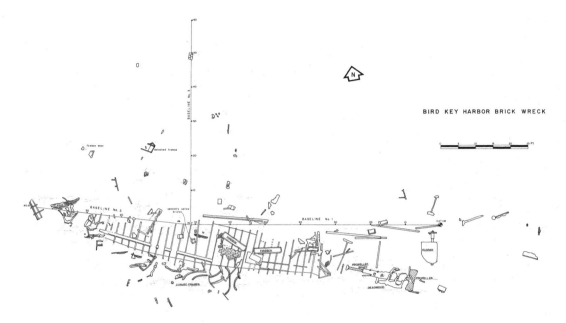

Fig. 14. Trilateration plan of the Bird Key Wreck, showing the extensive debris field and bricks associated with parts of the vessel's firebox. Dry Tortugas National Park, Florida.

The survey revealed that there were three types of bricks present on the shipwreck site. One type consisted of unmarked yellow bricks similar in size, shape, color, and texture to those used in the construction of the bastions, curtains, and other major parts of Fort Jefferson (and Fort Taylor in Key West). Table 1 summarizes the results of a t-test comparison of unmarked yellow bricks from the shipwreck site and yellow bricks selected at random from the exterior of Fort Jefferson. The results show low values for t when comparing length and width measurements, indicating that the two samples of bricks belong to similar or identical populations. The higher value for t in relation to maximum thickness reflects a significant difference between these two populations along this dimension. This difference can be attributed to weathering, which affected bricks on the fort's exterior surfaces to varying degrees. It was this same weathering, which exposed the bricks by eroding away their cement mortar matrix, that permitted the thickness measurements (something not always possible with bricks fully cemented in place). Unmarked yellow bricks were the

Table 1 *T-test comparison of Pensacola bricks from Fort Jefferson with unmarked bricks from the Bird Key wreck, Florida*

	No. of cases	Mean (feet)	Standard deviation	Standard error	T-value
LENGTH					
Wreck sample	38	0.7322	0.034	0.005	
					1.99
Fort Jefferson sample	38	0.7453	0.023	0.004	
WIDTH					
Wreck sample	38	0.3479	0.019	0.003	
					0.42
Fort Jefferson sample	38	0.3462	0.015	0.002	
THICKNESS					
Wreck sample	38	0.2097	0.022	0.003	
					6.84
Fort Jefferson sample	38	0.1831	0.010	0.002	

ship's primary cargo, although many more of these may have been present before salvage occurred.

Both of the other types of bricks present were refractory bricks used to line the ship's firebox. Portions of the firebox were found in a primary association with the hull structure of the ship and with firebricks laid in courses and mortared in place. Yellow firebricks formed the course facing the fire, while red bricks served as insulation between the layer of yellow firebricks and the iron walls of the firebox. A total of eighteen yellow firebricks marked "EVENS & HOWARD, ST. LOUIS," were found at the site, including two cemented directly into the firebox structure. These bricks were manufactured by the Evens and Howard Firebrick Company from 1857 to 1930 (Gurcke, 1987: 232). The red insulating bricks were similar in general appearance to red bricks used in parts of the post–1861 construction of Fort Jefferson. Had some of these not been cemented directly into the firebox structure or to each other as part of the shipwreck's primary association, it would have been easy to mistake the loose red bricks for part of the ship's cargo.

The firebricks marked "EVENS & HOWARD, ST. LOUIS" are securely dated and indicate that the ship could not have sunk before 1857.

The yellow bricks used in the construction of Fort Jefferson and present in the ship's cargo were manufactured by the firm of Raiford and Abercrombie from deposits of Escambia clay in and around Pensacola, Florida, under a contract with the army dated 24 August 1854 (Bell, 1925; Ellsworth, 1974: 251). Difficulties with production and quality control delayed the delivery of Pensacola bricks in significant quantities to the fort until 1858, following the development of an efficient brick-making machine. From then until the start of the Civil War the firm produced over 16 million bricks for the federal government, most of which were used in the construction of Fort Jefferson and Fort Taylor. Under secessionist pressure the firm stopped producing bricks for the federal government after 26 February 1861, and the brickyard was burned by Confederate forces in March 1862. The latest likely date for the cargo of Pensacola yellow bricks at the Bird Key wreck, therefore, is 1861, and the loss of the ship is presumed to have occurred sometime between 1857 and 1861. The primary association of firebricks with the Bird Key wreck was the key to distinguishing between bricks that were part of the ship's structure and bricks that were part of its cargo, leading to a date for the ship's loss.

Ships' cargoes present archaeologists with primary associations, too. On the East Key wreck and the Barrel wreck in the Dry Tortugas, cement barrel casts have been found resting in parallel, contiguous rows directly on top of a ballast layer and/or the ship's timbers. These barrel casts represent a primary association of materials in their original position as they rested inside the ship's hold, and they were in direct physical contact with primary elements of the ships' wooden structure.

Secondary associations occur when we encounter elements of structure that have become physically detached from the primary association of structural elements but can nevertheless be reconnected (on paper or using a computer) to some portion of the original structure. The fragment of starboard frames and planks from the Kyrenia wreck is an example of such a secondary association. In many cases, secondary associations occur in close proximity to primary ones. Refitting of secondarily associated hull components, machinery, hardware, and other elements to the primary association of the ship's structure offers a useful measure of the effects of postdepositional processes and can also produce a more detailed understanding of the ship's original structure. The same reasoning applies in certain cases to ship's cargoes. The loose yellow construction bricks manufactured by Raiford and Abercrombie and found in secondary associations in and around the Bird Key wreck are one example, and the Barrel wreck and the East Key wreck are others. Each of these two wrecks has large numbers of cement barrel casts that have become detached from their primary associations and are now dispersed over wide areas of the Loggerhead and East Key Reefs. A nearest-neighbor analysis was used to measure the dispersal of these barrel casts (Table 2), which were grouped into four "fields" or zones in terms of their degree of dispersal. Different depositional mechanisms, related either to immediate circumstances of wrecking or to later, postdepositional processes, accounted for each field.

The preservation of primary and secondary associations at these sites appears to depend mainly upon micro-topography such as dips and crevices in the reef that shield shipwreck remains from the force of storm waves and currents and upon localized trapping of silt that covers these remains and preserves them against shipworms and other disintegrating forces. Such processes run counter to conventional wisdom in underwater archaeology, which generally predicts poor preservation of wooden ship structure in situations of this kind.

Tertiary associations usually occur in highly dispersed contexts and may indicate mixed deposits from overlapping debris fields or isolated objects derived from other wrecks. At the Barrel wreck site there are several, large objects, including a boxlike item of iron plating, a large chainplate (iron straps used to attach the ship's standing rigging to the hull), and a deadeye, that are anomalous relative to the primary- and secondary-associated materials at the site. Two of these three items were situated relatively close to the primary-associated part of the wreck, but they occur farther from each other than any other objects at the site, including the most widely dispersed cement barrel casts. Further study is needed to account for the presence of these anomalous items at other wreck sites on Loggerhead Reef. What appear to be tertiary associations at the Barrel wreck site may eventually prove to be secondary associations that can be refitted to other shipwrecks or shipwreck scatters on the reef.

Tertiary associations challenge assumptions about shipwrecks as simple time capsules and direct our attention to the complexities of formation processes in the archaeological record. The magnetometer survey and visual inspection of the magnetometer "hits" during the survey have revealed the presence of large iron frames and other pieces of ship

Table 2 *Nearest-neighbor ranking of cement barrel fields at DRTO-036 wreck site, Dry Tortugas, National Park, FL*

RANK		Nearest-neighbor value
1. Field No. 1	=	3.38
2. Field No. 2	=	5.33
3. Field No. 3	=	6.14
mean	=	4.95
standard deviation	=	1.42
4. Field no. 4	=	21.44

Note: These figures include only detached barrels, not barrels in rows and in direct contact.

structure scattered across Loggerhead Reef to the northeast of the Barrel wreck in the general direction of the *Killean*, but preliminary indications are that none of these items, including the three noted at the Barrel wreck, came from that ship. They appear, instead, to be from a large, iron-framed wooden sailing ship and possibly from some other ships as well. To account for the tertiary associations at the Barrel wreck site it will be necessary to record and analyze the scattered ship remains across much of the adjacent area of the reef.

The archaeologist's primary task is to record the physical associations at a site as fully as possible and then to account for them as fully as possible, but this does not mean that all associations can in fact be explained. Many archaeologists are fond of using the jigsaw-puzzle metaphor to explain what they do, but sometimes they miss the point that the puzzle will always have at least some missing pieces. The full and complete picture of human behavior that produced a particular site assemblage in the past will never be fully known, either through archaeology or with the aid of written and other documents. The ideas that archaeologists produce about the past to account for the material assemblages that they record at sites should be viewed as approximations of what happened to produce those associations. These approximations are open to critical review and testing to see which ones best account for the remains that are present. There is no final answer or ultimate level of understanding in this process but only relatively better approximations of past reality.

Controls

Many aspects of underwater excavation will at first glance appear familiar to land archaeologists. The idea that techniques of underwater excavation are merely extensions of techniques used on land to the underwater environment is still widely accepted. The conduct of underwater excavation, however, compels archaeologists to acknowledge and adapt to unique conditions. For example, the use of a grid over the area of the site to be excavated is a common feature of underwater research, but in practice it may differ from those used on land. Since true stratigraphic excavation is not an option at many underwater sites, underwater archaeologists favor the use of devices like air lifts and suction dredges to remove silt and other kinds of sterile overburden that cover shipwreck remains. The grid frame confines and focuses the use of devices like these, but it tends to serve more as a positional aid for horizontal recording of artifact distributions and ship structure than as a framework for analyzing vertical stratigraphic sequences. There are, however, some notable exceptions, and in some situations devices such as suction dredges and air lifts can be used in a stratigraphically controlled manner.

Certain basic skills emerge in the conduct of underwater excavations and contribute to the level of control achieved at the site. For scuba divers, precise buoyancy control is essential, and experienced underwater archaeologists can hover over the worksite and maintain position with a minimum of movement. This allows one to view and record the horizontal positioning of artifacts and features without having to walk or crawl over the surface of the site. The advantages of being able to work in this way at sites containing fragile materials are obvious. Along with good buoyancy control, experienced underwater archaeologists have the ability to work without fins. Kicking with fins creates swirls and vortices in the water that can damage and dislodge delicate items such as timbers and portable artifacts. Another basic skill is hand-fanning – gentle, rhythmic and circular movement of the hand over an object or feature to remove loose sand and silt without dislodging or damaging the item. Sometimes hand-fanning can be used effectively with an air lift or suction dredge by fanning sand and silt into the end of the nozzle. This not only clears loose material from the object but removes this material as well. It also enables the excavator to keep loose items such as nails, ceramic sherds, and other potentially important materials from disappearing up the air lift. More powerful air lifts and suction dredges can be used to remove thick layers of sterile overburden, with the excavator controlling the movement and positioning of the nozzle and watching out for possible artifacts and structural features.

The effective application of these skills can occur only when one is accurately positioned over the site and is working within a controlled collecting and recording environment. The bed-frame grid works well in relatively shallow waters, allowing accurate trilateration in three dimensions. This technique was developed during excavations at the *James Matthews* shipwreck site in Cockburn Sound, Western Australia (Henderson, 1976). It was accomplished by driving stakes into the seabed at 1-meter intervals along the baseline. A bar was set up between two of these stakes and leveled. Then a pair of bars was mounted horizontally and at right angles to the baseline across the site to a second pair of stakes. In this case, the horizontal distance was 6 meters, but this can vary according to the size and shape of the site being excavated. After leveling the entire framework, a sliding H-shape was positioned so that its vertical arms moved along the parallel 6-meter bars while its crosspiece ran between the 6-meter bars above and across the site (Fig. 15). It was then possible to drop a plumb bob from this crosspiece to the points on the site that needed to be measured. The distance across the H-bar gave the x coordinate, the distance from the baseline to H-bar gave the y coordinate, and the vertical distance from the plumb bob point to the horizontal plane of the bed frame gave the vertical or z coordinate (Green, 1990: 69). While relatively time-consuming, this technique, like that of baseline trilateration in underwater survey, is relatively simple to use and can be extended in any direction across the site.

The discussion so far assumes that human divers carry out the tasks of excavation and site recording. As indicated earlier, however, there are limits to the depths at which divers can work effectively. Bass (1966: 143–60; 1976: 100–10, 185–96) has described some of the difficulties encountered in doing effective archaeological excavations at Yassi Ada, where the first season's work took place at a depth of 36 meters. Limited bottom times and the need for decompression stops were among the constraints encountered, and similar conditions apply to any archaeological excavations conducted close to the practical limits for safe diving. Beyond these limits,

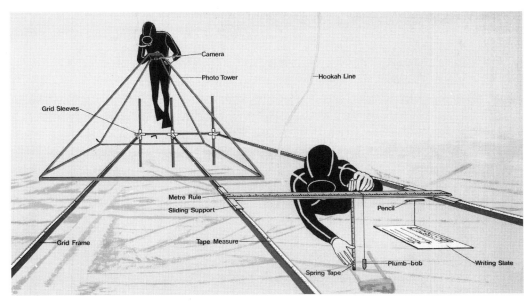

Fig. 15. Drawing of "bed frame" technique for three-dimensional site recording. Courtesy of the Western Australian Maritime Museum, Fremantle.

only small submersibles and ROVs can operate effectively. ROVs combined with accurate underwater positioning have already proven themselves in underwater archaeological survey and nondestructive recording. It remains to be seen how effectively such devices and even newer ones such as autonomous underwater vehicles can be adapted to perform true "blue-water archaeology," that is, controlled archaeological excavation and recording of material associations at depths and under conditions beyond the limits for human divers. Experience so far with these new technologies in underwater surveys suggests that the conduct of this new kind of archaeology will require controls of a different order from those now in use.

The key to such efforts will be accurate underwater positioning. More than any other, this requirement distinguishes archaeology from other underwater sciences, where the need for precise positioning is generally less acute. While more conventional methods of underwater excavation and site recording can be expected to continue in the shallower depths of the world's lakes, rivers, and oceans, important advances can also be expected as archaeologists learn to adapt new marine technologies and electronic positioning to the controlled excavation and recording of sites at greater depths.

3 · Ships and Shipwrecks: Basic Mechanics

As a historical science, underwater archaeology requires some basic understanding of the physical relationships between ship design and construction and the medium in which voyaging occurs. It also requires an organized approach to the physical context of the wreck – both the factors leading to the loss of the vessel and the factors that have affected the condition and distribution of wreck materials at the site. Many such relationships operate according to uniformitarian principles – that is, they can be assumed to have operated in the past in the same manner, though not necessarily at the same rate, as they do today.

Any ship other than a submersible operates simultaneously and continuously in two media, the sea and the air, while avoiding contact with a third, land, except under specific conditions such as docking or beaching. The combination of sea and air environments, fluid and ever-changing, dominates all maritime activities. Each of these media independently affects the movements of a ship at sea. Approaching a dock on a windy day, for example, with a current setting in one direction and a wind from another at different velocities, the vessel is affected differently above- and below-water. Docking under such conditions requires a high order of skill and experience, and the ship's ability to maneuver and change speed is critical.

Sea and air environments interact in complex ways. Wave action resulting from wind friction is probably the most obvious product of such interaction and is a constant concern to mariners. The surface of the sea also responds to long-term or distant wind effects by producing sustained waves, termed swells, that may persist in spite of contrary local winds, resulting in waves and swells of different amplitudes from different directions at the same time. Local conditions are also affected by interaction with adjacent landmasses. In some situations the wind may be blocked by a nearby land-mass (even though the wave action can continue). For ships under sail, such a situation can be hazardous, since the vessel may lose its ability to move and maneuver while still being affected by waves and currents close to shore. In other situations, strong wind gusts can occur close to shore as moving air accelerates across lee shore slopes toward the water, creating sudden upsets to vessels under sail. Close to a shelving or sloping shore, waves have a tendency to steepen, which can produce a combination of hazards involving the force of the waves themselves and the intermittent exposure of the seabed in shallow offshore areas. Under conditions of high waves in such locations, a vessel can run aground even in water that under quieter conditions is deep enough to permit it to pass safely. Tidal action can be a significant factor, too, by varying the depth of water beneath the ship and by creating local currents and eddies that can affect maneuvering.

Similar considerations apply to voyaging, although they usually apply to other aspects of the ship's performance. In a cruise mode, it is the vessel's sea-keeping abilities that are usually important in combination with relia-bility and economy of operation. For example, in sailing vessels it is important to be able to maintain as straight a track as possible through the water, whatever the wind direction. Excessive keel area for stability and straight tracking creates drag, which slows the vessel, but too little keel area may produce instability and a tendency for the vessel to be pushed sideways in the water (termed leeway). Similar considerations apply to weight and strength in ship construction. Robust construction protects against damage due to wave action but may exact penalties with regard to speed and economy. In short, ship design and construction represents compromises, often between safety and efficiency of operation.

Ship Design and Construction

The overriding fact of wooden ship construction is that no single piece of wood in the ship can exceed the size of the tree from which it came. Similar constraints apply to the shapes of individual pieces of wood, whether straight or curved (Fig. 16a–b). All wooden ships are therefore built up by joining numerous wooden pieces to form larger structures such

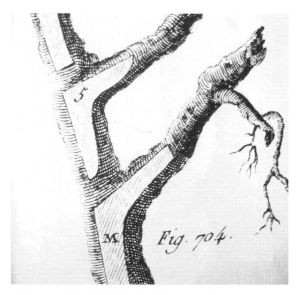

Fig 16a. "Knees from trees" – This drawing from an eighteenth-century French shipbuilding manual shows how ships' knees were cut from natural shapes found at the junction of tree trunks and branches.

Fig 16b. Hanging knees inside hull of three-masted schooner *C. A. Thayer*, at the National Maritime Museum at San Francisco Golden Gate Recreation Area. Published with permission of the National Park Service.

as hulls and decks. Much of what follows benefits from a useful discussion by the maritime archaeologist, J. Richard Steffy (1994: 8–20), and from various manuals and general references relating to shipbuilding (Desmond, 1919; Doyère, 1895; Paasch, 1890; Chapelle, 1967) and to methods of joinery in particular.

Steffy (1994: 10) points out that ships that transport freight can be considered as rectangular, boxlike shapes moving through the water, and this view could be extended to include all ships. Whatever the ship's contents or purpose, it must always have an enclosed space to contain the crew, passengers, weapons, cargo, and whatever specialized equipment it requires. Since ship's cargoes are often bulky, seagoing transports may present extreme examples of such boxiness. Because the flat end of the box would be grossly inefficient for passage through the water, most ships have a pointed or curved bow ahead of it. The principal exception is the barge. Such vessels may have optimal cargo capacity and are usually cheap to build. They can sacrifice efficiency of movement, however, because they usually operate in rivers, canals, or sheltered waters and at slow speeds that reduce the penalties for hydrodynamic inefficency and the pounding of water against the bow.

The aim of moving a boxlike shape through a fluid in accordance with the requirements of the ship's operators is central to ship design and construction. Ships intended for the transport of cargoes often have a rectangular box-shaped section enclosed within the hull, usually with crew quarters, galley, anchors, and other personal and operational spaces in the bow and stern areas outside the box. Although speed may be desirable for transports under special circumstances, as in the case of mid-nineteenth-century clipper ships (Chapelle, 1967: 321–397) and Civil War blockade runners (Wise, 1988), the economies of commercial transport usually place cargo capacity ahead of speed. The result is often a broad-beamed vessel with large holds or open spaces to accommodate freight and subtle lines to provide optimal efficiency of movement given the primary requirement to transport enough cargo to secure a profit. Narrow hull shapes could sometimes improve speed but always at the expense of cargo capacity (Fig. 17).

A broad-beamed hull has advantages beyond enhanced capacity. It usually improves side-to-side stability, though this, too, will vary according to other design features and circumstances. It can also provide good

Fig 17. Bow-on view of composite clipper ship *Cutty Sark* in Greenwich, England. Here tradeoffs in hull shape clearly favored speed over cargo capacity.

carrying capacity without requiring extreme depth below waterline, an important consideration in shallow-water operations. Early Dutch ship-builders were particularly innovative in this regard, and many of their traditional designs, intended for use in shallow waters in and around the North Sea, influenced English construction of smaller ships during the fifteenth and sixteenth centuries. The Dutch *fluyt*, related to the earlier *vlieboot* (flyboat), was a beamy, shallow-draft cargo carrier with a large hold and rounded bow and stern that evolved through most of the seventeenth century into a popular and profitable sailing transport (McGowan, 1981: 53). Early cargo ships often had to be beached for loading and unloading, since developed ports and docks were not always available, and therefore small size, sturdy construction, and relatively beamy hull shapes continued to offer commercial and practical advantages for sailing transports right through the nineteenth century. Some of these later types, such as the Dutch *galiot* and *schuyt* and their close relative, the Thames sailing barge, retained the rounded, beamy hull shapes and even the paddle-shaped lee-boards of the earlier ones (McGowan, 1980: 44–51). This long-standing Dutch tradition of building small, practical (and profitable) cargo carriers suited to local and regional conditions resulted in ships with hull shapes and other characteristics at the opposite end of the cargo-carrying design spectrum from the narrow-hulled war galleys of ancient Greece and the fast clipper ships of the mid- to late nineteenth century.

The evolution of ancient Greek oared warships from pre-Homeric times until the peak of their development in the form of the trireme or galley with three banks of oars by the time of the Battle of Salamis in 480 B.C. reveals the complex trade-offs between speed and maneuverability that are sometimes required of specialized ships. As the maritime historians Vernard Foley and Werner Soedel (1981) point out, the hydrodynamics of bow wave formation has important effects on the vessel's speed. William Froude's experiments during the 1870s with hull models of various shapes in a specially designed tank showed that at slow speeds a ship's movement through the water is not much affected by the bow wave, which has a short amplitude. As the vessel's speed increases, however, the amplitude of the bow wave lengthens, and as the wave passes under the ship's stern it can either add momentum (if it crests below the stern while the next bow wave is cresting under the bow) or slow the ship down (if the stern settles into the trough formed by the previous bow

wave, forcing the boat to move uphill along its back side). For greater
speed, therefore, the hull must be lengthened to defer the onset of this
unsynchronized condition (Foley and Soedel, 1981:148, 153). The long,
narrow fifty-oared Greek galleys (*penteconters*) that preceded the trireme,
with the oars arranged in two banks, appear to have been very well
designed for speed. With the advent of ramming as a naval tactic around
850 B.C., however, there was a need for greater maneuverability, and the
length that provided greater speed could interfere with the ship's ability to
turn quickly to face or fend off attack. By rearranging the seating for the
oarsmen, the ancient Greeks managed to add an extra bank of rowers
without greatly increasing the length of the ship's hull. The added rowing power offered extra speed when needed – though not necessarily at
the highest level of hydrodynamic efficiency – without sacrificing the all-
important ability to maneuver effectively in battle. By the sixth century
B.C. the trireme had become the leading warship of its day, with the ability to sprint at speeds of slightly over 9 knots and to cruise at 4 knots with
half the oarsmen rowing in alternating shifts. A trireme could also execute
a 180-degree turn in one minute within a turning radius of no more than
two and one-half ship lengths (Casson, 1991: 85). No one is suggesting
that the ancient Greeks used scientific tank-testing and hydrodynamic
science to calculate these effects and apply them to their warships. The
shape of ships during Classical times resulted from a more empirical
process, accomplished through practical experience of conditions at sea
and a good knowledge of shipbuilding techniques. This process ultimately resulted, however, in a Mediterranean tradition of building oared warships that continued through the Roman and Byzantine empires (Lewis
and Runyan, 1990: 1–40) and the war fleets of Spain during the sixteenth
century and spread to other localities later on. The last recorded use of
oared war galleys in battle involved Swedish and Russian fleets in the eastern Baltic in 1809 (Kemp, 1976: 336).

The nineteenth-century clippers were designed for the rapid transport
of high-value cargoes. Chapelle (1967: 398–414) reviews the factors that
led to improved speed under sail. Here the internal box for holding cargo
was narrowed and elongated within a refined hull shape. These refine-
ments included a high power:weight ratio (in this case, increased sail area
and attention to the placement of the masts and design of the rig versus
the displacement weight of the ship), efforts to reduce the wetted area of

the immersed parts of the ship (thus reducing skin friction, especially at slow speeds), and the displacement:length ratio (the fatter the hull, the lower the ratio and the greater the resistance). Perhaps the best overall index for evaluating the performance of the clippers was the speed/length ratio, calculated as speed (in knots) divided by the square root of the ship's hull length at the load line. The fastest clippers, such as the *Sovereign of the Seas*, the *Lightning*, and the *Great Republic*, all of which achieved speeds of between 19 and 22 knots, had speed/length ratios of between 1.26 and 1.45 (Chapelle, 1967: 409).

Chapelle is careful to point out, however, that any clipper ship with a speed/length ratio of 1.25 could realistically be considered capable of achieving the maximum potential for this type, since weather conditions rarely permitted higher speeds. He notes that practical conditions often intruded upon the mathematically based expectations of ship designers and operators. For example, calculations of wetted area were useful for creating efficient hull shapes, but roughness of the hull surfaces due to marine growth, uneven planking or sheathing, and other friction-producing features were usually more important in determining the vessels' speeds than small differences in wetted area. Here, as in the case of Greek oared warships, a review of the technical characteristics of a particular type of ship in relation to its use has revealed the nature of some of the trade-offs required in the vessel's design and construction.

Early documents with information about ancient ship design rules and practices are rare, partly because of a tendency toward professional secrecy on the part of individual shipbuilders and partly because of the craft nature of early shipbuilding (not to mention the fact that writing was not widespread). Early shipbuilding traditions did not rely upon scientific engineering and the application of hydrodynamic principles. Prior to the clipper ships and Froude's experiments, ship design involved trial-and-error and a tendency toward conservatism once a workable design had been achieved. One of the most intriguing examples of early design drawings for ships appears in Matthew Baker's *Fragments of Ancient Shipwrightery* (ca. 1586), where a profile view of a small galleon, intended to show the ideal shape for the below-water portion of the hull, has a fish superimposed on it. This much-cited drawing signaled changes in underwater hull design in English ships that may have given them advantages of speed and maneuverability during the battles with the Spanish Armada in 1588

(McGowan, 1981: 26–29). Although Baker's drawing pertained mainly to warships, the basic goal was the same as in the case of cargo ships, namely, creating an efficient hull within which to place the box (in this case containing guns, crew, and accommodations). The efficiencies in this case had more to do with speed, strength, and maneuverability than with capacity, but similar trade-offs applied to naval vessels generally. By the late seventeenth century manuals and written instructions as well as ship plans and models were more common. One of the most important was Anthony Deane's *Doctrine of Naval Architecture* (1670), which did much to standardize ship design and building practices then and now provides a useful baseline for archaeological comparisons of ship remains of that period (Abell, 1981; Steffy, 1994: 156–62).

While relative efficiencies of movement through the water have always been an essential part of ship design and construction, there are also factors of hull strength and safety to consider. Steffy (1994: 11–20) reviews various hull designs of ancient ships and boats with regard to seaworthiness and efficiency. As ships increased in size, so did their susceptibility to hogging and sagging. Hogging occurs when a ship's buoyancy exceeds its weight over roughly half of its midship half-length while the bow and stern are less buoyant. One reason for this is the tapered shape of the bow and stern, which reduces their buoyancy relative to their weight. This condition can occur as a long wave passes below the ship, causing the hull to float or arch upward roughly halfway along its length. Sagging occurs in the trough of a long wave, when the midship half-length of the hull bends downward in relation to the more buoyant bow and stern. Each type of motion creates stresses that affect the operational lives of large ships and are potential factors in their eventual loss (Fig. 18). During the nineteenth century, wooden ships, both civil and military, were becoming so large that extra reinforcement was required to protect hull structures against these stresses.

The formula used to calculate the bending moment due to hogging and sagging of a point along a ship's hull (Desmond, 1919: 33–34) assumed that the vessel was riding upright in the water. Such calculations were complicated by real-world factors encountered by a ship at sea, when rolling and pitching occurred simultaneously because of wave action. Such movement introduced additional strains on a ship's hull due to unequal stresses at various points along the hull as twisting occurred, especially

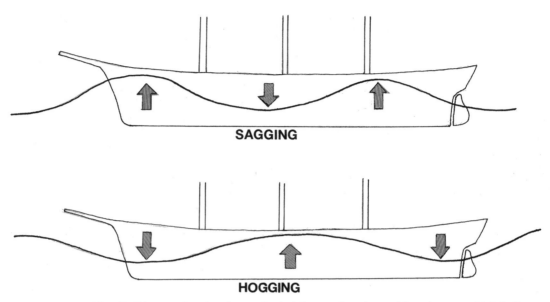

SAGGING

HOGGING

Fig 18. Diagram showing the mechanical forces of sagging and hogging on a ship's hull due to wave action.

when the ship was poised on the crest of a wave, with one side of the stern down while the opposite side of the bow was subject to upward pressure. As Desmond (1919: 34) notes, wooden ships, with their many joints, were especially susceptible to this kind of stress while at sea.

For large wooden warships there were added stresses caused by the concussion of the big guns and later by the vibration of steam engines, which strained the timbers around the stern (in ships with a screw propeller) or along the sides (in paddle-wheeled ships). One approach to this problem, involving a system of diagonal framing using heavy timbers to support the vertical frames, was introduced into Royal Navy ships from 1813 to 1832, along with the use of iron knees and strapping, by Robert Seppings (Lambert, 1984: 13–15). Later and even larger ships demanded more radical solutions, such as composite hull construction using a combination of iron frames and wooden hull and deck planking. These solutions produced mixed results and were most widely and successfully applied to civil cargo-sailing ships without guns or engines. But the problems of hogging and sagging were never definitively solved, even after the introduction of all-iron-hulled construction, and continue to affect ships today.

The long-term effects of hogging are especially evident in old wooden ships that have been preserved afloat as historical relics. The USS *Constitution*, launched in 1797, achieved important successes in battle during the War of 1812 and afterward and has been preserved. Now on display and open to the public in Boston, it shows some hogging. The *Constellation*, originally built in 1798 as a sister ship to the *Constitution* but a virtually new ship when reconstructed and launched again as a sloop of war in 1854 (Langille, 1998), is currently undergoing restoration in Baltimore. The mid-portion of the hull had hogged 0.9 meters when the ship was drydocked in 1996. In these cases, however, it is the curation of these ships as historical relics for over 200 years rather than normal use that has led to this condition.

Another basic factor affecting the performance of ships at sea is loading. Until the English Merchant Shipping Act of 1876, there were few standards for loading ships, and losses due to overloading sometimes occurred. This possibility needs to be considered by maritime archaeologists, who may be tempted to assume congruence between the size and weight of the cargo from a shipwreck and the ship's true capacity. In the latter half of the nineteenth century "coffin ships" – ships so unseaworthy and overloaded (and often overinsured against loss) that they placed their crews at risk – were becoming increasingly common (Kemp, 1976: 653). The dogged efforts of Samuel Plimsoll eventually led to the adoption of a mark, now known as the Plimsoll mark, on the sides of British merchant ships at the waterline to show the level to which the ship could be loaded safely under varying conditions. With such a mark, anyone could see whether a particular ship was loaded within the legal limits prescribed for the conditions under which it was expected to operate.

Rigidity of construction was always hard to achieve with wooden ships and was probably undesirable, since some degree of flexibility could reduce stresses on key elements. This basic fact that all wooden shipbuilding required joining small pieces of wood also set upper limits on the size of ships, although near the end of the history of commercial wooden ships under sail some remarkably large all-wood ships were built in Maine to compete with iron-and-sail bulk carriers built in England and Scotland and with steamships (Lubbock, 1987). Some of these wooden vessels were over 61 meters long and exceeded 2,000 (gross) tons of cargo capacity. Perhaps the most impressive wooden ships were the wooden steam-and-sail-powered battleships built for the British and French navies during the mid-nineteenth century, many of which carried over 3,000 tons of guns and material and displaced over 5,000 tons (Lambert, 1984:122–143), and the wooden-hulled motorships of 5,000-ton displacement built in the United States as transports during World War I (Desmond, 1919: 181–183). For all practical purposes, these were the largest wooden ships ever built.

Stability was also a major factor in ship design. Stability in a ship refers to its ability to return to an upright position after listing. A stable hull – an ideal condition found only in still water – is one in which the center of buoyancy, a product of all forces within the water that act to lift the submerged portions of the hull, are vertically aligned with the forces of gravity pressing straight down on the hull (Fig. 19). Under this condition, the center of buoyancy (CB) is located at a point below the waterline within the hull while the center of gravity (CG) occurs within the hull at a point at or above the waterline. When wind or waves cause a ship to depart from this ideal condition by causing it to list to one side, the hull's ability to return to an upright position after listing is determined by the distance between the center of gravity and a third point, the metacenter (MC), situated at the intersection of the hull centerline and a vertical line passing through the center of buoyancy. In a rolling or listing condition, the greater the distance of the metacenter above the center of gravity (the *metacentric height*), the more quickly the hull will right itself. If a ship is designed or loaded with the center of gravity above the metacenter, it will be unstable (Steffy, 1994: 9; see Fig. 19).

An extreme roll can cause the metacentric height to vary to the point of instability even in a well-designed ship. Good ship design requires that the ship's shape and size provide not only for positive stability when loaded and in still water but also for heeling caused by the conditions of sea and wind that the ship is likely to encounter. Sailing ships with tall masts, for example, may be subject to strong gusts that cause them to heel over sharply. Too much sail or too little ballast under such conditions will cause the roll to continue past the point of no return, capsizing the ship. As Steffy (1994: 9) points out, sailing vessels varied in metacentric height because of variations in rigging and hull shapes, while modern freighters tend to have metacentric heights that represent only a small percentage of the vessel's breadth. The theory of the metacenter in ship construction was

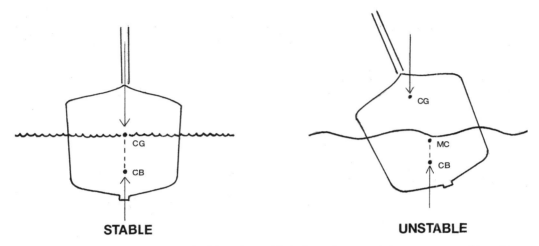

STABLE   **UNSTABLE**

Fig 19. Diagram of stable and unstable hull conditions and the contrasting relationship between the center of gravity and the center of buoyancy in each case (after Steffy, 1994).

developed by a French scientist and hydrographer, Pierre Bouguer, in the mid-eighteenth century; ships built earlier had had to depend upon a combination of trial-and-error and traditional shipbuilding practices to achieve hull designs that were positively stable.

The loss of the sixty-four-gun Swedish warship *Vasa* in Stockholm Harbor reveals how important stability can be in shipwreck studies. The ship was launched in 1627 with a displacement of approximately 1,400 tons and a sail area of 1,114 square meters, making it one of the major fighting ships of its day. When it began its maiden voyage on 10 August 1628, it was closely watched by King Gustav II Adolf and his court as well as by many ordinary citizens. Many of the crew had members of their families on the ship in addition to the ship's normal complement, 133 sailors and 300 soldiers (Franzén, 1962: 7). As some of the ship's sails were being set for the first time, just a few hundred meters out, a sudden squall struck, and it heeled so far over to port that water rushed in through the gunports, increasing the list and sinking it.

The ship came to rest in 33.4 meters of water in an upright position. Its loss was a national and very public catastrophe for Sweden, since many on board were drowned. A full-scale inquest produced no firm conclusion with regard to the ship's instability. One likely factor was the weight of its guns, many of which had been too heavy to be mounted on the upper deck and had therefore been arranged along two lower decks and provided with gunports. The gunports were opened when the guns were run out for action and should have been closed while the ship was under way. A serious effort had been made to place the guns low enough so as not to endanger the ship's stability, but the result was that the lower gunports were perilously close to the waterline. This problem plagued sixteenth- and seventeenth-century warships and was a factor in the loss of the *Mary Rose* (capsized in full view of King Henry VIII and his court on 19 July 1545, with major loss of life) and the HMS *Royal George* (capsized on 29 August 1782 while moored at Spithead, with a loss of about 900 lives) as well. Such disasters reveal that the problem of how high to position the guns of a great wooden warship was never satisfactorily resolved.

In addition to protection against hogging and sagging, other elements of ship strength played a role both in the loss of ships and in their preservation as archaeological features. For large wooden ships, the bow and stern were generally weaker than the midships area. Seppings's early-nineteenth-century reforms included rounded and greatly strengthened bow and stern construction for Royal Navy ships. The maritime historian Andrew Lambert (1984: 13–14) has noted that these reforms led to a practical increase of about 25 percent in their size and made possible the introduction of the ninety-gun, two-decker steam-powered wooden battleships of the 1850s. With the introduction of iron and, later, steel ship construction, the bow and stern areas were much strengthened by their triangular framing, and it was the midships areas that tended to be weaker.

Vertical bulkheads offered both internal strength and compartmentalization for ships' hulls. These partitions were arranged transversely and/or lengthwise and were a common feature from the beginnings of iron and steel ship construction. Transverse bulkheads have been present in wooden ships since at least the Kyrenia ship of the fourth century B.C. (Steffy, 1994: 52) and were a notable feature of wooden shipbuilding in Asia, especially in China, as seen in the hull of the Quanzhou vessel from the Song Dynasty (tenth to eleventh centuries A.D.) and comparable wooden remains from the Pattaya wreck in Thailand (Green and Harper, 1983). In the case of the Pattaya wreck, archaeologists found that each transverse bulkhead had a waterway to allow water to pass from one compartment to another, making extra hull strength the most likely reason for this feature. But the occurrence of bulkheads in wooden ship construction was generally spotty compared with the ways in which bulkheads were employed in ships of iron and steel. Here compartments created by bulkheads were also important for containing flooding within the hull in the event of a collision or a shore strike and for protection against the spread of fire.

Where considerations of efficiency and profit in the transport of bulk cargoes were important to shipowners, iron and steel ships, especially those powered entirely by sail, often lacked internal bulkheads and were strengthened instead with rail-like longitudinal stiffeners along the inside of the hull plating. By omitting bulkheads altogether, even for ships as large as the steel four-masted Finnish bark *Pommern*, with its length of 106.5 meters, 4,050-ton displacement, and cargo-carrying capacity of 2,266 tons (Svensson, 1988: 22), shipowners could transport large amounts of bulk cargo such as grain within a single enclosed hull space without the difficulties and delays in loading and unloading imposed by separate compartments. Many ships of this kind were built from the 1860s until the early 1900s, long after the advent of steam. The *Pommern*, built in 1903, survives today as a preserved ship at the Åland Maritime Museum in Finland. Preserved examples of iron and steel ships of this kind may also be visited in New York City, San Francisco, Honolulu, and elsewhere.

The Physical and Cultural Geography of Voyaging

While winds, currents, weather, and general sea conditions are universally acknowledged by mariners to be of paramount importance in voyaging, archaeologists have only recently begun to deal with these factors in a systematic way. One pioneering effort in this direction was the study by Levison, Ward, and Webb (1973), with voyaging simulations involving vessels with brown performance parameters in relation to data on winds, weather, and currents. The Southwest Pacific has attracted particular attention of this kind, spurred by archaeological interest in the initial voyages of colonization by the ancestors of the Polynesians. Such simulations have been continued and expanded by the archaeologist Geoffrey Irwin and his associates, Simon Bickler and Philip Quirke (1990). Irwin (1992: 133) refers to such studies as "voyaging by computer." Their simulations involved wind data for the months of January (midsummer) and July (midwinter) for all years for which data were available at the Marine Division of the Meteorological Office, Bracknell, England. Using this information, the researchers were able to estimate probabilistically what direction and intensity of winds would have been experienced by the simulated voyaging canoe on each new day of its voyage. Other data included sighting circles of different radii based on the size and elevation of the islands extending from Papua New Guinea to the west coast of America. A sighting circle represents the maximum distance that an island or other landmark would have been visible from the simulated voyaging canoe.

The rules of the simulation were based on a knowledge of traditional Pacific watercraft, seamanship, and navigation and addressed the conditions faced by ancient voyagers setting out for an unknown destination or making a return voyage from that destination. They did not include information that might have been obtained after an island group was colonized. The simulated canoes could start a voyage from any island with an allowance of up to thirty days of waiting time for favorable winds. The simulated voyage could last up to ninety days (a reasonable estimate of limits imposed by on-board provisioning), with hourly checks by the crew for previously unknown land after the first three days at sea. The canoes sailed at selected average speeds based upon the performance parameters of traditional Pacific watercraft. The course at sea could be chosen at random or by the navigator. Whenever tacking into a headwind, the heading into the wind would be the optimal one in relation to the desired course but never closer than 75 degrees to the wind. This figure is widely accepted as a practical sailing limitation of Pacific canoes generally and was established experimentally using replicate sailing canoes during trials prior to the initial voyage of the Polynesian double-hulled sailing canoe *Hokule'a* from Hawaii to Tahiti in 1976 (Finney, 1977).

The element of risk enters strongly into simulations of this kind. No prudent sailor would sail downwind toward an unknown destination, since it would be difficult if not impossible to return against the wind. In the event that no land was sighted, it was always necessary to have a way back. Irwin (1989) provides a schematic representation of the level of risk involved in exploring in different directions relative to the prevailing wind (Fig. 20). The safest course in such a situation would be into the wind

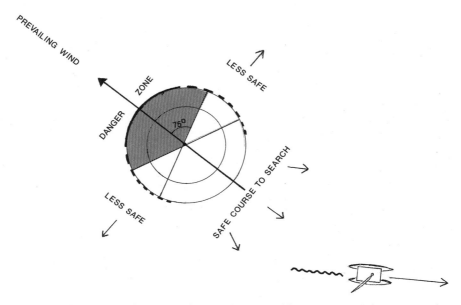

Fig 20. Plan showing the "upwind strategy" proposed by Irwin (1994) for voyages of discovery and colonization by the ancestors of the Polynesians.

within an arc defined by the canoe's ability to tack. This upwind strategy would allow the explorers to turn and sail safely up to 75 degrees downwind off the prevailing wind if they failed to find land within the time allowed by their provisions, with the best possible chance of making it back to their point of departure. Along with this upwind strategy, Irwin suggests that sailing up-latitude also would have provided a measure of safety, since the prevailing winds in the higher latitudes on both sides of the equator provide the canoe with a downwind component with which to make a return to the point of departure (Irwin, 1992: 57).

The combined use of upwind and up-latitude sailing proposed by Irwin provided a general theory of search-and-return that was incorporated into the computer simulations, enabling the researchers to simulate voyages from different islands to specific destinations – usually Pacific islands or island groups that seemed remote or otherwise difficult for early explorers to find. This is a two-way model for exploratory voyaging during the initial human colonization of the Pacific, and it owes as much to rational considerations of risk as it does to a desire to seek out new, unknown lands. On the basis of the experience of small-boat sailors in the Pacific, a voyaging canoe could safely allow one week of return sailing for every two weeks outbound, making for a fast trip home.

Irwin's two-way model implies a high order of planning and knowledge of winds and other conditions likely to be encountered at sea, although he is careful to note that uncertainties remained from the perspective afforded by this model.

> What has always seemed most marvellous about the settlement of the Pacific is that it went against the prevailing winds, for people interested in staying alive, it was taking that very direction that made it possible. Unsuccessful voyages of exploration were usually two-way, and successful ones were commonly as well, securing a navigational closure . . . (1992: 58)

Detailed knowledge of winds, currents, and other geographical factors affecting voyaging is of critical importance in archaeological analysis in the Pacific, where land archaeology has made significant progress in presenting evidence for the earliest movement of colonizing populations from west to east. This kind of analysis rests upon the assumption that geographical factors observable today operated to influence voyages of colonization 3,000 or more years ago as indicated by the presence in archaeological sites of Lapita cultural materials (especially pottery) that spread rapidly from the southwestern Pacific region through West Polynesia, with offshoots farther out into East Polynesia. Irwin's two-way model competes with earlier theories intended to account for the initial movement of colonizing human populations into Polynesia, such as Thor Heyerdahl's (1950) east-to-west theory (based upon the experimental drift voyage of the balsa raft *Kon Tiki* with the prevailing winds and currents), the accidental-voyaging model proposed by the ethnohistorian Andrew Sharp (1957), and the voyaging strategies based upon anomalous westerlies proposed by the anthropologist Ben Finney (1977; 1985; 1988). These competing theories directed attention to geographic factors in a systematic way that has transformed our understanding of the initial human settlement of the Pacific islands.

Ship Traps

From the beginnings of modern underwater archaeology there has been an awareness that shipwrecks tend to be concentrated in specific and relatively localized areas. Throckmorton (1964: 51–61) coined the term "ship trap" to describe a particularly hazardous area close to the small island of Yassi Ada, westernmost of the Chattal Islands between modern Greece and Turkey in the Aegean Sea. Noting the strength of the north-westerly wind (called the *meltemi* in Greek) that rises daily and dies down each night for three months every summer, Throckmorton offered a sailor's scenario for disaster when these winds could lead ancient sailing vessels onto the submerged reef immediately west of Yassi Ada. Subsequent underwater explorations in the late 1950s showed this reef to be littered with shipwreck debris, and excavations by George Bass and his associates followed soon after. Their work on the seventh-century Byzantine wreck found there (reported in detail by Bass, van Doorninck, et al., 1982) is widely regarded as one of the first scholarly efforts at controlled underwater archaeology. While we might now regard Throckmorton's initial assessment of the Yassi Ada ship trap as anecdotal and descriptive, it was based on a sound knowledge of local sailing conditions and their likely effects upon ancient vessels. The subsequent finds did not "prove" Throckmorton's idea, because it was presented not as a testable hypothesis, but they presaged scientifically controlled studies such as are currently being conducted in the Pacific and in the Mediterranean.

Ship traps capture the attention of underwater archaeologists by the sheer numbers of wrecks they contain. Estimates based upon historical documents, accounts by sport divers, and archaeological searches and surveys indicate, for example, at least 400 known wreckings in Bermuda since the Spanish discovery of the island group in the sixteenth century, and over 2,000 shipwrecks may have occurred since the sixteenth century off the three large capes of North Carolina – Cape Hatteras, Cape Fear, and Cape Lookout (Farb, 1985). As we have seen, the Dry Tortugas also qualify as an important ship trap.

Efforts are under way to identify and measure the relative effects of specific geographical and weather-related factors that produced shipwreck concentrations within the Dry Tortugas. Movements of water through the Straits of Florida are influenced by the Loop Current in the deeper waters of the Gulf of Mexico (Sturges, 1993). This current sweeps eastward through the Straits into the Atlantic in a path that varies with the time of year. Satellite data show the current path curving to the north of the Straits, close to the Dry Tortugas, in May and to the south of them in

December. Yet in May 1983 the current briefly shifted to its more southerly route. Although data are limited, the Loop Current is reported to move at approximately 1/2 to 1 knot. For mariners passing through the Straits, this means that the prevailing current is highly variable in its path, with its edge sometimes passing close to the Dry Tortugas. For eastbound ships the advantages of an extra boost in speed were sometimes, and unpredictably, offset by a current that could push them farther north and closer to the Dry Tortugas than intended.

Tidal currents are more difficult to assess, since there are few data for the Dry Tortugas. Captains of Florida Institute for Oceanography vessels report that strong tidal currents occur in the narrow channels but there are slack periods several hours long when passage through these channels is unhindered. Wind-driven currents also occur and may produce localized shallow-water flows, but these are less important than either the Loop Current's movements or tidal currents and eddies.

Prevailing winds in the Straits of Florida are from the east, sometimes creating anomalous combinations of currents and wind that could carry eastbound ships attempting a direct-line passage to Key West northward into the shoals and reefs of the Dry Tortugas. Here, as is so often the case at sea, a straight line is not necessarily the shortest distance between two points. Currents, tides, and winds represent more or less normal conditions for mariners in this region with real but generally manageable levels of hazard. Windstorms of various kinds increase the risks. Thunderstorms are frequent and may arise suddenly and be accompanied by tornadoes and waterspouts. Often these can be seen and avoided, but in the narrow confines of the Dry Tortugas channels vessels could be damaged or blown off course by such storms. Caribbean "northers" – rushes of cold continental air that swept in from the northwest during the fall and winter with powerful, gusty winds and rain – were another hazard. Christopher Columbus encountered what was probably a norther of this kind on 9 November 1492 near the Cuban coast (Millas, 1968: 25).

Much more intense however, were the hurricanes that tracked through this region from mid-May through November. Records indicate that from 1875 to 1958, 125 hurricanes struck Florida, averaging 1.7 storms per year, with wind speeds of up to 400 kilometers per hour and storm surges up to almost 12 meters. Almost 73 percent of these devastating storms occurred from August to mid-October, with southeastern Florida leading the United States in hurricane strikes. More recent data (Gentry, 1984) support the conclusion that there is long-term as well as seasonal periodicity to hurricane frequency, with cycles of increased hurricane activity roughly every twenty years.

At least twenty-nine hurricane-strength cyclones are reported to have struck or passed close to the Dry Tortugas between 1852 and 1935, yet few ship casualties are attributed to such storms. More have occurred during thunderstorms and northers (Murphy and Jonsson, 1993a:103). Perhaps the dramatic and visibly dangerous nature of hurricanes has encouraged mariners to be more cautious in dealing with them than with these other types of storms, but there may be a problem of sampling error here, too. Hurricane surge and water movement from northers are recognized as important in transporting sediments and altering the shapes and locations of the individual islets that make up the Dry Tortugas. Such storms not only interrupted the construction history of Fort Jefferson at least eleven times but also were factors in the virtual disappearance or reduction of Bird and Hospital Keys and significant changes to the southern end of Loggerhead Key. Storms, in addition to wave action generally, have sometimes produced radical changes in the shape and location of landmarks within the Dry Tortugas, thus presenting a hazard to navigation.

Murphy and Jonsson (1993a: 109) note that Loggerhead Key, North Key, and Pulaski Shoals presented especially high risks for ship casualties due to northers, while the southern shoals, such as East Key, Garden Key, and the southeast side of Loggerhead Key, were especially dangerous for vessels during hurricanes. An analysis of documented ship casualties in the Dry Tortugas from the earliest period to 1969 (Murphy and Jonsson, 1993b: 147) shows a total of thirty-two storm-related casualties, with fifteen resulting in ship losses. But these figures must be understood in relation to the limited data available about such casualties, since for only 43 of the 215 vessels was there sufficient information to indicate whether weather was a contributing factor. One can at least provisionally conclude from these data that when weather was a factor, the casualties tended to be serious.

Indirect indicators suggest, however, that weather may have been less important than other factors in accounting for ship casualties. Local geography appears to have been a contributing factor as well. Loggerhead Reef accounts for 58 (26.9 percent) of the total recorded casualties, and this finding correlates well with the assessment that the southern shoals were the most vulnerable to hurricanes. Adding the other southern shoals – East Key (6 percent), Garden Key (6.5 percent), and Bird Key (5.6 percent) – raises the total to 97 (45 percent) of documented casualties. One difficulty with this correlation is that weather is not often mentioned in relation to ship losses, so there may have been other factors operating to produce this result. The northern shoals, including Loggerhead Key, Pulaski Shoal, Northwest Reef, and North Key, accounted for a total of 43 (19.9 percent) of documented casualties. This could be linked to the effects of northers, but such a correlation is constrained by the same limitations of the documentary record as with hurricanes and remains speculative. While one cannot come to final conclusions about these correlations, it is apparent that data of this kind enable maritime archaeologists to begin to evaluate the relative hazard potentials within a complex ship trap.

The Loggerhead Reef system operated as a ship trap (Gould and Conlin, 1999). This reef extends approximately 2.9 kilometers south from the south end of Loggerhead Key. One of its most prominent shipwrecks was the Barrel wreck, which lies about two-thirds of the way along the reef on a sandy bottom at a depth of 7.6 meters. Its most visible feature is a compact cluster of 34 cement barrel casts resting in rows, formed when the ship sank and the natural concrete inside the wooden barrels hardened and set. Two small barrel clusters were also found at other locations. A scatter of at least 320 similar barrel casts runs in a generally north–northwesterly direction away from the main cluster for at least 91 meters, with some occurring over 300 meters away (Fig. 21). The main barrel cast pile at the wreck site directly overlay a layer of ballast stones which, in turn, rested directly upon a preserved portion of the ship's hull. These timbers were traced, cleared by a combination of hand-fanning and use of a suction dredge, and mapped in detail (Fig. 22a–b). Thanks to a slight alteration in the reef topography caused by the main barrel cast pile and currents across the site of from ½ to 1 knot, silt and sand have accumulated over the wooden timbers enough to stabilize the remaining ship structure and to protect the wood from invasion by shipworms.

Before such stabilization was achieved, the wreck was subjected to postdepositional processes characteristic of shallow and high-energy underwater environments. The absence of whole or complete dressed paving

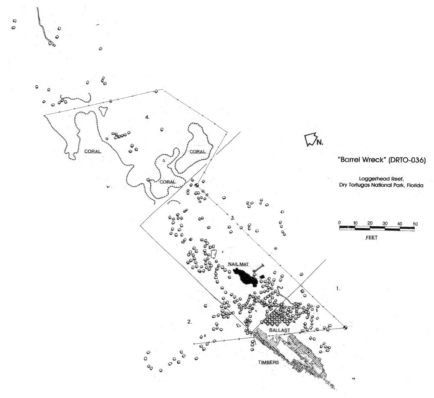

Fig 21. Trilateration plan of the "Barrel Wreck" site, Loggerhead Reef, Dry Tortugas, National Park, Florida.

stones and the occurrence of large areas of hull timbers not overlain by either cargo or ballast suggested salvage activity at the wreck. Whole paving stones, needed at Fort Jefferson, may have been part of the ship's original cargo and would have been easily salvaged in these shallow waters, while broken pieces would have been left at the site. Alternatively, paving stone fragments may have been part of the ship's ballast rather than of its cargo. But if the absence of whole paving stones remains problematic as evidence of salvage the absence of rigging (with the exception of a single broken chainplate) at the site is somewhat more convincing, since this was often the object of nineteenth-century salvage attempts. In short, salvage is a probable postdepositional factor in the patterning of some of the material associations at the Barrel wreck site, but it can be ruled out as a factor in the patterning of the cement barrel casts.

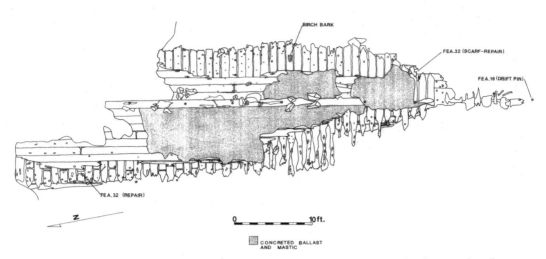

DRTO-036 TIMBER PLAN

Fig 22a–b*(opposite page)***.** Plan of ship's timbers and photograph of cement barrel casts at "Barrel Wreck" site, Loggerhead Reef, Dry Tortugas National Park, Florida.

To resolve the issue of how these barrel casts came to rest in their present locations on Loggerhead Reef, a nearest-neighbor analysis was performed on them to measure their concentration in different zones of the site. Zone 1, which contained fifty-eight casts, extended south from the line defined by the northernmost row of the central barrel pile. Barrels in this zone became detached from the central barrel pile as originally stacked in the ship's hold, either during the wrecking process or afterwards. Zone 2, which contained thirty-seven casts, extended westward from what was a portion of the ship's hull that had burned and collapsed outward during the wrecking event. This part of the wreck also had a large mat of iron nails that had corroded into a layer matching the curvature of the hull, upon which it had rested before the hull decomposed. In other words, the mat of corroded nails preserved a "ghost image" of the part of the hull that had burned and collapsed, spilling barrels to the west. This was the only zone without even a single row of barrels resting in contact with each other, suggesting the relative violence of the wrecking event at this point along the side of the ship's hull. Charred ceramics and melted-glass bottle fragments were found embedded in the nail mat.

Fig 22b

The central barrel pile rose high enough above the seabed to create a hump that caused the loose barrels on either site of it to roll off in opposite directions. Those that became detached and rolled to the north, 166 in all, were found in Zone 3. The presence there of a row of five barrel casts in contact with each other suggested the remains of another barrel pile located between the central pile and the corroded-nail mat – that is, barrels dispersed from another hold within the ship. The north end of the zone was defined by a row of prominent, jagged coral heads that formed an impenetrable obstacle to the postdepositional movement of barrel casts northward. The assumption here was that any casts found to the north of these coral heads could only have been deposited from a part of the ship that broke away, floated briefly, and sank after the ship struck the coral heads.

Zone 4, north of the coral heads, contained the smallest number of detached barrel casts (twenty-nine) and the widest dispersal of them. The presence of a single row of four attached casts supported the inference that a part of the ship with a hold containing more barrels stowed in rows sank here.

Storms were probably more important than salvage in accounting for the distribution of barrel casts across the site. Conlin (1994: 26) points out that the earliest storms acting upon the shipwreck would have had the greatest effect on the spatial patterning of wreck materials such as barrel casts. The issue, therefore, was one of establishing the relative importance of the wrecking process versus the effects of storms. The site plan shows that the barrel casts and other wreckage were distributed on both sides of a coral head, with some barrel casts resting on elevated portions of the coral reef formation above the level of the main barrel cast concentration or the wooden structure. This patterning suggests that the ship struck the coral head and split into two sections that floated a short distance before sinking and spilling out some of the cargo. The ship also burned, as is evidenced by charred timbers and scorched and melted items like glass and ceramics. The nearest-neighbor analysis, combined with the visual patterning shown on the site plan, indicated a complex combination of proximate factors connected with the wrecking event and postdepositional factors that acted to disperse the ship's contents more widely. The reef topography around the coral head and to the north was uneven, with crevices and hollows that effectively captured some of the barrel casts and limited their movement by storm waves, however powerful. It is likely, therefore, that the dispersal of barrel casts across the site was a product first of the wrecking process, as portions of the ship floated and then settled to the bottom in a more-or-less linear pattern along a north–south axis, and then of the differential capture of detached barrels by the uneven reef terrain.

By a systematic process of elemination, it was possible to rule out salvage and storm action as the most important factors in the patterning of cement barrel casts at the Barrel wreck site, leaving the relative movements of different parts of the ship during the wrecking process as the primary explanation for the position of these items shown in the site plan. This conclusion was possible only after recognition and systematic evaluation of the localized environmental and geographical features of this particular ship trap in relation to the ship's structural remains and contents. This stepwise kind of analysis is essential whenever there is evidence for multiple shipwrecks with overlapping debris fields, as is often the case at ship-trap localities like Loggerhead Reef.

Before and After the Wreck

Examination of the physical properties of ships in relation to sea conditions before wrecking and the physical conditions that affect ships after they are wrecked is necessary for the evaluation of any shipwreck site. Everyone knows, for example, that the *Titanic* struck an iceberg while traveling at high speed, and on the face of it this would seem to be a sufficient explanation. Yet unanswered questions persist. Conventional wisdom has always suggested that a massive gash or tear occurred below the waterline as a result of contact with the iceberg, passing along a distance of almost 72 meters and across five of the ship's sixteen watertight compartments. Yet expert opinions offered since the British inquest in 1912 have questioned whether such a continuous gash ever existed (Ballard, 1987: 196–197). Intermittent damage caused by contact with the ice may more likely have ruptured the joints between the hull plates, popping rivets and opening the seams to the sea. The exact nature of the hull breach is hard to determine today, mainly because the starboard side of the ship's bow where the damage occurred is deeply buried in silt. Further complicating the details of the *Titanic*'s wrecking sequence is the possibility that the steel used in the ship's hull plates was rendered brittle by the cold winter temperatures of the North Atlantic so that a crack could have spread almost instantaneously along the hull. Ship casualties due to a "fracture epidemic" in which hull structures and plating split disastrously on U.S. war-built merchant ships were a source of genuine alarm during 1942. Finally, in January 1943, the newly built T-2 tanker *Schenectady* broke in two and sank at its mooring in calm waters near Portland, Oregon, on a day when the air temperature was −3 degrees Celsius, dramatically calling attention to the problem. Subsequent research revealed that cracking casualties in steel at low temperatures had been documented as far back as 1884, in the early days of steel ship construction, and included such famous ships as the liner *Leviathan*, built in 1913, as well as steel bridges and storage tanks (MacCutcheon, 1989: 213).

This possibility raises two points of special interest for maritime archaeologists. First, it suggests that preexisting conditions of the ship's technology were factors in the ship's loss, and, second, it presents a clear example of the *principle of equifinality* – the recognition of more than one equally acceptable explanation for the same evidence. The specific issue of the proximate factors causing the loss of the *Titanic* has yet to be resolved. Scientific materials testing of the sort conducted in World War II during the fracture epidemic may one day be possible, however, on steel plates from the wreck of the *Titanic*, and this will allow archaeologists and maritime historians to support or rule out this possibility. The material properties of the ship's hull may be a key issue. This kind of materials-based study has been used successfully in land archaeology and should be extended to underwater research whenever possible as part of the "before and after" approach to shipwrecks. It reminds us once again that shipwrecks should not be regarded simply as historical events but as embedded in sociocultural and natural processes, with both antecedents and consequences that need to be examined at least as carefully as the proximate causes of the event itself.

4 · The Archaeology of Small Watercraft

Because the remains of early watercraft are often found in saturated soils and peat bogs, the archaeological record tends toward overrepresentation of log and wood plank boats, since these are better preserved than watercraft made of skins, reeds, or other, more perishable materials (McGrail, 1981: 6). Sometimes this bias can be overcome to a degree by the use of documentary and iconographic information, although such representations often lack detail and may be inaccurate. The biggest problem with the archaeology of small watercraft has been the tendency to resort to conjectural history to overcome the limitations and gaps imposed by the archaeological record. There are still serious questions about the use of ethnographic analogies in an attempt to understand ancient boatbuilding and use (McGrail, 1998: 3). Their value to archaeology was succinctly summarized by Muckelroy (1978: 236) as providing a wider range of possibilities for assessing how particular boat technologies may have been used than experimental reconstructions or computer-generated simulations. The archaeology of boats and early ships has come a long way, however, since Muckelroy's time, and today the archaeological evidence can support more empirically grounded analysis and interpretation.

Ephemeral Watercraft

The earliest direct archaeological evidence for small watercraft is a birchwood paddle preserved in peat and mud deposits at Star Carr, a roughly 8,000-year-old Mesolithic campsite in northeastern England (Clark, 1954: 23, Fig. 77, Pl. 21). The inferred boat, constructed using skins or birch bark over a wood frame, was probably the most technologically complex item in the material culture inventory of these ancient hunter–gatherers (Muckelroy, 1978: 3).

Intriguing but inconclusive evidence exists for prehistoric sailing rafts in the form of wooden models found in sites excavated by the archaeologist Junius Bird near Arica, Chile, and there are eyewitness accounts by European explorers such as William Dampier in the 1680s of large sailing rafts for transporting freight between Lima, Peru, and the Bay of Panama (Johnstone, 1980: 8). Historical examples of large rafts, either rowed or sailed, have been described from various locations in Asia and from Panama. These rafts appear to share certain basic technological features, such as a tapered shape, an uneven number of logs, and sometimes hardwood pins to fasten the logs together. It is tempting to suppose that rafts of this sort were used on initial voyages of colonization during the Pleistocene, especially to offshore destinations such as Australia/New Guinea/Tasmania and Japan, but so far direct archaeological evidence for this idea is lacking.

It has been suggested that bark canoes may be the most ancient form of constructed watercraft (Hornell, 1970: 17). Hornell proposed a progression of stages, from technologically simple to complex, based upon ethnographic and historical examples and then projected into the prehistoric past. As Johnstone (1980: 24–25) has pointed out, the dominant factor in the building of bark canoes would have been the presence of suitable trees, such as birch, beech, and certain eucalypts. One of the obvious problems with Hornell's scheme, aside from its lack of direct archaeological evidence, was the fact that bark boatbuilding was predominantly a New World tradition despite Europe's having suitable trees.

Similar problems of historical conjecture apply to skin and reed boats. Some limited archaeological evidence exists for prehistoric reed boats in the form of ceramic models of Chimu cultural origin in Peru from around A.D. 1200 and a miniature reed boat excavated from a burial in the Atacama Desert of the northern Chile coast, preserved by unusually dry conditions and claimed to be around 2,000 years old (Johnstone, 1980: 14). In historic times, reed boats were widely observed in use in Tasmania, New Zealand, and Easter Island, as well as in several New World localities (including Baja California, Mexico, and Lake Titicaca, Bolivia) and among the Marsh Arabs of Mesopotamia. Despite cautionary remarks concerning the use of ethnographic evidence to argue about situations many thousands of years ago, Johnstone (1980: 16) states that "these craft can be followed in an intermittent chain of modern survivals to Tasmania and to the west coast of South America." It is unclear to what extent these survivals are to be interpreted as the product of cultural evolution or as traits preserved from an earlier cultural diffusion. Such craft may have been useful during antiquity because of their simplicity of construction and buoyancy, but all of the ethnographic accounts agree that to compete effectively against large rafts for long voyages they would have required a supporting framework and other technical improvements to prevent waterlogging.

Skin boats are also widely reported ethnographically, with the best-known examples being the Eskimo kayak and umiak. The kayak was a light and agile craft, usually used by a single male for purposes of hunting and fishing, while the umiak (the "womens' boat") was a larger craft used for transporting people and goods. Johnstone argues that the watertightness of skin boats, including not only the Eskimo craft but also the Irish curragh and the *baidarka* of northern Russia, made them advantageous for use in cold northern waters (1980: 38–39). This functional argument is overshadowed, however, by his diffusionist and evolutionary speculations as to the spread of simple round boats comparable to the coracle of the British Isles and the later appearance of more complex skin boats requiring the preparation and sewing of skins and the construction of a suitable frame for the skin covering. As with rafts and reed boats, these arguments do little more than point to the scarcity of direct archaeological evidence for such watercraft.

Newer studies of ancient and traditional ethnographic boats and boat-building methods rely less upon evolutionist or diffusionist interpretations and avoid general explanations based on conjectural history. As the maritime historians Basil Greenhill and John Morrison (1995: 20) point out,

> Boats have developed all over the world in different ways and at different speeds. Their development has been conditioned by the geography of the local waters, climate, purposes for which the boat was needed, availability of materials for their construction, tradition of craftsmanship which grew up among the boatbuilders and the general state and nature of the culture of the people building them.

These scholars encourage a more adaptational perspective with regard to boats and boatbuilding in the distant past, cautioning against judging any boat against watercraft built by other peoples for other purposes. Their concept of "fitness of purpose" in relation to local conditions encourages the assessment of boats and boatbuilding traditions in terms of the particular opportunities and constraints of the place and time in which they appeared. This point of view is handicapped, however, by the tyranny of the archaeological record, which limits and skews the information available to scholars by permitting evidence about some varieties to survive while obscuring the remains of others.

For example, there is one notable exception to the dearth of archaeological information about skin boats. Archaeologists working in the Arctic have found prehistoric boat parts and, in one case, a nearly complete boat frame preserved in late pre-Eskimo contexts from both the eastern and western extremities of the geographical distribution of the Eskimo. Bark models and toys of kayaks and umiaks have been found in late prehistoric archaeological sites on St. Lawrence Island, in the Bering Strait (Collins, 1937: 158–159, Pl. 59, Figs. 1–3, 6), and at Point Barrow, Alaska, at the localities of Utkiavik, Nunagiak, and Birnirk (Ford, 1959: 156–158, Fig. 78). Wooden boat parts and a portion of a paddle blade were also found at Birnirk (Ford, 1959: 158–160, Figs. 79–80). Wooden parts from a kayak were identified at the Nukleet site at Cape Denbigh, Alaska, dating to around A.D. 1400 (Giddings, 1964: 81–83, Pl. 28). All of these finds resembled ethnographic Eskimo boats in most respects. Caution, however, is needed when interpreting finds of this kind, since it is often hard to distinguish the parts for skin boat frames from those of sleds. And, in the context of a treeless environment where wood was scarce, it was not unusual for Arctic Eskimos to recycle wooden items by reshaping or reusing them to other suit other purposes. Farther south, kayak parts have been reported from the archaeological site of Kar–716 on Kodiak Island (Clark, 1974), and kayak or *baidarka* frame pieces and paddle fragments were identified from the Palutat Cave site, Prince William Sound, Alaska (de Laguna, 1956: 245–248, Fig. 37, Pl. 57). The historical Chugach and Chenega people of this region used two- and three-man kayak-like skin boats referred to as *baidarka*. Unlike the Arctic Eskimo, these Southeast Alaskan coastal people did not use sleds for transport, so there is no danger in this case of confusing boat parts with sled pieces.

Aside from Thule-period (proto-Eskimo) kayak parts from the Mackenzie River Delta region (McGhee, 1974), relatively few prehistoric boat parts are reported from archaelogical sites across the Canadian Arctic. But in Peary Land in extreme northeastern Greenland Danish archaeologists in 1949 found and recorded the nearly complete frame of a late prehistoric (Thule-period) umiak together with a wooden paddle (Knuth, 1952: Figs. 1, 3–5). The boat had a heavy wooden keel plank with thirteen cross-pieces held together with lashings of baleen and large spikes of walrus ivory. Spruce and/or larch driftwood was used for the boat's construction, but a single piece of oak from the port gunwale suggests that the Eskimos using this boat may have encountered Europeans or the wreckage of a European ship during their travels. On the basis of this piece of oak, Knuth (1952: 23) suggested that this umiak could not be more than 300 years old. The boat, as measured in situ, was 10.86 meters long and was preserved over its entire length. The pieces from this boat were later recovered and are at the Danish National Museum, Copenhagen. As noted by both Ford and Knuth, there are close resemblances between this umiak and some of the boat parts found by archaeologists in the Alaskan Arctic sites.

None of the archaeological evidence found so far for ephemeral watercraft comes from underwater sites, nor is any of it very old.

Log Dugouts

Log dugouts appear more often in the archaeological record. Archaeological and ethnographic evidence for the use of log dugouts is found in nearly every temperate region of the world as well as in many tropical areas. A hollowed pine log that may have served as a watercraft was reported from Pesse, the Netherlands, with a radiocarbon date of around 6315 B.C. (McGrail, 1978: 9). The date places this find within the Mesolithic, during the final retreat of the Pleistocene glaciers from northern Europe. Although there is uncertainty as to whether this item was actually a boat, there is nothing improbable about the idea that prehistoric hunter-gatherers used dugout log craft. Ethnographic sources abound with accounts of log dugouts made and used by hunter-gatherers from relatively sedentary people like the Indians of northern California and the Northwest Coast, who used immense trunks of redwood, cedar, and fir to construct canoes for both river and offshore use, to mobile hunter-gatherers like the Aborigines of northern Australia and Queensland. In this latter case, dugout technology probably was adopted in late prehistoric times from Macassan islanders from Indonesia. Their fleets of small sailing craft left the Celebes to make annual visits to the northern coast of Australia to harvest trepang, a variety of sea cucumber much sought-after as a delicacy in Asian diets (Edwards, 1972: 10–14). In addition, some Queensland dugout canoes sprouted outriggers, perhaps due to influences by way of New Guinea.

Unambiguous archaeological evidence appears for dugout boats during the European Neolithic and early Bronze Age. With the worldwide rise of sea levels following the final retreat of the Pleistocene glaciers, many parts of northern Europe were cut off as islands, making some form of water transport essential. With the emergence of farming economies and increased trade in Europe after around 5,000 years ago, the occurrence of log dugouts in the archaeological record increases as well. Many of these boats have been dated by means of radiocarbon analysis, and efforts are continuing to provide absolute dates using dendrochronology as well. Fifteen dugout log boats of alder (*Alnus* sp.) were found in the Amose peat bog near Verup, Denmark, and the peat in which they were found was radiocarbon-dated to around 2000 B.C. Two other Danish log boats (one radiocarbon dated to 3310 B.C.) as well as one in France and one in Italy also have reported dates that place them in either late Neolithic or early Bronze Age contexts (McGrail, 1981: 14; 1998: 86).

Some of the log dugouts from this period may have been paired or constructed with multiple hulls attached by means of connecting poles and/or lashings to provide additional carrying capacity and stability. Ethnographic examples of double and multiple dugouts are reported in detail from Poland and Finland (Johnstone, 1980: 48–49; Boczar, 1966; Crumlin-Pedersen, 1967). The archaeologist Grahame Clark (1952: 288) noted that multiple dugouts could have provided the stability needed to transport livestock along and across rivers. Timbers fastened alongside the log hull were another way of improving stability, as were various techniques for expanding the beam of the dugout by heating and flaring the sides. These techniques are better-known through the study of ethnographic cases in Finland, the Baltic states, and India than from archaeological sources, so one must view with caution the interpretation offered by Crumlin-

Pedersen (1972: 208–34) that the expanded softwood dugout was the archetype for northern European planked boats.

The earliest log dugout reported from Britain is from Locharbriggs in Dumfriesshire (McGrail, 1998: 86), dated by radiocarbon to 1804 B.C. Other early examples include those from Appleby (ca. 1100 B.C.) and Short Ferry, Lincolnshire (ca. 846 B.C.). The Appleby boat is of special interest because of the probable use of wooden treenails in its construction (McGrail, 1978: 333) – a feature more generally associated with wood-plank craft. Treenails are round, dowel-like hardwood pegs that are inserted into drilled holes to join wooden elements, and they continue to be a key element of wooden boat and ship joinery today.

By far the largest log dugout found in a prehistoric archaeological context in Britain, however, is the one from Brigg, near the River Ancholme, unearthed in 1886 (McGrail, 1981: 17; 1983: 36–37). It dates to approximately the same period as the dugouts reported above. Recorded in detail before it was destroyed in a fire at the Hull Museum during the 1940s, it was shaped from a single, much larger oak log to produce a boat 14.8 meters long, 1.29–1.37 meters wide, and 1 meter deep at the stern. McGrail (1978) estimated that it could have carried two men standing and five men kneeling while drawing only 36 centimeters of water. Alternatively, it could have transported 10,000 kilograms of stone or other dead weight with a crew of two while drawing 88 centimeters and with a freeboard of 12 centimeters. It would, however, have been relatively unstable when lightly loaded. In contrast, a dugout craft from Poole Harbor, Dorset, dated to around 300–200 B.C., was constructed in such a way as to be stable with such a load. Its bow was carved into the shape of a stem, suggesting to McGrail (1983: 38) that its builders were familiar with plank boats possessing true stems. In contrast to the Brigg boat, it was made from a half log split longitudinally and could transport a load of 1,723 kilograms along with four crewmen. With a load of peat it would have had a higher center of gravity than with a load of stone of similar weight.

McGrail notes that thirty of a total of fifty European log dugouts so far dated are from after the first century A.D. In addition to these there are three as-yet undated oak log dugouts excavated from the Rhine River near Zwammerdam, the Netherlands. Two of these have holes in their midship section leading to a space enclosed by watertight bulkheads, suggesting a free-flooding fishwell inside each boat (McGrail, 1983: 37). There is archaeological evidence that log boats continued in use in many parts of medieval and postmedieval Europe, with twelve examples reported from Britain dating between A.D. 640 and 1335 and others from Scandinavia, Russia, France, and Italy dated from A.D. 450 to 1300 (McGrail, 1981: 27). Excavated examples of log dugouts have been reported from northern Szechwan in China dating from around the fourth century B.C. (Needham, 1971: 388–389; Johnstone, 1980: 187). At least some of these craft, which were about 5 meters long and 1 meter wide, contained human remains and had been used as coffins. These dugouts were flat-bottomed with near-vertical sides. Although they were large enough to have been used as watercraft on rivers and lakes, it is not known if they were initially used as boats and later recycled as coffins or intended as burial items. Log dugout technology is reported from burial sites in Vietnam about A.D. 375 and Malysia in the second century A.D. (Sieveking, 1954).

A dugout canoe encountered near Jamaica on Columbus's second voyage was estimated by his chronicler, Bernaldez, as 29.3 meters long and 2.4 meters wide, while another was described that could carry seventy–eighty men (McKusick, 1960). Log canoes of this size could easily account for archaeological evidence of widespread trade along the Mesoamerican coast and throughout the Caribbean prior to European contact there. In the Yucatan region of Mexico, Chontal Maya merchants dominated sea trade from Tabasco to Honduras via Cozumel during the Post-Classic Maya period until around A.D. 1450 (Sabloff and Rathje, 1975), and it was probably one of their large trading canoes that Columbus encountered near the Bay Islands of Honduras during his fourth voyage in 1502.

Large dugout canoes were also encountered by early European explorers along the British Columbia coast during the eighteenth century, and they appear not to have changed much in more recent times (Fig. 23). As indicated by nineteenth-century accounts, log dugouts were in use in many parts of the New World, including the Upper Amazon, northern California (Fig. 24), the Mississippi Valley, and other parts of the eastern United States. This distribution suggests that they were present in at least some of these areas prior to European contact, and this supposition is borne out by archaeological finds in several places. A log dugout made of

Fig. 23. Haida cedar dugout canoe. Published with permission of the American Museum of Natural History, New York.

Fig. 24. A Tolowa Indian, Mr. Sam Lopez, making modifications to a traditional Northwest California dugout river canoe in 1963. Specifically, he has flattened the peaked stem of the boat for an outboard motor.

white oak was recovered from Lake Erie and radiocarbon-dated to around 1600 B.C., and four pine-log dugouts with radiocarbon dates ranging from about A.D. 300 to 1300 have been reported from Florida (McGrail, 1981: 79). A collection of five small whole or fragmentary dugout canoes was recovered from Palutat Cave along Prince William Sound, Alaska (de Laguna, 1956: 241–245, Fig. 36, Pl. 56). These canoes were only 3.6–3.8 meters long and about 54.8 centimeters wide and could have been used only for short trips in sheltered waters, but they are of special interest because of their association with skin boat parts (from a kayak and/or *baidarka*) at the same site. Although not dated, the Palutat Cave materials probably belong to late prehistoric or early European contact period times, since they closely resemble the watercraft of the Chugach Eskimo of the region.

In the Southwest and Central Pacific there were dugout log watercraft with built-up planking and a variety of outrigger and double-hulled canoe types (Fig. 25a–b), often with particular stylistic or technical details that link the vessel's origin and use to a particular island group (Haddon and Hornell, 1975). It is in the Pacific that the temptation is the greatest to offer conjectural arguments about ancient boatbuilding practices based upon evolutionist and diffusionist theories. As with the study of ephemeral watercraft, there are claims regarding the technological evolution of wooden boats from log dugouts to built-up plank boats that so far have no archaeological support whatever. Some of these ideas, such as that built-up plank boats evolved from expanded dugouts, can be tested archaeologically and may eventually prove to be correct, but in the absence of such testing they remain speculative.

Planked Boats

Enough archaeological evidence exists for early planked watercraft in different regions to warn against evolutionist or diffusionist assumptions about their historical development. McGrail (1983: 41–42; 1998) points to a good example in his discussion of a fourteenth-century planked oak boat excavated from boggy soils in an old lakebed at Kentmere, England. This 4.3-meter-long rowing craft, excavated and described by archaeologist David Wilson (1966) in 1955, had plank sides built up from what appeared to be a logboat that had been damaged or had rotted. The

Fig 25a–b. Fijian outrigger canoe under sail at Ono-I-Lau, in 1991. Small canoes like this were commonly used for fishing and for travel close to shore. Fig. 25b. Fijian double-hull voyaging canoe at the Fiji Museum, Suva. This canoe was collected in 1918. The mast and sail are stowed along the starboard (right) side of the vessel, holding the steering oar in place. An older steering oar can be seen resting on the floor in the lower right-hand corner of the picture. Published with permission of the Fiji Museum.

clinker-built planking on the sides was secured by four birch ribs. "Clinker-built" planking involves a degree of overlapping of each plank with the next along either the top or the bottom. The appearance of this boat might seem to confirm the notion that planked hulls developed from expanded log dugouts, but in fact planked boats have been documented as far back as the Bronze Age.

In 1894 the French explorer-archaeologist Jean-Jacques de Morgan reported finding six wood-planked boats buried near a brick pyramid at Dashur belonging to the twelfth-Dynasty Egyptian ruler Sestostris III (1850 B.C.). Some uncertainty surrounds de Morgan's excavation reports, and only four of these boats are known to exist in museum collections. Two of these, one at the Field Museum of Natural History in Chicago and the other at the Carnegie Museum of Natural History in Pittsburgh, have been studied in detail by Cheryl Ward Haldane, whose results are summarized by Steffy (1994: 33–36). The Chicago boat is 9.8 meters long and 2.4 meters wide, and others are of comparable size. The hulls of all of these boats consist of edge-to-edge cedar planks closely fitted and smoothly rounded. There is no keel, nor are there any frames or flattened bottoms. The planks were attached to each other by mortise-and-tenon joints and dovetail fastenings, although the latter may have been later additions. Wood beams supported the hull laterally with rabbets (grooves cut into the upper surfaces to seat removable deck planks). Abutting plank edges were beveled for a close fit, and there are no signs of lashings for edge joinery below the waterline. There is no mention of caulking for the Dashur boats, although Steffy (1994: 36) quotes a fifth-century-B.C. account of Egyptian boat construction by Herodotus that includes the use of papyrus-fiber caulking.

Steffy (1994: 36) cautions that these were funerary boats, and there is no assurance that this was exactly the way commercial craft were constructed in the same period and region, but he also points out that they were constructed well enough for travel on the Nile and probably reflect at least some of the boatbuilding practices of the time. Depictions of boats in use on the Nile River abound in Egyptian wall paintings and bas-reliefs. Despite their often stylized, spoon-shaped appearance, these images provide enough detail to show that both wood-planked and reed boats were widely used throughout the history of ancient Egypt. To these images one can add model boats found in tombs. Wood-planked boats represented in this manner varied in size and function, from small craft for fishing and waterfowling to larger vessels used in royal excursions and even a massive barge from around 1500 B.C. shown transporting stone obelisks (Casson, 1971: Fig. 14). Images on rock surfaces and pottery from southern Egypt dating back to around 3200 B.C. are thought to include the earliest known representation of a sail (Casson, 1991: 3, Pl. 1). The great riverine boating tradition of ancient Egypt with the early use of sail depended in large measure on a unique combination of circumstances that enabled boaters to sail south, upstream, with the prevailing winds and drift back north with the river current (Casson, 1991: 13).

In England, four Bronze Age planked boats have been recovered from archaeological sites, none of them burials, and therefore this particular problem of cultural sampling does not apply in this case. The first of these boats to be discovered was the so-called Brigg raft, excavated in the shoreline mud along the Humber River in north Lincolnshire in 1888. Initially this find was described as a flat series of sewn oak planks with moss caulking and longitudinal laths at the seams of the planks and with timbers extending transversely through cleats that rose above the planks. When the craft was reexcavated in 1974 it proved to be the flat bottom of a planked boat or barge (McGrail, 1975; 1981: 18–19), and it has been radiocarbon-dated to around 650 B.C.

Remains of three sewn-planked boats were excavated in the tidal foreshore of the Humber River at North Ferriby, Yorkshire, by E. V. Wright (1976) intermittently between 1937 and 1963. Four radiocarbon dates place these boats between about 1217 and 715 B.C., making them the oldest planked boats known so far in Europe. The bottom of each of these boats consisted of three oak planks, some of which were composite with scarf joints, with the keel plank twice as thick as the other two flanking it. Ferriby was estimated to have an original length of 14.35 meters and was the most complete of the three. The two side planks along the bottom were attached to the keel plank by means of thin yew saplings, pounded and twisted into a cord and stitched through carefully drilled holes, with dry moss as caulking where the planks butted together. Wooden wedges were inserted to seal the holes and tighten the joints, and ash poles were inserted as transverse stiffeners through raised cleats in a manner comparable to that of the Brigg "raft." Of special interest were the remains of the first side strakes of boats 1 and 3 (Fig. 26), showing

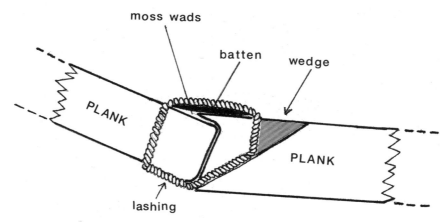

Fig 26. Diagram of sewn-plank joinery of the Ferriby 1 boat (after Steffy, 1994). However improbable this mode of joinery may appear, it is the earliest example known so far of plank-boat construction in Europe.

details of the attachment of the lowest side strake and the outer bottom plank (Steffy, 1994: Fig. 3–17). The tightness of this attachment and the generally smooth finish of these boats revealed a high order of boatbuilding skill.

The fact that all three Ferriby craft showed these features as well as resemblances to the Brigg "raft" indicated that this was not a chance occurrence (Johnstone, 1980: 146), but there are still questions about how representative these boats are of European Bronze Age boat construction. They could have been the work of an unusually skilled craftsman in this locality of Britain, or they could be the products of a regional vernacular boatbuilding tradition. Speculation abounds about the historical relationship of the Ferriby and Brigg boats to subsequent early European boat and ship construction techniques, mostly along the techno-evolutionary lines we have seen with regard to the hypothesized relationship between expanded log dugouts and planked boats (Johnstone, 1980: 150–151). There is little to suggest that the Ferriby and Brigg boats were historical antecedents of the Iron Age craft found archaeologically in England, the Netherlands, Switzerland, France, and England.

No planked-boat remains have yet been found in Asia that are as ancient as the Dashur boats from Egypt or the Ferriby and Brigg boats from Britain. Oracle bones from the Shang Dynasty in China (1766–1122 B.C.) contain incised pictographs showing curved, ladderlike shapes representing the word for boat (*chou*), which Needham (1970: 63) argues was a graphic representation of a sampan. The later appearance of planked wooden craft with the flat-bottomed, punt-ended shapes of Chinese, Japanese, and Southeast Asian sampans and junks is so far without archaeological antecedents before the appearance of a fragmentary wooden boat model from a tomb in Changsha, dated to around 50 B.C., and two ceramic model boats from the first-century-A.D. tombs near Canton (Needham, 1971: 447–448, Figs. 961–965 and 1036–1037). These models are ambiguous in details such as bulkheads, but they do show features such as a notch at one end for a steering sweep, poling galleries along the sides, and a unique type of rudder positioned under the overhanging stern.

One of the best archaeological examples of an early Asian planked boat or small ship comes from the Pattaya site in Thailand (Green and Intakosi, 1983; Green and Harper, 1983; Green, 1996). The site had been extensively looted by treasure hunters in search of pottery, especially porcelain, but portions of the hull structure remained intact and provided useful information about the vessel's construction. While no firm dates have been offered for either the vessel's construction or its loss, the excavators regard it as having fairly close parallels to the Song Dynasty Quanzhou ship (Green, 1983a). Like the Quanzhou ship, the Pattaya vessel was constructed of edge-joined planks attached with dowel fasteners. About 9 meters of the length of the hull was preserved along with 4.5 meters of the vessel's width. It had a definite keel and a pronounced V shape to the hull on either side of the keel. Further similarities to the Quanzhou ship included three layers of hull planking and the presence of bulkheads.

These findings are especially important when compared with historically recent Chinese sampans (Greenhill and Morrison, 1995: 81–83), which lacked keels and tended to be either flat-bottomed (the "duck sampan" of North China) or somewhat more round-bottomed, with a rounded turn of bilge where the sides met the bottom (the "chicken sampan" of South China). The modes of construction of the ancient Pattaya vessel and the Quanzhou ship differed significantly from those of historical or contemporary sampans except for the presence of transverse bulkheads. The post-European-contact period sampans of China are of considerable interest in their own right but are not a good guide for interpreting ancient Asian shipwrecks. As in the case of remains from Europe and the Mediterranean region, the evidence of underwater archaeology points to variation and changes in ancient boatbuilding that cannot be fully accounted for with reference to contemporary examples.

Nowhere do we find greater continuity between prehistoric and historical boatbuilding traditions than in Polynesia and Micronesia. Despite the experimental voyaging of the double-hulled canoe *Hokule'a* (Fig. 27), computer simulations of voyages, images of canoes depicted in rock art (Fig. 28), and a wealth of firsthand ethnographic accounts of boatbuilding, seamanship, and long-distance navigation (for example, Gladwin, 1970; Feinberg, 1988), there is only a single case so far of direct archaeological evidence of prehistoric canoe remains from this region. This find resulted from over ten years of archaeological salvage work undertaken by Yosihiko Sinoto, an archaeologist from the Bernice P. Bishop Museum of Honolulu and a specialist in Polynesian culture history, on the grounds of a hotel complex on Huahine Island, in the Society Islands, French Polynesia. Sinoto's painstaking efforts from 1973 to 1984 in the water-logged deposits of this large site produced a picture of an ancient settlement with what appear to be multiple task-specific localities including a canoe-making area, all radiocarbon-dated to around A.D. 700 to 1150 (Sinoto, 1983; 1988: 114). Two large side planks nearly 7 meters long, a steering paddle about 4 meters long, and remains of finished and unfinished bailers were exposed and identified. The planks had drilled holes for lashings, and the ends were shaped to form scarf-joints with the planks to which they were attached at either end. Sinoto (1983: 14) thinks that this row of planks formed a splashboard along the top of a dugout hull − a common practice among historical Pacific Islanders and one that makes it hard to know whether to classify such vessels as dugouts or as planked canoes. Analysis of the wood indicated that the planks were made from *Terminalia* sp., a hardwood that is common throughout the Pacific. There had been speculation that the planks were made of New Zealand-derived kauri wood, suggesting a return voyage from New Zealand to Huahine, but this identification effectively ruled out that interpretation (Sinoto, 1988: 125).

The size of the planks and steering oar suggested that canoes large enough for long-distance voyaging were being constructed at Huahine in prehistoric times. In another part of the site complex at Huahine, Sinoto's team uncovered a straight log 12 meters long that may have been a mast for a canoe, although it was found in deposits that were not clearly

Fig 27. Double-hull voyaging canoe replica *Hokule'a* shortly after its launch in 1975 at Kaneohe Bay, Oahu.

Fig 28. Rock engraving of outrigger canoe at Anaehoomalu, Hawaii. The petroglyph shows the canoe in plan view (lower left) and side view (upper right).

associated with the other canoe remains. These remains are fragmentary, but they are consistent with the current archaeological picture, based on land sites, of an initial west-to-east spread of human populations (makers of Lapita pottery and other distinctive elements of material culture) followed by further dispersals of Polynesian groups westward to New Zealand, northward to Hawaii, and southeastward to Easter Island (Kirch, 1984). The Huahine materials appear to have particularly close relationships to ancient Maori remains, supporting the idea that the Society Islands – especially the Leeward Islands of the Society group, including Huahine – were jumping-off points for the late westward voyages by Polynesian mariners to New Zealand.

In Central Europe we encounter the archaeological remains of planked boats from around 500 B.C. onward. One from a site near Ljubljana, Slovenia, discovered in 1890, is regarded by McGrail (1981: 21) as having some elements in common with the Ferriby and Brigg boats – among them a flat bottom and sewn planking. But this boat, about 30 meters long and 4.5 meters wide, also had iron nails used as fasteners and wooden knees and lacked the raised cleats of the planks of the Ferriby and Brigg boats. The general similarities between this boat and the Bronze Age British craft are not necessarily evidence for any historical connection between these boatbuilding traditions.

Denmark has proved to be an important area for preserved wooden boats, mainly because of its extensive peat bogs. One such boat, found at Hjortspring on the island of Als, was a lashed-plank craft dated (from the associated weapons) to around 300 B.C. It was 13.6 meters long, not counting an upward-curving projecting timber element, and consisted of five broad strakes of lime wood sewn together and caulked with resin. The boat had ten light frames of hazel lashed to cleats along the insides of the strakes. McGrail (1981: 22) points out that the Hjortspring boat from Denmark presents the earliest securely dated evidence for overlapping strakes, making it a possible forerunner of the Scandinavian clinker-built vessels. Overall, it impressed Johnstone (1980: 115) with its lightness and flexibility, and this and its double-bowed shape led him to suggest that it represented an evolutionary development from earlier skin boats. While he agreed with Crumlin-Pedersen (1972) that early planked boats in Scandinavia may have evolved from expanded log dugouts, he also seriously considered a development from skin-covered to clinker-built wood-planked boats in this region, pointing out that the Eskimo technique of sewing skins together, producing a blind seam that creates an overlapping joint is similar in appearance to the overlapping joining of planks in a clinker-built wooden hull. This suggestion of multilinear development in boatbuilding technology has merit and there is archaeological evidence for such development in the association of skin boat parts and dugout canoes at Palutat Cave and of wood-planked and reed boats in ancient Egypt. But evolutionary theories of boat construction are weakened by the paucity of antecedents in the archaeological record. The earliest wood-planked boats so far reported archaeologically, the Dashur boats from Egypt and the Ferriby and Brigg boats from England, show few indications that either of these hypothesized sequences of technological evolution occurred in those areas. One could just as easily hypothesize that the idea of building wood-planked craft diffused from either or both of these areas, but this would be equally unprovable. Given the present archaeological evidence for the earliest wood-planked boats, regional differences and chronological discontinuities in boatbuilding practices appear to outweigh similarities. Any attempt to regard ethnographically documented boatbuilding technologies such as the expanded dugout observed in the Satakunta district of Finland (Johnstone, 1980: 49–50) as survivals of ancient, transitional evolutionary stages in boat construction requires a continuous archaeologically documented sequence showing how the ancient form survived in that area. This sequence would also have to show evidence for historical antecedents leading to planked-boat construction in the same area. Although Crumlin-Pedersen (1972) presents several historical examples of the expanded dugout technique, including two fourth-century-A.D. grave boats from Slusegård on the island of Bornholm excavated by the maritime archaeologist and historian Ole Klindt-Jensen, such continuity is lacking in the archaeological record of early boatbuilding.

Archaeological evidence for historical continuity in the development of wood-planked boat construction in Scandinavia is stronger. Early sewn or partly sewn planked boats have been found in several Scandinavian localities, most notably at Halsnoy, Norway, and Björke, near Stockholm (Greenhill and Morrison, 1995: 176–177). The Halsnoy craft, a small rowing boat of clinker-built planked construction, may date to as early as 350 B.C. (Muckelroy, 1978: 85), although this date is not universally accepted. It was constructed with planks that had cleats carved from the same piece as the plank and protruding out from the plank surface – a technique that Muckelroy notes was wasteful of wood, since each plank was fashioned from an initial piece of timber more than twice as large. Light internal frames were attached to these cleats. The Björke boat may date to around A.D. 100 and consists of only three planks attached with iron fasteners.

The Nydam boat, a clinker-built craft (Fig. 29) excavated from a bog in Jutland, Denmark, by Conrad Englehardt in 1863, was recently dated by means of dendrochronology to A.D. 310–320. Like the Björke boat, the Nydam craft had a keel plank and iron fastening (the latter a feature of later Norse craft) but was neither as deep nor as strong as Norse boats (Johnstone, 1980: 115). It was 27 meters long and had fifteen oars on each side and a large oar used as a steering sweep. McGrail (1983: 46) notes that the keel was a plank (broader than deep) with ribs inserted and fastened after the side planking was finished. When compared with other, late pre-Viking remains such as the Sutton Hoo ship burial in East Anglia, England, and with numerous Viking-age ship remains, the Nydam boat is a probable precursor to the Norse shipbuilding tradition (McGrail, 1983: 46;

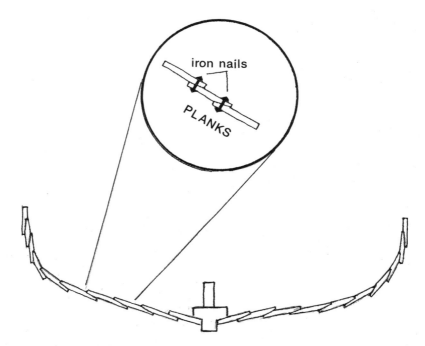

Fig 29. Generalized diagram of clinker construction. The hull planking is shown in cross section, with an expanded view to show how the planks were overlapped and nailed together.

Johnstone, 1980: 116), despite the fact that it shows no residual signs of the expanded-dugout stage hypothesized by Crumlin-Pedersen and Johnstone.

Further development of this boatbuilding tradition can be seen in the Gredstedbro boat from Denmark, dated to the sixth century A.D. This vessel's planks were attached to the frames with dowels rather than protruding cleats, although such cleats remained in use in some boats from this region as late as the tenth century A.D. Muckelroy (1978: 85) suggests that pre-Viking boatbuilders may have been reluctant to drill holes through the hull for dowels despite the economies of labor and wood offered by this technique. It is possible that such drilling might have weakened the hull. The somewhat anomalous Graveney boat, excavated in 1970 along a former branch of the Thames (Fenwick, 1978), dates to around 900 A.D. (McGrail, 1998: 203) A.D. and was originally 14 meters long and about 3.9 meters in beam. It was clinker-built like other vessels of Viking origin, but its heavy, closely spaced frames (added after the outer hull had been constructed) and raked sternpost, which formed an angle at its junction with the keel instead of a curved stem, set it apart from contemporary Viking craft. McGrail (1983: 49–50) suggests that the Graveney boat was capable of sea voyages with a cargo, probably a compact one such as stone, of 6–7 tons.

Iron Age boats in Europe are represented by at least twelve finds in the Rhine River region of Holland and nearby Belgium as well as finds from Switzerland, France, and England. All of these boats have a flat-bottomed bargelike character, although they vary in many details. The large size of some of them means that calling them boats rather than ships may be somewhat arbitrary, but they appear to have been intended mainly for use along Europe's rivers and lakes rather than at sea. Drawing on literary sources, depictions on bas-reliefs, and at least one archaeological example, Johnstone (1980: 161–62) proposed that these vessels were used largely to transport wooden casks, which might help to explain their shape. In the absence of port and docking facilities, their flat-bottomed shape also offered the practical advantage of making it easy to beach them. These utilitarian-looking boats have been labeled a "Celtic" tradition characteristic of the northern parts of the Roman Empire (Marsden, 1976, 1977; Johnstone, 1980: 163). What makes them of special interest is their lack of historical antecedents. Their technology cannot be traced continuously from either the Bronze Age craft of Egypt and England or the pre-Viking boats from Denmark, despite the fact that they constitute the largest and best-studied archaeological sample of inland watercraft known (Muckelroy, 1978: 140). Nor, with the exception of the County Hall vessel found in the south bank of the Thames in 1910, do they show similarities to Roman-age wrecks from the Mediterranean region.

One of these boats was found underwater at a depth of 2 meters in the Bay of Bevaix, Lake Neuchâtel, Switzerland, in the same region as the submerged Iron Age site of La Tène. The Bevaix boat was recorded and excavated in 1972, and a radiocarbon date of A.D. 90+/−70 was obtained for it (Arnold, 1974). The boat was made of oak planks in an unusual stepped sequence that angled obliquely across the entire hull length. The planks were fastened by twenty-two pairs of L-shaped frames and iron nails. The main structural nails were hammered in from the outside and then turned and driven back in to clench the planks. The planks were caulked with moss sandwiched between a strip of willow and a two-stranded thread, all compressed using a row of small nails. Some 4,000 nails were used in this boat's construction. The boat was flat-bottomed and lacked a keel, but it had a mast step near the bow. This mast step lay cross-wise, thus spreading the strain of the mast evenly over the flat bottom. Johnstone (1980: 164) suggested that this was for a towing mast rather than for a sail. Arnold's (1974) analysis indicated that the Bevaix boat was constructed by first lashing the bottom planks together before attaching the frames, then removing the cord lashings and filling the lashing holes with wooden treenails.

Three of the best-described of these boats were excavated at Zwammerdam, the Netherlands. Associated ceramics and other items of Roman origin indicated that they dated to the second century A.D. Reed caulking was used in some of these boats, with iron nails turned to clench the wood planks, but a Mediterranean-style mortise-and-tenon type of fastening was also reported (Johnstone, 1980: 163). The boat identified as Zwammerdam 6 was a large, flat-bottomed vessel that may have served as a ferry on the Rhine. Another important Iron Age boat was excavated from the bank of the Thames River at Blackfriars, London, in 1963. The Blackfriars 1 vessel was 18 meters long and 7 meters wide and was dated by means of associated pottery to the second century A.D. The archaeologist Peter Marsden, who excavated it, suggested that it was a sailing barge that sank while transporting a cargo of building stone from quarries in Kent (Marsden, 1966: 47). In its construction it resembled another Romano-British river barge found at New Guy's House in Bermondsey, South London. These vessels – possibly large enough to be considered ships – were constructed of oak planks clenched with bent-over iron nails and were flat-bottomed without keels. The Blackfriars vessel had a Roman coin resting at the base of the mast step. The bottom and side timbers lacked edge joinery and depended upon mushroom-headed iron nails and heavy wood frames for attachment. The Blackfriars and New Guy's House boats were probably seagoing at least to the extent of venturing out onto the Thames estuary.

Although these Iron Age vessels shared many features in their construction, such as the liberal use of mushroom-headed iron nails, keel-less flat bottoms, flush-laid bottom planking clenched by turned iron nails, and the absence of joinery to attach planks, they differed considerably. The

Thames boats in particular show characteristics resembling those described by Caesar and Strabo for the seagoing vessels of the Veneti, a Celtic society of the Breton coast in northwestern France (Casson, 1971: 338–340). None shows the clinker built planked construction of the Nydam boat or other pre-Viking craft from Scandinavia, although they shared with these craft the use of iron nails for fastening planks. Further complicating this picture is the County Hall wreck, the remains of which were dated by means of associated coins and ceramics to the third century A.D. It was built of oak planks and is estimated to have originally been between 18 and 22 meters long. The hull planks were edge-joined by means of pegged mortise-and-tenon joints, with the frames added afterwards and secured by oak treenails in a manner widely seen in the Mediterranean during Roman times. More than any other boat found so far in northern Europe from this period, the County Hall vessel bears the signs of Mediterranean influence (Steffy, 1994: 72).

In the Mediterranean region, widespread archaeological evidence of trade – especially of obsidian traced by neutron activation from sources on the island of Melos in the Greek Cyclades almost 10,000 years ago (Renfrew and Dixon, 1976) – implies the early use of watercraft. No ancient boat remains have been found prior to the fourteenth-century-B.C. shipwreck near Ulu Burun, at Kas, off the southern coast of Turkey, but three model boats made of lead were found on the island of Naxos and attributed to the Early Bronze Age. Controversies surrounding the authenticity of these models have been settled through an analysis of Cycladic metallurgy showing that lead was widely used during this early period (Renfrew, 1967). Disagreement persists, however, over the shape of these model boats, which appear to be narrower at the high, upward-curved bow than at the stern (which in two cases is relatively wide and flat-bottomed), and references to various representations of ancient boats on vases, mosaics, and stelae have not resolved questions about the shape and technical characteristics of the early Aegean boats they represented (Johnstone, 1980: 64–65). It is not even certain if these models represent planked watercraft, although the bow shape, which would have required some form of built-up construction with planking, makes this seem likely.

Later Classical boats of both Greek and Roman origin were widely depicted in carvings and paintings, although boat remains recovered archaeologically remain relatively rare and derive mainly from Roman times. In 1968 archaeologists excavated the remains of a boat from the shore of the Sea of Galilee (Lake Kinneret), Israel. This vessel, known as the Kinneret boat, is estimated to date from sometime between the first and second centuries A.D. About 9 meters long and 2.5 meters in beam, it was flat-bottomed in its midships area, with its maximum breadth occurring aft of that area (Steffy, 1994: 65). The cedar planking was edge-joined with mortise-and-tenon joints that produced an unusual pattern attributed to either a scarcity of broad timbers or recycling of used materials. The frames were oak and were irregularly shaped and positioned. The keel included a mixture of pieces of oak and cedar, and other kinds of wood were used in other places within the structure, further reflecting the expedient nature of the materials. Iron nails were used to attach the frames to the planks, and the hull was sealed with a covering of pitch. The Kinneret vessel was open except for small bow and stern decks. There were indications of a mast step for a sail, but the boat may have been rowed as well.

A boat of approximately the same date was found in excavations at Herculaneum, near Naples, Italy. This boat was found upside down and was preserved over the aft two-thirds of its length. The hull was carbonized, probably as a result of the eruption of Mount Vesuvius in A.D. 79. Only the exterior of the hull has been examined, but even this limited view has revealed that this was a better-built boat than the one from Kinneret (Steffy, 1994: 67). The hull planks extended all or most of the length of the boat, without any scarfs. The keel was rectangular in cross section, and a complex, two-piece wale (a longitudinal plank attached to the side of the vessel to provide stiffening) capped the top of the hull planking. Like the Kinneret boat, this vessel was built by fastening the outer hull planks first, using wooden-pegged mortise-and-tenon joints, and then adding the frame elements.

Although the sample of finds so far is too small to be considered representative of Roman boatbuilding practices, the Kinneret and Herculaneum boats suggest how differently boats may have been constructed within the same cultural tradition. Both vessels were produced within the Roman Empire at about the same time, but their construction differed according to local circumstances. The expedient character of the Kinneret boat, contrasts with the regular and well-finished planking of the Herculaneum vessel. Herculaneum was more centrally located within the empire than Lake Kinneret, and raw materials and experienced boatbuilders were, in

all likelihood, more readily available there than in Israel. This comparison
cautions archaeologists to be alert to situational responses in boatbuilding
technology and to be careful about attributing variability in boat construction to differences in cultural or historical traditions.

Like the Kinneret and Herculaneum boats and the County Hall vessel,
other small boat finds of Roman origin from localities such as Fiumicino,
Lake Nemi, and the harbor of Rome indicate a mode of construction
based upon the initial joining of hull planks with wooden-pegged mortise-and-tenon fastenings (Fig. 30) with the later addition of frame elements (Casson, 1971: 203). This shell-first construction has been generally
noted for shipwrecks of Classical antiquity and indicates a long-standing
and widespread though by no means uniform Mediterranean boatbuilding
tradition.

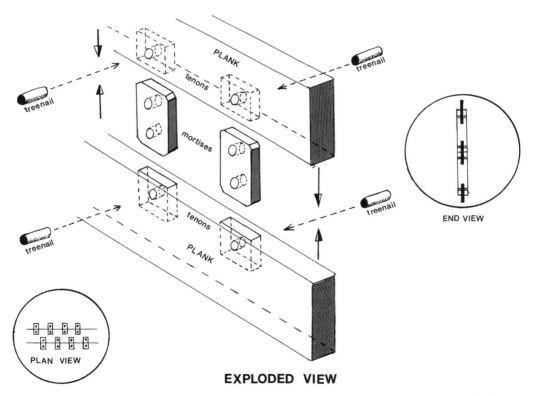

EXPLODED VIEW

Fig 30. Exploded view of Graeco-Roman mortise-and-tenon joinery of hull planks.
Note the alternating arrangement of the mortises shown in the plan view.

Boats and Behavior

Variations in boat construction and the historical relationships they bear to regional approaches in shipbuilding are receiving increasing attention in maritime archaeology. Studies of traditional contemporary or historical boatbuilding and use, from the pioneering studies by James Hornell to more recent observations by maritime scholars such as Ole Crumlin-Pedersen, Olaf Hasslof, and Basil Greenhill, have provided us detailed accounts of boatbuilding techniques that expand the range of known possibilities for constructing and using small watercraft. Muckelroy (1978: 234) has referred to this approach as "maritime ethnology," and he has pointed out its utility in suggesting technical parallels for the construction techniques seen in archaeological contexts. According to Muckelroy, one of the most useful aspects of maritime ethnology is the way in which it can free maritime archaeologists from the constraints of ethnocentrism – from unthinkingly applying modern concepts to past ship- or boatbuilding. For example, observations of planked boats powered exclusively by oarsmen such as the *oselver* of Norway and the *fourern* of the Shetland Islands, which bear close resemblances to ancient wooden boats known from the Viking era (Greenhill and Morrison, 1995: 208), provide useful information about the use-lives of different craft in relation to their size. For planked boats of the Scandinavian tradition, for example, simplicity and flexibility in hull construction were desirable up to the point where larger vessels were required for long-distance trade, warfare, colonization, and exploration.

While differing rates of change appear to have been characteristic of Scandinavian boat- versus shipbuilding traditions, ancient Egypt presented a different pattern of change through time. Throughout the history of Egyptian civilization, there seems to have been little change in boat or ship construction methods. Here the shipbuilding tradition seems to have been dominated by rules of construction that applied more appropriately to river craft. In other words, the shipbuilding of different cultural traditions seems to have followed different trajectories. At the very least, this limited comparison demonstrates that there is no unilineal, evolutionary progression of boat and/or ship technology that applies on a global level.

Ethnographic studies of ship and boat technology can provide maritime archaeologists with real-world cases of relationships between differential rates of technological change and the cultural and situational conditions that affect such change. The potential of such studies, however, has yet to be realized in full. A broader view of the context in which maritime technologies develop and function is capable of providing better models of technology and behavior for archaeological testing.

5 · The Earliest Ships

Shipbuilding and related industries often represented the highest technology of their time, and archaeologists have played a leading role in the process of understanding its nature and complexities. The literature on ancient shipbuilding is skewed, however, toward ships associated with cultural elites or with powerful historical associations, such as battles or other documented events and famous personalities. In the case of early ships, there is also a preoccupation with the earliest example of a particular shipbuilding tradition or, for that matter, of shipbuilding itself.

The recent history of archaeology offers on-land guidance here. Archaeological fieldwork in the late '40s and '50s initiated by archaeologist Robert Braidwood led to discoveries and claims for the earliest domestication in the Iraqi highlands, particularly at the ancient village site of Jarmo (Braidwood and Howe, 1960). Further research in this region by Kathleen Kenyon, James Mellaart, Frank Hole, and Kent Flannery, however, led to the recognition that early domestication was not a unique event but a process that was under way around twelve thousand to ten thousand years ago at more than twenty sites from Turkey to Iran and extending southward to Jordan and southern Israel. Subsequent archaeological research has sought to identify and evaluate the different cultural factors that drove this process. Archaeologists now assume that the origin of agriculture and settled communities in the Near East was a multifaceted process that took place over a wide but ecologically definable region and over a period of hundreds or even thousands of years – not a single event at a particular spot or attributable to a single cause. Similarly, for maritime archaeologists it is becoming clear that multiple factors interacting in complex ways are responsible for the development of the earliest ships. While the details of ship construction and technology continue to be the focus of much of their attention, geography and trade are emerging as major themes. The lesson of land archaeology concerning the earliest agriculture is that looking for evidence of the first ship may be as pointless as looking for the physical remains of Noah's Ark. Like agriculture, the earliest ships were products of sociocultural processes that can only be understood by adopting the broadest of perspectives.

Our knowledge of the origins of ship construction and use depends heavily upon the survival of organic materials, such as wood and fibers, under limited favorable conditions. Historical gaps and problems of cultural sampling and of representativeness persist. The most intriguing of these gaps is the absence of evidence for the voyages of colonization to Australia and New Guinea that occurred at least forty thousand years ago and the voyages involving transport of obsidian from the Aegean island of Melos throughout the eastern Mediterranean roughly ten thousand years ago. Maritime archaeologists are, however, obtaining direct evidence of how the earliest ships were being built from around four thousand five hundred years ago in Egypt through the Roman era and important information about the nature of voyaging at the time. Thanks to a series of major finds in the past few decades, we now have reliable information to compare with written texts and other historical sources. The story of seafaring in the eastern Mediterranean is as multicultural and varied as any set of human relations in the history of our species.

Ancient Egyptian Seafaring

In 1954 Egyptian archaeologists exposed the remains of a large wooden vessel within one of two sealed pits close to the Great Pyramid at Giza. These remains were attributed to Cheops (Khufu), second ruler of the fourth Dynasty of the Old Kingdom, and his son Djedefre, and they were dated, on the basis of associated emblems or cartouches from that dynasty, to about 2650 B.C. This date established the Royal Ship of Cheops (or Khufu), as the oldest ship yet known (Fig. 31). The ship was 43.6 meters long and 5.7 meters in beam at its widest point and had an estimated hull weight of 38.5 tons. It was originally found disassembled in stacks of timbers totaling 1,244 pieces, and five phases of reconstruction and

Fig 31. The world's oldest known ship – the royal ship of Cheops on public display at Giza. Photograph by Dr. Elizabeth B. Gould.

restoration were required over a period of fourteen years. The reconstruction program was supervised by the Egyptian ship restorer Hag Ahmed Youssef Moustafa. A detailed account of it and drawings and plans of the ship were later published by the maritime archaeologist Paul Lipke (1984).

It is uncertain whether this vessel was used on the Nile or served a purely symbolic function related to funerary activities and the Egyptian concept of the afterlife (as a "solar bark"), but, Lipke (1984: 125) argues that "the ancient Egyptians could have, and almost certainly did, build vessels of similar type, technique and quality for active riverine, marine and solar [symbolic funerary] use." It is unlike anything known from ethnographic sources, although there are general parallels with royal barges and the Chinese "dragon boats" used for ritual races on the Yangtze River (Johnstone, 1980: 193). There is no evidence of sails, but the oar arrangement, if correctly interpreted, would have been awkward for propulsion and may have been limited to a steering function (Lipke, 1984: 125–26). It is possible that it was towed by other vessels and may also have been assisted by the Nile current when traveling downstream.

The Khufu ship's planked hull was built up before the frames were added, providing the earliest example so far of shell-first construction. The keelless narrow bottom, consisting of eight cedar planks, was assembled first, using a mortise-and-tenon technique along the plank edges for fastening. Watertightness, however, depended as much upon battens along the insides of the seams as it did upon skillful joinery involving hundreds of mortises (Steffy, 1994: 26). Each seam was capped by a semicircular half-section of light timber running longitudinally along it inside the hull (Fig. 32). This arrangement of battens and caps continued for the side planks, which were added next. Lashing for both bottom and side planks was accomplished through 227 V-shaped holes that permitted the lashings to run continuously in and out of the holes from one plank to the next as well over each of the seam caps. Lashing of this kind lends itself to rapid assembly and disassembly, supporting the idea that vessels constructed this way may have been dismantled for overland transport. Alternatively, however, it may be that, like many kinds of Egyptian grave goods, it was intended to be assembled for use in the land of the dead.

Several planks were scarfed, and different methods of attaching the lower edge of the first side strake to the bottom plank were used according to the changing angle of the joint at different points along the hull.

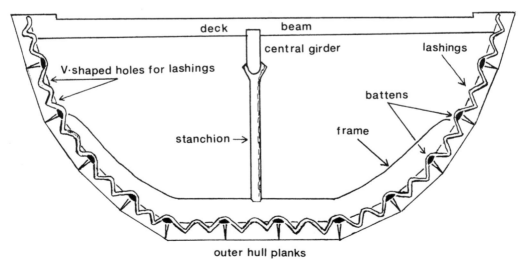

Fig 32. Cross-section diagram of hull of the royal ship of Cheops, showing the complex arrangement of lashings and battens used to join the planks (after Lipke, 1984). Not shown are the mortise-and-tenon joints that were used in some places as well.

The entire hull was stiffened by a complex arrangement of deck beams across the hull joined to a central girder running lengthwise, supported by side girders above and below the beams and drawn together with vertical lashings. Internal frames were added at intervals, and vertical posts were used on top of these to support the central girder. Each vertical post or pillar had a Y-shaped top upon which the central girder rested. The decks and superstructure were added last.

The hull form of the Khufu ship was basically similar to that of the Dashur boats but more complex. It relied mainly upon lashing as its primary fastening system, presenting problems of alignment in the lashing holes and planks during initial construction and from the wear and tear of normal use. This was an extremely labor-intensive mode of construction, and Steffy (1994: 28) suggests that the result "was not a ship at all; it was a very luxurious barge."

The maritime historian Lionel Casson (1971: 20) notes that the earliest archaeologically dated depiction of seagoing Egyptian ships appeared around 2450 B.C. (about 200 years later than the Khufu ship). It was a detailed bas-relief commissioned by Pharoah Sahure to depict the transport of an overseas military expedition and shows two large sailing craft. Despite general resemblances in overall hull shape and construction to the Khufu ship and to the Dashur boats, these ships differed from them in important ways. The most obvious was the presence of a hogging truss consisting of a thick rope running the full length of each ship and looped around each end. This rope was elevated above the deck and could be tightened by inserting a wooden billet and twisting it like a tourniquet (Casson, 1991: 14). With tension applied in this manner, the bow and stern ends of the vessel could be stiffened and prevented from sagging. If one assumes that the planked hulls of these seagoing boats were lashed together in the same way as that of the Khufu ship, extra stiffening would clearly have been required at sea. Another unique structural feature visible in this relief is a band of netting running horizontally along the exterior of the upper part of the hull. Casson identifies this as a girdle intended to keep the hull planks from spreading outward, although he considers the alternative possibility that this netting served as chafing gear to protect the outer surface of the hull and lashings.

Low bas-reliefs from the temple of Queen Hatshepsut (ca. 1500 B.C.) at Deir-el-Bahari, near Thebes, showed fleets of oceangoing vessels on a trading expedition in the Red Sea. These large, graceful ships were generally similar in appearance to the ship shown on the earlier relief but lacked the net girdle, apparently relying for hull strength upon cross-beams that extended through the hull planks (Casson, 1971: 21). The true mast had also appeared, replacing the earlier bipod mast, but, considering that almost a thousand years had elapsed between Sahure's and Hatshepsut's ships, the similarity of these ships is remarkable. Not only did they present the same general hull configuration but they even retained the overhead hogging trusses (Fig. 33). Casson's (1991: 13) observation that Egyptian ships appear to have been oversized Nile riverboats turned into seagoing vessels would help to account for devices such as hogging trusses and net girdles to overcome stresses imposed by oceanic conditions. Another factor that may help to account for this type of construction is the relative scarcity of timber in and around the Nile Valley, resulting in the use of smaller pieces of wood and the production of a relatively weak vessel. Egyptian ship- and boatbuilders were able to overcome this problem to a limited extent by obtaining larger timbers from overseas,

Fig 33. Model of Egyptian sailing craft, showing the hogging truss, steering oars, and characteristic use of a yard at the top and a boom at the bottom of the sail. Unlike earlier Egyptian ships, this vessel has a true mast instead of a bipod structure to support the sail. Crabtree Miniature Ship Collection, published with permission of the Mariners Museum, Newport News, Virginia.

especially from the Levant, but scarcity of suitable timbers was a constant constraint.

By 1500 B.C. Egyptian shipbuilding had reached its peak, and by 1200 B.C. seagoing vessels from other parts of the eastern Mediterranean were increasingly appearing in Egyptian art. Egypt's overseas trade was flourishing in this period, with commerce extending to Cyprus, Nubia, Turkey, and Syria. Ships depicted in this period are of generally Egyptian appearance but without hogging trusses, and rowing galleys are shown as well. The cultural origins of these vessels and the accuracy of these depictions are open to question, but what is certain is that during or around this period other societies were also venturing to sea in the eastern Mediterranean.

A painted frieze from the island of Thera, near Crete, dated to around 1600 B.C. and depicting several large galleys, one with a mast and furled sail, shows that the early Minoans were becoming established as long-distance oceanic voyagers and traders. Casson (1991: 17–19) believes that this frieze represented ships of the Minoan navy and that the tomb inscription of Rekhmire, a high official under Thutmose III around 1500 B.C., describing "The People of the Isles in the midst of the Sea," referred to the Minoans. But so far no archaeological remains of Minoan ships have been found.

Earliest Shipwrecks of the Mediterranean: Ulu Burun

The oldest dated seagoing ship found underwater so far anywhere in the world (Bass, Frey, and Pulak, 1984) is the wreck from Ulu Burun, off the south coast of Turkey, first explored in 1982 by the Institute of Nautical Archaeology (INA) and excavated beginning in 1984 under the joint direction of George Bass and Cemal Pulak. Provisionally dated by associated artifacts to around 1350 B.C., this wreck lies in 45.7–51.8 meters of water. Excavations and recovery of artifacts have been continuing since the initial discovery, and analysis and conservation of the materials are taking place at the INA facilities at Bodrum Castle in Turkey and at Texas A & M University. The results so far must be regarded as interim rather than final.

The artifacts recovered from the wreck, including copper and tin ingots, (Fig. 34) pottery, amphorae, and massive stone anchors, have attracted the

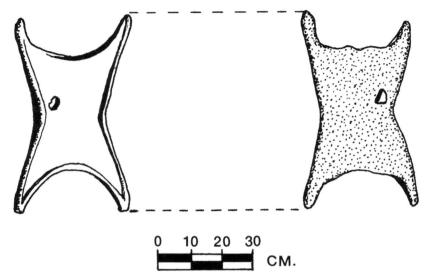

Fig 34. Copper "ox-hide" ingot No. 33 from the Late Bronze Age shipwreck at Cape Gelidonya. Note the rough texture on one side.

most attention. Of special interest both for artistic reasons and for purposes of dating are cylinder seals, scarabs, pendants, and other objects of gold (including a gold chalice), amber of Baltic origin fashioned into beads of Mycenaean style, bronze swords, and a Mycenaean seal (Pulak, 1988), along with other portable artifacts such as jars containing pomegranate seeds. Some of the tin ingots were cast in the characteristic ox-hide shape referred to earlier and are the earliest dated examples of such items so far reported. The amphorae, along with other objects such as lamps, indicated Canaanite origins from the Levantine area of the eastern Mediterranean. Even a cursory review of the portable artifacts from the Ulu Burun wreck reveals a cosmopolitan array of materials and styles.

Despite emphasis in the reporting so far on finished artifacts and art objects, the ship's primary cargo consisted of raw materials. In addition to the ingots and amphorae already mentioned, the ship carried glass ingots. Analyzed at the Corning Museum of Glass, these dark-blue ingots were found to be chemically similar to fourteenth-century-B.C. glass objects from Egypt and Mycenae, among the earliest in the world (Pulak, 1988: 14). In close association with the copper ingots there were hundreds of snail opercula (horny plates that closed off the open end of the shell) identified as belonging to the species *Phyllonotus trunculus*, or murex. This species was used to produce a dye known as Tyrian purple that was highly prized and may have been used for incense and for medicinal purposes. Murex shell deposits indicating production centers for the dye have been identified at sites on the North African, Israeli, and Lebanese coasts. A submerged coastal settlement at Aperlae in Turkey was recently reported by the underwater archaeologist Robert Hohlfelder of the University of Colorado that contained a midden of murex shells associated with what may have been breeding tanks (*Science* vol. 274, 13 December 1996), further expanding the known extent of this industry. The snail materials on the Ulu Burun ship were probably a by-product of the purple-dye industry and may have been part of a small cargo stored in a bag for use as incense (Pulak, 1988: 5). Copper ingots underlying the amphora layer were found resting upon a layer of thorny burnet (*Sarcopoterium spinosum*). This plant probably served as dunnage (packing material), and remains of it have been reported from at least three other ancient shipwrecks along the south coast of Turkey (Haldane, 1986). Although the analysis of the Ulu Burun shipwreck materials is still in the preliminary stage and has been artifact-oriented, botanical studies like this offer the promise of new information about the cargoes and the conduct of ancient maritime commerce in the eastern Mediterranean.

The size of the anchors and the timbers recorded so far, along with the bulk of the cargo, suggest that this was a large vessel for the period (Steffy, 1994: 37). The shipwreck rested upright on the seabed, with most of the surviving structure covered by cargo and other contents. Limited structural remains have been reported so far, including a heavy keel of fir with two adjacent plank strakes. These strakes were edge-joined with mortise-and-tenon attachments to each other and to the keel. Initial indications suggest that the Ulu Burun ship was a robust and ancient example of the shell-first mode of construction that was to dominate the construction of wooden ships in Classical antiquity and to influence later ship construction in that region as well. The ship may have resembled the Levantine ships depicted in a fourteenth-century-B.C. Egyptian tomb painting commissioned by an official under Pharoah Amenhotep III (Casson, 1991: 15–16, Fig. 2) and showing the arrival of a trading fleet at an Egyptian port. The Ulu Burun evidence and the Egyptian tomb painting suggest that by this time commercial ships of Levantine origin were considerably more seaworthy than their Egyptian counterparts, which retained their lashed hull planks and hogging trusses.

The Cape Gelidonya Shipwreck

From a historical point of view, the excavations begun in 1960 on a small Bronze Age wreck at Cape Gelidonya, off the Turkish coast, by George Bass, Peter Throckmorton, Frederick Dumas, and Joan du Plat Taylor were a landmark in the technical development of maritime archaeology. This was the first time that underwater shipwreck recording and excavation were conducted according to the same standards and using the same controls as archaeology on land. The Cape Gelidonya ship, dated by associated artifacts to around 1200 B.C., was a small cargo vessel which, like the Ulu Burun ship, had been transporting various raw materials, including copper ingots, copper scrap, pieces of unshaped crystal, a lead disk, slab- and bun-shaped ingots of copper, and beads. The remains include cylinder seal, balance weights, and tools (including an anvil). Few structural remains were preserved at the Cape Gelidonya wreck site, so most inferences about the ship's construction were based on the size and physical distribution of the cargo and other portable artifacts on the seabed. A few disarticulated planks, some with treenail holes, were found along with 116 kilograms of ballast stones, and there were brushwood twigs that were probably the remains of dunnage. The vessel was probably around 10 meters long and carried at least a ton of cargo. In part, its badly broken condition can be related to the steeply sloping and uneven underwater topography of the wreck site.

The Kyrenia Shipwreck

Approximately a thousand years after the shipwreck at Ulu Burun, another cargo ship, probably of Greek origin, was wrecked off the north coast of Cyprus, near the town of Kyrenia. This wreck site was excavated in 1968–69 by a team under the direction of the underwater archaeologist Michael Katzev, with analysis and reassembly of the wreck materials performed at the Crusaders' Castle in Kyrenia. The ship's principal cargo consisted of over four hundred amphorae (chiefly for transporting wine) of eight different types along with other items including millstones, coins, a large copper cauldron, and other portable artifacts. Steffy (1994: 43) and Casson (1991: 113–114) regard the Kyrenia vessel as fairly representative of the smaller trading vessels operating in the Aegean and eastern Mediterranean region at about the time of Alexander the Great.

Over half of the ship's hull survived intact on the seabed, with timbers representing at least 75 percent of it (Steffy, 1994: 43). On the basis of this unusually complete assemblage of hull remains, Katzev and his associates set about reconstructing the vessel using materials such as Aleppo pine and Turkey oak to match the materials identified from the wreck. The hull was constructed shell-first by edge-fitting the planks with mortise-and-tenon joints for attachment. The tenons were made of the stronger oak and acted as stiffeners at each joint. The hull had a broad, rounded shape, avoiding the sharp curves and acute joints that, given the mortise-and-tenon technique of plank attachment, would have been points of weakness. It was built up plank by plank with braces, clamps, and other internal and external devices to maintain its shape as the planks were added and attached. The keel was attached to the hull planks by means of garboard strakes and chocks (pieces of wood inserted to support larger elements), but there was no keelson or other supporting structure riding above the keel. No caulking was driven between the planks. (The exterior of the hull of the replica was, however, coated with pitch just before launching.)

Once the planks were fitted and joined, the internal frame timbers were added. These were fitted vertically against the interior of the hull and attached to the hull timbers with copper nails driven from the outside of the hull and then clenched to the interior face of the frame. About three thousand copper nails were used in the hull construction – at least 75 percent of them for attaching the frames to the hull. The frames were spaced about 25 centimeters apart and arranged so that one frame line spanned the entire bottom and sides while the adjacent frames spanned the turn of the bilge but did not cross the bottom (Steffy, 1994: 52). This floor-and-half-frame method continued to be a common feature of wooden ships well into the nineteenth century. The frames on the Kyrenia ship were not directly attached to the keel, nor were the futtocks scarfed to the frames and half-frames. This was a relatively weak form of framing, but Steffy (1985: 89) pointed out that the deep V-shaped trough of planks descending toward the keel, with lateral chocks every half-meter, produced a girder-like structure of sufficient strength to support the hull. His analysis of the keel revealed an ancient engineering solution to a structural problem common to wooden ships. Ceiling planks (used to line the interior of the vessel's hull) and a stern bulkhead were added after the frames, but these did not add significantly to the strength of the hull. Using the construction of the replica as a guide, Katzev and Steffy estimated that a ship built on these lines and with a cargo capacity of four hundred amphorae would have been about 15 meters long and relatively broad-beamed.

Information from both the wreck of this small cargo vessel and the construction of the replica provides the most detailed picture available so far of ship construction during Classical antiquity. The strength of the hull depended primarily upon the tightly fitted joinery of the hull planks and their attachment to the keel. This technology was a paragon of skilled carpentry, and many aspects of the construction seen on the Kyrenia wreck continued into the later vernacular boatbuilding traditions of the Aegean and the eastern Mediterranean. While it is hard to say definitively whether or to what extent the Kyrenia ship was typical of commercial ships of its period and region, every shipwreck known so far from Classical antiquity in the Mediterranean region was constructed in the same shell-first manner (Casson, 1971: 203), albeit with some important variations.

While probably adequate under most conditions encountered in the Mediterranean, this type of ship was not the strongest possible. Since the hull depended for its strength upon mutually supporting planks and joints, any break in it could have caused rapid and total collapse. Such ships could be extremely vulnerable to damage due to grounding or collision with rocks and reefs. Shell-first construction also required a high level of skill in carpentry; without driven caulking between planks, watertight integrity depended upon the planks' having a close, tight fit. The archaeological remains of the Kyrenia ship included a step for the mast but offered no direct information about the mast and sails; the replica's single mast and rectangular sail were conjectural. For a vessel of shell-first construction like the Kyrenia ship, the mast step was an obvious point of stress, especially when the keel was relatively light and unsupported by the frames. The shell-first method of ship construction was also profligate in the use of wood, requiring perhaps three times as much as the frame-first method (David Conlin, personal communication).

The Kyrenia ship had been repaired and altered many times. Major repairs included replacement of a rotten floor timber near the bow using a single wooden element that combined the chock and the floorboard in a single piece, a keel repair using a wooden block to span the break (possible in this case only because the frame elements were not attached to the keel), and replacement of several rotten strakes (Steffy, 1994: 55–56). After some major repairs to the bow sometime shortly before the ship sank, a sheathing of 1-millimeter-thick lead sheets was fastened to the outer part of the hull, extending well above the waterline, in an attempt to reduce damage by shipworms. While it is impossible to specify how long this vessel operated, a subjective impression based upon the repairs suggested that it had a long use-life and was pushed to continue in service even after extensive damage by shipworms and other kinds of maritime wear and tear. If so – and such an interpretation is admittedly conjectural – it would be the earliest archaeological evidence for rigorous economies in commercial ship use.

Variability in Ancient Ship Construction

A wreck tentatively dated to around 400 B.C. that is currently being investigated off the shore of Israel near Kibbutz Ma'agan Michael and the Bon Porte I wreck off the coast of southern France near Saint-Tropez (the latter probably of sixth-century-B.C. date and Etruscan cultural origin) both show evidence of shell-first hull construction. The Ma'agan Michael vessel presents the first known use of iron fasteners in Mediterranean shipbuilding. Both ships used mortise-and-tenon joinery and wooden treenails for attaching planks and other elements, but there was also evidence of extensive use of lashing in certain parts of the hull. Lashing holes were especially evident in the stern timbers of the Ma'agan Michael vessel. As Steffy notes (1994: 40), techniques involving lashed planks coexisted with other joinery methods such as treenails, mortise-and-tenon, and iron fasteners, raising the possibility that this mixture of construction methods might in some way have been transitional between the two.

If, however, as seems to be the case, the Kyrenia, Ma'agan Michael, and Bon Porte I vessels were fairly close contemporaries, the persistence of mixed construction may not be part of an evolutionary sequence of technological development. Instead, it may be more a matter of localized shipbuilding practices or situational responses to the particular types of wood used, the parts of the ships involved, or other factors of that kind. For example, the holes drilled for lashings appeared only in the structures at the ends of the hull of the Ma'agan Michael wreck, while lashings were used for joining planks, in combination with mortise-and-tenons, more generally throughout the hull of the Bon Porte I wreck. These variations in the use of different joinery techniques suggest a wider range of possibilities than a unilinear sequence of stages in ship construction can explain. Further examination of the structure of the Ulu Burun vessel assumes special importance in relation to this issue, since this shipwreck presents the best-documented historical antecedent so far for these three later wrecks. If, upon further examination, the Ulu Burun wreck does not show evidence of lashing, it will be hard to claim that this mixed mode of construction in the same region was somehow transitional from an earlier stage of shipbuilding that required lashing. The discovery of mixed use of lashing and mortise-and-tenon joinery on the Ulu Burun wreck would not prove that such an evolutionary transition took place, but the occurrence of mortise-and-tenon joinery there without the use of lashing would rule out such an explanation.

Graeco-Roman Warships

Archaeological reporting of ancient ships from the Mediterranean has clarified information previously only ambiguously understood from texts. Casson's (1971: 217–219) discussion of the building of Odysseus's boat used information gained from archaeology about shell-first hull construction and use of mortise-and-tenon joints to explain the section of the *Odyssey* in which Calypso aids him in building a boat to leave Ogygia. Literary historians have disagreed about the nature of Odysseus's boat, with some arguing on philological grounds that it was a raft. For those who recognized it as a true boat, the mode of construction was unfamiliar; the text descriptions did not follow the rules of frame-first wooden shipbuilding. Casson's analysis of this text in relation to archaeological findings of shell-first-built ships explained it more parsimoniously than before. The oral traditions that produced the Homeric epics preserved a description of ancient boat construction in Odysseus's adventure that is congruent with a shipbuilding tradition observed in the underwater archaeological record. Although the archaeology of Bronze Age ships and boats in the Mediterranean is still spotty, present evidence indicates that Casson is on firm ground.

By contrast, there is a dearth of archaeological information about naval warfare and warships in the ancient Mediterranean. With one (possibly two) notable exceptions, we lack direct archaeological evidence for the earliest warships of Classical antiquity. Various explanations for this gap are possible. Ancient warships were specialized craft that depended heavily upon oarsmen, and fleets tended to fight their battles within sight of land. The practice of fighting fleet actions close to shore continued to dominate naval warfare until after world War I, when the rise of naval aviation and widespread use of submarine warfare contributed to truly oceanic warfare (Keegan, 1989: 272).

Unlike ships of commerce, ancient oared warships did not cruise as often or cover as great distances, and they were probably drawn up on shore when not in use. Fleets were usually raised as needed to combat piracy or to defend against attack and sometimes as quickly disbanded. Therefore the chances of ancient warships' finding their way into the archaeological record were relatively poor. To this may be added the possibility raised by the maritime historians John S. Morrison and J. F. Coates (1986: 128–129) that Greek triremes were positively buoyant and instead of sinking floated and drifted or were towed away after being rammed. The maritime archaeologist Honor Frost (1973: 33) has also pointed out that because warships kept their decks cleared for action and did not transport cargo, archaeologists are denied the pile of amphorae and other bulk items that so often covers and marks the remains of an ancient vessel on the seabed. Not only would such shipwrecks be difficult to locate, but their wood structures would have been relatively unprotected against shipworms and other destructive elements unless they had been quickly buried in silt or sand.

The Battle of Salamis in 480 B.C., a decisive naval victory for the Athenian Greeks over the Persian fleet, marked the supremacy of the trireme, a war galley propelled by three banks of oars and armed with a ram projecting from the bow. The trireme remained the dominant warship of the ancient Greeks until the death of Alexander the Great in 323 B.C. Although competing against other types of warships from then on, it persisted into late-Roman and Byzantine times and was sometimes adapted for use as a troop or horse transport or to make use of special weapons such as catapults and Greek fire. Historical references to triremes abound, as do partial images depicted on painted vases and murals and in sculpture (Casson, 1991: 84). A stone bas-relief fragment of a Greek trireme from the late fifth century B.C. discovered in 1852 by the French archaeologist Charles Lenormant presented a side view of a galley with three banks of oars, with the uppermost row of oarsmen clearly visible (Morrison and Coates, 1986: 139–141). Some of the best information about ancient Greek triremes comes from excavations of the Athenian dockyard at the Bay of Zea in Piraeus (Casson, 1971: 363–364: Fig. 197; Morrison and Coates, 1986: 4–5, Fig. 9, 35). Docking slips there measured about 37 meters long by 6 meters wide, representing the upper size limit for such vessels and revealing a roughly ten-to-one ratio of length to beam.

The trireme was built around its specialized weapon, the ram, which was intended as a weapon for sinking enemy ships in fleet actions. The Battle of Salamis was only one of several decisive fleet actions fought by triremes, usually involving large numbers of ships. The use of relatively specialized warships like the trireme in such battles was organized around fleet tactics. Favored tactics for organized ramming by the ancient Greeks (Casson, 1991: 91) included the *diekplus* (or "breakthrough" out of one's own line of ships to sail through the enemy's) and the *periplus* (or "sailing around" by outflanking the enemy's line, mainly in open waters). These tactics were met by countermeasures such as drawing one's line of ships close along a shoreline, thus denying maneuvering room to the attackers, and adopting a radial formation with sterns inward to form a circle from which ships could dart out to attack when their opponents approached.

Historical antecedents of the trireme included oared galleys without rams, depicted as early as 2500 B.C. in ancient Egypt (Casson, 1971: Fig. 63) and later in the Medinet Habu battle frieze, involving Egyptian and Levantine vessels, produced during the reign of Ramses II in 1186 B.C. (Casson, 1971: 36, Fig. 61; Greenhill and Morrison, 1995: 137–139). Minoan seals and painted pottery also showed oared galleys without rams dating to around 1600 to 1400 B.C., but these representations were highly stylized and provided few details. These and other early depictions indicate that the earliest attempts at naval warfare were essentially land battles fought on the water. Oarsmen maneuvered and propelled their galleys into physical contact with the enemy's vessels and then abandoned their oars for combat by boarding. Some of these early depictions also showed archery as a weapon in such encounters, and therefore at least some ships carried soldiers to support the oarsmen in attacking and boarding other vessels.

An engraved pin dated to around 850 B.C. from Athens contains the earliest depiction so far of a ram (Casson, 1991:76), although large galleys without ram bows continued to appear on painted Greek pottery as late as 550–530 B.C. The practice of ramming one's opponent at sea introduced a complex new set of engineering problems for shipbuilders. Experiments in 1987 with a full-scale replica of an Athenian trireme named *Olympias* (Morrison and Coates, 1986; Coates, 1989) showed how it was possible to arrange the oarsmen – 170 in all – efficiently into three banks within the narrow confines of the hull and to reproduce the levels of ship performance recorded in ancient texts.

One frequently cited historical account by Thucydides (1951:172) described an event of high drama in 427 B.C. An Athenian trireme was dispatched to the city of Mitylene on the island of Lesbos to put down a revolt. The distance from Athens to Mitylene is 345 kilometers, and the ship proceeded there at its cruising speed. The following day, however, the Athenian assembly reversed its order, and the Mitylenian ambassadors in Athens quickly arranged for another trireme to overtake the first and countermand the order. The second trireme left Athens about twenty-four hours after the first and rowed continuously through the night:

> Wine and barley-cakes were provided for the vessel by the Mitylenian ambassadors, and great promises were made if they arrived in time; which caused the men to use such diligence upon the voyage that they took their meals of barley-cakes kneaded with oil and wine as they rowed, and only slept in turns while the others were at the oar.

The pursuers reached Mitylene shortly after the first trireme, just in time to forestall the massacre, having completed the trip in less than twenty-four hours at an average speed of almost 9 knots.

The trireme replica effectively matched this kind of sprint performance using triads of rowers seated in elevated positions that permitted efficient power strokes without interference between the oars. This kind of rowing required coordination and physical strength but no special training or skill. Frictional drag along the wetted area of the hull and drag due to the increasing length of the bow wave both increased exponentially with speed, and this required a virtual doubling of effort by the oarsmen at speeds between 8 and 10 knots. Thus calculations based on the *Olympias* replica showed that in order to sprint in the manner described in Thucydides's account the trireme must have been pushing the limits for speed under oars for any sort of large vessel and moving only slightly more slowly than a modern racing shell.

Stability was important in trireme warfare. Estimates based on the known dimensions of Greek triremes suggest that they had a metacentric height of only about 0.4 meters, which meant that they tended to be unstable (Foley and Soedel, 1981: 158). The amount of ballast, if any, carried by triremes is unknown, and it is possible that they were lightened before battle by removing ballast in order to gain speed at the expense of stability. Like modern racing shells, triremes may have depended in part on their oars for stability in such situations, assuming that sea and wind conditions permitted. When sea conditions and winds might adversely affect stability but speed was less important, greater amounts of ballast may have been used.

The trireme experiments, along with those of the "Kyrenia II," were replicative in nature and reveal how such accomplishments in ship construction and operation were possible. Experiments of this kind have been widely used in in maritime archaeology. They enable archaeologists to visualize the construction and performance of certain types of vessels, often under particular conditions. They are different, however, from controlled, laboratory-like experiments that test alternative hypotheses about human behavior in relation to basic mechanical and geographical factors.

The trireme experiments provided insights into how the warships of Classical antiquity were propelled, manned, and steered, and they replicated construction methods known for that period through written and iconographic sources, but they still did not fully address the question of the trireme as a *weapon*. Ramming at sea imposed special stresses on ships that were not encountered in normal use. Nothing less than a controlled collision at sea, ramming was a radical tactic, and it was also a clear indication that naval warfare was becoming increasingly directed at disabling or destroying enemy ships as opposed to disabling the opposing crew. With the ability to turn quickly and steer in any direction regardless of the wind – both demonstrated by the trireme experiments – came the opportunity to employ this tactic, especially in massed formations of warships.

But the trireme experiment also replicated the relatively vulnerable shell-first mode of hull construction with pegged mortise-and-tenon joinery, raising the question how ancient triremes achieved sufficient hull strength to withstand the shock of ramming in battle.

Several partial answers to this question are possible. One has to do with the nature of ramming under the conditions of ancient Classical warfare. Casson (1991: 88) noted that triremes were lightly constructed and tended to have short use-lives, and he argued that ramming was difficult to carry out effectively. Foley and Soedel (1981) and Coates (1989) also stressed how light the trireme was for its size, estimating the weight of a 121-foot-long example at under 40 tons. But lightweight construction for the sake of speed would have left the trireme vulnerable both to the shock of ramming and to a ramming blow. Early rams were pointed and risked becoming stuck in the opposing ship's hull; trireme rams were blunt, with a squared-off face, and were intended to pound and shatter the planks in the opposing ship's hull rather than punch a hole through it. The attack speed for ramming at the final moment had to be fast enough to prevent the opposing ship from escaping but slow enough to keep the ram from becoming wedged in the opposing ship's side, which would risk immobilizing the attackers and exposing them to ramming by other opponents. Casson (1991: 90) described these ancient battles as slow-motion affairs, with soldiers shooting arrows at enemy oarsmen while complicated maneuvering took place, so perhaps ramming occurred at such slow speeds that damage to the attacking craft was minimized.

Foley and Soedel (1981: 149) have called attention to the practice of running transverse cables around the trireme's hull at intervals along its length and adjusting their tension with winches to reinforce the hull before the ships were placed in the water. They focused on the stresses of rowing and the tight packing of the oarsmen within the ship's lightly constructed hull, but ramming would have been at least as stressful. This use of external ropes to support the hull under stress is reminiscent of the much earlier Egyptian use of external rope girdles on their larger ships' hulls along with hogging trusses – parallel solutions arrived at independently but not necessarily for the same reasons. Could such measures have imparted enough strength to the hulls of these ancient triremes to enable them to ram an opponent successfully during battle and survive?

As is so often the case in archaeology, no firm or final conclusions are possible yet, especially since no wrecks of ancient Greek triremes have been found. It is possible (though admittedly unlikely) that some of these triremes were built frame-first to give them greater strength for ramming in battle. Such alternatives, however improbable, must be considered and ruled out whenever direct archaeological evidence bearing on ancient triremes becomes available. Archaeologists cannot assume that all the warships of Classical antiquity were constructed shell-first. From the information available it seems clear that the design and use of the Greek trireme represented a bundle of trade-offs between speed and stability, maneuverability and strength, and speed and endurance (occasioned by the large number of oarsmen and limited space for provisions). Compromises between these performance factors, some only partly understood on the basis of existing evidence, may have led to structural modifications in different situations.

The Isola Lunga Wreck

Two shipwrecks from the Mediterranean provide important information about oared warships in Classical antiquity. One is the wreck of what may well have been a galley off the west coast of Sicily close to Isola Lunga, near Marsala (ancient Lilybaeum), dating to the mid-third century B.C. (Frost, 1973; Steffy, 1994: 59). The other consists of the remains of a bronze ram with associated bow timbers, found along the shore near Athlit, Israel, and attributed to a large oared warship of Roman origin with multiple banks of oars from the second century B.C. (Casson and Steffy, 1991; Steffy, 1994: 59–62). It is apparent that this ship was rowed on occasion, making it different from the Kyrenia vessel, which relied exclusively on sails for propulsion. Like the Kyrenia ship, the Isola Lunga craft was extensively sheathed with lead over the exterior of its hull. Unlike the Kyrenia ship, it was constructed with iron nails as well as the usual dowels and mortise-and-tenon joinery. As in other Bronze Age ships, leafy branches had been laid along the inside of the hull to protect the hull planking from ballast stones. No cargo was found on the wreck, and therefore this brushwood of various kinds of *Phyllyrea*, along with myrtle and fern cannot be regarded as dunnage. A wide variety of timber was used in the ship's construction, including pine planks and oak frames, dowels, and tenons as well as cedar, pistachio, beech, and maple (identified from a mass of what were probably wood chips packed into the keel cavity). This eclectic tendency to use timbers found throughout the Mediterranean region was seen on other early wrecks as well, suggesting that ancient ship-builders often imported wood for their use.

The Isola Lunga wreck site did not produce any evidence of a ram bow, but the ballast pile contained the concretion of a spearhead, supporting the interpretation that this was a war galley. The limited number of amphora sherds, sixty in all, indicated that the ship was probably not transporting cargo at the time it sank. The amphorae they represent are perhaps best explained as containers for crew provisions. The ballast consisted of vol-canic tufa stones from the island of Pantelleria, a convenient stopover and port of call for any vessel traveling between Africa and Sicily. A fragmen-tary anchor of an unusual form associated with Punic warships was found close to the ballast pile (Frost, 1972a: 114, Figs. 5 and 6).

Remains of the wood structure were preserved from one end of the vessel along the keel and on one side adjacent to that end of the keel. In contrast to most wooden shipwrecks, this one preserved the end structure better than the midships. The keel-stern (or stem-) post angled upward to present a raked extremity. This angled structure differed from depictions of Classical warships with a ram at the bow and a curved stern and from images of Roman-era merchant ships with rounded extremities (Basch, in Frost, 1973: 48). Only a Roman merchant galley from the first century A.D. shown in a bas-relief of the draining of Lake Fucino (Casson, 1971: Fig. 139) presented an angled bow comparable to the sternpost configu-ration of the Isola Lunga wreck. The overall shape of the vessel's hull was also angular compared with that of the Kyrenia ship, and Frost (1973: 38) estimated the ship's overall length at around 25 meters.

While there is evidence to support the idea that this vessel was a Punic war galley, it could almost as easily have been a merchant galley traveling empty or carrying a perishable cargo that decomposed or floated away fol-lowing the wreck. If it was a warship, it presents the possibility of an early mode of combat alternative to that represented by ram-equipped galleys like the trireme. With vessels like the Isola Lunga ship we can see the possible emergence of commerce raiding by single vessels of more gener-alized design, with a combination of sail and oars but without a ram. In such cases the capture of enemy vessels and their cargo (virtually a form of government-sanctioned piracy) may have been as important as the destruction of enemy ships, which undoubtedly occurred whenever circumstances required or when there was a compelling need to deny the enemy the use of its ships and cargoes. Speed and maneuverability combined with sufficient size to carry personnel to overwhelm resistance during boarding would have been essential for commerce raiders to operate effectively during attacks on single vessels and to escape from fleet units sent to hunt them down. The Isola Lunga ship may be the first archaeological harbinger of a doctrine of naval warfare that competed with the concept of naval superiority based on disciplined and organized fleets of warships.

The Athlit Ram

In 1980 a cast-bronze ram weighing 465 kilograms was discovered protruding from sand at a depth of 3 meters some 200 meters offshore near Athlit, Israel. Sixteen timbers were found preserved inside its casing. After the ram and timbers were excavated and placed in conservation at the University of Haifa, J. Richard Steffy undertook the complex task of detachment and disassembly of the timbers from the ram and the subsequent analysis of the bow structure of this vessel. So far this remains the only archaeological example of an ancient oared warship with a ram bow. When analyzed, the bronze ram and attached timbers revealed a bow that was heavily reinforced with two thick wooden wales or supporting timbers, one on each side, and a ramming timber forward of the keel, all extending into the bronze casing of the ram itself. Wooden planks on either side of the keel would have absorbed some of the shock of ramming. The wales, bottom planks, and keel were joined with 1.1-centimeter thick tenons (twice as thick as the tenons on the Kyrenia ship) and large mortises, with wooden treenails to lock the ship's stem into the ramming timber. Bronze nails attached the aft end of the ram to the ship's wooden bow. Steffy (1994: 59) concluded that "the entire bottom of this ship was essentially the weapon."

In contrast to other scholars who have claimed that the trireme was a lightweight and agile ship for its length, Steffy (Casson and Steffy, 1991: 33) inferred from his study of the Athlit ram that the ship was more heavily constructed than the Kyrenia ship and other ancient cargo carriers. He estimated that the very lightest trireme capable of militarily useful tasks would have had to contain about 0.75 ton of material per meter of length – heavy enough, perhaps, for ramming but still with thin hull planking and light frames and bracing. The Athlit ship would have been heavier than this hypothetical trireme, with a displacement weight greater than 1 ton per meter of hull length, but his estimate for its overall weight is still very close to those of other scholars for oared warships. He points out, too, that the keel of the Athlit ship was small for a warship with a half-ton ram.

Steffy's analysis of the Athlit ram suggested that most of this weight was concentrated in strong, heavy timbers, like the starboard and port wales, and along the vessel's shallow bottom, with lighter construction in the upper portions of the hull. This kind of arrangement would have reduced or even eliminated the need for ballast. One can only speculate on the shape of this ship's keel and supporting timbers aft of the ram. But Steffy has called attention to the importance of the ram and its supporting structure as evidence of an ancient weapons system, and he has shown how these oared warships of Classical antiquity may have differed in their design and construction from ancient cargo vessels. The *Olympias* experiment helps us to understand some of the practical solutions required to operate an ancient trireme, but the archaeology of the Athlit ram demonstrates that there is more to a complete understanding of the trireme than that experiment can provide.

Roman Merchant Vessels

Ancient Rome is best known for its land empire, but Roman-era shipwrecks in the Mediterranean and Black Sea region reflect a high level of activity in maritime commerce (Fig. 35). At least 407 wrecks have been identified from 300 B.C. to A.D. 300 (Parker, 1980: 50–51). As Anthony Parker points out, their predominantly western Mediterranean distribution results mainly from chance finds in and around harbors and rivers and by scuba divers after World War II. The greatest concentrations of wrecks are along the southern coast of France and the nearby islands of Corsica and Sardinia. In part this may be the result of attractive conditions for sport divers and treasure hunters and bottom conditions that favored good preservation of wrecks, and therefore one cannot assume that these geographical distributions necessarily reflected the intensity of maritime commerce.

Fig 35. Generalized model of a Roman merchant ship. Crabtree Miniature Ship Collection, published with permission of the Mariners Museum, Newport News, Virginia.

The scale of maritime trade in the Roman era is shown more clearly by the size of ships' cargoes at various wreck sites. Although seen in substantial numbers on earlier Bronze Age shipwrecks in the eastern Mediterranean, amphorae now appeared on shipwrecks in larger numbers than ever before. For over a decade French underwater archaeologists excavated a large merchant ship that was transporting between 6,000 and 7,000 amphorae, totaling 300–350 tons of cargo, when it sank near the port of Toulon between the first and the second century B.C. This shipwreck, the Madrague de Giens, has provided a wealth of information on the contents and construction details of a large Roman merchantman. Three layers of amphorae were identified in the ship's hold. A cork or clay stopper was cemented in place to seal the contents of each. Each amphora contained between 19 and 38 liters and weighed around 23 kilograms when empty and about twice that when filled. In terms of the chronological sequence for Roman amphorae established by Heinrich Dressel, they belonged to Dressel type 1B, dating to the mid-first century B.C. They contained traces of wine and were stamped with the name of a pottery kiln south of Rome (Parker, 1980: 54).

Large quantities of marble were also transported on Roman-era ships, and archaeologists have been able to trace some of these cargoes to quarries in different parts of the Mediterranean region (Parker, 1980: 58–59). Several cargoes of marble found on shipwrecks totaled around 300 tons each, and in one case a single block for a stone column weighed 40 tons. Twenty-three semifinished stone sarcophagi came from a ship that sank sometime around A.D. 200–250 near the southern Italian port city of Taranto. This vessel, the San Pietro wreck, was excavated by Peter Throckmorton in 1964.

Bulk grain shipments by sea, especially from Egypt, were a major part of maritime commerce during the Hellenistic period and continued in Roman times through the third century A.D., but these have not survived in shipwreck sites. The scale of the Roman grain trade is indicated by records revealing that the annual amount of grain shipped from Egypt to Rome totaled around 135,000 tons (Casson, 1991: 207). Grain ships used the northwesterly summer winds to sail directly downwind to Alexandria from Ostia (the port of Rome) and other Roman ports in Italy, but they followed a different return route via the Turkish coast, Rhodes, Crete, and Sicily, sailing laboriously back into the northwesterlies on a much longer course. This meant that a ship could expect to complete only a single trip in a season. Because Rome depended heavily upon these imports of grain, special ships capable of transporting 1,200–1,300 tons of grain operated on this route. One such ship that was blown off course in bad weather turned up in Piraeus, near Athens, during the second century A.D., where it was seen and described in detail by Lucian (Casson, 1991: 208–209):

> What a size the ship was! One hundred and eighty feet in length, the ship's carpenter told me, the beam more than a quarter of that, and forty-four feet from the deck to the bottom, the deepest point in the bilge. The way the sternpost rose in a gradual curve with a gilded goose-head set on the tip of it, matched at the opposite end by the forward, more flattened, rise of the prow with the figure of Isis, the goddess the ship was named after, on each side! And the rest of the decoration, the paintings, the red pennant on the main yard, the anchors and capstans and winches on the foredeck, the accommodations toward the stern – it all seemed like marvels to me! The crew must have been as big as an army. They told me she carried so much grain that it would be enough to feed every mouth in Athens for a year.

While the great Roman-era grain ships and cargo carriers operated throughout the Mediterranean, significant amounts of shipping extended to northwestern France and southern England. This commerce is known mainly from archaeological finds of trade objects such as amphorae of Dressel type 1A at land sites at Hengistbury Head, near the present city of Bournemouth, from the end of the second century B.C. These finds, which were distributed over a 150-kilometer radius of Hengistbury Head and its nearby port of Christchurch Harbor, suggest that this locality was a major port of entry for commerce from the French mainland (Muckelroy, 1980b: 66). The Iron Age boat remains from southern England provide a glimpse of some of the construction techniques that may have been used for cross-channel trade in the Roman era. Although the familiar Mediterranean-style pegged mortise-and-tenon fastening was present in the County Hall vessel, other wrecks from the Thames, in particular the Blackfriars 1 and New Guy's House craft, were heavily timbered and framed in oak and used clenched iron nails for fastening planks – building techniques of a distinctly non-Mediterranean character. These were probably not cross-channel transports, but their frame-first construction does point to regionally varied approaches to boat- and ship-building within the empire.

The archaeological evidence from these wrecks helps to account for Julius Caesar's much-cited description of the heavily framed vessels of the Veneti as relatively flat-bottomed, with high bow and stern, leather sails, foot-square timbers, and iron anchor chains (Casson, 1971: 339) – just the sort of robust craft that could sail in the heavy seas of the channel and still make it across the shoals and mudflats of the English coast. After the Roman conquest in A.D. 43, large amounts of Samian ware, a high-quality pottery of Roman origin, appeared in land sites in Britain and in underwater sites such as Pudding Pan Reef, near Whitstable, Kent. Although this wreck was not excavated, it was dated to around A.D. 160 and provided further evidence for a lively cross-Channel trade in Roman imports that began before the conquest and continued well afterwards (Muckelroy, 1980b: 66–67).

No unequivocal remains have yet been found of the great Roman grain ships, but wrecks of several large merchant ships of the Roman era have been studied in detail. French archaeologists led by Andre Tchernia and Patrice Pomey (1978) showed that the Madrague de Giens vessel was double-planked – that is, planks covered both the interior and exterior of the ship's frames – and that at least some of the planks were fitted to the frames rather than the other way around (Muckelroy, 1978: 64). Pegged mortise-and-tenon joinery was still used for the hull, and Steffy (1994: 65), noting the absence of a full-length keelson for longitudinal support, regarded the outer hull joinery as the primary source of the vessel's strength. Thanks to the relatively complete preservation of this ship's hull, its capacity has been reliably estimated at 400 tons. Like the Blackfriars 1 and New Guy's House vessels, it showed early signs of a departure from the strictly shell-first mode of construction, and this in a region where shell-first construction had been dominant since the Bronze Age.

Other, smaller Roman-era shipwrecks from the Mediterranean were more conventional in their construction. The Chrétienne C vessel, discovered in 1954 near Anthéor in southeastern France and excavated for three seasons by the French maritime archaeologist Jeanne-Pierre Joncheray, produced the remains of a relatively small cargo ship, about 15.5 meters long, containing about 500 amphorae. Associated amphora seals, a coin, and other pottery enabled the excavators to date the loss of this vessel to 175–150 B.C. It was constructed using pegged mortise-and-tenon joinery, with planks varying in thickness by over a centimeter, probably from planing after fitting to achieve a smooth-lined hull (Muckelroy, 1978: 61). But the ship also possessed a more V-shaped hull-bottom cross section than one normally associates with cargo vessels. Muckelroy has suggested that rampant piracy in the Mediterranean prior to Pompey the Great (106–48 B.C.) placed a premium on speed for merchant vessels and may help to account for this vessel's hull form. The wreck of L'Anse des Laurons 2, the remains of another relatively small ship from the coast of southern France dating to the end of the second century B.C., presented a more complete picture of the vessel's construction. This ship was about the same size as the Chrétienne C vessel but had a flat bottom and gently rounded bilges. The hull was similarly constructed shell-first using pegged mortise-and-tenon joints spaced every 10–12 centimeters. Although thin-planked, the vessel had relatively heavy framing, with upward-curved stem and stern structures (Steffy, 1994: 72–73).

The Roman-era ships of commerce represented at shipwreck sites present a varied picture, with hints of frame-first construction and large ships comparable in size to late-eighteenth-century European frigates. Traditional canons of shipbuilding based on shell-first construction were being varied to suit different circumstances of weather and sea conditions, as in the cross-channel trade, or perhaps cultural factors such as piracy in the western Mediterranean and economic imperatives such as Rome's appetite for Egyptian grain. In the latter years of the empire the nearly three-thousand-year-old tradition of shell-first ship and boat construction in the Mediterranean region was showing signs of regional variability and change.

A Roman Anomaly: The Lake Nemi Vessels

Sometime during the reign of Emperor Caligula (A.D. 37–41), two massive barges were built and set afloat in Lake Nemi, a small lake about 32 kilometers south of Rome (Ucelli, 1950). The existence of these vessels had been known for a long time, but it was not until the 1920s and 1930s that the Italian government embarked upon a program to drain the lake and restore them. They were placed in a museum on the lakeshore and had been recorded and documented in detail before they were burned by the retreating German army in 1944.

Although the superstructures of both vessels were gone, the hulls were well preserved and massive. One was 73 meters long and 24 meters wide and the other was 71.3 meters long and 20 meters wide. Their unique location, together with associated artifacts and materials including marble veneering, mosaic tiles, and bronze furnishings, suggested that they were floating villas. As in the case of the Khufu ship, they cannot be viewed as representative of Roman watercraft, but it is still possible to compare details of their construction with the corpus of archaeological information already available on the earliest ships of antiquity.

Both vessels were constructed shell-first using pegged mortise-and-tenon fastenings for the hull planks. They were flat-bottomed with a main keel and four smaller keels, and the frames all extended continuously across the hull. Frame spacing was 50 centimeters When compared with the mean maximum measured frame spacing of 20.9 centimeters (standard deviation 7.8) for 16 other shipwrecks of Bronze Age and Roman-era origin, the Nemi vessels presented by far the widest frame spacing for any Classical shipwreck recorded so far from Classical antiquity. Perhaps the fact that these barges were intended merely to float in the quiet waters of Lake Nemi can account for this difference. Their hulls were sheathed in lead to the gunwales even though shipworms were not a problem in this freshwater environment. As Steffy (1994: 72) points out, the Kyrenia ship's hull was the first known to have been completely sheathed in lead, and the Nemi barges were the last.

Variability in Shell-First Ship Construction

No other known ships in antiquity ever looked like the Nemi barges, but these unique vessels were built at about the same time as the other large Roman-era ships recorded archaeologically. These examples show how adaptable the Romans and their client cultures were at pushing the ancient shell-first mode of construction to its limits of size and shape. The relatively large number of Roman-era shipwrecks allows us to sample the variety of ships constructed according to this tradition and conclude that they were fairly heterogeneous. At present, the archaeologically known ships of Classical antiquity are a bundle of technological anomalies loosely tied together by the tradition of shell-first hull construction. While at one extreme we can identify situational factors that may have influenced variability in the construction of Roman-era boats such as the Kinneret and Herculaneum craft, at the other extreme we can infer the operation of socioeconomic factors of status and power to account for the Nemi barges. Ship construction in Classical antiquity appears on present evidence to have been adapted to a wide range of situationally and culturally derived requirements, all within the structural limits imposed by shell-first construction.

6 · Shipwrecks and Our Understanding of Ancient Trade

Underwater archaeology offers a unique perspective on ancient trade. Shipwrecks provide information about trading behavior and relationships *at a distance*, in contexts that differ sharply from those on land.

The archaeologist, Colin Renfrew (1975: 4) noted that trade, ". . . requires organization as well as commodity," and he went on to develop a comprehensive theory of ancient trade. His theory was based on a model of exchange involving 10 different modes of trade. Each of these postulated different kinds of patterning of material items in the archaeological record as the result of different ways of organizing trade. This was a land-based model and emphasized the archaeology of destinations or nodes of exchange (Renfrew, 1975: 41–44). For martime archaeology, however, Renfrew's is applicable only to ports of trade and other shore-based facilities.

For maritime archaeologists, the principal loci for evidence of ancient trade occur at points **between** the nodes of exchange in Renfrew's model. The Bronze Age wrecks at Ulu Burun and Cape Gelidonya and the Roman-era wreck at Madrague de Giens (along with scores of other Roman-era cargo transports) were the remains of vessels wrecked while en route between ports and not necessarily near the node of exchange. Renfrew admitted that (1975: 45) "Maritime trade virtually excludes certain modes, such as mode 4 and it is a truism that rivers or seas may be regarded either as barriers or as easy channels of communication according to the transport available."

Later, Renfrew proposed distance-decay relationships between items of trade and distances of those items from their source. His Law of

Monotonic Decrement (Renfrew, 1977: 72) essentially predicts that, all else being equal, frequency of materials from a particular source decreases in a regular, monotonic fashion with increasing distance from the source. Renfrew reviewed a series of distance-decay fall-off models, noting that similar final results (in this case, distance-decay fall-off curves) can appear in the archaeological record even when initial conditions are different and when exchange of commodities is accomplished in different ways – an outcome he referred to as *equifinality*. In other words, qualitative differences in trade and exchange behavior within or between different human societies can produce essentially similar patterning in the archaeological record.

For archaeologists who base their studies of maritime trade on land sites, Renfrew's 10-part model and his Law of Monotonic Decrement can be useful analytical concepts, but their applicability in the context of maritime transport and trade is limited. He introduced the idea of *effective distance*, which is not necessarily the same as the direct distance between two points (Renfrew, 1977: 72). The flow of trade along pathways structured by seasonal winds, currents, storm patterns, and sea hazards like reefs and shoals in relation to the available technologies of transport and navigation is the essence of seaborne commerce.

The archaeologist A. J. Ammerman, together with C. Matessi and L. L. Cavalli-Sforza (1978), in a study of the transport of obsidian during the Neolithic from sources on the island of Lipari, off the northeast end of Sicily, and Calabria, on the Italian mainland, pointed to the potential effects of geography on seaborne obsidian trade (pp. 191–92):

> It is likely that the trip to and from an island such as Lipari was a relatively demanding enterprise using primitive, Neolithic boats and may have only been undertaken during certain seasons of the year. In terms of the distance covered, the initial step in an exchange system here tends to be a giant one. For Lipari, the nearest land area of any size is the north coast of Sicily which is located some 30 km away. On the other hand, the sea also offers certain opportunities in the sense that obsidian can be transported in various directions from the island with more or less the same degree of difficulty. It is not necessary for example, to think that obsidian could only reach Calabria by travelling over the shortest possible sea route . . .

Although their model of prehistoric obsidian trade remained essentially land-based, Ammerman and his associates proposed ways for archaeologists working in southern Italy to test for the flow of obsidian directly from Lipari to Calabria as opposed to a shorter sea route via Sicily and the Straits of Messina. Recognition and control of geographical factors like these can provide better explanations for particular shipwreck assemblages related to trade than land-based models, such as those of Renfrew (1975, 1977). As a footnote to this argument, it is of interest that Lipari is in the Aeolian Islands, the legendary (Homeric) home of the winds, suggesting one possible factor other than distance that influenced the flow of the ancient obsidian trade.

The central fact of the archaeology of maritime trade is that it relates directly to transport and only indirectly to exchange. How commodities were transported over water in the context of both physical-geographical and socioeconomic factors constitutes the first order of analysis. It is the ship as an instrument of trade and its contents as data bearing on the conduct of trade that command our attention. Therefore the limitations of interpretation due to equifinality will have to be overcome by specifying why one particular explanation of the archaeological evidence is more compelling than the alternatives. The best archaeological evidence so far for the earliest maritime trade comes from the study of the cargoes and contents at of the Cape Gelidonya and Ulu Burun wrecks described earlier and the cultural affiliations of the artifacts in those cargoes.

Bronze Age Trade in the Mediterranean

The historian Fernand Braudel (1972: 133) visualized the geography of the Mediterranean as consisting of two vast, empty stretches or "solitary wastes" at the eastern and western ends divided by Sicily and bordered in some areas by relatively smaller and almost enclosed seas such as the Tyrrhenian and Adriatic that constituted virtually self-contained lakes for commerce. He identified two main kinds of commerce that were established in the Mediterranean by the fifteenth century: *destination-conscious shipping* of cargoes across long stretches from one point to another (such as the shipping of grain from Egypt to Ostia) and *tramping*, a kind of slow-motion shipping between more closely spaced ports. Tramping offered advantages of simplicity of navigation, protection against offshore winds, ready supplies of water and other provisions, and harbors for protection if pursued by pirates, and it could be conducted by small ships that were relatively inexpensive to build and easy to maintain. But, above all, tramping afforded special opportunities for commerce: "The round trip, which could last several weeks or months, was a long succession of selling, buying, and exchanging, organized within a complicated itinerary. In the course of the voyage, the cargo would often have completely altered its nature" (Braudel, 1972: 107)

As we have seen, the earliest shipwrecks of the Mediterranean Bronze Age were cargo vessels, and serious efforts have been made to explain the nature of Bronze Age trade by studying their cargoes. It will be recalled that the Cape Gelidonya wreck included at least thirty-four ox-hide copper ingots and baskets of copper scrap along with other copper items, presumably of Cypriot origin. Other artifacts associated with the wreck site suggested that Cyprus was merely one of many stops made by this small cargo vessel in its voyaging through the eastern Mediterranean. A cylinder seal of Syro-Palestinian origin suggested contacts with Phoenicia and even the possibility that the merchant was Syrian and the ship of Phoenician origin (Bass, 1967: 165). Bass was careful to note that a single find like this cannot be used to reinterpret Bronze Age trade in the eastern Mediterranean, but he favored the idea that prevailing views of Mycenaean dominance in maritime trade needed to be reevaluated in light of evidence of Phoenician activity.

Other items associated with the Cape Gelidonya wreck point to the tramping described by Braudel. In particular, the presence of balance-pan weights, tools, and stone anvils indicated that there was a smithy on board. While this smithy may have assisted in repairs to the ship during its voyages, the weights indicate commercial activity as this small vessel made its way from port to port. Pottery found with the wreck reveals a cosmopolitan variety of sources, including items of Palestinian, Syrian, Mycenaean, and Cypriot origin (Hennessy and du Plat Taylor, 1967: 122–125). Bronze tools, including at least twenty-four socketed picks and assorted fragments, were also present and generally resembled items found in Cyprus, while bronze hoes and socketed blades appeared to have their closest parallels to objects found on the Greek mainland and in Palestine (Bass, 1967: 84–93). While definitive sourcing of the pottery and bronze objects will have to await more rigorous materials testing, typological evidence supports the argument that this was a well-traveled Bronze Age tramping vessel in the eastern Mediterranean.

The Ulu Burun wreck presents a picture that is somewhat harder to interpret. The artifacts here were more diverse than those from the Cape Gelidonya wreck, ranging as we have seen, from copper and tin ingots in the largest numbers found so far from any Bronze Age wreck site to items made of gold, silver, amber, elephant and hippopotamus ivory, and faience (Pulak, 1988). The ingots were high-priority trade items that were probably hauled overland from the mines and smelting facilities in the hinterland of Cyprus or the Near Eastern mainland for transshipment to the vessel. Copper ingots appeared in a variety of shapes in addition to the ox-hide, including asymmetrical, trapeziform, and bun-shaped (Pulak, 1988: 7–8). They also varied considerably in size. The Ulu Burun and Cape Gelidonya wrecks have yielded a large enough sample to permit an outline of the range of variability present in this class of materials. A total of twenty-seven ox-hide-shaped copper ingots had been excavated at Ulu Burun by 1985, with at least eighty-three visible when the preliminary count was made in the 1983 survey; preliminary estimates suggested a total at the wreck site of around two hundred. By 1985 thirty-nine bun-shaped copper ingots had also been recovered there. Initial tests on some of the ox-hide- and bun-shaped ingots showed that both types were cast of nearly pure copper, but it is uncertain if they resulted from primary smelting of the raw material or remelting of copper scrap. The ox-hide ingots showed the same pattern of rough texture on one side and smooth on the other noted in the Cape Gelidonya specimens.

This and other archaeological evidence for the distribution of copper ox-hide-shaped ingots has led to arguments in favor of trade organized by some kind of centralized authority: "The widespread occurrence of the basic ox-hide ingot shape, from Sardinia to Mesopotamia and from Egypt (as representations) to the Black Sea, has suggested to some a central authority exercising control over the production and the trade in this important commodity" (Pulak, 1988: 8). Various suggestions have been offered for the locality and identity of this centralized authority, ranging from Cyprus (Maddin, Wheeler, and Muhly, 1977) to Syria (Bass, 1986) and the Aegean (Catling, 1964). Pulak's suggestion, however, that "the shape itself probably evolved merely for its ease of transportation over long distances on pack animals" (1988: 8) is more parsimonious. This interpretation is supported by variations in shape and size of the ox-hide copper ingots from the Ulu Burun and Cape Gelidonya wrecks that suggest situationally adaptive behavior in response to the requirements of land transport and transshipment. Some other kind of evidence for centralized control will be needed to make a convincing case for it.

This utilitarian view of trade is supported by the presence of at least forty tin ingots and ingot fragments at Ulu Burun, seventeen of which were in ox-hide form. Of these, sixteen had been sectioned into quarter-ingots, each with one handle or corner preserved, while one specimen was sectioned into a half-ingot with two handles at one end preserved. One of these tin ingots, cleaned for inspection, was found to have a mark on its surface that was also seen on most of the bun-shaped copper ingots. Pulak (1988: 10) has suggested that similar production techniques rather than control of metals production and trade by a central authority should be considered to account for the characteristics of these ingots. Initial measurements support Pulak's utilitarian view. The bun-shaped copper ingots and tin quarter-ingots fell into roughly the same size range, while the copper ox-hide ingots were consistently longer, wider, and thicker. When the complete measurements of these specimens are published it will be possible to test these differences for statistical significance, but it appears that the cargo of metals aboard the Ulu Burun vessel was divided into two broad size categories.

Measurements of the ingots from the Cape Gelidonya wreck also revealed two broad size groupings, one consisting of complete ox-hide-shaped copper ingots and half-ingots of ox-hide shape (the "jumbo size") and the other of bun-shaped and slab copper ingots (the "regular size"). The mean weights of these categories differed significantly from each other while showing consistently low standard deviations within each category.

In addition, sixteen quarter-ingots of tin, produced in the ox-hide shape but with only a single handle element, were reported. (No weights were published for these specimens, so we cannot tell if they were in fact one-quarter of the full weight.) Some specimens were incomplete and required estimates based on assumed weights for missing corners, handles, etc. Corrosion and marine growth on some of the items also affected these measurements. In extreme cases where such factors were observed, the specimens were eliminated from the sample, and therefore the measurements that remained can be regarded as close approximations of the original weights of these specimens. A preliminary comparison of the Cape Gelidonya ingot data with descriptions provided for the Ulu Burun collection showed that the five complete copper ox–hide–shaped ingots measured so far from Ulu Burun were longer (73–82 centimeters) and slightly wider (37–40 centimeters) and thicker (5–6 centimeters). The largest ox–hide–shaped copper ingots found at Ulu Burun weighed 28.8 kilograms and 26.4 kilogram and the smallest 17.9 kilograms – comparable to those from Cape Gelidonya. Ox–hide–shaped ingots with forms showing less well developed handles were smaller – 29 to 33 centimeters long, 20 to 25 centimeters wide, and 4 to 5 centimeters thick. The bun–shaped copper ingots, in contrast, were 22 to 30 centimeters long, 11.7 to 15 centimeters wide, and 3.5 to 3.6 centimeters thick, with 70 percent reported as "small," with an average diameter of 23 centimeters.

This information suggested that the bun–shaped copper ingots from Ulu Burun were comparable in size with their Cape Gelidonya counterparts but significantly smaller than any of the ox–hide–shaped ingots from either wreck. In other words, a trial comparison based on limited data so far available from Ulu Burun suggested that, with respect to the shape and size of ingots of copper and tin, form more or less followed function. The heaviest and largest specimens also showed the most exaggerated handles, suitable as aids in lifting during transshipment and for stowage on pack animals. Preliminary indications, then, are that there was some standardization in the shapes and sizes of these metal preforms during the Late Bronze Age in the eastern Mediterranean but this standardization probably resulted more from the practical requirements of transport than from any centralized control of trade.

Ceramic materials from the Ulu Burun wreck appeared to be dominated by types originating in Syria-Palestine, although examples of these pottery types have also been found archaeologically from as far afield as Akko, in Persia, and Mycenae. So far sixty-seven amphorae have been excavated, and it is estimated that this figure represents about half the total. Residues of a yellow resin were found inside forty-five of these amphorae. Analysis by Curt Beck at the Vassar College Amber Laboratory indicated that this resin belongs to the family Burseracacea (which includes frankincense and myrrh). Additional samples submitted to the National Gallery of London laboratories, however, were reported to be *Pistacia* resin, and this may help to account for the presence of pistachio leaves and fruits inside some of these amphorae. Either or both of these plant products can be viewed as *priority cargoes* comparable to the copper and tin ingots on board. Such commodities were processed and/or packaged in archaeologically identifiable ways that set them apart from unprocessed or unpackaged *bulk cargoes*. Processing, packaging, and transport applied to priority cargoes represented a greater investment of energy and capital than was devoted to bulk cargoes, and evidence of these activities often appears in the archaeological record in a manner that allows one to evaluate the nature and importance of the cargo. In the case of the Ulu Burun wreck, there was evidence as well for contents that indicated the presence of *sumptuary cargoes*, specialized and highly valued objects associated with elite status. Sumptuary items were usually finished products. They were often small and highly portable and could also be made of unusual or exotic materials (that is, distant from their original source). The nature of the association between sumptuary cargoes and elites in the context of shipwreck studies is an important domain for archaeological analysis. The archaeological value of sumptuary items of cargo associated with shipwrecks is based on the information they can yield about the social relations of trade. Sumptuary items, either as cargo or as personal articles of people on board the vessel, can be viewed as extreme instances of the potential for high valuation due to increased distance from the source or from one entrepôt to another, especially when valuations in one entrepôt differ from those in another because of scarcity and the prestige associated with it. Viewed this way, the ship serves as a conduit between points of high and low value potential.

Other ceramic items found at Ulu Burun contributed to the cosmopolitan character of the ship's contents and suggested that like the Cape Gelidonya vessel it was engaged in tramping. Stirrup jars and a one-handled cup of Mycenaean origin were found along with two lamps and four pilgrim flasks of Syrian origin. Short bronze swords of differing types, bronze daggers and/or dirks, and arrowheads and larger bronze projectile points of types seen widely throughout the Aegean and Syria-Palestine in the Bronze Age were also present in the Ulu Burun wreck assemblage, along with a varied assemblage of bronze adzes and chisels that could have served either as items of trade or for shipboard use. One of these items, a necked adze, resembled adzes reported from the eighteenth or nineteenth Dynasties in Egypt, and other necked adzes from the wreck also showed Egyptian affinities.

The cultural affinities of the gold chalice have remained uncertain, but a gold pectoral from the wreck appeared to be of Syro-Palestinian origin, as did three silver bracelets. Other important items of jewelry included numerous stone and amber beads as well as gold pendants and roundels, with some showing general stylistic parallels with Syrian and possibly even Egyptian craft traditions. A scarab attributable to the Second Intermediate Period of Egypt (ca. 1786–1567 B.C.) was found associated with the Ulu Burun wreck materials, although such items commonly occurred as well in the Syro-Palestinian region, where they may have been made or used as late as the fifteenth century B.C. Also found at the wreck site was an inscribed stone plaque with hieroglyphic inscriptions to the Egyptian god Ptah that presented similar problems of cultural attribution. Such plaques began to appear during the Second Intermediate Period and continued to appear in later centuries in localities outside Egypt such as the Palestinian site of Lachish. Although these have yet to be described in detail, reports from the 1986 field season indicated that further portable artifacts, such as a gold scarab of Queen Nefertiti, two cylinder seals, and scrap jewelry items of Syro-Palestinian origin, have been found at Ulu Burun. While most of the sumptuary items on board the Ulu Burun vessel suggested affinities with Levantine and, ultimately, Egyptian centers, a bronze pin pointed to possible early Greek (Mycenaean) contacts as well.

While many of these items were finished pieces, there were also pieces of scrap gold and silver derived from finished objects that had been cut, flattened, or otherwise prepared for smelting. A collection of twenty-two balance-pan weights, mainly of hematite and bronze, suggested that, as with the Cape Gelidonya ship, commercial exchanges were conducted during the course of the voyage. Despite (or perhaps because of) the wealth of portable artifacts found with the Ulu Burun wreck, it is hard to say with assurance which sumptuary items were the personal belongings of people on board and which were cargo. The Ulu Burun ship's contents resembled those of the Cape Gelidonya vessel with respect to the priority cargo of copper and tin but differed significantly in the quantity of sumptuary items present. While it is generally assumed that the copper ingots on board both vessels were originally taken aboard in Cyprus, the cosmopolitan character of the rest of each assemblage made it difficult to infer either ship's port of origin.

Alternative Hypotheses on the Origins of Bronze Age Trade

The Ulu Burun and Cape Gelidonya assemblages indicate the existence of an open social system of exchange. Centralized control of seaborne trade has been repeatedly invoked by archaeologists studying the eastern Mediterranean Bronze Age and critiqued by others (e.g., Knapp 1993). It is apparent from the two wrecks just examined that alternative explanations are possible. Knapp, citing studies by archaeologists Andrew and Susan Sherratt (1991), drew attention to the role of emergent cultural elites seeking to acquire goods that would enhance their social status. He proposed that trade in the eastern Mediterranean Bronze Age began as the transport of high-value, compact luxury items and changed over time to incorporate economies of scale that involved bulk exchange of non convertible commodities. Knapp and the Sherratts saw eastern Mediterranean exchange during the Bronze Age as evolving through the expansion of regional exchange networks that began as specialized trade by elites, perhaps through formal gift-exchanges operating independently of more utilitarian forms of trade within or between cultural systems. Their theory was an attempt to reintegrate ideas about ancient trading strategies into the wider range of cultural incentives operating in the region, and it proposed that the initial impetus for this activity was the pursuit by elites of goods with special social significance (Sherratt and Sherratt 1991: 376):

> Inter-regional trade [in the Bronze Age] was often "Inter-regal trade", conducted in the language of gift exchange between kinsmen: but it was capable of mobilising specific kinds of export commodities and obtaining specific goods in return. Moreover, it allowed considerable scope for individual initiative on the part of stewards and emissaries, and such mercantile activity particularly developed on the fringes of the command economy. Royal trade and individual enterprise thus went hand in hand . . . The palace economy of the Bronze Age gave way to one of two Iron Age alternatives: the territorial empire or the mercantile city state.

This interpretation could account for the presence of significant amounts of sumptuary items in the earlier of the two wrecks and their relative absence in the later one, where trade may have been proceeding in relation to the exchange networks established earlier but not necessarily to the elites that had established these networks. The archaeological evidence allows but does not mandate such an explanation. The Knapp–Sherratt theory requires the appearance over time of standards of exchange and measuring systems, but evidence of these was found on both vessels. Standards may have been just as important for the postulated early exchange of luxury items as they were for market-based exchanges involving priority cargoes such as metal ingots. It is possible that sumptuary items and priority-cargo commodities circulated within separate economic spheres, each with its own agreed-upon standards of exchange. And, as we have seen, the shapes and sizes of ingots may have been structured more by practical considerations of transport and transshipment than by either standards of exchange or centralized control.

Given the limited sample of evidence represented by the two principal shipwrecks bearing on this issue, Cape Gelidonya and Ulu Burun, it is impossible to choose between these alternative explanations, but they can serve as sources of testable hypotheses to guide further shipwreck studies in this region. If additional wrecks contemporaneous with or earlier than the one at Ulu Burun are found that do not contain significant amounts of sumptuary items associated with priority cargoes, they will effectively disprove the Knapp–Sherratt hypothesis. Conversely, if shipwrecks contemporaneous with or later than the Cape Gelidonya wreck are found that contain significant amounts of sumptuary items, either as cargo or as personal possessions, along with ingots, ceramic containers, and other evidence of priority cargoes, it will show that sumptuary exchange in relation to cultural elites persisted well into and perhaps even beyond the point where more market-based and/or entrepreneurial modes of exchange became established. So far no archaeological evidence from shipwrecks for transport or trade of true bulk cargoes has appeared in Bronze Age contexts. As studies proceed on other wrecks of Bronze Age origin in this region, such as the wreck at Sheytan Deresi along the southwestern coast of Turkey (Wachsmann, 1998: 205) and the recently reported Iria wreck off the southern coast of the Argolid of Greece (Lolos, 1993; Wachsmann, 1998:205), it will be important to see which of these alternative explanations of trade best accounts for dated associations of the material remains of exchange represented by ancient shipwrecks and their contents.

Argonauts of the Western Pacific

Argonauts of the Western Pacific, (Malinowski, 1922), addressed the nature of maritime trade in a non-Western culture. Among other things, Malinowski's descriptions provided a seminal analysis of the conduct of this trade within the total structure of Trobriand Island society. Anthropologists have long regarded Malinowski's studies as a defining example of the substantivist view of human economic relations (Dalton, 1975), while both archaeologists and anthropologists (Weiner, 1976, 1988; Leach and Leach, 1983) have discussed and debated Malinowski's functionalist analysis of the Trobriand interisland exchange system – the *kula* – ever since.

For maritime archaeology, the value of examining the kula rests with an understanding of the structural properties and conduct of trade of this kind rather than with any kind of direct archaeological payoff. No wrecks or physical remains of the types of watercraft involved in this activity have yet been found, and the archaeology of trade and exchange in this region remains essentially a land-based enterprise. But the kula directs attention to the organizational and systemic properties of this kind of exchange behavior that, in turn, can serve as a basis for archaeological explanation.

The Trobriand Islanders offer an example of the sumptuary trade invoked by the Knapp–Sherratt model. Renfrew (Renfrew and Bahn, 1991: 309), for example, has identified the Trobrianders' kula as an example of reciprocity involving the overseas exchange of valuables, attended by ceremonies and conferring prestige upon the participants. Malinowski's (1922) original description of the kula was of a vast interisland circuit of specialized exchanges between lifelong male partners. Kula participants distinguished between valuables and more mundane goods, and within the category of valuables they identified two classes of objects – long necklaces of red shells (*soulava*) and bracelets of white shell (*mwali*) – that moved in opposite directions (*soulava* clockwise and *mwali* counterclockwise). Items of one class were exchanged for items of the opposite class, and every exchange was accompanied by ritual. One did not simply hand over one kind of valuable and receive another; instead, valuables were presented in an orderly and ritualized manner with the expectation of a return gift of equivalent value at some later but not-too-distant time. Prestige accrued less from possession of valuables than from participation.

Kula activity was marked by periodic overseas expeditions involving large quantitities of valuables accompanied by trade in more mundane goods known to be in demand at the destination. Return voyages included cargoes of goods of this sort that were valued or needed back home. On some kula visits, the visitors obtained the desired materials or items for themselves. For example, Dobuans visiting the Trobriands would catch fish there before returning to Dobu, and visitors from Sinaketa would dive for *Spondylus* shells at Sanaroa Lagoon. This suggests a degree of separation between spheres of exchange involving kula items and more mundane commodities, and this in turn suggests that the exchange of valuables ritually extended the visitors the right to harvest local resources. It was Malinowski's (1922: 84) contention that no individual participant perceived or understood the totality of the kula system-only analysis by the ethnographer could discern the total pattern (Fig. 36).

Further study has produced fine-grained ethnographic accounts that challenge many of Malinowski's assumptions about the kula. The anthropologist Annette Weiner, who worked on the Trobriand Island of Kiriwina in the early 1970s, noted that some valuables were redirected into a different kind of trade that was integral to the kula but operated

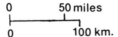

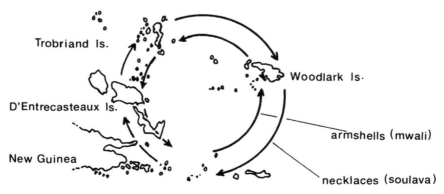

Fig 36. Schematic model of kula exchange system (after Renfrew and Bahn, 1996).

according to different principles. Known as *kitoma*, this kind of exchange drew valuables out of the one-way flow of the archetypal system and usually occurred when a kula participant wanted to provide his children with special decorative items of value. In such cases, the valuables in question tended to circulate within a limited area of the local community (Weiner, 1976: 129). In the case of overseas kula exchange, moreover, such valuables, were accumulated and collectively referred to as *kitoma* because they were not yet part of the kula but were expected to be soon (Weiner, 1976: 180–81). Newly acquired valuables could be fed into the kula if they were equivalent in value to kula items. *Kitoma* exchanges allowed for competition and entrepreneurship within the kula. The discovery of *kitoma* exchanges did not necessarily invalidate the basic picture provided by Malinowski, but they did complicate it, and the lesson here for archaeologists is that ethnographic analogies must be checked against the empirical realities upon which they are based. The map of the kula in the 1970s drawn by the anthropologist Jerry Leach (1983: 20–21), updating the "received model of the kula" based on Malinowski's studies, was more complex than either Malinowski's original map (1922: 82) or a later schematic map by Renfrew and Bahn (1996:337), but it raised the question of what the kula circuit really looked like when Malinowski conducted his field research.

Edmund Leach (1983) accepted the idea that individual participants in the kula believed in the opposite-circulation rule, at least insofar as it applied to particular kula exchanges, but he saw these exchanges as part of a more generalized model of asymmetrical exchange (p. 536):

> in the geographical zone which has come to be regarded as the kula area there is a certain general similarity about the ways non-utilitarian "valuables," consisting of such things as armshells, shell necklaces, boars' tusks, stone adze-blades and the like, are "traded around." In the process of such "trading," individual items may sometimes acquire "economic value" of a straightforward sort. But this is not always the case. A variety of different kinds of "value" are involved in the total complex of exchange relationships that are to be observed . . . Any network of social relations is a structure of indebtedness. The value that attaches to a kula valuable at any point in its wanderings is the value of the debt relationship which it has most recently served to express.

For archaeologists it is important to keep in mind that patterned exchanges of specific items of material culture occurred with sufficient regularity to have been noted by both early and recent ethnographers in the Trobriand region. There are compelling reasons to accept a minimalist view of this behavior as a real system of exchange and interaction that operated between islands and within island communities without necessarily adopting Malinowski's normative model of the kula ring (which, as he noted himself, was an ethnographer's construct). Leach was right to question the assumptions underlying the Malinowskian conception of the kula ring, but from an archaeological perspective all this means is that a better idea or construct of Trobriand overseas exchange may be needed.

The nonutilitarian character of the valuables that circulated in the kula suggests that the patterned exchange in question was something more than simple trade in commodities. Social values were clearly a dominant factor in structuring this exchange. But an empirical review of kula exchange must also consider the exchange of more strictly utilitarian items that accompanied kula transactions – the so-called secondary trade described by Malinowski. Taking Leach's skepticism one step further, it is appropriate here to suggest that Malinowski's "secondary trade" may have been a *primary* factor in the kula and could have played a role in determining which islands engaged in it. A useful effort at historical reconstruction was provided by Raymond Firth (1983) in relation to the scale of kula-related voyaging and the kula-related goods transported during these voyages. Firth estimated, on the basis of Malinowski's information, that about sixty canoes were available for kula-related voyaging in the Trobriand segment of the kula ring in 1918. In one well-documented case in September 1917, Malinowski recorded a kula voyage of forty-two canoes from the Trobriands (eight from Sinaketa, twenty-four from Vakuta, and ten from the Amphletts) to Dobu. Another voyage from Dobu to Sinaketa in March–April 1918 was accomplished with a fleet consisting of at least eighty-four canoes (sixty canoes directly involved with large-scale, competitive kula activities plus twelve canoes from the Amphletts and twelve from Vakuta). According to Malinowski, each canoe had a crew of nine or ten, but only about half were participants. Overall totals for this latter trip thus furnished estimates of men voyaging from Dobu to the Trobriands of 750–850 men, of whom only about 150–200 were directly engaged in the kula. How are these figures to be reconciled with the primacy accorded by Malinowski to kula exchanges? Although the leadership role of kula participants as elite members of the society who initiated and organized these voyages is not seriously in doubt, we need to know more about the 75–80 percent of the personnel who were not participants. For example, how much was their presence due to general "excitement" or kin-based obligations and how much to their involvement in so-called secondary trade?

Firth (1983: 96) estimated that at least three thousand bracelets and necklaces were in circulation in the kula circuit in 1918. Like the sumptuary cargoes of Bronze Age vessels in the eastern Mediterranean, these items were portable, high-value objects associated with cultural elites. As such, they would not have taxed the cargo capacity of voyaging canoes on kula-related expeditions. The principal type of voyaging canoe in use in the Trobriands for kula expeditions was a dugout averaging about 7.6 meters long with a single outrigger and built-up plank sides (Haddon and Hornell, 1975: 271). Another, larger canoe was reported in use for kula voyaging between Tubetube and Gawa (Malinowski, 1922: 144; Haddon and Hornell, 1975: 269) but was relatively uncommon at the time of Malinowski's field studies. The built-up plank sides of both canoe types increased their cargo capacity and improved their general seaworthiness. The poles used to attach the outrigger to the hull extended horizontally across the top of the hollowed-out log hull through the wood planks on both sides, forming a series of ten–twelve internal compartments that were used for stowage of provisions and cargo.

For kula-related voyages the central compartments (from one to three, depending upon the size of the canoe) were partitioned into a hold for stowage of valuables along with a small bundle of representative trade goods (such as a comb, a lime pot, a packet of betel nuts, and a plaited armlet) imbued with magical properties. The rest of the trade items were placed on this bundle to fill the remainder of the hold, with bundles of personal belongings of the voyagers piled on top. Since a kula expedition sailed mainly to receive gifts and not to give them and since kula exchanges never took place simultaneously (Malinowski, 1922: 210–11), valuables were transported only on return voyages, and therefore for one leg of a voyage all of the hold capacity could be reserved for secondary cargo. As for the other leg of the voyage, in their early 1918 visit to the Trobriands the Dobuans received 648 pairs of bracelets, nearly 11 per canoe if one counts only the sixty participating canoes (Firth, 1983: 93). Eleven such items in the hold of a canoe would have occupied no more than about 1.35 cubic meters or 35 percent of the capacity of the hold. Thus the early 1918 kula voyage from Dobu to the Trobriands of eighty-four sailing canoes would have had a total "secondary" cargo capacity of about 322.6 cubic meters when no kula valuables were being transported and 241.6 cubic meters when kula items were present.

In light of Malinowski's many anecdotal references to secondary trade during overseas kula expeditions, it is hard to believe that any voyaging canoes traveled with empty or nearly empty holds. On the return trip of the Sinaketan fleet from Dobu in 1918, Malinowski (1922: 366–367) reported a secondary cargo consisting of *Spondylus* shells, obsidian, pumice, basalt hammerstones, red ochre, and fine silica sand (the last used for polishing stone blades) – all materials unavailable in the Trobriands but much used there. Although *Spondylus* was available in the Trobriand area, shells from the lagoon at Sanaroa, near Dobu, were preferred for their color. Therefore a special collecting expedition was formed when the Trobrianders voyaged to Dobu to obtain *Spondylus* shells for transport back to the Trobriands to be fashioned into necklaces. Accounts like this make it clear that raw materials and key resources were not uniformly distributed throughout the archipelago. Trade in such materials and in items fashioned from them, such as axes in the Trobriands made of greenstone from Woodlark Island, suggest that, quantitatively or in bulk, the flow of materials in the so-called secondary trade on overseas voyages surpassed that of the kula valuables by a factor of at least three to one even when kula valuables were present in the cargo.

For maritime archaeologists the kula offers both opportunities for understanding the nature of ancient trade and cautionary lessons about achieving that understanding. Even a cursory review of Malinowski's information about kula-related voyages reveals gross quantitative discrepancies between his claim for the primacy of kula exchanges in the conduct of these voyages and the personnel and cargoes they involved. The association between kula-related exchange, involving sumptuary cargoes and patterned interaction between elites, and the transport of more utilitarian cargoes suggests a possible socioeconomic model for the kind of archaeological associations found in the Ulu Burun wreck. The Sherratts' hypothesis takes Malinowski's conclusions about the kula more or less at face value and applies them to Bronze Age maritime trade in the eastern Mediterranean, but the kula's complexities remind archaeologists to be wary of models that oversimplify such exchanges. A quantitative reinterpretation of Malinowski's observations of the kula provides a hypothesis that differs from Malinowski's and the Sherratts', namely, that this trade was driven primarily by a demand for utilitarian cargoes consisting mainly of priority items, with sumptuary exchanges playing an important but secondary role.

There is an even more immediate archaeological lesson to be gained from the kula. The archaeologist Stephen Chia and the chemist-archaeologist Robert Tykot, analyzing some two hundred obsidian flakes excavated in 1994 at levels dated to about six thousand years ago at the site of Bukit Tengkorak, in northeast Borneo, were able to identify the sources of the obsidian at localities in the Admiralty Islands and New Britain, about 3,500 kilometers to the east (*Science*, vol. 274, 20 December 1996: 2012–2013). A small percentage of the obsidian at Bukit Tengkorak was also attributed to probable sources in the Philippines. These results suggest that sea trade was established in the Melanesian and island Southeast Asian region about 2,500 years before the appearance of the Lapita culture, generally regarded as the earliest archaeological presence of seaborne migrations into eastern Melanesia and Polynesia. The Field Museum archaeologist John Terrell has suggested that this new evidence indicates a "voyaging corridor" at an early date involving traffic in both directions and not just from west to east. Bennett Bronson, also at the Field Museum, supports Terrell's interpretation and has commented that the obsidian sourcing at Bukit Tengkorak "suggests that the early migrations come out of an early commercial system at a surprisingly early date capable of sophisticated navigation" (*Science*, vol. 274, 20 December 1996: 2013).

Of special interest here is the fact that these ancient obsidian sources occur in the same general area as the kula. The ancient obsidian trade was not necessarily structured in the same way as the kula, but the indications are that there was trade in priority utilitarian materials whether or not other articles were also being exchanged between elite members of these different island societies. It is also clear that boat construction, sailing, and navigation had reached the point by six thousand years ago that this kind of long-distance seaborne trade was possible.

7 · Sailing Ships of the Middle Ages

Shipbuilding Traditions under Sail

Elements of conservatism are sometimes implicit in contemporary treatments of maritime technology under sail. While conservative adherence to shipbuilding rules and practices was undeniably present at the level of distinguishable cultural traditions such as the Vikings, there was another level within these traditions in which shipbuilders revealed their adaptability in relation to changing circumstances of commerce and conflict. Underwater archaeology has substantially increased our appreciation for this finer-grained level of analysis and has made the different maritime traditions appear less monolithic to maritime culture historians.

Sailing craft in various parts of the world today retain certain features of ancient boats and ships. For example, Greenhill and Morrison (1995: 221) suggest that, "although clinker-building for large vessels went out of use, it persisted for boats and small ships down to the end of wooden boat-building and remained the principal tradition in Britain and Scandinavia and parts of North America." They go on to present a parallel case for the historical survival of a European-based flat-bottomed boatbuilding tradition founded ultimately on the Baltic cog and continuing to the modern dory, a type of boat widely used by fishermen along the northeastern coast of North America (Greenhill and Morrison, 1995: 229–40). Their argument is muddied, however, by recognition that the functional advantages of flat-bottomed boats and ships – simplicity, cheapness of construction, and suitability for operation in shallow waters and on beaches and mud-flats – led to the adoption of this design in many parts of the world, and one cannot tell to what extent these claimed survivals were due to the retention and transmission of the principles of a particular culture-historical tradition or to convergent abilities within different culture-historical traditions to adapt in similar ways to similar circumstances. With the development of underwater archaeology, enough direct information is appearing about medieval ships to begin to explain these so-called survivals.

We must be careful not to assume a one-to-one correlation between particular shipbuilders and their products. The apparent cultural conservatism noted at times in the early history of sail may have been more true of the ships than of the builders, who at least in some cases were well acquainted with a variety of different techniques and were prepared to use them as needed – sometimes, perhaps, even in the construction of a single ship.

Maritime archaeologists sometimes find it hard to resist the temptation to treat shipwreck remains as disembodied cultural traits, without regard for the behavioral realities that structure them. That is, they may limit their view of these items to an understanding of them as material objects, usually for purposes of classification or chronology. The opposite extreme, more commonly encountered in land archaeology, is the use of concepts like the *mental template* to define the cognitive limits of acceptability of particular technologies or aesthetic designs within a social or ethnic group (Deetz, 1967: 45–46). Taken to extremes, this view sometimes tends to objectify concepts instead of artifacts as disembodied cultural traits. In reviewing the archaeology of sailing ships we can avoid these extremes by adhering to the archaeologist Kent Flannery's (1967: 120) dictum that the archaeologist's concern is not with the artifact alone or with the person behind the artifact but rather with *the cultural system behind both*. We need to remember that even in such traditions as the Graeco-Roman–Byzantine and the Viking there may have been sufficient technological flexibility and expertise to adapt to new situations. This, together with our ability to recognize interaction between different cultures and the selective adoption of introduced technologies by different cultures, can help us to account for the complexities of the archaeological record without recourse to concepts such as the notion of survivals.

The Seventh-century Yassi Ada Shipwreck

Yassi Ada is a small, barren island in the southeastern Aegean, not far off the coast of Turkey, and can be regarded as a classic ship trap. During the late 1950s sponge divers reported the presence of a Byzantine shipwreck to diver-archaeologist Peter Throckmorton. Following this lead, a team of archaeologists led by George Bass, then at the University of Pennsylvania, undertook a series of underwater excavations from 1961 to 1964. Subsequent analysis and publication of these materials has produced some of the most detailed information to date on any shipwreck site in the world. Two wrecks of Byzantine origin, one a fourth-century-A.D. vessel and the other dated to the seventh century A.D., were found there along with other wreckage. The seventh-century wreck has been described in detail and provides important insights into an otherwise little-known period of maritime history.

The seventh-century shipwreck at Yassi Ada was a small Byzantine merchant vessel whose cargo, structural features, and other contents generally fit Braudel's model of tramping. Bass inferred that the ship was sailing southeasterly before a *meltemi* wind, probably between the end of May and the end of September, sometime shortly before A.D. 625, when it struck and sank on the southeast side of the reef at Yassi Ada (Bass, 1982a: 311–19). The wreck lay on a steeply sloping seabed at depths between 32 and 39 meters. Significant portions of the ship's wood structure were preserved below the siltline, while a cargo of more than 850 amphorae was present in a fairly concentrated area over the wreck site.

Most of these amphorae were large and globular, a newly introduced style in the eastern Mediterranean at the time of the ship's loss. They are thought to have held wine, an important priority cargo. No grape seeds or other direct evidence of wine was found in these amphorae during the initial excavations, but nine of the sixteen amphorae raised during a 1980 revisit of the site did contain grape seeds. Bass considered the alternatives that the ship's cargo was empty amphorae or wine that was sold at various ports along the way with the empty amphorae remaining on board. Although Bass (1982b: 165) favored the idea that the whole cargo of wine was lost in the wreck, its having been being sold off gradually as the ship proceeded from port to port is more consistent with the idea of tramping and with the wreck assemblage as a whole.

Other portable artifacts included fifty-four copper and sixteen gold coins. While Bass noted that the amount of money present was not large – suggesting to him that the merchant had not yet sold off his cargo – there is no way to know how many of the coins originally present on the ship were found by the excavators or how many had been carried off the vessel before it sank. While useful for purposes of dating and possible information about the ship's routing and cultural contacts, the coins cannot resolve the issue of whether the ship was on a direct point-to-point voyage or was tramping through the eastern Mediterranean.

The wreck site also produced weighing implements, including eight bronze balance-pan weights, a glass pendant weight, two lead weights, and several bronze balances and accessories. These latter items included at least three steelyards (the beam portion of the balance), various hooks, and a lead-filled counterweight in the shape of a bust of Athena. A detailed analysis of these implements (Sams, 1982) revealed the calibrations of each steelyard and the weight intervals represented by the weights, which were compared with historical information about Graeco-Roman weights and measures and their continued use in Byzantine times. Although the balance-pan weights and steelyard calibrations were internally consistent, they reflected different weighing systems. There is no single convincing explanation for this difference, but, as with the contents of the amphorae, the difference appears to be consistent with the requirements of a tramping voyage between ports with varying systems of weights and measures.

A wide variety of miscellaneous portable artifacts were found, including a bronze cross and censer, personal items related to clothing (bronze buckles and pins), items related to food preparation and cooking (a cauldron, a pitcher, a jug, and a stone mortar and pestle, as well as possible food remains in the form of edible mussel shells and pottery related to food storage and preparation), assorted items of lead including bars and scrap as well as numerous lead fishing weights, glass bottle fragments, twenty-four terracotta lamps and lamp fragments, remains of iron tools such as hoes, spades, billhooks, axes, mattocks, adzes, hammers, files, chisels, gouges, punches, and a carpenter's compass, iron nails, tacks, and bolts, and wooden items including a possible fishing-net spreader. A bronze or copper spoon bowl was also found coated with lead, suggesting possible use for stirring and dipping molten lead for making lead objects such as hull patches, fishing sinkers, and net weights. Viewed as a whole, these portable artifacts provided a glimpse into some of the daily activities of the crew.

The iron objects required special efforts at recovery involving plaster casting of each corroded item inside the concretion that formed around it after submergence (Katzev, 1982). This process revealed a comprehensive collection of woodworking tools and hardware, some of which was suitable for maintaining a wooden ship during a voyage. Van Doorninck (1982b: 96), however, noted that these tools and the fishing gear associated with the wreck would also have been suitable for setting up temporary camps on land and foraging for firewood and water. This is another argument in support of the idea of the Yassi Ada vessel as a coast-hugging tramper rather than as an oceangoing cargo sailer.

Another touch of domesticity aboard the vessel was revealed by the remnants of the ship's galley near the stern, which was reconstructed in detail (van Doorninck, 1982b: 87–120). Curved tiles were used to cover the roof and flat tiles to line the hearth. The flat baked-clay tiles here may be the earliest extant example of one of the longest-lived technologies of the age of sail. Flat baked-clay tiles, varying somewhat in size and shape, appear often in shipwrecks until the nineteenth century. Flat galley tiles are one of the most durable types of materials on shipwreck sites, where they survive even when the ship's cargo and wood structure have disappeared. They are also good indicators of the effects of postdepositional processes on a wreck site, since it is fairly safe to assume that they were concentrated in the galley area at the moment of the ship's loss. One of the most detailed and useful aspects of van Doorninck's analysis of the archaeological associations in the galley area of the Yassi Ada wreck has to do with the distribution of the various kinds of tiles at the site in relation to the ship's original structure and its collapse on the seabed after wrecking.

A significant portion of the ship's wooden keel and portside hull structure was preserved under the sand, where it was protected from shipworms and could be recorded in detail (van Doorninck, 1982a: 32–64). This recording effort was followed by a reconstruction of the ship's hull, aided by model-building and plan drawings developed from the site data (Steffy, 1982: 65–86). The ship had a deck length of 20.5 meters and a keel length of 12 meters, indicating considerable flare to both the bow and stern. It had a maximum beam of 5.2 meters and an estimated displacement of 73 tons. The hull was fully decked. The ship was small and relatively narrow-hulled, with an estimated capacity for cargo, passengers, and crew of approximately 60 tons in calm weather (but more like 50 tons in rougher conditions) and a breadth/length ratio of 1:4. If all the amphorae found on the wreck were filled with liquid, the cargo would have weighed about 37 tons (Bass, 1982a: 316).

After the ship's keel was laid, the hull was built up shell-first, using planks of variable width to adjust for the curvature of the hull. These planks were attached along their edges by mortise-and-tenon joints in a manner reminiscent of the ships of Classical antiquity. Half-frames were then installed, followed by ceiling planks to line the interior of the hull. The installation of half-frames included futtocks that extended upward along the sides of the hull; planks were connected to the upper part of the hull exterior with iron nails attached directly to the futtocks as in frame-first construction. In other words, whereas below the waterline the Yassi Ada vessel was constructed shell-first, relying heavily upon mortise-and-tenon joinery, above the waterline it followed frame-first principles, using nails instead of mortise-and-tenon plank attachments. Bass (1982a: 312) regarded this unique combination of techniques as a transitional stage in the evolution of ship construction in the Mediterranean, but it is equally reasonable to suggest that seventh-century Byzantine shipbuilders had a range of construction methods at their disposal which they employed in response to changing factors of labor, cost, and market demands. Elements of frame-first construction were already practiced during the Roman era and may have been known to shipbuilders over a wide area of the eastern Mediterranean and elsewhere.

The fourth-century wreck at Yassi Ada made use of mortise-and-tenon joinery throughout the hull and appeared to be better-made than the seventh-century ship. Iron nails instead of wooden treenails above the waterline and the use of unfinished timbers in the seventh-century ship suggested the presence of economies of labor and cost not evident in the earlier vessel. Steffy and Bass interpreted the construction details of the later ship as an indication of the shift in maritime trade in the eastern Mediterranean from the great 1,200-ton Roman grain carriers that sailed between Egypt and Ostia to smaller vessels based on more modest capital investments by private entrepreneurs. A larger sample of shipwrecks from this era will be needed to determine whether this is the case.

Vikings under Sail

Until recently, most information about Viking ships came from spectacular burial sites excavated under conditions of exceptional organic preservation. In particular, the Gokstad ship, excavated at a burial mound near Oslo in 1880, and the Oseberg ship, from a burial mound near Tonsberg, Norway, in 1905, have commanded special attention. As the Norwegian maritime archaeologist Arne Christensen (1996: 80–81) notes ". . . all real Viking ships were though to be of 'the Gokstad type' meaning sleek and open oared warships, sometimes with a single sail." To these well-known finds we could add the Sutton Hoo ship burial excavated in 1938–39 in East Anglia, although its cultural attributions are more Anglo-Saxon than Viking (Green, 1963; Evans, 1994: 107–108). These and other Viking ship finds are commonly referred to as "longships" because of their characteristically long, narrow hull shape. The precursors of this Scandinavian longship tradition discussed earlier (the Hjortspring and Nydam boats) were clinker-built, and this method dominated Viking and other Scandinavian-influenced shipbuilding. Although shell-first, it was very different from the shell-first method seen in the ancient Mediterranean, and because of the lightness of the ships it produced it was not well suited to the use of sail. The Oseberg ship is so far the earliest example of a clinker-built Scandinavian ship with direct evidence of the use of a sail. It was built sometime between A.D. 815 and 820, and the wood for its burial chamber was cut in A.D. 834 (Christensen, 1996: 79). If one takes the Nydam boat as a starting point and accepts the Oseberg ship as the earliest known use of sail by the Vikings, this tradition of boat and ship construction may have lasted 500 years before sailing was adopted.

Gokstad, Oseberg, and Sutton Hoo were all burials containing rich grave goods marking the special treatment of high-status individuals, and they present problems of cultural sampling and representativeness similar to those encountered with the Khufu ship. Christensen (1996: 79) refers to the Oseberg vessel – and, by implication, the other burial ships as well – as "more of a state barge than a ship for ordinary use." Because all three of these major finds were made on land, our sample of Viking ships may have been skewed by the exceptionally good preservation of the wood and the relative accessibility of land sites before the beginnings of true underwater archaeology. Exploration of land sites containing Viking or

Viking-related ship remains continues and has recently produced useful results – the most important, perhaps, being the Ladby ship from the island of Fünen in Denmark, a grave boat that, like the Sutton Hoo vessel, was preserved as an impression or "ghost" in the soil.

Greenhill and Morrison (1995: 175) note that there are over 420 graves known in northern Europe and Iceland in which a boat was buried. To these we can add an undetermined number of boat-shaped stone effigies or "ship-settings" (Fig. 37) in the eastern Baltic region, especially from the Swedish island of Gotland and from the Åland Islands of Finland (Kivikoski, 1967: 58, Pl. 23; Dreijer, 1986: 52–53, 82). Some of these may have served as memorials to important individuals lost at sea in pre-Viking and Viking times. Archaeologically excavated Iron Age (Viking-era) burial mounds in the Åland Islands contained large numbers of boat rivets and charred human remains, indicating true boat burials in which the individual was burned on the pyre inside his boat (Kivikoski, 1967: 129). Land and wet-site archaeology can be expected to continue to play a significant role in the study of Viking-related ships.

Recently, however, underwater archaeology has entered the arena of

Fig 37. Prehistoric stone ship setting, Åland Islands, Finland. These are thought to have been memorials to captains and crews of ships lost at sea. Note the elevated, Viking-like prow.

Viking studies, and the results have dramatically changed our understanding of ancient Scandinavian ship construction and use. Between 1957 and 1962 the remains of five Viking vessels were excavated at Roskilde Fjord in Denmark. Some of these vessels were well preserved partly because the low salinity of the Baltic is a poor environment for shipworms. These vessels all appeared to have been sunk deliberately in shallow water to block access to a channel around A.D. 1000. Referred to as the Skuldelev ships, their remains were analyzed and reconstructed in detail and are currently exhibited in the Viking Ship Museum in Roskilde. In addition to providing new information about Viking-era ships, these vessels have expanded the sample of Viking sailing ships beyond the domain of mortuary assemblages. Two of these wrecks, Skuldelev 1 and 3, were probably trading vessels, while Skuldelev 2 and 5 appear to have been warships. Skuldelev 6, the smallest of the five vessels, was an open boat 11.6 meters long that could have been either rowed or sailed and was probably used for fishing (Christensen, 1996: 85). The Skuldelev wrecks provide an archaeological assemblage that departs significantly from these of previously known ships from the Viking maritime tradition. All five ships were open, clinker-built vessels with many of the same features seen in the other Viking ships but without the elaborate grave goods present at localities such as Oseberg and Gokstad. These vessels were sunk at about the same time and thus represent a unit of contemporaneity from a period when Viking ship construction was well developed. Whatever variability appears among these vessels cannot be due to differences in ethnicity or to change. Skuldelev 5 showed signs of extensive repairs and was probably an old ship when it was sunk (Steffy, 1994: 112). Even with good maintenance, however, the use-life of wooden ships was generally less than fifty years, so the chances are that the Skuldelev vessels were all contemporaneous to within a century.

The Skuldelev ships date to approximately the time of the Norman conquest, and several of them may have looked much like the troop-carrying vessels depicted on the Bayeux Tapestry of A.D. 1066 (Fig. 38), regarded by many art historians as an unusually explicit representation of the Norman invasion of Britain. The transport vessels shown in the tapestry presented a typically Viking profile, complete with ornamented prow and stern and a steering oar but propelled by a single sail. Beginning in A.D. 911 for two hundred to three hundred years Normandy was a

Fig 38. Sailing ship of Viking tradition shown on the Bayeux Tapestry as part of William the Conqueror's invasion fleet of 1066.

Nordic-Frankish duchy (Brøndsted, 1960: 244–45; Jones, 1989: 76), so the Viking character of their ships is not surprising.

Skuldelev 2 was a large warship built of thin oak planking, and Skuldelev 5 was a smaller vessel of the same form. Both show the high breadth/length ratios (1:7.3 and 1:6.7, respectively) characteristic of long-ships intended for speed, particularly when rowed, and like other known Viking warships they were lightly constructed – probably another concession to speed under oars. The number and positions of the stationary thwarts indicated that Skuldelev 5 was rowed by twenty-four men, but the presence of a mast step made it clear that a sail was sometimes used. The mast step was badly damaged, suggesting that the relatively light construction of Viking warships provided poor support for the mast and did not combine well with the use of sail.

Skuldelev 1, however, presented a different picture altogether. Here we see the relatively well-preserved remains of a beamier ship (breadth/length ratio of 1:3.6) with a heavier system of internal frames (added after the clinker shell was built up) than was present in Viking longships, pointing to its use as a deepwater cargo vessel. The hull was deeper, too, at 2.1 meters, than other Viking ships, with an open hold amidships providing internal capacity for cargo and provisions (Christensen, 1996: 84–85) estimated at around 24 tons (Greenhill and Morrison, 1995: 218). While most Viking ships were planked with oak, Skuldelev 1 used pine planking, with oak for the frames and other elements (Steffy, 1994: 111). Skuldelev 3 was a smaller but better-preserved ship with a mast step and a cargo hold of an estimated 4.6 tons capacity. It had a breadth/length ratio of 1:4.0. Both Skuldelev 1 and 3 had some oarports, probably for maneuvering close to shore, but were small merchantmen that relied principally on sail for open-water travel. Although clinker-built and constructed according to the general principles of the Viking shipbuilding tradition, these two ships were dramatically different from the warships found in Viking burial sites and more like the robust sailing vessels depicted on the Bayeux Tapestry.

The Skuldelev wrecks revealed a wider range of variability in ship construction than anything previously known from the Viking tradition. These ships varied as much or more in size and building materials than the burial ships, and the cargo vessels were more heavily constructed and more dependent on sail for propulsion. By at least A.D. 1000 the Vikings were moving beyond raiding and conquest and engaging in long-distance colonization and commerce, especially in the Baltic region but extending across the North Atlantic to England and France, and into Russia (Fig. 39) along the Volga River and Caspian Sea (Jones, 1989: 145–311). This expansion was accomplished entirely by ships, which, thanks to the research on the Skuldelev wrecks, we know were built according to a recognizable but flexible shipbuilding tradition that included oared vessels, ships that combined sails and oars, and true sailing ships. As has been suggested for the seventh-century Yassi Ada ship, there are archaeological indications of adaptability in construction methods by shipbuilders working within definable culture-historical traditions that stretch our ideas about the shipbuilding traditions of the past.

Shipwrecks of the Hanseatic Period

A visitor to nineteenth- and tenth-century A.D seaports such as Birka, near the modern city of Stockholm, or Hedeby, on the Baltic coast of the Jutland peninsula, would have seen clinker-built ships of Viking origin alongside examples of another, quite different type of vessel – the precursor of the Baltic cog. Evidence in the form of ships depicted on early

Fig 39. Sailing replica of Viking warship at Viipuri (Vyborg), Russia, showing clinker-planked hull and ornamented prow.

coins, references in written texts, and direct archaeological evidence from excavations at Birka of about sixty typical cog nails associated with thousands of rivets from Viking ships points to the beginnings of another maritime tradition in the Baltic region (Ellmers, 1994: 34–40).

The ships shown on coins from Hedeby were especially important, because Hedeby was a port where cargoes were transshipped overland from the North Sea to the Baltic. Hedeby, the site of major but intermittent investigations by German archaeologists from 1900 until the outbreak of World War II (Brøndsted, 1960: 141), was a bridgehead for trade eastward from the Frisian and Dutch coasts and was under Danish and Swedish political control during the ninth and tenth centuries – hence the large number of coins showing Viking ships. Some ninth-century coins also showed single-masted, flat-bottomed sailing ships with reversed clinker construction – that is, with the lower hull planks (strakes) overlapping the upper ones, a practice never seen in ships of Viking origin (Ellmers, 1994: 37). Archaeological excavations at the Wurt Hessens, at the present-day port of Wilhelmshaven, have identified a seventh-century slipway constructed for flat-bottomed boats at least 2 meters wide and a steering oar of a type associated with early cogs. It appears to have originated somewhere along the Frisian-Dutch coast, where its flat bottom would have been useful for sailing among the shoals and mud flats of that coastline (Ellmers, 1994: 34).

By around A.D. 1150–1250 there is evidence that trade carried on in Viking ships was giving way to the use of the cog, with the port of Hedeby in decline as new seaports appeared along the Baltic coast of Germany from Kiel to Elbing. Three early seals from one of these port cities, Lübeck, dating from 1224 to 1281, show a vessel described as a cog in contemporary documents and with a type of steering oar associated with early cogs but with Viking-style dragonheads at the tops of the curved stem- and sternposts (Ellmers, 1994: 37). Ellmers regarded these as depictions of early cogs, but they could just as easily reflect interaction between late Viking and early Hanseatic shipbuilding traditions. Clinker-built cargo vessels based on earlier Viking techniques continued to be built in the Baltic region after the Viking period and are represented by several archaeological finds, so it it would not be surprising if elements of Viking shipbuilding had persisted into Hanseatic times.

Excavations at Tyskerbryggen, near Bergen, in 1962 uncovered a large clinker-built vessel that may have been damaged or destroyed by a fire in 1248 (Greenhill and Morrison, 1995: 217). The ship was estimated to have had a cargo capacity of 200 tons, and its measured and estimated dimensions (breadth 9.5 metres, length 30 metres, breadth/length ratio 1:3.2) make it the largest extant vessel of Viking origin. This vessel had a thick mast and clearly operated under sail. Other clinker-built Viking-style wrecks that pertain to this period include the Hedeby 3 ship, thought to be of eleventh-century date, and the Lynaes ship, near Copenhagen at the north end of Roskilde Fjord, from the mid-twelfth century. The Hedeby 3 vessel was estimated to have a cargo capacity of at least 40 tons, while the Lynaes ship could transport about 60 tons of cargo. With breadth/length ratios of 1:3.2, 1:4.4, and 1:4.2, respectively, these three ships were also comparable in their proportions to the Skuldelev 1 and 3 wrecks (Crumlin-Pedersen, 1991; Greenhill and Morrison, 1995: 218).

Taken together, the Lübeck coins and late clinker-built ship remains from Bergen, Hedeby, and Lynaes suggest that Viking shipbuilding methods continued to exert a visible influence even as the cog became the predominant type of trading vessel in the Baltic. Another example of this persistence and the combination of these elements of construction appeared in a thirteenth-century clinker-built boat from the harbor at Kalmar Castle, Sweden, discovered during archaeological studies conducted there in 1934. This boat, a small coastal trader 10.9 meters long and 4.6 meters wide, had a straight and near-vertical sternpost with attachments for a true rudder – a most un-Viking development and one that may have been added during the boat's use-life (Roberts, 1994: 23–24). By the thirteenth century, sternpost rudders were already in use with cogs. Thus, on the basis of the limited archaeological evidence available so far, it appears that cultural influences in ship- and boatbuilding from the Viking and Hanseatic traditions were flowing both ways and being recombined in opportunistic ways that fitted the needs of each culture.

The city of Lübeck and the Hanseatic League, a community of Baltic seaports and trading centers in which merchants swore oaths of partnership and assisted each other's commerce, were both founded in 1159. The seals struck to commemorate the founding of Lübeck, Elbing, and other cities often depicted cogs. Trading bonds of this kind did much to reduce the commercial uncertainties inherent in tramping. Instead of sailing from one coastal port to another hoping for sales and cargoes along the way, merchants could travel between ports with a clear idea of what to expect from their trading associates at each location. The rise of the cog as a trading vessel became linked to the routinization of commerce between Hanseatic seaport towns. Remains of a wrecked cog at Vigso, on the Skaggerak coast of Denmark, included goods from western Europe such as bronze fingerbowls, while another cog wrecked in 1370 at Vejby in northern Denmark was reported to have been carrying fine textiles, cooking and eating utensils, and coins (Ellmers, 1994: 42) – all priority cargoes. Between 1250 and 1400 bulk cargoes were still a marginal proposition for Baltic merchants because, among other things, of the effects of the Black Death on grain prices (Unger, 1980: 169).

Depictions of these vessels often showed profile views of a high-sided, single-masted vessel with reverse-clinker planking and a straight stem and stern, often angled steeply outward from the waterline to the peak. A centerline stern rudder, attached with hinges to the sternpost, replaced the older steering oar. During this period, similar ship images appeared in wall paintings in churches, (Fig. 40a–b). Documentary sources and the iconography of seals and church murals, while useful, tend to be somewhat generalized and are always at one level removed from the ships themselves. As the maritime archaeologist and historian Detlev Ellmers (1994: 29) has pointed out,

> The term "cog" only appears in written sources for ships of the Hanseatic League from about A.D. 1200, but in the course of the fifteeenth century this type of ship disappeared so completely from the sea that nobody after the Middle Ages knew precisely what a cog looked like. In Hanseatic towns around 1900 people just knew the term, but used it for any wooden sailing vessel more than a century old.

The fortuitous appearance in October 1962 of wooden ship remains during dredging operations in the River Weser near Bremen led to a series of excavations by the maritime archaeologist Siegfried Fliedner and the recovery and detailed restoration of this vessel, which presented many of the features seen on the seals and murals. The ship, known as the Bremen cog, was 23.2 meters long, with massive oak timbers forming vertical pillars and horizontal throughbeams inside the hull. A single oak log 11.4 meters long and weighing 600 kilograms was fitted over the floor timbers to form a kind of keelson that contained the mast step. The hull was flat-

Fig 40a, b. Two depictions of Baltic cogs on the walls of a thirteenth-century church at Finström, Åland Islands, Finland. Published with permission of Finström Church (St. Mikaels kyrka).

bottomed, with broad planks attached in normal clinker fashion to the sides and flat-laid planks along the bottom. The ship had a weather deck supported by heavy beams and a deeper hull (4.3 meters) and higher sides than any known ships of Viking origin. Although overlapping in the formal manner of clinker-style construction, the Bremen cog's planking was unlike that of the Viking ships, with far fewer strakes and with generous caulking with moss, animal hair, and tar (Steffy, 1994: 119–20). The ship's bow- and sternposts were straight and angled rather than curved in the Viking manner. The ship's cargo capacity was estimated at 80 tons. It had a centerline rudder attached to the sternpost and an aftercastle (a built-up structure on the stern) with a wooden windlass on top. Dendrochronology of the Bremen cog's timbers indicated that the oak trees used in the hull structure were cut in the autumn of 1378 (Ellmers, 1994: 30), making this a relatively late example of this type of ship.

Once the Bremen wreck was identified as a cog, it was apparent that other, earlier archaeological finds, in particular, Wreck 5 from the ancient harbor at Kalmar, may have been those of cogs as well. Additional archaeological work since the Bremen finds has also produced fragmentary remains of cogs from Holland, Germany, Denmark, and Sweden. The earliest archaeological example of a cog so far found is the wreck sunk off Kollerup at the north end of the Jutland peninsula, which has been dated to around A.D. 1200. This find and others have produced evidence of cooking facilities on board (Ellmers, 1994: 41). The Kalmar cog excavations produced fragmentary remains of a wooden ship's pump, and the Bremen cog, while lacking a pump, had an outlet under the stern that suggested that a pump had been installed. As Ellmers (1994: 42) has pointed out, some arrangement for pumping or drawing off water from inside the hull was necessary given the fact that the deck planks were laid at right angles to the sides, forming a less-than-watertight joint. Instead of collecting on the deck, water from rain and spray drained into the hold and bilges, improving stability but also making conditions below decks extremely wet. It appears that the Hanseatic shippers relied heavily upon barrels to keep the cargo dry aboard these ships, and the use of barrels as containers also helps to account for the prominent capstan on the stern deck of the Bremen cog.

One of the most complete examples of a cog or coglike ship was excavated from a bog near Almere, the Netherlands, in 1968. This vessel was an even later example of cog construction than the Bremen ship and was dated by means of associated coins to between 1422 and 1433 (Steffy, 1994: 121). Reconstruction by the maritime archaeologist Frederick Hocker showed this to be a flat-bottomed ship just under 16 meters long and 4.2 meters wide, with an estimated cargo capacity of 24.5 tons. It had the same kind of angled, straight stem- and sternposts as the Bremen ship but more vertical sides. The hull planks were broad and were fastened in clinker fashion with caulking, again as in the Bremen ship, but little remained of the deck except for portions of the supporting structure. From his analysis, Hocker was able to infer a kind of bottom-to-top sequence of construction for cogs and coglike vessels in which the heavy bottom planks were temporarily fitted together first to form the flat bottom, then unfastened to allow the attachment of the frames and side planking. According to Hocker this kind of building sequence, with variations, could be viewed as an essentially different mode of construction from either shell-first or frame-first methods.

In the Almere vessel, as in other cogs or coglike ships, the hull planking was made from sawed planks instead of planks split from logs using axes and wedges. This practice reflected a major technological change then taking place in northern and western Europe involving the widespread use of hydraulic sawmills. Sawed planks were more economical with timber as well as with the labor needed to produce them. Split-log planks were stronger, but this advantage was more than offset by the ease and economy of production with sawed timber and the medieval shipbuilder's ability to strengthen the hull in other ways, using internal beams. The use of sawed timber in prodigious amounts for many purposes, of which shipbuilding was only one, contributed to the rapid and widespread deforestation that transformed the landscape of Europe north of the Alps during the thirteenth and fourteenth centuries (Darby, 1962: 190–199).

Neither the Bremen cog nor the Almere ship shows the reverse-clinker type of hull planking shown on early Hanseatic seals, suggesting that even greater variability in this tradition can be expected as shipwreck archaeology continues in places such as the Dutch polders. Larger cogs began to appear, providing a marked increase (especially over ships of Viking design) in carrying capacity for cargo without a corresponding increase in the size of the crew needed to man them and thus increasing the return for investment. For example, a late Viking-style cargo ship of

50 tons cargo capacity required a crew of twelve–fourteen men, while a cog capable of transporting 200 tons of cargo needed eighteen–twenty men. This return was further improved by greater economies of scale as the volume of goods shipped rose (Unger, 1980: 139).

Although primarily a ship of commerce, the cog also possessed characteristics that made it a good candidate for use as a warship. Its high sides, particularly when they angled outward as in the Bremen ship, gave it a marked advantage of height over contemporary warships of Viking design. Not only did this make it difficult for boarders, but it allowed archers and spearmen standing on the high weather deck and elevated stern to shoot their missiles downward into the relatively unprotected open hull of the Viking-style ship (Unger, 1980: 139–40). A Viking vessel might have been able to outrun and and outmaneuver a cog by sprinting and dodging under oars, but the cog had the defensive advantage of greater height. It could also carry large numbers of soldiers, making it useful as a troop transport.

Personal weapons such as daggers were found associated with the cog wrecks at Bremen, Kalmar, and Kollerup, but this does not mean that they were true warships. Sailors on cargo ships presumably needed to protect themselves from attack by pirates and others. Historical documents show, however, that cogs were requisitioned by Hanseatic towns such as Lübeck (in 1234 and in 1239) to fight naval battles against the king of Denmark. During the trade wars between Hanseatic merchants and the king of Norway in 1284, cogs were used for blockading Norwegian ports. These cogs were fitted with crenellated wooden platforms on the forward and rear decks, a device adopted from English ships of that period (Ellmers, 1994: 43). These miniature wooden "castles" provided even greater advantages of height for archers, especially crossbowmen, necessary now because cogs were sometimes engaging other cogs. Eventually these platforms were enclosed and integrated more closely into the ship's hull and deck. Although cogs did not show these specialized adaptations for warfare until much later, it seems likely that armed cogs serving as ad-hoc fighting ships had a history extending back to the ninth century (Runyan, 1994: 47). A documentary survey of ships used in the early part of the Hundred Years' War (1337–1360) showed that about 751 out of 1,300 ships identified were cogs. An English military fleet of 1299–1300 was recorded as including 15 cogs raised at the Cinque Ports (Hastings, Romney, Dover, Hythe, and Sandwich) as part of their royal service in exchange for trade concessions and relief from taxes (Runyan, 1994: 51). So in addition to their ability to transport cargoes, cogs were an important component in medieval warfare at sea immediately prior to the advent of gunpowder.

The Transition to Post-Medieval Ships

Of the major maritime traditions examined so far, only the Vikings were truly oceanic in the scope of their voyaging. As their competitive relationships with the Hanseatic League intensified, it became apparent that open, clinker-built ships of Viking style were not ideally suited for trading over long distances or for sustaining colonies in remote areas such as Greenland or North America. This makes it all the more remarkable that the Vikings were able to explore, colonize, and trade as widely and for as long as they did. Much of their voyaging was done within sight of land, however, and this was almost exclusively the case for medieval sailing in the Baltic and Mediterranean regions. The cog, with its single square sail, had very limited ability to sail into the wind and could not be rowed – an advantage still retained by the Vikings in most if not all of their ships. The proliferation of Hanseatic ports along the coast of northern Germany and Poland and among the islands and southern coastlines of Scandinavia was due, in part, to the need for overnight stopovers and places of refuge during storms and periods of contrary winds. Like so many of their Mediterranean contemporaries, these ships were mainly coast-huggers that sailed in a start-stop fashion according to the vagaries of wind and weather.

As trade revived and expanded after the Black Death, the cog grew larger and was transformed into the more seaworthy carrack, especially in the shipyards of Venice and Genoa, and the emergence of ships with multiple masts and more varied sailing rigs was under way by 1400. Cogs were being constructed using carvel-built methods, in which planks were laid edge-to-edge and attached directly to the frames rather than overlapping (Unger, 1980: 221–23). This change economized on the amount of timber used in ship construction and encouraged the production of larger ships.

As the maritime historian Richard Unger (1980: 221) has noted, the maximum practical size for a square sail is about 500 square meters. Therefore, as cogs and carracks grew larger, there was a need for more sails (with more masts) and for a "divisible" sail plan – sails of different shapes on multiple masts to provide better speed and control when sailing at different angles to the wind. Frame-first construction combined with carvel planking appeared in northern Europe during this period, although frame-first construction had appeared earlier in the Mediterranean and was already expanding rapidly there. Construction started on the first carvel-built ship with three masts in the port of Gdansk in 1473 (Unger, 1980: 222). This development signaled that Baltic shipbuilders were producing vessels comparable in size and sophistication to their Mediterranean counterparts by the late fifteenth century and that European maritime cultures were about to embark upon another, more decisive round of oceanic voyaging.

Most of the information about this transition in Europe comes from historical documents and paintings and drawings rather than from archaeology. Because such transitions tend to occur quickly, with new designs appearing in small numbers and varying so much that they defy classification, it is hard to find shipwrecks that are truly transitional in nature. Once designs become established they tend to be produced repetitively and in large numbers over fairly long periods of time, and this may create a false impression of extreme conservatism. Time lines in the history of ship construction are marked by long periods of relatively little change punctuated by spurts of rapid innovation and adaptation in which important new developments appear in historical documents but are poorly represented archaeologically.

What archaeology provides is a kind of before-and-after perspective on this transition. As we have seen, elements of frame-first ship construction were already present in the Mediterranean, especially in the case of the seventh-century Yassi Ada vessel. A small shipwreck in the eleventh century at Serçe Limani Harbor, opposite Rhodes, revealed even more extensive use of frame-first methods. Although the hull planks were butted flush against each other, there was no evidence of mortise-and-tenon joinery. Instead, the planks were nailed directly to the frames, providing a watertight "skin" for the hull as opposed to serving as the primary source of its strength (Steffy, 1994: 91). The ship was flat-bottomed with flaring sides somewhat like those of Baltic cogs, but it had upwardly curved bow- and sternposts that in no way resembled the cog's and effectively precluded the installation of a rudder. Steffy (1982) has argued that this vessel's shape would not have been possible without the prior use of mortise-and-tenon construction methods in earlier ships of that region.

Associated coins were used to date the loss of the Serçe Limani vessel to A.D. 1024 or 1025. The ship was transporting a primary cargo of Muslim glassware and broken glass suitable for remelting along with 110 old Byzantine amphorae when it was wrecked. Some Muslim pottery was also found along with fifty javelins, twelve spears, and a few swords. This rather eclectic cargo, including both bulk and priority goods, suggested trade between the Islamic and Byzantine empires and raised the possibility that the ship was Muslim-built (Pryor, 1994: 61).

A more definitive precursor of frame-first construction was uncovered in 1898 during the construction of a canal at Rovigo in the Po River delta, Italy. The remains of two ships and a boat were well preserved in the mud and were recorded with unusual care for that period. These wrecks became known as the Contarina ships and the Logonovo boat. Subsequent research by the maritime archaeologist Marco Bonino (1978) has provided more recent information about them. One of the ships was a two-masted vessel about 21 meters long and 5.2 meters wide. It is tentatively dated to around A.D. 1300 mainly because of its resemblance to images shown in floor mosaics dated to A.D. 1225 and to drawings and specifications in *Fabrica di galere*, an Italian treatise on shipbuilding from 1410. The ship was built entirely frame-first, with closely spaced overlapping futtocks joined to the ends of the floor timbers. The frames and planks were oak, with stringers of larch. There was no sign of a rudder, but the hull had more rounded curves than the Serçe Limani wreck – suggesting that it was built by people who were already experienced with frame-first construction. This ship is generally regarded as a small lateen-rigged *nave* (Steffy, 1994: 91; Smith, 1993: 31; Unger, 1980: 203). The remains of the Logonovo boat were found preserved in the muck of the Po delta near Ferrara in 1958, and it is thought to date to the early fifteenth century (Bonino, 1978; Steffy, 1994: 93). The boat was about 10 meters long and 2.6 meters wide and was, like the Contarina ship, made entirely of oak except for stringers of larch. It, too, was built entirely frame-first and was generally similar to the two ships in construction, including steps for two masts for lateen sails, suggesting that it was a small Italian *barca* – a sort of miniature version of the Contarina ship just described. Finally, the second Contarina ship is tentatively dated to the mid-sixteenth century, mainly on the basis of associated pottery. (Unfortunately, the pottery found at the wreck site was known to have been in use for over a century, so the precise dating remains uncertain.) Like the other two, this vessel was built entirely frame-first, and like the other Cantarina ship it used iron bolts to join the ribs. It was 20.5 meters long and 6.3 meters (wide), with a breadth/length ratio of 1:3.3 – making it measurably the beamiest of the Po delta wrecks and more like other rounded-hulled ships of that period. It had a horizontal through-beam on top of every third futtock, but these were not directly attached to the futtocks and remain something of a mystery. Perhaps they were a holdover from earlier shell-first construction, when through-beams like these were used to maintain the shape of the hull before adding the internal frames (Smith 1993: 193).

The historical importance of these three small Italian wrecks lies in their chronological position as archaeological representatives (though not necessarily typical) of the era of round ships. The Mediterranean round-ship tradition is represented in a variety of documents including contracts with shipyards in Genoa, Venice, and Marseilles by King Louis IX of France for ships to transport troops and horses for his two Crusades (1248–1254 and 1270). The maritime historian John Pryor (1994: 64) points out that despite serious difficulties with these documents they can be used for basic information about these remarkable ships. The ships were built in two-decked and three-decked classes, with the larger, three-decked variety displacing up to 806 metric tons. The three-decked versions had an overall length of 35.2 meters and a maximum width of 9.5 meters and were propelled by two immense triangular lateen sails, each with a yard longer than the ship itself. Each ship was guided by two massive steering oars and carried as many twenty-five anchors. When under way, they towed a large ship's boat astern and carried up to three more on board. The largest of these vessels reportedly could carry over a thousand passengers (Pryor, 1984; 1994: 64).

Documentary evidence of this kind is supported by a variety of images in manuscripts, paintings, murals, and on ceramics, all showing a heavy dependence on triangular lateen sails in preference to the square sails of Graeco-Roman, Viking, and Hanseatic ships. Iconographic evidence suggests the complete dominance of this rig throughout the Mediterranean from the ninth to the fourteenth centuries (Pryor, 1994: 67). Documents describing specific voyages in lateen-rigged round ships between A.D. 867 and 1254 indicated that these vessels were generally slow and made poor progress when sailing into the wind. A total of seven passages in the Mediterranean running with the wind over distances ranging from 868 to 2,000 nautical miles averaged 2.53 knots in speed, while on three recorded voyages against the wind over distances from 1,300 to 1,900 nautical miles these ships averaged a speed of 1.14 knots (Pryor, 1994: 73). Still, even this limited capability for upwind sailing was superior to that reported for ancient Graeco-Roman ships. The slow passages reflected by these figures meant that medieval round ships were dangerously exposed to bad weather and to spoilage of provisions. Anecdotal historical accounts by pilgrims and Crusaders of the trials of such voyages abound.

No shipwreck remains dated earlier than about 1530 are available so far to provide direct documentation of this transition to post-medieval ships. Smith (1993: 190–93 and Fig. 3.15), however, reviews research on a votive ship model from the Catalonian town of Mataro. The date of the model is open to question, as is its scale. Spanish scholars appear to agree that it represents a Mediterranean cog (locally termed *coca*) of the type introduced into southern Europe by the beginning of the thirteenth century. Smith, however, considers it more likely that this is a model of the medium-sized, single-masted fifteenth-century carrack called a *nao* in Spain. The carrack was a type of round-ship descendant of the cog that later saw development toward larger, three-masted ships. If Smith's interpretation is correct, the Mataro model holds special interest for maritime historians, since Columbus's largest ship on his 1492 voyage to the New World, the *Santa María*, was recorded as a nao, as were two ships the (*São Gabriel* and *São Rafael*) used in a voyage of exploration to India by Vasco da Gama in 1497. The appearance of the Iberian nao and its contemporaries (Fig. 41) could be viewed as marking a decisive shift away from the tendency to voyage within sight of land and take refuge in sheltered coves during inclement weather, adverse winds, and at night – the medieval approach to voyaging – and toward more regular voyaging beyond sight of land on a truly oceanic scale.

The Great Age of Asian Seafaring

Seaborne commerce on a large scale in Asia dates to the Song Dynasty of China (A.D. 960–1270), and the Mongols (the Yuan Dynasty, ca. A.D. 1271–1368) took over the Song ships and went on to build even more ships on a grand scale. Marco Polo described four-masted seagoing merchant ships with watertight bulkheads and crews of up to three hundred during his stay at the imperial court from 1275 to 1292 (Levathes, 1994: 49). Early in the Ming Dynasty (A.D. 1368–1644) there was an expansion of seaborne trade with the construction of an immense treasure fleet (reported to consist of 317 ships when it was assembled in Nanjing in 1405) that made trading cruises throughout the Indian Ocean and the China Seas (Levathes, 1994: 82). Ming seaborne commerce declined rapidly during the mid-fifteenth century as a result of conflict between the court and the merchants over control of it. The emperor eventually declared the construction of any ship with more than two masts a capital offense, authorized the destruction of all oceangoing ships and the arrest of merchants who sailed them, and declared it a crime even to go to sea in a multimasted ship (Levathes, 1994: 174–75).

Although shipwreck archaeology is relatively new in Asia, important finds are pointing the way toward the broader use of archaeological evidence in relation to the documentary history of this era of Chinese maritime expansion. The documents cannot always be assumed to be detailed or accurate. As Worcester (1971: 22) pointed out,

> No writer of nautical experience has described these vessels [large ships of the Mongol Dynasty] or provided us with information on which reliance can be placed. Writers on shipping were, or seemed to be, practically unknown in those days; the few that refer to it are so inaccurate and laconic, or both, that their works have little real value, and so everything relating to the ships of the period is in a great degree a matter for conjecture.

This view was shared by no less an authority than Joseph Needham (1971: vol. 4, p. 3, 380), who pointed out that "systematic nautical treatises did not arise in Chinese culture, or at least did not get into print." Furthermore, European observers of medieval-era Chinese ships, including Marco Polo, were characteristically impressed by their seaworthiness but at the same time described them in Eurocentric terms on the basis of what they lacked – such as keels, stemposts and stemposts, centerline rudders attached to the sternpost, and masts that were not positioned along the ship's longitudinal centerline (Keith and Buys, 1981: 121). Often the interpretation based upon such observations was that Chinese shipbuilding evolved in isolation from the rest of the world and especially from the West: "As in so many other areas of activity, the craftsmen of China developed their own designs and techniques, owing little if anything to outside influences and having surprisingly little impact on ideas in neighboring lands" (Muckelroy, 1978: 136).

It remains to be seen how isolated Chinese shipbuilding was during its zenith in the Song, Mongol (Yuan), and Ming Dynasties, but it seems appropriate here to remind archaeologists to be wary, once again, of the fallacy of affirming the consequent. Instead of assuming cultural isolation on the part of historic Chinese shipbuilders and sailors, perhaps we should be using archaeological evidence to find out whether this was the case. The Australian maritime archaeologist Jeremy Green (1983a: 260) points out that following the imperial ban on overseas voyaging during the Ming Dynasty, shipping increased along China's inland waterways and coasts. This suggests that historical accounts of later Chinese ships, mainly from the nineteenth and early twentieth centuries, were biased toward shallow-water craft intended for use on canals, rivers, and close to shore – quite a different maritime tradition from this earlier period in Chinese history.

The best archaeological evidence available so far for this period comes from the wreck found during canal dredging in 1973 of a large ship buried in muck at Houzhou, about 10 kilometers from Quanzhou, an important trading port of the Song Dynasty in what is now Fujian Province. The hull remains of the Quanzhou ship were excavated and reported by People's Republic of China archaeologists in a series of reports (Editorial Committee, *Wen Wu*, 1975), and are now on display at the Overseas Communications Museum at Quanzhou. The ship was 34.6 meters long and 9.8 meters wide with a displacement of 374.4 tons. A total of 504 copper coins were found associated with the wreck, 70 of which were minted during the Southern Song period (ca. 1127–1279), with the latest ones dating to 1272. The ship probably sank soon after that date. This evidence revealed a ship as large as any merchant vessel known from Europe during this period (Keith and Buys, 1981: 124). Remains of the hull were preserved up to the waterline, permitting detailed study of important elements of the ship's construction.

The ship had a pine keel constructed in three parts, with the fore- and aft-ends sloping upward along the ship's longitudinal axis. The hull was covered with double layers of planking from the keel up to the start of the turn of the bilge and triple layers of planking upward from that point. All hull planks were made of cedar. The attachments for this planking were complex and combined elements of carvel and clinker joinery. There were twelve vertical wooden bulkheads arranged across the bottom interior of the hull to form thirteen compartments. These were not, however, watertight, since an opening or waterway was present at the base of each bulkhead except for the ones at either end of the hull. Half-frames were attached to each bulkhead and extended partway up the inside of the hull, but no evidence was found of futtocks extending farther up the hull interior (Green, 1983a). Overall, the ship's hull was V-shaped, indicating its seagoing character. Two mast steps were found set in line along the keel and supported by beam elements comparable to those seen in the Pattaya wreck (Green and Harper, 1983: 40). Both masts had square sockets to accommodate a tabernacle for lowering the mast when necessary. No wooden treenails or mortise-and-tenon joinery were found on the Quanzhou ship. Instead, flat L-shaped iron fasteners were widely used. The stern had a square transom with a round, vertical groove for mounting an axial rudder that could be raised and lowered while in use (Green, 1983a).

Associated with the ship remains were 2,300 kilograms of fragrant wood, probably from either mainland or island Southeast Asia, and assorted materials such as cowrie shells, ambergris, cinnabar, betel nut, pepper, and tortoise shell, attributed to sources in Somalia (Green, 1983a: 259) – in other words, a priority cargo. Although historical accounts of Chinese seaborne commerce described organized trading expeditions, these archaeological associations could just as easily have resulted from tramping or even sustained cross-cultural trading partnerships. Remains of supplies relating to the ship's provisioning and operations were also found, including faunal remains of possible food animals (bird, fish, goat, pig, and cow) and dogs and rats (eaten, too?) as well as plant remains of food items (coconuts, olives, lychees, peaches, and plums). Portable artifacts included an axe, a wooden ruler, and a bronze ladle (all useful items for maintaining the ship during its voyages) and assorted celadon bowls, a stoneware wine jar, Chinese chessmen, glass beads, and other personal items and tableware.

The presence of transverse bulkheads agrees with early historical accounts such as Marco Polo's, but in other respects, such as the claim for alternately stepped masts and the absence of a keel, the archaeological findings differ from literary sources and ethnographic sources. The archaeology of the Quanzhou ship presents evidence of an oceangoing commercial vessel comparable in size to the largest known European ships of its time that was engaged in trade in priority goods around the Indian Ocean from East Africa to the southeast coast of China. The archaeological associations of both the ship's structure and its contents are ambiguous about the conduct of the trade beyond the general implications of long-distance commerce and about whether the ship followed a coastline route or engaged in true oceanic voyaging.

How typical or representative was the Quanzhou ship of Asian ships of its time? While the process of archaeological comparison has only begun and will require more data, additional information is available from two important shipwreck sites in South Korea. From 1976 to 1982 archaeologists excavated a rich cargo from a submerged wreck near Shinan, and this initial work was followed by excavation and recovery of the ship's remaining structure. These remains are now undergoing conservation treatment at the Mokpo Conservation and Restoration Center of the Cultural Properties Research Institute (Hoffman, Choi, and Kim, 1991), and a one-fifth-scale model has been built at the Mokpo Center to aid in the analysis of the ship's structure (Green, 1983b; Green, 1996: 100–101). The shipwreck was dated by an associated wooden cargo tag to 1323 and by coins, the latest of which were minted in 1310, and may be of South Chinese origin (Green and Kim, 1989).

The ship had seven internal bulkheads that created eight compartments with waterways in each bulkhead. The hull planking was unusual, involving a single layer of planks that were joined at the edges by butting into closely fitted rabbets (half-grooved and countersunk joints), giving the outward appearance of clinker construction over most of the hull but smoothed to a carvel-like external appearance near the bow (Green, 1996: 100–101). The rabbeted hull planks were supported by attaching them to the internal bulkheads with pointed wooden pegs driven from the outside of the hull — somewhat like the nails used on the Quanzhou ship but clearly involving a different technique. The Shinan ship, like the Quanzhou ship, had a keel with two mast steps. It had a pram bow, and the keel showed signs of hogging. The center of the keel was 22 centimeters higher than the bow and stern ends; this may have been an original feature of the ship, a result of hogging during the ship's use-life, or the product of postdepositional processes at the wreck site. While the bulkheads and keel structure revealed certain similarities to the Quanzhou ship, the mode of hull planking and plank attachment differed enough to suggest a less-than-uniform shipbuilding tradition in East Asia at the time.

So far, it is this ship's cargo that has attracted the most attention. This included at least sixteen thousand ceramic items and over seven million brass-bronze coins (totaling 26.8 tons). These coins provided a dramatic example of recycling and reuse in the archaeological record, since the oldest coin in this collection dated to A.D. 14. A similarly impressive priority cargo was recovered from the other major early shipwreck in South Korea – the Wando ship, discovered in 1984. This vessel was carrying a cargo of at least thirty thousand pieces of celadon ceramics that have been traced to a kiln in Haenam Province and probably date to A.D. 1050–1100 (Green, 1996: 101).

The construction of the Wando ship differed in some important ways from the other medieval Asian shipwrecks investigated so far. It had no keel; it was flat-bottomed, with five heavy longitudinal planks pinned together with complicated mortise-and-tenon joints. The side planking was attached to the outer bottom plank on each side with planks that had an L-shaped cross-section, producing a hard-chined hull shape. The side planks were rabbeted in clinker fashion in somewhat the same way as in the Shinan ship. The timbers were fashioned from the wood of trees native to Korea, and the general construction techniques were common to Korea as well (Green, 1983b), so its Korean origins seem clear. A log dugout boat excavated in South Korea in 1992, the Jindo logboat, had six transverse bulkheads and a mast step and was originally about 19 meters long and 2.3 meters wide. Its sides were built up with the same general kind of rabbeted planks seen in the Wando and Shinan vessels, but it was made of camphor wood of South Chinese origin. Coins associated with the Jindo boat provided a date of A.D. 1111–1117, while radiocarbon-dated timbers indicated A.D. 1260–1380.

Taken together and in comparison with the Pattaya wreck from Thailand, these ships show evidence of considerable diversity in shipbuilding methods even when cultural links with China were strong. The Quanzhou and Shinan ships and the Pattaya ship from Thailand all had V-shaped hulls with keels, and transverse bulkheads were one of the most distinctive elements of this shipbuilding tradition. The isolation attributed to this tradition may be more apparent than real, since even the limited archaeological evidence available so far reveals a series of wrecks that were historically linked by eclectic building methods that overlapped over a wide geographical area extending at least from Thailand to Korea.

As for its isolation from medieval European shipbuilding cultures, we see striking differences – most notably in the use of transverse bulkheads about five hundred years before the practice was widely adopted in European ships – that are not surprising given the distances involved and the barrier created by Islamic conquest of the intervening territory. What is especially interesting is the parallel Asian use of certain techniques that appeared at various times in early European shipbuilding, such as the keel-and-V-shaped-hull combination, in-line masts, and mortise-and-tenon joinery (in the case of the Wando ship). Rather than being due to any sort of direct historical contact between Europe and East Asia at that time, these parallelisms are more easily interpreted as the product of convergent technological responses to similar circumstances by shipbuilders whose levels of skill and craft knowledge were also similar.

Nothing in the archaeological record so far provides direct evidence for anything like the Ming Dynasty's treasure ships, and the same empirical skepticism normally used in evaluating archaeological claims must be applied to accounts of these ships. Did nine-masted ships over 120 meters long really accomplish these fabled voyages? The possibility has fascinated Chinese scholars and resulted in the construction of a hypothetical model of such a ship in 1985 at the Zeng He Research Institute in Nanjing (Levathes, 1994: 80–81). Literary sources suggest that the treasure ships combined the characteristics of the *fuchuan*, a multimasted seagoing type of vessel with a keel, V-shaped hull, multiple decks, and elevated bow and stern (for greater height in fighting, similar to the northern European cogs adapted for fighting) and a type of shallow-water boat with a flat bottom and squared-off prow called the *shachuan* (Levathes, 1994: 78–79). The Quanzhou ship could be the remains of a *fuchuan*-type vessel, comparable in size and general character to the largest contemporary medieval European cogs and carracks but nowhere near as large as the treasure ships described.

Estimates of the treasure ships' size are based on literary references in texts pertaining to the first of the Ming emperors, Zhu Di (1402–1424). His reign was known for grandiose projects such as the monumental tomb built for his father, which was intended to include a stone tablet so large that it could not be moved from its quarry at Nanjing to the tomb site. In other words, ship construction and overseas trading expeditions on a grand scale would have been consistent with the known behavior of this ruler. The calculations were based on units of measurement used in ship-building during the Ming period, which, if correctly understood, described ships of 119 to 124 meters long and 49 to 51 meters wide (Levathes, 1994: 80). If correct, these dimensions record by far the largest wooden ships ever built. Even the biggest of the 5,000–6,000-ton wooden battleships of the mid- to late nineteenth century (Lambert, 1984) and the 5,000-ton wooden motorships constructed in the United States during World War I (Desmond, 1919: 181–182) did not exceed 102 meters in length or 18 meters in width. The longest of these ships, the Mersey-class frigates, were unsuccessful, and one, HMS *Orlando*, showed signs of structural failure after an 1863 voyage to the United States (Lambert, 1984: 140). The *Orlando* was scrapped in 1871 and the *Mersey* soon after. Both the Mersey-class frigates and the largest of the wooden battleships, the 121-gun Victoria class, required internal iron strapping to support the hull (Lambert, 1984: 122), as did many other ships of this kind. In short, the construction and use histories of these ships indicated that they were already pushing or had exceeded the practical limits for the size of wooden ships.

How did the Chinese shipbuilders construct and operate wooden ships that were 40 percent longer and 65 percent wider than the largest wooden ships known to have been built at any time anywhere else? Since no special construction techniques such as iron strapping for supporting the wooden hulls of these treasure ships were reported, there is something inherently improbable about the claims made for them in the Ming texts. Perhaps these texts only describe a grandiose dream and the overseas trading voyages of the early Ming Dynasty were in fact accomplished with large numbers of smaller ships. Or perhaps one or more ships of this kind were built at the Longjiang shipyard outside Nanjing but never sailed. As with the tomb slab for his father, Zhu Di's ambitions may have outstripped reality. More convincing documents or direct archaeological evidence will be needed to demonstrate that his treasure ships ever operated as claimed. Although maritime archaeology in East Asia does not yet support extreme claims for the grandeur of medieval Chinese shipbuilding, it does reveal an energetic and varied maritime cultural tradition that flourished until it was abruptly cut off in the Ming Dynasty. It will be especially important now for archaeologists to see just how effective and complete the Ming ban on oceangoing commerce was after A.D. 1550.

Lessons from Medieval Ships

As the pace of underwater archaeology has increased in recent years, so has the level of detailed understanding about how early ships were built and used. An archaeological comparison of shipbuilding traditions during the Middle Ages leads to some general conclusions susceptible to testing. The evolution of medieval and early post-medieval ships was cumulative but nonlinear; advances in technology based on preexisting abilities occurred within each maritime cultural tradition, but these advances did not always follow a single line.

With the seventh-century Yassi Ada shipwreck, we find a combination of shell-first and frame-first construction that simultaneously reflected eclecticism and opportunism. There was nothing truly new about this ship when it was built, but to the archaeologist it presents a unique combination of shipbuilding technologies that coexisted in the Byzantine world. It remains to be seen whether this vessel represented a trend from shell-first to frame-first construction and from large-scale transport of bulk cargoes toward small-scale shipping controlled by individual entrepreneurs and small partnerships. The seventh-century Yassi Ada ship may have been a tramper, picking up and discharging priority cargoes as it poked along the eastern Mediterranean coast, but there may also have been larger ships then that carried priority and/or bulk cargoes more directly from one destination to another.

In the case of the Vikings, we have seen how long it took for sail to become established as the primary mode of propulsion. The practical difficulties of footing a mast efficiently for sail and the light, clinker-built structures of the earlier oared Viking-type ships are part of the explanation. When sails became more important, ships with more robust structures also appeared, partly to provide better masting and greater reliance upon sail but also because of the need for beamier and bigger ships to use as transports and cargo vessels. This shift in maritime technology, which seems to have occurred fairly quickly, reflected a general changeover from raiding and exploration to conquest and trade as the Viking expansion reached its peak. For the Viking maritime tradition, from the early Hjortspring and Nydam boats to the ships depicted in the Bayeux Tapestry, change was not only nonlinear but also uneven in rate. Maritime archaeology suggests that at some point after sails were adopted, pathways in Viking shipbuilding branched into two major lines; longships that were used for fighting and raiding and continued to rely heavily on oars and relatively beamy transports that relied more on sails and could carry cargoes and people to distant colonies such as Greenland and Iceland.

Neither of these classes of Viking-type ship could compete in the long run, however, with the sturdy but less elegant cog and its cousins of the North European Hanse. In securing the economic niche for transport of priority and bulk cargoes in the Baltic region and between there and Western Europe, cogs were easier and cheaper to build and man relative to overall ship size and cargo capacity than their largest Viking-derived rivals. The Viking cargo ships may have been faster and more maneuverable in some circumstances, but ultimately economics won out. The maintenance of reciprocal trading partnerships between the Hanseatic ports and their hinterlands required a more reliable, expandable, and efficient class of merchant ship than the Viking clinker-built tradition could provide, even when pushed to its limits as seen archaeologically in the Bergen ship.

Although too few coglike shipwrecks have yet been documented to demonstrate in detail how this shipbuilding tradition evolved, the two principal wrecks reported so far, the Bremen cog and the Almere vessel, differ in one important respect from many of the iconographic representations of such ships: they both lack reverse-clinker planking. This suggests that the maritime tradition that characterized the Hanseatic League was more complex than the documentary evidence suggests. This contrast between the archaeological record and historical sources hints at a variable and opportunistic series of adaptive responses to trade opportunities and to new materials for ship construction such as mechanically sawed as opposed to hand-split lumber for planking. This aspect of northern European maritime archaeology is now receiving the attention it deserves, and it should not be long before additional shipwrecks from this important period and cultural tradition are reported and analyzed.

Asian seafaring in medieval times, while best represented archaeologically in China by the Quanzhou ship, extended over a wide geographical area and can be studied in relation to shipwrecks from Korea and Thailand. While this maritime tradition may have been relatively isolated from those of the West at the time, it communicated broadly across East Asia in distinctive ways and should not be viewed as cut off from other, non-Chinese sources of innovation. The most distinctive element of Asian shipbuilding in the archaeological record so far is the use of transverse bulkheads, but unique methods of planking and joinery both distinguished this tradition from its European contemporaries and connected it with others across East Asia. Serious dissonances arise between the historical, documentary sources on ancient Chinese ships and what has been learned so far from archaeology, and it remains to be seen if direct evidence for any significantly larger vessels than the Quanzhou ship will be found. Systematic, regional efforts at controlled underwater and shipwreck archaeology will be necessary to support or rule out the historical reality of the Ming Dynasty treasure ships or anything comparable to them in medieval times.

8 · Ships of the Great Age of Sail

It has been suggested that if a sailor from the days of the Spanish Armada could have been transported forward through time to the deck of a sailing ship in the mid- to late nineteenth century, he would have been familiar with the sails, rigging, and general character of the ship and could have proceeded about his duties without delay. The various European cultural traditions that emerged during this period eventually settled on a class of ship, the galleon, that was to dominate overseas colonization, trade, and war, for three hundred years. The galleon was the product of processes of cultural selection during the course of numerous voyages of exploration, fishing, whaling, and initial colonization that encompassed the New World, Africa, and Asia (with a few unplanned excursions to Australia). Events in Europe also had a direct bearing upon the course of overseas empire, especially in the head-to-head competition between Spanish and English seafarers, and underwater archaeology has profoundly influenced our understanding of the nature of this competition.

The final phase of the European transition from medieval to post-medieval maritime culture, from the fourteenth to the mid-sixteenth century, received a strong impetus from the exploration, commerce, and warfare of the societies of the Iberian Peninsula – the Spanish, Portuguese, and the Basques – along with the Genoese and the Venetians.

Most of our information about Iberian ships and sailing practices of this period is based on literary and documentary sources, with the best archaeological information coming from shipwrecks that date to the late part of the transition. Historical sources indicate that explorations were usually conducted with small flotillas of ships of different types, including the nao

(Fig. 41) and the smaller caravel, a shallow-draft and maneuverable vessel that could operate along coastlines and up rivers supported by one or more naos for their provisioning and maintenance. This was a combination that Iberian explorers refined as they extended their voyages, especially after the experiences of Bartholomeu Dias during a difficult 1487–1488 trip around the southern tip of Africa (Smith, 1993: 32). The lateen-rigged caravel was most likely a development of a long-standing Mediterranean design comparable to the first Contarina ship. Historical sources from the early fifteenth century suggest that the antecedents of the early Portuguese caravels were small ships of 25–30 tons and were only partially decked, with two masts and quadrangular sails but also with the capability for rowing as needed (Smith, 1993: 37). Lateen sails were adopted when the need for better upwind sailing became apparent, but oars were retained for movement close to shore and in calm conditions. Along with this change, the caravel was constructed with finer lines (increased length relative to width) and was improved in other ways to make it faster and more maneuverable, producing the *caravela latina*. While he did not actually invent this type of ship, Prince Henry the Navigator and his sponsorship of voyages of exploration to Africa and the Atlantic Islands have been associated with their use (Smith, 1993: 40). The improved version of this type was about 20–30 meters long and 6–8 meters wide, with a main sail yard as long as the ship. The *Niña* and the *Pinta* were square-sailed versions of this type, known as the *caravela redonda*, and were able to keep up with the *Santa María*, a square-rigged nao (Pastor, 1992: 7–18), when sailing with the trade winds. As Smith (1993: 42) notes: "Since caravels were relatively light ships, their rigs were extremely flexible and could be altered to suit various nautical situations."

Square-rigged caravels grew larger over time, with multiple sails, crow's nests (small observation platforms partway up the mast), and guns. State-supported fleets for conquest and commerce grew during the sixteenth century, with armed caravels increasingly serving as fast scouts and escorts to the larger merchantmen, and they also became popular with pirates. Columbus came to rely more and more upon caravels in his voyages after 1492 (Smith, 1993: 43–46). A disproportionate amount of effort has been expended by maritime archaeologists in searching for the remains of Columbus's ships. Although no convincing evidence has yet been found for these vessels, their status as historical icons has prompted research on

Fig 41. Sailing replica of the *Matthew*, a nao–like vessel used by John Cabot in his 1497 voyage to North America. This ship sailed from Bristol, England, to Bristol, Rhode Island (where it was photographed), in 1997 and was featured in a BBC television documentary. The exact details of the *Matthew* are unknown, so this vessel must be viewed as a generalized representation of ships of that type and period.

shipwrecks throughout the Caribbean, Florida, and Gulf Coast regions where Columbus's voyages were centered. Shipwrecks of Iberian origin, however, have also been found from Labrador to the Seychelles Islands as well as in European waters. Over the past fifteen years, the remains of at least eight sixteenth-century shipwrecks of Iberian origin have been identified and recorded in varying degrees of detail.

The information gathered by archaeologists so far has added greatly to our understanding of this maritime tradition and the early colonial enterprise it supported. The ships and guns left by these early Iberian-based colonial enterprises define a phase of expeditionary exploitation (Weigand, Harbottle, and Sayre, 1977: 18–19) that preceded mature colonialism. Expeditionary exploitation was characterized by the use of relatively small armed ships to locate, process, and extract valued resources for transport as priority cargoes back to the parent country. Shore stations tended to be small and relatively task-specific. The arming of ships was necessary because of the predation of rival powers and pirates, but armed conflict was more along the lines of guerrilla warfare than of naval battles. In the Caribbean and Gulf region, the transition toward fully developed colonial exploitation, involving larger and more permanent settlements and regular shipments of priority cargoes back to the parent country using larger ships in planned, armed convoys, occurred quickly. In the Canadian Maritime region, however, no durable colonial phase appeared in the sixteenth century.

Two shipwrecks are candidates for the earliest evidence so far of expeditionary exploitation by Iberian sailors. At Molasses Reef, in the Caicos Bank, and at Highborn Cay, in the Exuma Islands of the Bahamas, the maritime archaeologist Thomas J. Oertling has recorded shipwreck remains that present evidence bearing directly on this earliest wave of Iberian activities in the New World.

The Molasses Reef ship carried at least nineteen guns, all of breech-loading design, and two small muzzle-loaders, making it a heavily armed ship for its size (estimated at 20 meters long and at least 7.5 meters wide). The approximately 35 tons of stone ballast recorded at the site would have sufficed for a ship of 100 tons, in other words, either a small nao or a large caravel (Oertling, 1989a: 241). The ballast was excavated with special care not only for the information it could provide about the ship's origins and movements but also because it overlay a substantial amount of wooden structure. The wood was almost all white oak, and a detailed analysis was possible for a section of the keel and adjacent timbers. Of special interest was the use of filler pieces between futtocks above the ends of the floor timbers and dovetail joints to attach the floor to the futtocks. These techniques have been seen on other sixteenth-century shipwrecks of Iberian origin and appear to be diagnostic of this shipbuilding tradition (Oertling, 1989a: 233). Similar comparisons of rudder gudgeons (iron lugs projecting from the aft end or sternpost to support the rudder) from the wreck revealed resemblances to contemporaneous Iberian shipwrecks as well. No trace of the ship's cargo was found, but some of the ballast stones have been tentatively traced to the Lisbon area as their source.

The Highborn Cay wreck was found under similar conditions to those at Molasses Reef, with a stone ballast pile covering the preserved elements of the ship's wooden structure. The ship's keel, which had largely vanished by the time the wreck was excavated, gouged an impression in the hardpan upon which it rested, allowing Oertling (1989b: 252) and his associates to estimate the vessel's overall length at 19 meters and its maximum width at 5.0–5.7 meters. Comparison with documentary sources suggests a small ship of about 150 tons. Filler planks between futtocks to complete the ceiling planking and dovetail joints for attaching floor planks to futtocks were similar to those on the Molasses Reef ship, although the dovetail joints were oriented in the opposite direction. Remains of a mast step based on an expanded keelson were also found, and this method of mast stepping proved to be closely similar to that observed at the wreck of the *San Juan*, a Basque whaling vessel wrecked in 1565 at Red Bay, Labrador, the Cattewater wreck near Plymouth, England, thought to have been sunk around 1530 (Redknap, 1984; 1985), and Vessel A from Rye, in Sussex, England. As Oertling (1989b: 249) observed, "More than anything else, the mast steps of these ships identify them as belonging to a single type or shipbuilding tradition, possibly of Iberian origin, since most of the ships have an association there." Two breech-loading guns similar to those from the Molasses Reef vessel and thirteen smaller swivel guns were found with the wreck along with associated breech blocks and iron breech wedges. The Highborn Cay ship appears to have been more lightly armed than the vessel at Molasses Reef. The relatively compact distribution of the guns and associated gun-related materials at both wreck sites led archaeologists to infer that small ships of this period stowed their heavy guns belowdecks during voyages, perhaps to improve the ships' stability at sea (Guilmartin, 1988: 40; Smith, 1993: 201).

The wide distribution of this shipbuilding tradition is shown by a wreck from the Seychelles (Blake and Green, 1986) and by the *San Esteban* and two other naos sunk at Padre Island, Texas, in 1554 (Arnold and Weddle, 1978), but the most detailed information about it comes from the *San Juan*, which sank along the northwest shore of the Strait of Belle Isle with a cargo of nine hundred to one thousand barrels of whale oil. This vessel and associated boat remains have been studied in detail since 1978 by underwater archaeologists from the Marine Excavation Unit of Parks Canada led by Robert Grenier. The adjacent whaling station on shore was excavated and recorded by workers from Memorial University of Newfoundland led by the archaeologist James A. Tuck. Documentary evidence from sixteenth-century Basque sources in Spain played an important role in this research as well (Tuck and Grenier, 1981). These sources reported the loss of the *San Juan* with a cargo of whale oil at "Grand Bay" just before it was to return to Spain.

Variously referred to as a large nao (Smith, 1993: 198) and a galleon (Waddell, 1986; Steffy 1994: 139), the *San Juan* was a three-masted ship with a cargo capacity of about 250 tons. The weather deck was 22 meters long, and the ship was 7.5 meters wide. The straight part of the keel was fashioned from a single plank of beechwood 14.7 meters long, while the ship's beam measured 7.5 meters, producing a keel-length-to-beam-breadth ratio of 0.5:1. Although it has been suggested that these dimensions "revealed a whaling ship with fine lines, far removed from the round, tubby shape commonly thought typical of 16th-century merchant vessels" (Renfrew and Bahn, 1996: 93), a comparison with documents on ship construction during the Elizabethan period shows that the preferred ratio then was between 0.4:1 for commercial galleons (Lavery, 1988: 10) and 0.3:1 for naval galleons (Kirsch, 1990: 21). Relative to other galleons of the period 1586–1605 for which data are available, the *San Juan* was slightly beamier than most but finer-lined than conventional wisdom or some early depictions have suggested.

The origins of the galleon are obscure. Documentary sources indicate the appearance around 1528 of a new type of sailing ship built by supervisor Matteo Bressan at the Arsenal in Venice. It was called a galleon (confusing, since large, oared *gallioni* had been used by the Venetians for river patrols since the fourteenth century [Phillips, 1994: 98]) and was intended for use by the city of Venice against pirates. By the time the *San Juan* sank in 1565 this type of ship was being imitated widely in a variety of forms outside the Mediterranean, Spanish galleons being mentioned in historical sources by 1540 (Kirsch, 1990: 3–7). The emergence of the galleon as a warship is associated in the popular imagination with the Spanish Armada battles of 1588, in which this type of ship was employed by both combatants. The magnitude of this historical event has tended to overshadow the role of commercial galleons (Fig. 42), which were often armed but not intended primarily as warships. The *San Juan* is the best extant archaeological example of a sixteenth-century commercial galleon.

Maritime historians have suggested that the fighting galleon was developed from the carrack in 1570 by Sir John Hawkins, one of Elizabeth I's principal captains during the Spanish Armada battles and a major figure in the naval reforms of the time (Kemp, 1976: 335). Hawkins is credited with improving their performance by reducing the high stern- and fore-castles of these earlier fighting ships. Historical sources, however, along with a sixteenth-century bronze cannon found in English waters (the well-

Fig 42. Sailing replica of the *Susan Constant* at Jamestown, Virginia. Like the *Matthew*, relatively little is known about the original ship built in 1605, but a serious effort was made to produce a detailed example of a commercial galleon of that period.

documented Yarmouth gun), point to strong and sustained contacts between England and Venice prior to the Spanish Armada (Tomalin, Cross, and Motkin, 1988: 84), supporting the Venetian origins of the galleon and its spread as an early example of technology transfer. Hawkins's contribution to the evolution of the fighting galleon should not be underestimated, but it came later, after armed commercial galleons from the Iberian Peninsula were already operating widely across the world's oceans.

The archaeological work at Red Bay has produced the most detailed direct information so far on the early construction of the commercial galleon. Except for the beechwood keel, the ship's hull timbers were made of white oak, with various softwoods used in building the fore- and stern-castles. The ship had a flat stern transom with diagonal planking and three full decks. It was built frame-first, with dovetail joints and distinctive mast steps along with artifacts including a capstan, bilge pump, compass, and binnacle – all pointing to a common Iberian ancestry with the Molasses Reef, Highborn Cay, Padre Island, and the Cattewater and Rye A wrecks. The two latter wrecks, found in English waters, could have been built either somewhere on the Iberian Peninsula or in England following Iberian practices. Although the portable artifacts point unmistakably to a ship of Iberian origin of this period, too little of the ship's structure at the Seychelles wreck site was found to permit detailed comparison. This ship, however, did reveal a unique feature in the use of lead strips for caulking plank seams in place of the more usual fiber (Blake and Green, 1986: 5).

Putting aside for the moment the remains of the great English warship *Mary Rose* (sunk in 1545), at least six wrecks in the New World as well as the Cattewater and Seychelles wrecks have produced early artillery of sixteenth-century Iberian pattern, with the Molasses Reef ship presenting the largest assemblage, consisting of twenty-one pieces of ordnance (Simmons, 1993). Taken together, these finds constitute the earliest direct evidence so far for guns at sea. There were two main types of guns in use aboard the Molasses Reef ship, *bombardetas* and *verso*, both indicative of established gun-making practices as distinctive as the shipbuilding methods of this tradition and just as instrumental to Iberian overseas exploration and conquest.

Early bombardetas had been taken to sea aboard Portuguese caravels since at least 1430, mainly for defense against pirates (Smith, 1993: 153).

Guns of this type were tubes formed from wrought-iron bars welded along the edges and reinforced with wrought-iron rings that shrank during cooling to form a gas-tight hollow cylinder A separate chamber containing the gunpowder charge was inserted and wedged into the breech at one end of the tube and ignited through a touchhole, propelling stone, lead, or iron shot. Built-up guns of this kind were already becoming obsolete by the time of the Iberian voyages of exploration, mainly because they were labor-intensive to produce and because the larger pieces were prone to crack or explode when fired. The Molasses Reef wreck site contained two small, matched examples of this type of weapon along with at least fourteen breech blocks that varied in the size of the charges they contained but were all of the same bore diameter. This evidence suggested that they were interchangeable for use with these guns, allowing the gunners to vary their firepower as needed (Keith, et al., 1984: 55). These bombardetas are estimated (Guilmartin, 1988: 36) to have been capable of firing a cast-iron ball weighing 1.8 kilograms. Historical sources indicate that bombardetas were mounted on low wooden carriages, but these particular weapons were found resting parallel to each other in association with the ballast pile and were probably stowed belowdecks when the ship sank. No trace of their gun carriages was found.

Versos were smaller than bombardetas and came in three sizes. They were all swivel guns (Fig. 43a–b), mounted on an oarlock-shaped spike at the gun's balance point to make them easy to elevate and aim by gripping a tubular iron bar extending behind the breech. The swivel spike was set in a hole, probably along the ship's rails or gunwales, and the gun was used to repel boarders and for other fighting at close quarters. Like the bombardetas, these guns were made of wrought iron but with a narrower tube and without the iron hoops found on the larger, built-up guns. At least sixteen of these weapons were found at the Molasses Reef wreck site, along with forty breech blocks (Simmons, 1988: 25).

A single example of another gun type was found at Molasses Reef. This was a *cerbatana*, a smaller version of the bombardeta. Its association with the site is open to question, since it was recovered by salvors before the site was excavated archaeologically. The gun was used to fire a 0.79-kilogram iron shot. Other weapons found at Molasses Reef included a matched pair of small antique swivel guns commonly referred to as *harquebuts*, nine hollow cast-iron globes that were filled with gunpowder

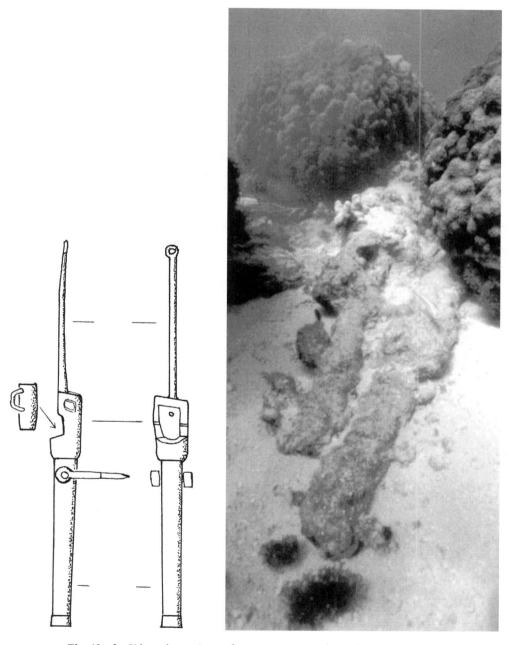

Fig 43a–b. Side and top views of a verso-type swivel gun from the Molasses Reef wreck, Caicos.

and are thought to have been hand grenades (Guilmartin 1988:36), at least two harquebuses, and parts from two or more crossbows – these latter indicating that archery was still practiced at sea.

Deck pieces (bombardetas and related weapons) and swivel guns were recovered from other sixteenth-century wrecks of Iberian origin, but in many cases the sites had already been damaged by salvors. The guns from the Highborn Cay wreck resembled those of the Molasses Reef ship but suffered from this problem, as did the guns attributed to the Seychelles wreck. A single verso was recovered from the *San Juan*. Three bombardetas, with fifteen breech chambers, a verso, and a smaller swivel gun, along with seventeen iron breech chambers for use with swivel guns were recovered from the Padre Island shipwrecks of 1554 (Arnold and Weddle, 1978: 240–250), but there is evidence that bronze cannons on these wrecks may have been removed by salvors at an early date. Some crossbow parts were present in the Padre Island wrecks.

Evaluation of these armaments is complicated by obscure and complex terminology indicating a less-than-standardized approach to arming these sixteenth-century vessels. In this respect, the Molasses Reef wreck stands out both in terms of its archaeological documentation and in terms of the coherence of the armaments present. Close examination of the touchholes showed few signs of erosion, which indicated that these guns were new and had seen little use (Simmons, 1988). The matching pairs of bombardetas and harquebuses also suggests that these guns were made at the same time and that their presence aboard the ship was planned. As the maritime historian J. F. Guilmartin Jr. (1988: 40) describes it:

> the Molasses Reef ordnance represents someone's idea of how a ship designed to go out intending serious mischief in the Caribbean should have been armed. Sixteenth-century ships' gundecks tended to be armed with a hodgepodge of types and sizes of ordnance; coherence therefore implies quality and, since the ordnance in question is of wrought iron and new wrought iron at that, antiquity.

It would be a mistake to view these armed ships as true naval vessels or to imagine them engaged in anything like the sea fights of the Spanish Armada or other organized ship-vs.-ship actions. In the Caribbean, rivalry between the Spanish, French, Dutch, and English as well as independent corsairs during the sixteenth century took the form of skirmishes involving amphibious raids on shore settlements, stealing ships from their moorings with cutting-out parties, and other activities in which small ships and war galleys were more useful than galleons. Sometimes a larger ship served as a floating base of operations for smaller boats engaged in such raids. Later on we start to see organized attacks on Spanish treasure convoys and stand-up naval battles, but initially these ships "were not warships in the modern sense. They were designed and fitted out for a guerrilla war at sea. That war was largely amphibious in nature and involved trade, extortion, and smuggling more than naval warfare in the modern sense" (Guilmartin, 1988: 41). Every sixteenth-century shipwreck site of Iberian origin has produced guns, and it is apparent from the archaeological evidence that gunpowder at sea was as much an instrument of overseas exploration as the ships themselves. These shipwrecks provide a technological indicator of the realities of early overseas expansion by the European powers, in which armed violence played a key role.

Historians such as Carlo Cipolla (1965) have recognized the decisive role played by the technological combination of seagoing sailing ships and artillery in the process of overseas colonial expansion during this early, formative period. Cipolla's analysis emphasized naval vessels and their use in major battles. The evidence of underwater archaeology in the Caribbean region presents unmistakable evidence to support his views but with the important caveat that organized naval warfare followed a period of small-scale, guerrilla-like skirmishing. It remains to be seen to what extent this same sequence of colonial competition and domination by armed ships also occurred in the Indian Ocean, the East Indies, and other overseas arenas of early European expansion.

The initial penetration of the Caribbean and Canadian Maritime regions by Iberian-based seafarers appears to have been based on searching for and extracting valued resources (gold and other precious metals in the former case, whale products and codfish in the latter) that required at least some preliminary processing and packaging at relatively small and specialized shore-based stations before shipment as priority cargoes. These cargoes had to be defended as well as transported, since predatory behavior by rivals was commonplace. Only later, when more permanent residential settlements by people from the parent countries and scheduled, large-scale shipments of processed materials to these countries became established, do we see the appearance of larger vessels and the frequent use of armed convoys that marked the colonial phase. The Padre Island shipwrecks were the remains of three ships lost in a four-ship convoy while transporting 6,750 kilograms of silver from the newly opened mint in Mexico City along with 225-kilogram barrels of cochineal, resins, and sugar to Spain in 1554. The quantities involved here can be viewed as an early indication that the colonial phase of exploitation of the region was beginning. In contrast, the Iberian-based whaling station at Red Bay did not persist beyond the expeditionary phase.

The Wreck of the *Mary Rose*

The *Mary Rose* was much larger than the ships just described, with a displacement of about 600 tons. At least twenty big guns and about sixty lighter guns were recovered from the wreck, but historical sources indicate that the ship had a total armament of ninety-one guns shortly before the time of its loss (Rule, 1982: 27). The ship was built for Henry VIII beginning in 1509 along with several other "great ships" intended to provide defense in home waters, primarily against the French. It was extensively rebuilt in 1536 and sank on 19 July 1545 in full view of the king and his entourage encamped around Southsea Castle during an action against the French fleet off Portsmouth. One can only imagine the stunned disbelief on shore as the ship took in massive amounts of water through its lower gunports and sank quickly after hoisting sails and heeling to one side. Although eyewitness and other accounts differed on the number of men aboard at the time (five hundred to over seven hundred), all agreed that few survived.

The *Mary Rose* was one of several large carracks in use by the English at that time, although it was by no means the biggest. It was dwarfed by the *Henry Grace à Dieu* (or *Great Harry*, as the ship was more commonly known), launched in 1514. At about 1,000 tons' displacement, with a crew of seven hundred men, and carrying 21 heavy and 231 light guns, the *Great Harry* was the largest warship of its day and was present in the same engagement as the *Mary Rose* at Portsmouth. The Tudor preference at this time for "great ships" was also reflected in the *Sovereign*, an 800-ton warship built in 1488 and rebuilt in 1509. Some articulated ship's timbers found buried at Woolwich, along the Thames, in 1912 are believed by maritime archaeologists (Rule, 1982: 22; Steffy, 1994: 141) to be the remains of this ship. If indeed they are, this raises questions about an important feature of the *Mary Rose*'s construction. There are definite indications that the *Mary Rose* was initially built with some or possibly even all of its outer hull of clinker rather than flush planking. The Woolwich ship also showed signs of having been constructed in this manner, but the clinker planks had later been removed and replaced by flush planking, The *Mary Rose*, too, had had its clinker planks replaced with flush planks, presumably during the 1536 rebuilding. In general, flush planking was considered a stronger method of construction, and other "great ships" were rebuilt in this manner during this period. But why would Tudor shipwrights modify one ship (the *Sovereign*) in this way and then immediately begin construction of the *Mary Rose* in the older, clinker fashion? The ultimate explanation clearly rests upon the identification and chronology of the Woolwich ship, but the question is a good example of how underwater archaeology has brought a new level of detail and precision to the questions we can ask about how these historic ships were built and used. The *Mary Rose* was transitional in other ways, too. Along with other "great ships" of this period, it had four masts and high stern- and forecastles bristling with guns. And the maritime archaeologist Mary Rule (1982: 15) notes that

> It was customary in the fifteenth century to consider large ships as having a dual purpose, enabling them to be hired out as merchant ships in time of peace but allowing them to be fitted with guns above the bulwark rail whenever necessary in time of war . . . the fire-power of fifteenth-century ships was limited by the weight of guns which could be carried without seriously affecting the stability of the ship.

Rule (1982: 17) points out how important it was in these ships to position the guns lower in the hull, which required gunports that could be sealed when closed during sea passages. Clinker-built hull planking did not readily accommodate this; whereas edge-to-edge planking did. Although edge-to-edge-planked hulls had been in use in northern Europe since Romano-British times (as is evident, for example, from Caesar's description of the Veneti ships and from the Blackfriars wreck), Rule contends that the impetus for this widespread changeover in planking methods was the need for gunports for larger guns set lower in the hull. She even raises the possibility that the gunports on the *Mary Rose* were not added until the 1536 rebuilding.

Detailed examination of the ship's structure revealed evidence, too, of what appears to have been hasty reinforcement of the hull through the use of internal stiffeners such as riders fitted over keel bolts as well as poor alignment and flawed carpentry of other stiffening elements. These features did not appear to be part of the ship's original design and suggested to Rule that in 1536 the military situation was urgent enough to require temporary measures instead of a thorough reconstruction of what was surely a rotting and weakened hull.

Despite the large number and variety of guns found with the *Mary Rose*, archery still played an important role in battles at sea. Some of the most important finds from the *Mary Rose* consisted of longbows, arrows, and related equipment. Several boxes were found containing arrows, and one of these found on the main deck of the ship was examined during conservation and found to contain a total of 1,248 arrows stored tip-to-tip in bundles of 24 wrapped with thin cords. About 2,000 arrows in all were found. Most of these arrows were made of poplar wood, which contemporary documents on archery regarded as inferior for this purpose (Rule, 1982: 176). Some of these arrows were found inserted in leather spacers with twenty-four holes, presumably for ready use during battle and to keep the feathers from being crushed. Rule likens these leather spacers to modern ammunition clips, assembled at the ready on the main deck shortly before fighting commenced.

At least 138 longbows of yew wood of three different types were also found. The lightest bows may have been for sniping, perhaps from the rigging. The larger bows could have been used for firing arrows en masse (English longbowmen were famous for their high rate of fire of twelve or more arrows per minute). A program of experimental archaeology is under way to test the mechanical strength and drawing power of the best-preserved examples as well as of replicate bows. An act of Parliament in 1542 required that all men twenty-four years of age be able to shoot at a mark of at least 200 meters, although no requirements for accuracy were specified (Rule, 1982: 173). It will be worthwhile to see to what extent the replicate bows from the *Mary Rose* can meet this requirement.

Finally, an assortment of archery gear including eleven wrist guards of leather and one of horn was found preserved aboard the wreck. Three of these were embossed with the Tudor rose, the fleur-de-lys of Henry VIII, and the pomegranate and castle (the latter the emblem of Catherine of Aragon). Rule (1982: 173) points out that the loss of the ship occurred thirteen years after the annulment of Henry's marriage to Catherine and nine years after her death, so the archaeology of the *Mary Rose* provides a precise and well-documented example of retention or reuse of artifacts in which practical considerations took priority over symbolic factors. On the eve of battle there was clearly a need for large numbers of archers with whatever equipment could be assembled. The use of poplar arrow shafts and some wrist guards with Catherine of Aragon's emblem suggests an urgent effort to acquire archery materials in the interests of meeting the needs of the moment. It also cautions archaeologists to recognize situations in which symbolic associations do not necessarily provide direct indications of symbolic meaning. It would be easy in a situation like this to misread the past.

The *Mary Rose*'s guns were an eclectic assortment of ancient forged-iron breech-loaders and more modern bronze-and-cast-iron muzzle-loaded cannon. Some of these guns were recovered from the ship's exterior during salvage operations by Charles and John Deane in 1836–40 and were preserved in various museums, while additional guns were brought up during the 1979–82 excavations directed by the *Mary Rose* Trust and supervised by Margaret Rule. Wrought-iron gun tubes generally similar in technology to the bombardetas described earlier were found with enough associated materials to permit a reconstruction of their low wooden-block carriages. It is generally assumed that the guns of this type on the Molasses Reef ship and other, related wrecks were mounted in a manner similar to those aboard the *Mary Rose*, although the presence here of what by 1545 were technological relics raises interesting questions.

In the case of the Spanish and other Iberian wrecks described earlier, the presence of guns of this kind could be explained in relation to the nature of warfare in the expeditionary context. If we assume, at least provisionally, that the dominant mode of warfare in such cases was predatory and guerrilla-like in scale, then there was little need for first-class guns when skirmishing was the order of the day. Size was a factor, too, since the relatively small size of ships during this initial phase of expansion effectively precluded the use of the newer, larger cannons of the sort one also finds on the *Mary Rose*. On the *Mary Rose*, the circumstances were different. It had big first-class guns, including six of the latest types in cast bronze, five of which were mounted on carriages. One especially fine example contained an inscription indicating that it was cast by John and Robert Owen at their London foundry in 1537. As Rule (1982: 157) points out, "The random mixture of Henry VIII's newest weapons of cast bronze with antique, stave-built, wrought-iron guns was difficult for some scholars to accept." The presence of the ancient wrought-iron guns found by the Deanes was rationalized in some quarters as being due to their being included in the ship's ballast. The fact, however, that all of these guns were found loaded and ready to be fired indicated otherwise (Rule, 1982: 157). During their underwater research in 1979–82, the *Mary Rose* team found several large spoked wooden wheels more commonly associated with field artillery on land than with shipboard gun carriages, along with remains of other gun carriages with four small wheels of a type that came to be more or less standard for naval guns. With the carriages, as with the guns aboard the *Mary Rose*, there is the same curious combination of ancient and modern.

Rule (1982: 156) suggests that this mixture of technologies was evidence of making do in an emergency. She sees the presence of the older type of wrought-iron guns as a rational measure to increase the close-in firepower of the ship; such weapons would have been effective in repelling boarders. The large-wheeled gun carriages, however, would have been awkward to control and reload on a moving ship's deck and are harder to explain. Perhaps this was an extreme example of ad hoc preparations for battle. The Spanish, however, made fairly regular use of large-wheeled gun carriages at sea, as is evidenced by shipwrecks of the Armada of 1588, and these were no less awkward (Martin and Parker, 1988: 223). Whether or not it was entirely practical or consistent with the requirements of shipboard fighting, there are archaeological indications of the persistence of this inefficient method of mounting seaborne artillery on large warships throughout much of the sixteenth century. Overall, with the notable exception of breech-loaded swivel guns, the guns from ships of this period seemed closely tied to their land-based antecedents, especially with respect to the way they were mounted.

Reloading artillery was always a bigger problem at sea than on land. Swivel guns could be reloaded fairly easily and achieved relatively high rates of fire, but the same cannot be said for the big muzzle-loaders. After the first salvo, which was probably the "main event" as ships closed for battle, the big guns had to be run in on their carriages for reloading, and if they were fixed in place someone had to climb out and reload them from outside. This latter activity, called "outboard loading," was something of an acrobatic feat and was dangerously exposed from the gunner's point of view. Early depictions of naval warfare portray this practice, with the gunner perched on the gun tube outside the gunport while he rams in the charge (Konstam, 1988: 19).

A comparison of the ships and seaborne guns of the shipwrecks reviewed suggests not only that the development of these technologies was nonlinear but that their rates and modes of change differed as well. The sixteenth century was a period of relatively rapid change in gun-making technology. Initially, many of the bigger guns at sea were reduced-sized counterparts of siege weapons used on land, but in the sixteenth century there were serious efforts to install larger, muzzle-loaded weapons on the "great ships." At first these guns were cast bronze, but during Elizabeth I's reign the English improved their methods of casting iron guns to such a degree that this technology was closely guarded against foreign imitation. Increased reliance upon cast guns as opposed to built-up guns of wrought iron was a major technological shift. At the same time, the use of small-wheeled naval gun carriages spread as their advantages in running in big guns for reloading became apparent. One possible explanation for the retention of breech-loaded or chambered guns at sea was their capability of being reloaded relatively quickly and without the requirement either for running in or outboard reloading. Instead of interpreting the mixed array of weapons on board the *Mary Rose* in 1545 as making do in an emergency, one could view it as a broad approach to warfare at sea that used every available technology with perhaps some tactical indecision as to how to use each best.

Ships changed less radically than guns. If one accepts Rule's interpretations concerning alterations to the *Mary Rose* during the ship's career, ad hoc modifications related to a changing military and political situation during the reign of Henry VIII were more significant than linear trends in the evolution of ship design and construction. There were more general changes to ships, too, especially in a decreasing reliance upon oars and in the adoption of edge-to-edge instead of clinker planking. While these were important, the basic use of frame-first, multimasted ships with a divisible sail pattern was already established before the sixteenth century and continued afterwards, and the same can be said for the reduction of the stern-and forecastles and other improvements to the English galleons. The archaeology of the *Mary Rose*, like that of the sixteenth-century wrecks of Iberian origin, tells us that the history of both shipboard weapons and ships during this period was not an orderly process of evolutionary progression but involved combinations of ancient and modern technologies.

The relocation, excavation, and recovery of the *Mary Rose* was an epic of archaeological investigation that produced spectacular results including a major public exhibit at the Portsmouth dockyard. The excavations were conducted under difficult conditions involving currents and poor visibility, but the work produced a model for archaeologists in the controlled study of seabed conditions to account for both the preservation and associations in some parts of the ship and the loss of other parts. The subsequent lifting of the entire remaining hull structure on a specially constructed frame and its present location in a structure on shore for public viewing, however, has more to do with tourism and Britain's "heritage industry" than it does with archaeology. Along with the ship remains, there are supporting exhibits of guns and portable artifacts relating to diet, medicine, clothing, and other aspects of shipboard life, presented mainly to satisfy an insatiable public interest in items historically associated with the events of Henry VIII's reign. Only time will tell whether lifting and preserving the complete remains of the ship will provide archaeological information about the wreck that would not have been available through the study of the shipwreck *in situ*.

The Spanish Armada of 1588

Although much has been written about the Armada battles and their consequences, recent work in underwater archaeology has made a dramatic difference to our understanding of this important episode. Since all of the shipwrecks were Spanish, the knowledge gained through underwater archaeology complements the historical information about global seafaring by Iberian-based sailors in the sixteenth century. The Armada was assembled by Philip II, whose armies occupied and controlled much of the European continent at the time, with the aim of transporting an army under the command of the Duke of Parma from the Spanish Netherlands across the English Channel in order to establish Catholic church rule (and

Spanish influence) in England (see Laughton, 1895; Mattingly, 1959; Lewis, 1960; Fallon, 1978; Martin and Parker, 1988, and Fernández-Armesto, 1989).

A military venture on an unprecedented scale, the effort involved ships, men, and materials from every corner of Spain's empire and was largely financed by gold and other valuables acquired from its New World colonies. The Armada battles were the first major sea engagements to be dominated by guns instead of boarding, and for underwater archaeology they represent an identifiable event resulting in a coherent set of physical associations on the seabed that affords one of the largest-scale approximations anywhere of the "Pompeii premise."

Four principal shipwrecks have been excavated and provide direct archaeological information about the Armada that upsets popular myths about the conduct and outcome of the conflict. In part, these myths are instances of an ethnocentrism that has tended to glorify English prowess and to devalue the abilities of the Spanish. Historical estimates place Spanish losses at between 50 and 70 ships and at least 20,000 men out of a total of 130 ships and 30,656 men that departed from Lisbon on the "Enterprise of England" in May 1588. By contrast, the English lost no ships, and fewer than 100 men were killed. These much-cited figures, however, are not the only ones that matter. For example, English guns probably accounted for only about 600 of the total Spanish casualties, with most of the losses resulting from wreckings due to autumnal gales and the dangerously exposed routings around the western side of Ireland taken by most of the Spanish ships after forcing their way northward through the Channel.

Recent underwater archaeology has contributed to a renewed appreciation of the Spanish efforts. Maritime historian Tom Glasgow (1964: 177) describes one of the dominant myths surrounding the Armada as, ". . . the legend of the Elizabethan Galleons, lively little vessels with big guns and sharpshooting gunners which blasted the gigantic Armada away from England's shores." Yet Historical documents have shown that all of the thirteen English ships over 500 tons were heavily armed galleons, one of them the 1,100-ton *Triumph*, larger than any similar galleon on the Spanish side (Martin and Parker, 1988: 195). The English fighting galleons generally had reduced fore- and sterncastles and were superior in their upwind sailing and maneuvering than their Spanish counterparts, but they were not smaller or less well-armed. The largest Spanish ships were generally not fighting galleons but armed transports with poor handling qualities. Three of the four Armada wrecks studied in detail by archaeologists were large transports of 650, 945, and 1,100 tons, while the fourth, *La Girona* (Sténuit, 1972), was one of only four galleasses known to have been with the Armada. This was an unusual, hybrid design of Mediterranean origin which combined features of the oared galley and the sailing galleon. The Armada galleasses – including *La Girona*, which was wrecked near the Giant's Causeway in northern Ireland – displaced about 600 tons and proved ill-adapted to sea conditions in the North Atlantic. This assemblage of shipwrecks generally supports the historical accounts of large Spanish invasion transports and smaller warships, although La *Girona* was admittedly atypical of the Spanish warships escorting the Armada.

It has been widely accepted that the Duke of Medina Sidonia, who was placed in charge of the Armada by Philip II after the death of the Marquis de Santa Cruz, was incompetent. He himself wrote Philip II asking to be relieved of the appointment noting that he was in poor health, was prone to seasickness, had little in the way of financial resources, and lacked experience in war or at sea (Mattingly, 1959: 206). But, as a cousin to Philip II, he was well connected and in a position to require the loyalty of his officers and men. Medina Sidonia's first task was to prepare the Armada for sailing, and historians disagree about how well he did this. Garrett Mattingly (1959: 206) describes the situation:

> In the mad week or so preceding the marquis' death, guns and supplies had been tumbled helter-skelter on the ships and crews herded aboard with orders to stand by for instant departure, and on no account to go ashore. There were soldiers and mariners on most of the ships without money or arms or proper clothing. There were crews – who had practically no food. Some ships were laden far too deeply for safety; some floated practically empty. In the wild scramble towards the end, every captain had apparently grabbed whatever he could get his hands on, particularly in the way of additional ordnance. Some ships had more guns than they had room for; others had almost none. One galleon had several new bronze pieces stowed between decks amidst a hopeless clutter of kegs and barrels; one Biscayan scarcely bigger than a pinnace had a huge demi-cannon filling most of her waist. Some had guns but not cannon balls; some had round shot but no guns to fire them.

Following major reorganization, the Armada's first attempt to sail on 18 May was foiled by contrary winds and an outbreak of dysentery. Medina

Sidonia and his officers, however, reassembled the fleet, repaired the damage, and had the Armada on its way again by 12 July. During this grace period they redistributed the guns and ammunition, trying especially to increase the percentage of big "ship-killers" in relation to the smaller, man-killing weapons that were more common throughout the fleet. One of the ships that needed major repairs at this time was the *Santa María de la Rosa*, whose mainmast had collapsed and had to be restepped. This matter was raised specifically by Medina Sidonia in a letter to Philip II on 10 July 1588 as part of a plea to delay the departure long enough to complete these essential tasks.

Archaeological evidence has been found that directly challenges the image of Medina Sidonia's incompetence. One of the Armada's large, armed merchantmen, *El Gran Grifón*, was wrecked at Fair Isle, between the Orkney and Shetland Islands, in a rocky cove called Stroms Hellier. A team led by the maritime archaeologist Colin Martin of St Andrews University, Scotland, mapped the site in 1970 and recovered twelve guns (or gun parts) and ninety-two pieces of cast-iron shot along with other artifacts from the wreck site (Martin, 1975: 156–187). Identification of the wreck was based largely upon circumstantial evidence in relation to historical documents and was less definite than that of the other Armada wrecks. According to historical documents, *El Gran Grifón* was a second-line fighting ship and was intended to play a purely defensive role. Martin's analysis of the cannons and other materials from the wreck site supported this view. He pointed out that the ship's armament consisted entirely of relatively small guns, long-range weapons using light shot, rather than the big guns that fired heavy shot at close range. By the standards of their day, these guns were obsolescent at best and could not match the firepower of the first-line fighting ships. Analysis of the guns from the wreck led Martin (1972: 69) to conclude:

> The armament of *El Gran Grifón* is clearly tailored to a defensive, second-line role, with protective rather than offensive firepower as the paramount consideration. The front-line ships of the fighting squadrons, on the other hand, were equipped with formidable and aggressive armaments . . . So clear and sensible a policy of distributing armament according to role implies deliberate and closely considered strategic planning before the Armada sailed . . . The urgent reorganization that took place between February and May, when the fleet sailed, was clearly due to the energy and administrative genius of Medina Sidonia himself.

Although controversy surrounds his direction of the Armada during its slow trip northwards through the English Channel, no one has ever accused Medina Sidonia of cowardice, even when he ordered the Armada to return to Spain by sailing north and then via open sea to the west of Ireland. By this time the Armada had fought a series of sharp but inconclusive encounters with the English, losing some ships but maintaining its formation intact. At Gravelines, however, it was driven by Sir Francis Drake's fire ships to cut anchor and attempt to escape individually, leading to a close-range battering by the English guns and the final abandonment of the mission. At this point it is estimated that the Armada had expended 123,790 rounds of great shot without sinking or inflicting serious damage on a single English ship. Considering the total inability of these square-rigged and rather cumbersome ships to sail back through the Channel against the wind, no other option remained but to attempt the dangerous journey to the northwest and around the British Isles.

As the weather worsened, Medina Sidonia's ships became separated. Some had been damaged by English guns during earlier battles and were plagued by spoiled provisions and lack of water. They were also rendered vulnerable by their relatively light construction. Another hazard of the voyage was the navigators' lack of knowledge of the coast in this region. Most of the Spaniards who came ashore after wrecking on the Irish coast were summarily executed by parties of English soldiers or handed over for execution by Irish under English control.

In this context, the wrecks of the *Santa María de la Rosa* and *La Trinidad Valencera*, both lost on the west coast of Ireland, are especially important. As noted earlier, *La Trinidad Valencera* was an armed transport of Venetian origin. The hull construction of this ship presented details, such as the use of iron fasteners and their attachment in straight lines, that indicated mass production and a short designed use-life. The expedient nature of many of the ships requisitioned for the Armada is further illustrated by the wreck of the *Santa María de la Rosa*. Eyewitness accounts indicated that this ship sank almost instantly after striking Stromboli Reef in Blasket Sound on the Irish west coast. The ship was of generally light construction – frame-first but with many close-fitting and interlocking components that formed a relatively solid, self-stressing shell (Martin, 1973: 449). Whereas the Armada's ten new "Atlantic"-type galleons of the Castilian Squadron, which were constructed of fewer but more massive components, suffered only 10 percent casualties, the Levant Squadron, of lighter, Mediterrranean-type construction, suffered 80 percent.

The loss of the *Santa María de la Rosa* has been documented in extraordinary detail. Archaeologists working on this wreck discovered a splintered rectangular box along the keel 11 meters from the ship's bow. This appeared to be the mainmast step, and the break described by Medina Sidonia and the efforts to repair it were visible because of the preservation of the timbers along the keelson. These repairs were also indicated by the way in which ballast had been cleared from the stepping area and the shoring needed to keep the area clear (Martin, 1973: 446). These findings indicated urgent, makeshift repairs to what was otherwise a well-constructed ship, and they pointed to the repaired mainmast step as a weak spot in the hull. Overstrained by its mast, the *Santa María de la Rosa* was vulnerable to the kind of "cracked-egg" damage that could account for the rapidity with which it sank.

Debunking myths about Medina Sidonia's character and competence may be of interest to historians, but the results of underwater archaeology are of more general social-scientific interest in revealing a well-organized effort at rational planning under exigent circumstances. The distribution of guns aboard *El Gran Grifón*, the construction details of *La Trinidad Valencera*, and the repairs to the *Santa María de la Rosa* are archaeological signatures of the practical trade-offs involved in the preparations for Philip II's "Enterprise of England."

Baltic Sea Wrecks

Because its brackish water is generally inhospitable to shipworms, the Baltic has preserved an array of shipwrecks spanning a wide range of time periods (Cederlund, 1983; 1985). Systematic efforts at archaeological recovery began in the 1930s, when it was still performed by helmeted divers with surface-supplied air and through the use of direct lifting methods with limited results. The most important of these pioneering efforts was the study of the *Elefanten*, a large warship uncovered in 1938 by a team led by the Swedish naval officer Carl Ekman. The ship was built in 1559 and sank at Bjorkenas, north of Kalmar on the Swedish coast, in 1564. Although about 50 meters of the lower part of the ship's hull structure was found, only the stern section was recovered and conserved. The remainder, however, was drawn in plan, and detailed sketches were made of structural features. Later, in the 1950s, the ship's timbers were exposed and photographed, and the stern elements were reconstructed and exhibited at the Swedish National Maritime Museum until 1953. Overshadowed later by publicity surrounding the spectacular raising of the Swedish warship *Vasa* in 1961, the work on the *Elefanten* was, in fact, the first major scientifically controlled underwater archaeological investigation in Sweden (Cederlund, 1983: 53) and was certainly one of the earliest anywhere in the world as well.

The ship, a close contemporary of the *Mary Rose*, was carvel-built, with heavy frames and edge-to-edge outer planking and no sign of clinker planking at any earlier stage in its history. More detailed information about Baltic shipbuilding is available from a total of eight seventeenth-century shipwrecks, six in Sweden and two in Denmark, the best-preserved of which is the *Vasa*. The *Vasa* achieved its celebrity-shipwreck status when it sank in Stockholm Harbor before the eyes of Gustav II Adolf of Sweden and his court. This catastrophe occurred on 10 August 1628 during its maiden voyage, when a gust of wind caused the ship to heel over to port until water flooded through the lower gunports, which were open (Fig. 45), and sank it in an upright position in about 30 meters of water. The loss of the *Vasa* was followed by salvage attempts in 1664 which recovered most of the guns; then the shipwreck's location was forgotten until 1956, when it was relocated by the Swedish officer and maritime archaeologist Anders Franzén using grapnels from a boat on the surface. Swedish Navy divers explored the wreck site in 1957 and began tunneling through the mud underneath the hull in preparation for lifting and moving the complete vessel (Franzén, 1961). In retrospect, this was dangerous both for the divers digging their way under the wreck in constant danger that their tunnels would collapse and for the ship which could have been sliced into sections by the lifting cables in the manner of the *Cairo* described earlier. The success of the effort was due at least as much to luck as to skill.

From 1959 until 1961, a massive operation was undertaken to move the intact hull from its original location to a depth of 15 meters closer to shore and finally to lift the entire ship on cables laid underneath the hull between two salvage barges using heavy winches. Thereafter continuous efforts were required to keep the ship's timbers saturated and to begin the laborious process of conservation (Håfors, 1985). After removal of mud and loose objects from the hull interior, the *Vasa* was moved to a special temporary museum in Djurgården, where conservation and restoration continued until the ship was moved to a more permanent pavilion for public exhibition. A visitor to the Vasa Museum today encounters the closest thing there is to King Tut's Tomb in underwater archaeology (Fig. 44).

As with the *Mary Rose*, the recovery and exhibition of the *Vasa* had as much to do with tourism and Swedish national pride as it did with scientific archaeology (Kvarning, 1985), but the vessel is important to archaeologists both in itself and for the impetus it provided for underwater archaeology in the Baltic region. A full technical account of the *Vasa*'s construction has yet to appear, and therefore comparisons with other shipwrecks of that period are necessarily limited. Historical sources indicate that Dutch shipwrights played an important role in building the *Vasa*, and one, Hein Jacobsson, was called as a witness at the inquest following the ship's loss. The court of enquiry came to no firm conclusions about the cause of the disaster, and neither have archaeologists.

The *Vasa* was a fairly conservative example of a large naval galleon of Dutch design but was distinguished by prodigious amounts of ornate

Fig 44. Upper deck of the Swedish warship *Vasa*, showing excellent preservation of the wooden structure. Note the two gun carriages in the background. Published with permission of the *Vasa* Museum, Stockholm.

carvings and decorative elements. The ship was 50 meters long and 12 meters in beam, with a breadth/length ratio of 1:4.3 – in other words, comparable to that of other fighting galleons of the sixteenth and seventeenth centuries. The *Vasa* was larger than most, however, with a displacement of about 1,400 tons. The ship was armed with sixty-four guns, most of them heavy cannons. It is possible that the proximate cause of its loss was incorrect storage or placement of guns, ballast, and other heavy items on board in a manner that raised the vessel's metacentric height above safe limits (Franzén, 1961: 11). There are no obvious signs that the *Vasa* was built or sailed in a manner that would have contributed to the disaster.

The ship was heavily built of oak and differed from contemporary English ships in cross section, with a sharper turn of the bilge and less deadrise (rise of the floors above the horizontal). The gun decks were supported by massive hanging knees and deck beams, and true naval gun carriages and gunports were used (Fig. 45). With its large size, ornate carvings running from stem to stern, heavy armament, and an estimated

Fig 45. Lower gunports of the Swedish warship *Vasa* with the gunport lids in the raised and open position. Open gunports close to the water line like these were an invitation to disaster for early, broadside battery wooden warships. Published with permission of the *Vasa* Museum, Stockholm.

1,100 square meters of sail, the *Vasa* was classified as a *regalskepp* (royal warship) and would have been as imposing as any of the largest warships of its period.

Wrecks of the Dutch East Indiamen

The Dutch origins of the *Vasa* are a reminder of the influence of the Netherlands on seventeenth-century maritime activity. The Dutch East India Company (*de Vereenigde Oost-Indische Compagnie*, often abbreviated as the V.O.C.) emerged to secure a monopoly in trading for spices in the East Indies and armed Dutch merchantmen followed in the path of Portuguese traders and explorers and by 1692 had organized themselves into the V.O.C. Ironically certain small Indonesian islands like Banda became the primary European source for nutmeg and other spices during the seventeenth century. Islands that once loomed so large in the economic and geopolitical consciousness of Europe thanks to the efforts of the V.O.C. are barely known to Europeans today. The V.O.C. rapidly established entrepôts from the Moluccas to the Coromandel Coast, with Batavia (modern Jakarta) as the principal center. In addition, it engaged in expeditions to find faster routes to and from the Netherlands. Its ships faced difficulties ranging from rivalries with the Portuguese, who controlled Mozambique, to navigational hazards such as the shoals and reefs of the central Indian Ocean. In 1610 the Dutch sailor and explorer Hendrick Brouwer determined that an outbound trip across the southern Indian Ocean, taking advantage of strong winds from the west, could shorten the trip by as much as six months, with the return voyage by a more northern Indian Ocean route using favorable winds from the east. The new southern route placed heavy demands upon the limited navigational abilities of this period. Latitude could be established fairly accurately using instruments like the astrolabe, and it was possible to turn the ships on an eastward heading before the winds as far as 40 degrees south. Longitude, however, could be estimated only by dead reckoning, and this meant that errors could not be detected astronomically and tended to be cumulative.

The hazards this presented were not fully appreciated until the company's ships inadvertently encountered the southern continent of Australia. In 1616 the *Eendracht*, under the command of Dirck Hartog, delayed too long in turning north toward the Indies and arrived at what is now Shark Bay on the west coast of Australia (Henderson, 1986: 18–19). Soon thereafter, other Dutch ships sighted the Australian coast at various places from Cape Leeuwin, at the southwestern tip of Australia, to the Houtman Abrolhos. Dutch sailors in a small pinnace called the *Duyfken*, commanded by Captain Willem Jansz, had discovered the Cape York Peninsula of northeastern Australia as early as 1606, but the shape and size of Australia were poorly understood and the *Duyfken*'s discovery provided little guidance for ships approaching from the west.

The Dutch East Indiamen faced navigational hazards closer to home as well. In winter it was generally preferable, despite the risk of stormy weather, to pass the British Isles to the north and west; the shorter southbound route through the English Channel presented contrary winds and was dangerous in wartime (Playford, 1996: 11–15). Taken together, these two hazardous routings account for many of the shipwrecks studied by maritime archaeologists. At least six Dutch East India Company wrecks have been found in British waters (Bax and Martin, 1974: 81), while four are known from waters off the west coast of Australia (Henderson, 1986: 19). These wrecks range in their dates of loss from 1629 to 1781, with the earliest being the *Batavia*, wrecked at the Houtman Abrolhos.

The *Batavia*'s history places it among the most celebrated maritime disasters of the seventeenth century. Of a total of 316 people on board, only 116 survived, with most of the deaths occurring on shore after the wreck. Mutineers led by a supernumerary named Jeronimus Cornelisz had already been conspiring to seize the ship and use it for piracy before it struck the reef. After surviving the wreck by clinging to the bowsprit mast for two days, Cornelisz made his way to one of the islands, where he discovered that the leader of the expedition, Francisco Pelsaert, and the ship's captain, Ariaen Jacobsz, had left for Java with forty-six officers, crew, and passengers in the ship's longboat to seek help for the stranded victims. Cornelisz's mutiny led to the massacre of 125 of the shipwreck victims. When Pelsaert returned he was able to capture the mutineers, hanging some, including Cornelisz, on the spot and marooning others on the Australian mainland or transporting them to Batavia for execution or imprisonment. Efforts were made to salvage as much as possible of the *Batavia*'s cargo, which included twelve chests of silver coins, jewelry, and assorted trade goods. Eleven chests and many other items were recovered, but the twelfth chest could not be moved and was left in place and marked with a cannon and an anchor (Henderson, 1986: 23).

In part, perhaps, because of its historical associations but more probably because of the valuables reportedly left at the site, the *Batavia* was subjected to blasting and removal of artifacts by treasure hunters until 1970. A major effort was mounted then by the University of Western Australia to protect the wreck site and to record and preserve the ship remains and materials from the wreck. This effort led directly to the leading role of the Western Australian Maritime Museum since then in underwater archaeology and conservation. The Maritime Archaeology Act of 1973 extended this protection to other Western Australian shipwrecks, including those of Dutch origin such as the *Vergulde Draeck* ("Golden Dragon"), the *Zuytdorp*, and the *Zeewijk*.

The remains of the *Batavia* were located in a shallow depression on Morning Reef at depths between 2 and 6 meters, in an area exposed to strong wave action and surge. Conventional wisdom in underwater archaeology had suggested that shipwrecks in high-energy environments like this were poor candidates for preservation, especially when it came to the all-important remains of the ship's wooden structure. As we have already, seen, however, some shipwreck sites, such as those in the Dry Tortugas and the Punic wreck in Sicily studied by Frost (1973), contained structural remains that were preserved in spite of strong wave action and unstable sea conditions. In all of these cases, the microenvironment immediately around the wreck site provided good protection and was sometimes enhanced by the very conditions that seemed to threaten the wreck (such as the rapid deposition of silt over ship's timbers due to surge and currents). Because of the exposed location of the *Batavia* wreck site, however, it was necessary to excavate, record, and raise the wreck in sections before storm damage could occur. The ship's stern transom appeared largely intact and was studied in detail before recovery. Later this portion of the ship was reassembled and placed on display at the Western Australian Maritime Museum (Fig. 46). The *Batavia* had the flat-backed stern that was fairly typical of early seventeenth-century ships (Green, 1975: 53). A complete photomosaic was made of the hull timbers at the north end of the site (Green, 1989: 23), and drawings were made of the individual timbers as well. Thanks to this careful recording, it is clear that the *Batavia* was built shell-first (Green and Parthesius, 1989: 34). The

Fig 46. Stern section of the seventeenth-century Dutch East India armed merchantman *Batavia* displayed at the Western Australian Maritime Museum, Fremantle, after excavation and conservation. The squared-off transom is visible at the right. Published with permission of the Western Australian Maritime Museum.

futtocks were not joined laterally, which meant that the complete frames could not have been set up and the outer planks attached to them afterwards. Nor were there indications of any lateral connections between the futtocks in the well-preserved stern third of the ship. A scale engineering model at the Western Australian Maritime Museum reveals details of this construction technique (Fig. 47).

The persistence of the shell-first technique of ship construction until the seventeenth century may appear surprising, but the evidence from the *Batavia* is unmistakable and points to the complexities of ship construction during the great age of sail. Green and his associates further discovered that the *Batavia*'s hull was double-planked with an additional outer sheathing of thin pine boards. This technique was linked in historical sources with shell-first construction, suggesting that the latter was widespread at the time (Green and Parthesius, 1989: 34).

Over 3,000 artifacts were recovered and recorded from the 1973 and 1974 field seasons at the site. These included 128 shaped limestone blocks

Fig 47. Model of the *Batavia* showing shell-first construction techniques. Published with permission of the Western Australian Maritime Museum.

weighing a total of 27 tons that turned out to be building stones for an arched portico (Fig. 48) probably intended for the walled settlement at Batavia (Green, 1989: 182–183). There was an impressive collection of ceramics, including numerous examples of the ubiquitous Beardman jug, a mass-produced vessel seen widely in early seventeenth-century overseas Dutch settlements and elsewhere as a trade item. Four astrolabes, one in good condition with the inscribed circles and gradations preserved, were also found at the site.

Although the *Batavia* was not a warship, it was well armed. A total of five bronze, nine iron, and two composite guns was recovered from the site, along with the remains of one of the wooden gunports. The shipwreck site was known to have contained at least twenty-eight guns, but many of these had been raised by treasure hunters before archaeological research there got under way. Large numbers of cannon balls, usually covered with concretions, were also found. The bronze and iron guns and gun-related items from the *Batavia* were analyzed in detail (Green, 1989: 25–72) and exhibited a range of idiosyncrasies and variability similar to that of the armaments from other early shipwreck sites.

Fig 48. Monumental gate reassembled from shaped stones from the wreck of the *Batavia*. Published with permission of the Western Australian Maritime Museum.

The two composite guns from the *Batavia* were formed by a series of thirty iron hoops shrunk onto a series of flat iron staves to form a gun barrel comparable to the bombardetas from the Molasses Reef and Highborn Cay wrecks. There, however, the resemblance ends. The entire iron gun tube was enclosed in a casing of rolled sheet copper, with the spaces between the copper case and the gun tube filled in with molten solder (Green, 1989: 37). Each of these guns had a chamber of complex construction, suggesting that they may originally have been breech-loaded and only later converted into muzzle-loaders. Archival research unearthed a patent issued in Amsterdam to Jan de Rycker in 1627 and to Bartlet Cornelis Smidt in 1633 for a gun "made of various metals" by a complicated technique that parallels the details of the two *Batavia* guns and proposes the advantage of lighter weight and ease of handling compared with more conventional guns firing shot of the same weight (Green, 1989: 38).

Other gun-related items from the *Batavia* wreck included bar-and-canister shot, a copper shot-gauge, a powder ladle and powder measuring cups, copper cartridge containers, touchhole prickers, a gunpowder bag, wooden bore plugs or tampions with fabric wadding, and a variety of small-arms items including a blunderbuss and a wooden gunstock. The rich and diverse array of weaponry found at the *Batavia* site indicated that these ships of commerce were prepared to fight in situations ranging from ship-to-ship battles to guerrilla-like engagements ashore against indigenous populations, pirates, and possibly European rivals in the spice trade. Cipolla's observation that armed violence based on sailing ships and guns served as the backbone and principal defining element of early European colonial expansion during the great age of sail is amply supported by the guns of the *Batavia*.

The Archaeology of European Colonial Expansion

The great age of sail from the sixteenth through the seventeenth century saw the overseas movement of several major European powers in their first great wave of expansion and consolidation. Maritime archaeology has provided significant new information about this process. The earliest known shipwrecks in the New World – the Molasses Reef, Highborn Cay, and Red Bay ships – all point to a period when small, armed vessels explored unfamiliar regions in search of valued resources that could be processed and transported as priority cargoes back to the parent country. In the case of the Caribbean examples, these ships operated in an uncertain and hostile environment, and they were armed accordingly, with an eclectic mix of weapons intended to ward off attacks by indigenes, rival colonial ships, and pirates and to conduct limited assaults on shore locations. These ships were not designed or armed for ship-to-ship fighting on any large scale. They were vehicles of direct, limited location and exploitation of resources. In the Canadian case, the shore-based Basque whaling station at Red Bay appears to have been fairly short-lived and did not lead directly to a sustained, developed colonial enterprise.

With the Padre Island shipwrecks, however, we see how, by the mid-sixteenth century, the Spanish were making the transition toward a more mature, developed mode of colonial exploitation that involved fleets of large, armed ships traveling in convoys. With fleets came permanent shore settlements and more regular routings and schedules for shipping priority and even sumptuary cargoes back to the home country. As this pattern evolved, the transfer of cargoes and personnel proceeded in both directions, with the new colonies receiving supplies and additional colonists as these merchant fleets shuttled back and forth. The Padre Island ships were bearing outbound cargoes when they were wrecked, but the *Batavia* was on its way from the Netherlands to Java when it was wrecked and provides an example of an inbound cargo destined for the colony itself. Like the Padre Island wrecks, the *Batavia* and later Dutch East India Company wrecks along the coast of Western Australia present examples of this developed phase of colonial exploitation, only by a different European power and in a different direction.

With bigger ships came bigger guns, including more muzzle-loaders of bronze and cast iron to supplant earlier breech-loaders of wrought iron. Armed merchantmen like the *Batavia* were comparable in this regard to the armed transports, *La Trinidad Valencera*, the *Santa María de la Rosa*, and *El Gran Grifón*, that sailed with the Spanish Armada. Thanks to maritime archaeology, a fine-grained picture is beginning to emerge of the coevolution of sailing ships and gunpowder as a critical element of European expansion during this period. As is indicated by the wreck of the *Mary Rose* and by historical and archaeological information about the Spanish Armada, large warships carrying the heaviest guns available were active mainly in or near home waters, where fleet actions were fought within sight of land. Shipwreck studies have resolved many issues about how the conduct of such conflicts changed. Great warships actually became smaller as top-heavy and sluggish carracks like the *Mary Rose* gave way to galleons that were more maneuverable and seaworthy. The reduction of the stern- and forecastles, in particular, appears to have paralleled a shift in emphasis toward reliance more on big guns than on longbows and crossbows. By the time of the Armada battles, gunnery at sea dominated naval warfare completely, in tandem with almost total reliance upon sail for propulsion. The oared galleasses like *La Girona* that participated in the Armada events were anachronisms that proved ineffective and vulnerable to damage and loss at sea.

Shipwrecks like the *Mary Rose, Vasa*, and those of the Armada all demonstrate the value of archaeology as a way of identifying and evaluating the preparations for war by different, competing European powers of the period. In the archaeological associations of these shipwrecks we can see evidence both for rational efforts to prepare for battle (for example, the way arrows were bundled for ready use on deck aboard the *Mary Rose* and the way in which guns were allocated for use aboard *El Gran Grifón*) and for errors (the pervasive problem of open gunports in the loss of the *Mary Rose* and *Vasa* and the inadequacies of Mediterranean-derived methods of ship design and construction in the events of the Armada). The underwater archaeology of the great age of sail has emerged as a potent approach for gaining new information and providing fresh and convincing interpretations of historical processes.

9 · The Transition from Sail to Steam in Maritime Commerce

In contrast to the cargoes of earlier times, which consisted largely of sumptuary and priority goods, mid-nineteenth-century maritime trade increasingly involved bulk cargoes of commodities, and the ships that carried them tended to be propelled by steam rather than sail and to be built of iron and later steel. Underwater archaeology is proving a potent and effective tool for understanding this transition. Archaeologists studying this period cannot always expect to find preserved cargoes, even with ships known to have been used as freighters or transports, but with cargoless wrecks, analysis of the ship's structure can be as informative about the conduct of trade as it is about ship technology. Two areas discussed earlier as notorious ship traps, the Dry Tortugas and Bermuda have provided exceptional opportunities for studying the maritime commerce of this time.

The *Killean*

Underwater surveys and documentation sponsored by the Park Service in the Dry Tortugas have enabled maritime archaeologists to identify two basic categories of mid-nineteenth-century shipwrecks there: construction wrecks, the remains of ships that were engaged in bringing building materials to Fort Jefferson between the 1840s and late 1860s, and en-route wrecks, the remains of vessels transporting cargoes through the Straits of Florida. Examining cargo casualties among the 103 documented cases of known total or partial losses in the Dry Tortugas, the Park Service research team found that they were dominated by lumber, cotton, and agricultural products including grain, sugar, molasses, phosphate (for fertilizer), and hogs. Cotton was a priority cargo because of the special processing and packaging it required and its higher value. Priority cargoes of manufactured goods, including construction materials and general merchandise, followed in importance, with additional bulk categories (oil and coal, fish) behind that. Bulk cargoes predominated, with 58 percent of the total. Cotton was subject to postdepositional loss at the wreck site in the same way as bulk materials and could be said to behave archaeologically like a bulk cargo. Adding it to the figure for bulk cargo would raise the proportion of this type of cargo to 73 percent.

Analysis of historical materials on cargoes led the team to some limited conclusions about the directionality of trade in relation to Dry Tortugas wrecks. Construction materials and general merchandise were generally imported into the Gulf region, usually from ports in the northeastern United States, while lumber, agricultural products, and cotton were exported to United States ports outside the Gulf and to overseas destinations. About half the known cargoes of cotton were mixed with agricultural or lumber products, but bulk cargoes were generally not mixed. Cargoes of construction materials bound for Fort Jefferson were not always distinguishable from similar cargoes being carried past the islands. The fact that Fort Jefferson was a destination in its own right from the 1840s until the late 1860s may increase the relative importance of bulk cargoes during this period; Murphy and Jonsson (1993b: 156) estimated that over 60 percent of vessels lost in the Dry Tortugas were inbound to Gulf destinations, including Fort Jefferson. Most losses occurred during 1830–60, when construction activities at Fort Jefferson were most intense. Three of the shipwrecks surveyed so far from this period – the Bird Key wreck, the East Key wreck, and the Barrel wreck – were construction wrecks. With the possible exception of the Bird Key wreck, which sank so close to Fort Jefferson that it could be said to have arrived there, these ships were lost while inbound to their destination. For the later peak period of losses, 1885–1905, construction had ended at Fort Jefferson and only en-route wrecks have been recorded.

Two important wrecks that were lost close to this later period have been located in the Dry Tortugas; the *Killean*, sunk on Loggerhead Reef in 1907, and a second ship that appears to date from 1860–80 (Souza, 1998). Other possible wrecks in the Dry Tortugas of large sailing cargo ships from the late nineteenth and early twentieth centuries include the

Iron Ballast wreck at the north end of Loggerhead Key (Murphy, 1993a: 201) and a wreck (designated BO13–030) with a steam-operated capstan of late nineteenth-century design and a windlass of a type introduced in the 1870s. No trace of the cargo was present at any of these wreck sites, suggesting that the ships were transporting perishable bulk cargoes or were in ballast when they were lost.

The construction and use of merchant ships driven entirely by sail persisted long after the appearance of the first practical steamboat to operate commercially, invented by John Fitch in 1790 and employed in scheduled service on the Delaware River (Flexner, 1944: 186–87). In the United States, for example, the registered tonnage of steam vessels did not overtake that of sailing vessels until the 1880s, and it was not until sometime during the decade 1900–1910 that the number of steam vessels built in the United States exceeded the number of sailing vessels. According to *Lloyd's Register of Shipping* and contemporary sources such as the British Board of Trade, in 1860 there were 25,663 sailing ships afloat with a total registered tonnage of 4,204,360 as compared with 2,000 steamers with a total of 454,327 tons (Lubbock, 1927: 116). By 1868, worldwide sail tonnage had begun to decline in relative terms, with a total of 4,691,820 registered tons as opposed to 824,614 for steam. In that year U.S. and British commercial ship construction totaled 1,697 registered sailing vessels as compared with 468 steamships (Souza, 1998: 2–4, and personal communication). For ships built in England in 1882 (Cornewall-Jones, 1898), steam decisively overtook sail by both measures, with 130 sailing ships (141,685 registered tons) as opposed to 650 steamships (1,090,132 registered tons).

The *Killean* was a product of this transitional period between sail and steam. Built by John Reid and Company, Glasgow, for Mackinnon, Frew and Company of Liverpool in 1875, it was constructed of wrought iron and its original dimensions and specifications are summarized in Table 3. In common with other early examples of its class, the *Killean* retained some of the fine lines and clipper-like bow of its immediate wooden predecessors, although its iron construction increased its cargo capacity.

It was sold to the French firm A. D. Bordes et Fils in 1893 and renamed *Antonin* in 1894. At this point it was probably used to transport nitrate fertilizer, since A. D. Bordes et Fils was then one of the principal companies in this highly profitable trade (Murphy, 1993b: 249). It was sold again in

Table 3 *Dimensions and specifications of the Killean*

Length	261.4 feet (79.7 meters)
Beam	39.3 feet (12 meters)
Length-to-beam ratio	1:6.65
Draft (estimated)	17.5 feet (5.3 meters)
Freeboard (estimated)	7.0 feet (2.1 meters)
Gross tonnage	1,862 tons (as originally built)
	1,761 tons (after renamed *Antonin*)
	1,818 tons (after renamed *Avanti*)
Under-deck tonnage	1,676 tons
Permanent cement ballast	75 tons

1902, by this time being too small to offer economies of scale in the bulk trade. In the final phase of its career, as the *Avanti*, it was probably sailing as a tramper. Newspaper accounts mentioned the *Avanti* as one of about a dozen vessels stranded and damaged in a hurricane in Pensacola, a major shipping port for lumber at the time, on 28 October 1906, and this also suggests that the ship was hurriedly repaired prior to its final voyage.

At the time of its loss three months later, the ship was outbound for Montevideo and most likely being driven by a strong northwest storm of the kind that frequently occurs in the Gulf during January–February. The shipwreck is in 5.5–6.4 meters of water. If one assumes that the *Killean* was carrying a full load of lumber, its draft at the load limit set by Lloyd's 1875 American Rules was 5.3 meters, and even if it was not fully loaded it could have taken on water that increased its draft before it struck Loggerhead Reef. The port anchor was missing from the wreck site, suggesting that it was deployed farther offshore in an attempt to stop the ship's progress toward the reef. Evidence from the site thus suggests that the ship was taking on water while being subjected to strong winds as it attempted to avoid the reefs. As reconstructed archaeologically by the Park Service team, the shipwreck shows the disadvantages of pure sail propulsion as opposed to steam. Vessels under sail were always at greater risk than steamships during this period (U.S. Life Saving Service, 1885–1909).

The *Killean* was an example of a type of iron ship built in the late nineteenth century to transport bulk cargoes in competition with steamships. These were sometimes referred to as "iron clippers" (Lubbock, 1927: 118), although carrying capacity was increasingly emphasized over speed. Other examples of this class of ships that survive as wrecks or abandoned vessels are the *North Carolina* in Bermuda, the *County of Roxborough* in French Polynesia (Fig. 49), the *Golden Horn* in the Channel Islands off the coast of southern California, and other ships in Chile (*County of Peebles, Falstaff*), the Falkland Islands (*Lady Elizabeth*), and South Georgia (*Bayard*). Others survive as preserved ships, among them the *Wavertree* in New York and the *Falls of Clyde* in Honolulu. Wooden and composite wood-and-iron sailing ships also competed with steam in this period. The best-known of these were the large clippers, some of which, like Donald McKay's first clipper, *Staghound*, and Samuel Pook's *Surprise* (both introduced in 1850), had displacements approaching or exceeding 2,000 registered tons, comparable to the *Killean*. The design of the clippers, however, emphasized speed more than the big iron cargo carriers that followed later, since these fine-lined ships were intended to transport priority cargoes (tea, china, Oriental crafts, etc.) across the Pacific. One of the ironies of this period was the conversion of some U.S. and British steamers to sail. The long, narrow hulls of these steamers produced relatively high speeds,

Fig 49. Wreck of the *Country of Roxborough* on Takaroa Atoll in the Tuamotu Islands, French Polynesia. This 2,120-ton iron clipper was deposited on shore during a Pacific typhoon on 8 February 1906, where it remains today as one of the best-preserved shipwrecks of this type.

leading at least one maritime historian to suggest that the distinctive hull shape of American clippers was derived from them (Chapelle, 1967: 365).

The California grain trade from 1865 to 1886 encouraged the construction of big wooden cargo sailers termed medium clippers, in which capacity was given a higher priority while still retaining considerable speed. So many of these ships were built in Maine and in other New England shipyards, where timber and skilled shipwrights were readily available, that they were also commonly referred to as "Down Easters" (Lubbock, 1987; MacGregor, 1993: 22). During the peak year of 1882 a total of 559 ships carried 1,128,031 tons of grain and 919,898 barrels of flour from California ports (mainly San Francisco) around Cape Horn to the eastern United States. Of these ships, 154 were U.S. vessels, including 12 wooden sailing ships of over 2,000 tons displacement (Lubbock, 1987: 3–4). In U.S. shipyards, an average of 90 wooden, square-rigged cargo ships were constructed each year from 1865 to 1870, declining to an average of 28 each year from 1871 to 1886.

Large sailing cargo ships thus presented a mixed collection of wooden, composite, and iron vessels. Sailing cargo vessels of all the major nations involved in bulk shipping in 1882 (Britain, France, Germany, Norway, Italy, and the United States included 703 wooden and composite wood-and-iron ships and 816 of iron. Collectively, iron ships like the *Killean* were commonly referred to as "windjammers" because of the large amounts of sail they carried and their ability to maintain speed by carrying sail in strong winds. This was possible because of the extensive use of iron masts and yards, standing rigging of wire rope, and steam deck machinery. The *Killean*, along with other three-masters, still retained some of the fine lines of the clippers but had greater cargo capacity (from 14 to 18.6 percent more in the case of oak hulls to 21.5 percent more in the case of fir hulls in ships of the same registered dimensions) because of the greater strength of iron construction (Ville, 1993: 54). Iron hulls also required less upkeep and lasted longer than wooden ones, further contributing to their profitability, and they were less susceptible to fire (Cornewall-Jones, 1898). The principal drawback of iron hulls was their tendency to require frequent cleaning to remove marine growth (Ville, 1993: 56).

Another technological irony of this period was that while military ships such as the early ironclads adopted steam propulsion but made little use of steam machinery to assist in heavy, labor-intensive tasks such as hauling anchors and raising sails, these iron sailing ships bypassed steam propulsion but employed steam instead for deck chores to reduce the high cost of crew labor. The maritime historian Basil Lubbock (1927: 119) commented about these early iron sailing ships:

> in 1870 a 1500-ton ship was a big ship; 10 years later 1800 tons was about the mark, and 20 years later few ships of under 2000 tons were being built. Though ships steadily increased in size, their crews did not, mechanical improvements as much as the need for economy being the reason for this anomaly.

Instead of a linear progression in technology during the second half of there was a branching in the tradition of steam technology. Economies of scale played a key role in the case of commercial iron sailing vessels like the *Killean*. These big iron sailing ships were designed to transport bulk cargoes in competition with steam and to sacrifice speed for profit. (Steamships, generally faster and safer but with less cargo capacity, tended to specialize in priority cargoes and passengers.) The question is whether the relatively narrow profit margins of the bulk trade led to shortcuts and risk-taking in either the construction or the use of these vessels.

In relation to the economic requirements of the bulk trade, the *Killean* became obsolete soon after it was launched. By 1875 there were iron four-masters, often with larger displacements and fuller lines to increase cargo capacity. Ships such as the *Falls of Clyde*, built by the Russell & Co. yards in Glasgow in 1878, with a cargo capacity of 1,809 registered tons, increasingly came to dominate the bulk trade. The fact that the three-masters were prone to dismasting – possibly because of the tendency of shipowners and masters to press on with sail in strong winds in order to maintain their speed – gave further impetus to the introduction of the four-masters. The dismasting of eleven three-masters during a twelve-month period in 1873–74 led to a government investigation and the ultimate reduction of their yard length and mast height (Murphy, 1993b: 265), which reduced their utility.

The site plan (Fig. 50) of the *Killean* wreck site shows the bow and stern areas of the ship relatively intact and resting about 30.5 meters apart, with large sections of the ship's midships hull structure and assorted items like the freshwater tank and some of the masts and yards on the seabed in between. This distribution of wreckage indicates that the ship began to break up when it was wrecked, probably after striking the reef broadside. The northwesterly wind, combined with wave action, pushed the vessel to the east until the anchor set, tilting the hull to starboard with the deck into the waves. The bow section was buoyed up somewhat by its lumber cargo and pivoted on the starboard anchor into its present position (Fig. 51). The foremast rests over the bow portion of the hull, indicating that it fell only after the hull had sunk and collapsed. The stern was pushed about 4.6 meters in the opposite direction, probably also at the moment of wrecking. Further movement of the stern section, perhaps due to storm effects, was indicated by pieces that became separated from the stern and by distortion in the shape of the stern structure. Thanks to their triangular framing, both the bow and the stern of the *Killean* were better-preserved than the midships area, which collapsed outward on both sides and rested in flat sections on the seabed. The capstan was hand-operated and now rests inside the starboard hull near the bow, where it settled after being torn from its mount, probably during the wreck. Together with the stud-link chain-cable drawn directly from the starboard hawse pipe to the anchor, dug into the seabed about 17 meters from the hull, this is evidence of a desperate last-ditch effort to save the ship. Instead of relying upon the ship's windlass to secure the anchor chain to the ship once the anchor held, the crew brought the chain out of the forecastle and wrapped it around the starboard bitts (deck fixtures designed to stop and hold chains). The anchor chain-cable connecting the anchor and capstan appears to have ripped the capstan from its mount and dragged it into the bow structure as the ship was straining on it while being driven onto the reef.

The midships wreckage field revealed a box keelson (a structure resembling two I-beams attached in parallel fashion) riding over the frames. This type of structure was strong but was difficult to inspect for internal corrosion during the life of the ship. Foremast chainplates were visible along portions of the hull sides. These were flat on the lower end for riveting to attach them to the bulwarks and round along their upper body, with rounded ends corresponding to wooden deadeyes at the top. A hull section with chainplates broke away and lay on a piece of outer hull with a mast resting on top of it, indicating that the hull sides collapsed inward before the mast fell. Closed deadlights (hinged metal plates with screw clamps used to cover portholes in heavy weather) on intact portholes

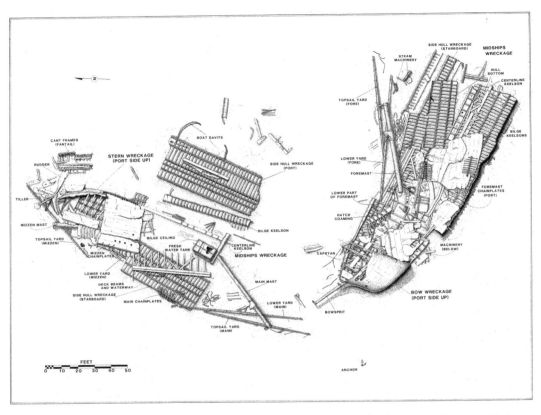

Fig 50. Trilateration plan of the *Killean* wreck, Loggerhead Key, Dry Tortugas National Park, Florida. Published with permission of the National Park Service.

beneath the foremast show that the ship was secured for heavy weather before it was wrecked. The exposed portholes shown in the site plan were removed after the ship sank, either by salvagers or by relic collectors.

According to documentary sources the *Killean* had one bulkhead and 75 tons of permanent cement ballast, but neither of these features was located or identified archaeologically. Cement found in the hull of the wreck of the *County of Roxborough*, an iron four-master built in 1886 and driven ashore on Takaroa Atoll in French Polynesia in 1906, formed a layer on the inside of the hull plating from the bilge up to the waterline and could have served as ballast and also as a sealant against saltwater seepage into the cargo hold. Further research at the *Killean* wreck site may produce evidence of cement ballast, but the failure to find it so far is at odds with the

Fig 51. Bow area of the *Killean*. Note how the triangular frames of the bow structure have enabled this part of the shipwreck to retain its three-dimensional shape. This was also true for the stern of the ship, while the midships area broke up and now lies flat on the seabed.

documentary record. The interior hold of the *County of Roxborough* had no bulkhead despite the fact that the hull was relatively intact (Fig. 52), so it is possible that the *Killean* had no bulkhead (unless one counts the transverse structure near the forecastle).

The *Killean*'s masts appear to have been of iron. The standing rigging was made of wire rope with turnbuckles (rigging screws) inside the bulwarks. There were no signs of topmasts and topgallants that could be telescoped to reduce weight aloft, a feature introduced for ships of this type in 1869, and this suggests that these masts were made of wood (Lubbock, 1927: 120). Assorted items of steam machinery were found at the site, especially near the midships cabin area, but many items of machinery, along with portholes and other collectables, were removed from the wreck by salvors and/or relic collectors after the ship went down. One of the best-preserved items was a double-riveted pressure vessel from a steam-powered cargo winch (Fig. 53). A cargo winch warping hub (a concave drum for winding cable taken in by the winch) in good condition rested on the hull side in association with other steam machinery. An 11,340-

Fig 52. Interior of the *County of Roxborough*. Notice the absence of transverse bulkheads or any other structural elements to divide the space inside the hull. This entire space could be filled with bulk cargo as long as it did not exceed weight limits.

Fig 53. Pressure vessel from steam deck machinery on the *Killean*. Evidence of this kind abounds, showing that these iron clippers made extensive use of steam for lifting and hauling tasks in order to reduce the number of seamen but did not use steam for propulsion.

liter iron tank for fresh water was found near the midships area and would originally have been located in the ship's hold.

Looking at the total picture afforded by the physical remains of the *Killean*, and with due regard for the effects of postdepositional factors such as storms and salvors, it appears that this ship was old before its time. Sailing ships in the late 1800s were evolving rapidly to compete with steam in the still-profitable field of bulk-cargo transport. They probably changed faster and responded more quickly to newly introduced technologies during this period than in the entire two hundred or so preceding years. In contrast, the *Killean*'s obsolescence deepened as its career progressed. The ship retained the fine clipper lines and bow of the 1850s wooden sailing ships, but its cargo capacity, fairly impressive in 1875 when it was launched, quickly fell behind that of comparable ships. With the introduction of four-masted and steel-hulled construction in large sailing cargo ships, along with innovations such as steel masts and yards, the *Killean* was outdistanced even in its own class and probably operated on narrow profit margins. Whether or not the ship was insured, its destruction in 1907 may have been a relief to its owners, although the loss of its cargo, of lumber would have been another matter. During its career and certainly by the time of its loss, the *Killean* was outclassed by other ships against which it had to compete in the bulk-cargo trade, where economies of scale were critical. Ironically, its sharpest competition came not from steamships, which at that time were adapted to a commercial niche involving priority cargoes and passengers, but from other ships of its same general type.

Some uncertainty surrounds the unfinished last voyage of the *Killean*. Was the ship exposed to excessive risk on its last trip? In one sense, it had been at risk for a long time, given the apparent unwillingness of a succession of owners to invest in improvements such as steel masts and yards or telescoping topmasts to reduce top-heaviness and overall weight. But more immediate risk factors can also be identified, such as the time of year and the location of the wreck. Winter storms and the difficult reefs and shoals of the Dry Tortugas were already recognized hazards along its route, yet the ship sailed in spite of them. And what of the hasty repairs made after hurricane damage to the ship in Pensacola? No direct archaeological evidence has been found to connect these repairs to the ship's loss, but an element of uncertainty remains.

Social Conditions at Sea in the Late 1800s

In order to move beyond the proximate causes of the loss of the *Killean*, we need to consider the social and economic context in which this ship and others like it operated. The period 1875–1907 was a time of industrial expansion in Europe and in the U.S. In Britain the initial impetus of the Industrial Revolution, based largely on textiles, had begun to decline but was overtaken by a new expansion of exports based on coal, iron, and steel, along with massive construction of railways. Industry expanded in the U.S.A. as well during this period, although this had more to do with internal, domestic markets than with exports. In England the social order that evolved during this period has been described as the "mid Victorian social pyramid" (Hobsbawm, 1969: 157). It was a highly stratified society with a strongly developed distinction between the skilled "labor aristocracy" and a mass of unskilled and poorly paid workers and with the main populations concentrated by 1881 in rapidly growing cities. For the "labor aristocracy" of engineers, managers, technicians, and other people with special skills that were in demand, this was a relatively prosperous period. But for the bottom 40 percent or so of unskilled workers whose labor remained cheap and in limited demand, conditions were much worse. The stagnation of this exploitive social order continued well into the 1880s in England despite improvements in diet and increased availability of consumer goods from about 1860 on. To an extent, we can view the social order aboard commercial ships both as an extension and as a delayed version of late Industrial-Revolution socioeconomic conditions on land. The slow but general improvement of working-class conditions in England from about 1870 onward was not immediately matched by the experience of sailors on merchant vessels.

The extent and importance of class structure in determining crew status aboard American vessels is less clear than it was aboard English ships and may have had more to do with recency of immigration than with a static European social order. We do know that flogging on American merchant vessels was not outlawed until 1850, and the U.S. Congress did not act again on the merchant sailors' behalf until 1871, when physical conditions aboard some vessels became so bad that a law was passed authorizing revocation of licenses of officers found guilty of mistreating their crews (Bauer, 1988: 284). Then there were the "crimps," or shipping masters who operated seamen's boarding houses on shore. They furnished room and board to sailors at exorbitant rates by collecting large advances on the sailors' wages upon delivering them to captains in need of crews. A seaman caught up in this system was already indebted to the ship when he signed on. New York State attempted to license these boarding houses in 1866, but the U.S. Congress did not act against them until 1872. Even so, the practice of sailors being "shanghaied" (unwittingly or forcibly signed on by a crimp to collect the sailor's advance) continued in spite of reforms introduced by the Dingley Act of 1884.

During the late-nineteenth century, sailors were also subject to arrest as deserters if they left their ship, no matter how bad the conditions on board. Not until the White Act of 1898 was this penalty finally abolished for sailors who were U.S. citizens. Prior to this, the U.S. Supreme Court held that the Thirteenth Amendment to the Constitution, which prohibits involuntary servitude, did not apply to seamen (Bauer, 1988: 285). Not until the LaFollette Act of 1915 was this protection extended to sailors who were not U.S. citizens. This same legislation introduced other improvements, such as the two- and three-watch systems for sailors and for the engine room gang, respectively. Clearly, social reform aboard American ships was slow in coming.

Unionization among American seamen began around 1875, especially in the Great Lakes where it achieved early success. Sailors' unions were strongest on the Pacific coast in the 1880s. As with legislative reforms, improvements in wages and working conditions were slow in coming, and union organization was spotty and uneven. Attempts at strikes as early as 1850 in San Francisco, before formation of seamen's unions, failed, as did a longshoremen's strike in 1851.

Anecdotal accounts abound concerning the harsh working conditions and difficult life in general on board merchant ships of the late 1800s, with the "windjammers" receiving a particularly bad reputation for being undermanned and for having overworked crews. For example, Lubbock (1927: 44), referring specifically to these ships, described how: "Very often the weak scanty crews of later days were quite unable to take in sail, so that it had to be allowed to blow away or else the men were sent aloft with sheath knives to cut it adrift from the jackstays."

Lubbock's account went on to describe how a 2,000-ton, four-master of the 1890s usually had a crew of only eighteen to twenty seamen. If we add to this twelve ship's officers and assorted personnel (cook, boatswain, carpenter, apprentices, etc.) for a total of thirty-two, we can calculate that ships of this kind could operate with approximately one person per 63 registered tons. By way of contrast, the manning requirements for a contemporary class of Royal Navy sail-and-steam warships (corvettes of 2,473 tons displacement) averaged one person per 7.8 tons, which was fairly typical for warships of that size and general type then. That is, contemporary warships of comparable size required slightly more than eight times the personnel to operate them. Dramatic as this difference was, wooden sailing warships of the previous century (1740–1775) of about this size (1800–2090 displacement tons) averaged about one person per 2.4 tons (based on Rodger, 1986: Appendix I). In general, the manning requirements of the iron and steel sailing cargo ships of 1870–1900 contrasted almost as dramatically with those of earlier commercial sailing vessels. Estimates of "tons per seaman" for eighteenth-century merchantmen, before the advent of steam propulsion or auxiliary machinery, varied from 20 tons per man for coastal traders to 10 tons per man for West Indiamen (Rodger, 1986: 40). In other words, iron and steel merchant sailing vessels of the period 1875–1900 intended for oceanic transport of bulk cargoes had over six times the tonnage per man as their pre-iron and -steam predecessors a century earlier. All of these estimates must be viewed as approximations, since they are based on different, though roughly comparable, measures of tonnage.

In addition to their routine duties at sea, like chipping rust, painting iron plating, and calls to go aloft and handle sails, crewmen serving on iron "windjammers" were often compelled to work as laborers on shore – especially in the guano trade. Barren islands off the West African and South American coasts contained vast deposits of bird guano which commanded high prices as fertilizer in Europe and America. This trade did much to encourage the use of large iron and steel sailing ships. Sailors had to excavate the guano deposits and carry the material to their ship. The work was hard, unpleasant, and dangerous. Lubbock described one incident on an island off the West African coast where a guano excavation pit collapsed, killing seven men, and he noted that such accidents were common. As one might expect, shipowners and captains varied greatly in their regard for their crews, with some individuals who stood out in their concern for their crews' well being. The provisioning scale introduced in

1870 by Thomas Charmichael, a Clyde shipowner whose firm operated several iron "windjammers," was a positive step toward improving the seamen's diet, although, as Lubbock (1927: 83) noted, "a mean captain, a rascally steward or a bad cook often nullified the intentions of a liberal owner." The main problem with this system, of course, was that it left the sailors' welfare up to the whim of the shipowners and operators, whose approach was usually less enlightened than that of Thomas Charmichael and was more concerned with cutting costs.

There are archaeological indications that the *Killean*'s loss was related to the economic and social conditions of the late Industrial Revolution. The *Killean* had been in continuous service for thirty-two years and was still operating with its original equipment when it was wrecked. No effort had been made to replace its heavy iron masts and yards with lighter ones. The undivided interior of the cargo hold, without protective longitudinal or transverse bulkheads, meant that the crew could not control internal flooding effectively during the high winds and waves before the ship struck the reef, and it explains why the hull gave way easily when the ship swung broadside onto Loggerhead Reef. Iron windjammers were generally regarded as robust ships with strong hulls, but their lack of bulkheads and compartmentalization rendered them vulnerable to exactly these hazards. In short, the ship's basic design compromised safety for the sake of capacity and efficiency in cargo transport. Although conditions were changing during the late nineteenth century in both nations, the reforms came too late to affect the design of the *Killean* in 1875 or of other iron "windjammers" of that brief era. The *Killean*'s original features were retained throughout the ship's career as it was passed from one owner to another without significant changes, even when such changes were known to be beneficial.

The wreck of the *Killean* can be interpreted as a material example of the effects of late Industrial Revolution assumptions and attitudes on the conduct of maritime trade. The extension of capitalist mercantilism from the context of a land-based society to seaborne trade is best described in terms of "one-more-voyaging" (Murphy, 1983); shipowners of the time were tempted to operate their vessels one more voyage beyond their designed or normal use-lives. The wrecks of ships "captured" in ship traps provide opportunities for archaeologists to identify and evaluate those parts of the ship that failed in a physical and geographical environment in which it is possible to control for risk factors. The *Killean* appears to have been a case of a commercial vessel that was pushed one voyage too far by its owners in order to squeeze profits from an increasingly competitive bulk trade. Further archeological testing of this principle is currently under way.

Blockade-Runners and Condemned Ships

The archaeology of modern maritime commerce shows us that commercial and military activities cannot be regarded as separate domains. The development of large iron sailing ships like the *Killean* for transporting bulk cargoes occurred within the so-called Pax Britannica, and one could argue that the bulk trade carried on by these vessels flourished under the protection of an umbrella provided by the Royal Navy. But this broad military context cannot explain the archaeological associations of the *Killean* shipwreck or the structural characteristics of the other large commercial sailing vessels that were the *Killean*'s contemporaries. For such defining relationships we must look to shipwrecks that were more closely tied to the conduct of war during the mid-nineteenth century.

The strategy of the northern states in the American Civil War was broadly guided by the Anaconda Plan formulated by General Winfield Scott. Named after a tropical snake that kills its victim by constriction, the plan was to cut off the secessionist southern states, which relied heavily upon exports of cotton and other agricultural products for revenue and purchase of needed war materials, by blockading them. The Confederacy was short of vessels to challenge the blockade, but it rose to the occasion in September 1861 by bringing the steamer *Bermuda* past the blockade to Savannah, Georgia, with a cargo of rifles, cartridges, cloth for uniforms, shoes, and two field guns (Wise, 1989: 50–51). Sailing cargo ships were easily intercepted by the blockaders, and therefore their role in this trade quickly diminished.

The *Bermuda*'s financial success on this and later trips was a powerful incentive for further efforts to slip priority cargoes past the Union blockade, and it was also a spur to the Union Navy to tighten the blockade. Confederate purchasing agents in England quickly obtained the iron-hulled screw-propeller steamer *Fingal* and succeeded in delivering a much larger shipment of war goods, including two Blakely cannons. Meanwhile the Union blockade grew tighter as combined operations campaigns were mounted against Confederate seaports and along the western rivers (Reed, 1978) and as the Union added more ships.

Further attempts to run cargoes past the blockade showed that small but fast shallow-draft steamers had better chances of success than large-capacity ships. Not only were smaller vessels harder for the blockaders to see, but they could use the maze of stream channels at the entrances to key Confederate ports, many of them still unguarded, to evade detection. The disadvantages of such vessels were their limited cargo capacity and range, and transshipment of cargoes became necessary at intermediate locations such as Bermuda, Havana, and Nassau. The profits reaped by these voyages more than offset the costs of transshipment, repeated dashes through the blockade, and losses to blockaders, groundings, and other hazards.

Initially the ships used for blockade running were adapted from pre-existing vessels, but by late 1863 British shipbuilders on the Mersey and Clyde Rivers were constructing ships especially designed for this purpose. These vessels, while not identical, shared certain diagnostic features that distinguished them from more conventional steam-powered cargo vessels of the early 1860s. Although a particularly successful British-built block-ade-runner, the *Banshee*, had showed the value of narrow hull lines for speed early in the war, British shipbuilders recognized that excessive narrowness would lead to structural weakness and poor seaworthiness and would restrict the size of the engines and the cargo capacity. These British-built blockade-runners were beamy and strong enough to contain oversized engines and reasonable amounts of cargo while retaining fine lines for speed and the small silhouettes for avoiding detection demanded by this specialized trade. The resulting design was a unique class of ships that combined the fine lines of the *Banshee* with the seaworthiness of Clyde ferryboats (Wise, 1989: 145). Among other things, some of these blockade-runners were the first ships in the world to be painted gray to enhance their stealth at sea, and the fastest among them achieved sprint speeds of around 18 knots (Watts, 1989).

It is some measure of the success of both the initial blockade-running by the Confederacy and later efforts using more of these purpose-built vessels that over 75 percent of all attempts by steamers to run the blockade during the Civil War were successful (Wise, 1989). Since the domestic industries of the southern states supplied less than half of the Confederacy's military needs, the cotton-for-arms trade through the Union blockade was essential to make up the difference. At least 60 percent of the South's modern arms was supplied from overseas through the blockade, and this trade also furnished cloth for uniforms, blankets, shoes, medicine, and food. In the opposite direction, blockade-runners are estimated to have transported around 350,000 bales of cotton past the Union forces, along with agricultural products such as tobacco and naval stores. The average blockade-runner survived just over four trips (two round-trips). At the end of the war 136 had been captured and another 85 destroyed (Wise, 1989: 226).

Although technically neutral, Britain did not extend the concept of neutrality to include control of the transshipment of goods from England to the Confederacy. With the emergence of St. George's and Hamilton as ports of transshipment and coaling depots, commerce in cotton-for-arms briefly made Bermuda one of the busiest entrepôts in the North Atlantic. In addition to blockaders off the major southern ports, the Union Navy sometimes operated a squadron in the vicinity of Bermuda to intercept blockade-runners outside British territorial waters.

On 5 January 1864, the iron paddle steamer *Nola*, on its maiden voyage from England, struck a reef and sank in about 9.1 meters of water near the Western Blue Cut, off Bermuda's West End. A large part of the ship's cargo of dry goods was salvaged and auctioned off later at Mangrove Bay to compensate the owners and underwriters. The ship was 750 registered tons with engines of 260 nominal horsepower. On 16 May 1864 another blockade runner of similar design, the *Mary Celestia*, struck a reef and sank in 18.3 m water near Gibbs Hill Lighthouse, along the South Shore of Bermuda (Fig. 54). The *Mary Celestia* had successfully run the blockade on at least five round trips between Bermuda and Wilmington, North Carolina, and was bound for Nassau with a cargo described as 534 containers of "general merchandise" along with 125 boxes of bacon when the ship struck a reef close to shore and sank within eight minutes. As in the case of the *Nola*, at least some of the *Mary Celestia*'s cargo was salvaged and auctioned off for the owners. The ship was small, even by the general standards of the blockade runners' trade, at 207 registered tons. No trace of the cargo remained at either shipwreck site, although numerous pieces of broken ceramics were present at the *Nola* wreck site that may have been either part of the original cargo or in use aboard the ship.

Fig 54. A contemporary watercolor showing the loss of the Confederate blockade runner *Mary Celestia* on 16 May 1864 off Gibbs Hill Lighthouse (at left). Photographed at the Bermuda Maritime Museum and published with permission of Mr. and Mrs. Thomas Godet, Bermuda.

Both ships were built for speed. The *Nola* was 72 meters long and 7.7 meters wide, with a breadth/length ratio of 1:9.4, while the *Mary Celestia* was 67.4 meters long and 6.7 meters wide, with a breadth/length ratio of 1:10. These narrow-lined ships were powered by twin oscillating-cylinder steam engines driving large paddles of a special design that included mechanically operated feathering paddle blades (buckets). Paddles of this kind were intended to break the suction as each bucket rose out of the water, improving the efficiency of the paddle and increasing the ship's overall speed and economy of operation. This design element became a feature of many of the late-model blockade runners, despite the increased acceptance of screw propellers for propulsion more generally by the 1860s. Side-paddle wheels worked well in shallow water and provided good maneuverability − both needed when moving across sandbars and along stream channels − although some successful blockade runners had screw propellers. The side-paddle wheel persisted as a mode of propulsion for ships in sheltered waters like Long Island Sound and the Hudson River well into the twentieth century. At least one large paddle steamer, the

Ticonderoga, with feathering paddles similar to those on the *Nola* and *Mary Celestia*, operated as a commercial passenger ship on Lake Champlain until 1950 (Whittier, 1987: 36–39; Bellico, 1992: 284–85).

The *Nola* and *Mary Celestia* shipwrecks were surveyed nondestructively in 1983–86 by research teams from East Carolina University led by the maritime archaeologist Gordon Watts (1988, 1993). Although little remained of the hull structure of the *Mary Celestia*, preserved elements of the engines, box boilers (Fig. 55), and paddles were present at the site. There were two large horizontal fire-tube boilers, which dominated the midships area, along with one paddle wheel in an upright position (Fig. 56) and another lying on its side. Each paddle wheel retained its feathering bucket mounts along with the eccentric spider gear that rotated the buckets when in use. These pieces of machinery were the most durable remains at the site, with only a small piece of the bow structure with the anchor windlass, some hull plating and frames from the ship's sides adjacent to the machinery, and a portion of the stern visible above the siltline.

More could be seen of the remains of the *Nola*. Unlike the *Mary Celestia* site, where silt covered most of the surviving hull and deck structure, the *Nola* wreck occurred in a narrow sand channel surrounded by reefs and was not covered with sediment. More of the hull, including the bow and stern, was intact. As in the case of the wreck of the *Killean*, both the *Nola* and *Mary Celestia* had better-preserved bow and stern components than midships hull structures which showed extensive signs of structural collapse. But for both of these iron steamers, in contrast to the *Killean*, there was relatively well-preserved machinery present in the midships area, along with coal from the ship's bunkers. The triangular iron-framed structure of the *Nola*'s bow, found resting on its starboard side in a section about 9 meters long extending back to the watertight forecastle, was encrusted with marine growth and had lost its wooden decking but was otherwise relatively intact. The *Nola*'s machinery, like that of the *Mary Celestia*, consisted of two large boilers and the remains of the steam engine, in this case two inverted oscillating-cylinders and associated items such as a smoke pipe. The sides of the hull had fallen away from the engines, and both paddle wheels were found resting on their sides overlying the collapsed hull plating. The paddle wheels were of the same feathering type as seen on the *Mary Celestia* but showed signs of damage due to salvage, as did the ship's machinery.

Fig 55. Box boiler of the *Mary Celestia*. Like the ship's narrow lines and feathering paddle wheels, the oversized boiler and engines were intended to gain speed over Federal blockaders during the Civil War.

Fig 56. Upright feathering paddle wheel at the wreck of the *Mary Celestia*, Bermuda. Photographed by Dr. Eugene T. Rowe and published with his permission.

Historical sources indicate that there was controversy over the loss of the *Mary Celestia*. The ship was brought in close to shore near Gibbs Hill Lighthouse in order to drop off the shipowner and the pilot. Items appearing in the *Bermuda Royal Gazette* at that time alleged that a dispute arose between the ship's captain and the pilot, a Bermudian, over the dangers of proceeding into an area known to contain hazardous reefs. According to these accounts, the captain finally relinquished his authority to the pilot, and the collision with the reef occurred soon afterward. It was also claimed that the "general merchandise" on board the *Mary Celestia* included military goods for the Confederacy and that the pilot was in the pay of the Union Navy. Archaeology has not yet resolved this controversy, although it might one day if excavations were to locate remains of weapons or other military goods among the ship's contents that may have been missed by salvors and relic collectors. But this evidence suggests that divided authority under hazardous circumstances was a factor in the ship's loss.

These two shipwrecks provided material evidence of specific shipbuilding techniques intended for the unique circumstances of the blockade-runners' trade. The exaggerated narrow lines of both vessels revealed their requirement for speed, as did the large engines and feathering paddle-wheel buckets. Their small size and cargo capacity would have been unprofitable in almost any other kind of trade, but with the inflated demand structure of the Confederate economy they allowed at least some shipowners to reap substantial profits with only a few successful voyages. With the end of the Civil War and the resumption of normal mercantile commerce, this type of ship virtually disappeared from the seas.

The Bird Key ship, sunk near Fort Jefferson in the Dry Tortugas some-time between 1857 and 1861, was another cargo vessel whose operation and loss occurred in the context of preparations for the American Civil War. Unlike the well-designed blockade-runners *Nola* and *Mary Celestia*, the Bird Key wreck presents a picture of an expedient approach to wartime profits. As tensions between the North and South increased shortly before the Civil War, the U.S. War Department made serious if somewhat belated efforts to build up key coast defense installations such as Fort Jefferson in the Dry Tortugas and Fort Taylor in Key West. General Winfield Scott's visit to Fort Taylor during its construction short-ly before the outbreak of the war may have imparted a sense of urgency to these preparations and suggests that he saw these coast defenses as an integral part of his Anaconda Plan. The only construction material that was locally available for this work was crushed coral sand, which was mixed with cement for concrete. Everything else – bricks, ironwork, paving stones, cement, lumber, nails, and provisions for workers – was shipped in. Initially the bricks were brought in from Pensacola, but this traffic ended in 1861 with the Confederate seizure and destruction of the Raiford and Abercrombie brickworks. The bricks found associated with this wreck indicated, as we have seen, that the ship sank before the U.S. Army Corps of Engineers had found it necessary to ship bricks in from the North. When the Raiford and Abercrombie brickworks began producing bricks for these forts by the millions it found that its two schooners were inadequate to transport them, and the War Department then contracted with the Key West firm of Tift and Company to find shipping for the construction materials. A study of the correspondence between the Tift brothers between September 1859 and June 1861 in the Tift Company Letter Book at the Historical Archives of the Monroe County Library, Key West, revealed that, while eager to get this contract, they came to view it as a mixed blessing. Although it provided steady income through the large-scale shipment of bulk cargoes, it also tied up vessels that could sometimes have been more profitably employed in the cotton trade. Efforts to keep costs to a minimum in this context included, as we have seen, operating uninsured vessels at considerable risk.

Although the Bird Key vessel has not yet been firmly identified, it was clearly a small steamboat built according to local or vernacular methods somewhere in the late pre-Civil War South. It was probably one of the earliest seagoing, propeller-driven steamboats to be used in this region. The wreck was located in shallow water, 1.2–2.7 meters deep at mean tide, on Bird Key Bank, approximately 1,554 meters southwest of the Fort Jefferson lighthouse. (Figs. 12–14). It was recorded intermittently by Park Service teams in 1985 and 1988, with more complete surveys by a mixed team of Brown University students and volunteers under my direction in 1989–90 (Gould, 1995). As noted earlier, the hull was flat-bottomed and angular, with no keel, and was of composite iron and oak construction. Its four-bladed solid iron propeller was of special interest because of its good condition and its flared blades with squared blade-tips.

The ship was driven onto Bird Key Bank with its engine running. The bow struck at more or less a right angle to the sandbank and folded like an accordion as the vessel hit, with the forward part breaking off. The ship stopped and came to rest as the propeller struck the seabed, tearing the deadwood away from the main part of the lower hull and leaving a 2.4-meter gap where separation occurred in the hull forward of the thrust bearing and propeller shaft. The deadwood was twisted over onto its starboard side at an angle of 32 degrees, while the main part of the lower hull came to rest more or less intact and tilted to starboard at an angle of 12 degrees. The ship's rudder was torn off at this time and came to rest flat on the seabed a short distance to starboard of the propeller. After the wrecking event the ship was extensively damaged by salvage efforts and later by storms, the combined effects of which produced a scatter pattern of debris extending to the north of the main hull structure. There were also indications of relic collecting of portable artifacts. Nothing of the ship's engine and little of its machinery remained, but there were boiler and firebox fragments that showed the effects of dynamite blasting, probably during salvage.

Surviving elements of the wreck revealed a minimum length for the lower hull from the bow to the propeller of 33 meters and a beam of

4.2 meters, giving it an estimated breadth/length ratio of 1:7.7. Remains of curved iron sponsons (frame extensions that flared out horizontally from the hull) were found resting alongside the lower hull, indicating that the main deck of the ship was broader than the lower hull. This vessel had a shallow draft that, together with its flat bottom, probably made it easy to operate in the shallows and reefs of the Dry Tortugas but also rather unseaworthy. From an engineering point of view, the propeller was hydrodynamically inefficient, with relatively flat, paddle-like blades that must have produced intense vibration and torque in the stern area of the ship. Evidence of these effects was present in the form of heavy wood-and-iron strapping that covered the deadwood area along the full length of the propeller shaft. The strapping created a composite iron–wood–iron laminated sleeve with a V-shaped cross section that fitted over the ship's deadwood keel – clearly added after the ship was completed and had been operating for some time. This feature represented an exaggerated effort to reinforce and strengthen the ship's stern, but it also revealed the area of the ship's greatest structural weakness. The break in the hull that occurred after the vessel grounded was at the forward end of the strapping-reinforced deadwood, the point along the hull where the extra protection ended.

The workmanship in the Bird Key vessel's construction was generally good, with regular plating and framing and closely fitted, riveted joints. But the ship's design reflected manufacturing techniques of a basic nature limited to the use of flat iron plates and simple angle irons. All iron-covered hull surfaces were flat and angular. The ship's design features were out of touch with the mainstream of ship construction of the time. The overall impression is one of a ship built by a local ironworks that did not specialize in shipbuilding but was familiar with early propellers like the Loper model and could generally imitate them. The details of the Bird Key wreck's structure and engineering were consistent with the philosophy of mercantile expediency expressed in the Tift brothers' correspondence. In some ways, the Bird Key vessel was a better example of the "one more voyage" concept than the *Killean*.

The search for profits in the context of the American Civil War produced shipwrecks that allow us to perceive two contrasting approaches to commercial ship construction and use: specialized ships like the *Nola* and *Mary Celestia*, designed for the speedy transport of priority cargoes past the Union blockade, and expedient vessels like the Bird Key ship for bulk cargoes. Blockade-runners depended upon high profits to offset the risks of the trade, while the Tift brothers of Key West, who operated on narrower profit margins, used ships of all sorts, including at least one that was condemned by its underwriters. Both kinds of shipwrecks demonstrate the value of maritime archaeology in addressing the sociocultural processes underlying the preparations for war.

In all these cases, historical accounts focused on specific details of social history that could be examined and evaluated in relation to the archaeological record. Even where no excavation or permanent recovery of submerged material remains was carried out, archaeologists were able to achieve a level of specificity and detail that could be connected convincingly to larger issues of social and economic behavior during a period of rapid change. The importance of these details – the failure to upgrade the masts on the *Killean*, the lean-hulled and over-engined configuration of the *Nola* and *Mary Celestia*, and the expedient nature of reinforcement to the stern structure of the Bird Key wreck – lies in their relationship to sociocultural processes having to do with the economies of technology, labor, and risk during the period in which the Industrial Revolution went to sea. These details of ship construction and related associations on the seabed should be viewed once again, as archaeological signatures of the socioeconomic relationships that produced them.

Although the archaeological studies in Bermuda and the Dry Tortugas were all carried out with a full awareness of postdepositional factors that could alter the archaeological record and thus our understanding of the sociocultural processes at work when these shipwrecks occurred, this does not, of course, mean that all possible postdepositional factors have been identified. The results presented here will be subject to reexamination and evaluation as analytical techniques improve. Further, a limited array of shipwreck studies, no matter how carefully controlled, cannot be assumed to be a representative sample of the period, and therefore the conclusions offered here are simply the best approximations possible today.

10 · New Technologies and Naval Warfare

Given the limitations of large, square-rigged ships of war, the line of battle – a column of heavily armed ships in parallel columns opposite each other at close range – was the preferred way to bring as many guns as possible to bear at once against an opponent during fleet actions at sea. The movements of these ships were constrained by the wind, since square-rigged ships had limited capabilities in upwind sailing and maneuvering. Their masts and rigging also interfered with the radius of fire by their guns. It was difficult to place guns on the upper deck where they could rotate and fire freely in any direction. Instead, the main gun batteries were arrayed in rows on either side of the ship, where they fired through open gunports. This arrangement, which shipwrecks like the *Mary Rose* show was in use by at least the sixteenth century, meant that individual guns were restricted in their ability to elevate and traverse. The positioning of one's ship relative to one's opponent was more important than the aim or accuracy of the gun. Another limitation imposed by this mode of warfare at sea was that the black powder used produced prodigious quantities of smoke that enveloped fighting ships after their first broadside. This often made it difficult for opposing ships to see each other well enough to maneuver and train their guns. Although boarding of enemy vessels during fleet actions at sea declined after the Spanish Armada battles, it was uncommon for a warship to be sunk by gunfire alone. Wooden ships were hard to sink, and, except for a lucky hit in a magazine or a major fire, a ship-to-ship battle was usually concluded when one vessel succeeded in dismasting the other, leaving it helpless in the water and unable to fight effectively.

Despite the obvious difficulties involved in fighting this way, the broadside-battery, line-of-battle sailing ship was the centerpiece of European nations' battle fleets and the key to their naval supremacy until the 1840s. In the course of this period two principal strategies emerged. One was the *fleet-in-being*, consisting of capital ships that could exert supremacy through direct action (or the threat of action) against comparable fleets, through the use of blockade, and through their support of combined operations involving land and sea units. The other was *commerce raiding*, and the French naval planners who favored it designed warships that were well enough armed to defeat any likely opponent at sea but fast enough to outrun a fleet sent against them (Ropp, 1987).

Throughout this period Britain was the leading naval power in relation to fleet actions (Kennedy, 1976). Sweden's fleets dominated the Baltic, although Russia presented limits to this challenge, and Russian and Turkish battle fleets fought each other for control of the Black Sea. Commerce raiding became the strategy of choice for nations whose fleets were not strong enough to ensure victory in fleet actions. In the United States the frigate emerged during the late eighteenth and early nineteenth centuries as a potent commerce raider. Three-masted, full-rigged ships of this kind were widely used in many navies and were fast, maneuverable, and well armed (with from twenty-four to thirty-eight guns carried on a single gun deck, later versions carrying up to forty-four guns). These two dominant strategies persisted into the age of steam.

The design and construction of warships were radically altered in the mid-nineteenth century by the advent of three new industrial technologies: big guns firing exploding shells, steam propulsion, and wrought-iron armour. These new technologies led to a debate and indecision over tactics elements of which persisted into the twentieth century. The history and archaeology of ships from this transitional period reveal multiple, branching lines of development that challenge popular notions of a linear evolution of naval technology culminating in the modern battleship.

Historical hindsight has tended to regard the development of ironclad ships as destined to affect the balance of seapower in a manner comparable to the wooden battleships that preceded them, namely, as the dominant elements of battle fleets at sea. However, the ironclads only rarely played this role. On 27 May 1905, the Japanese fleet ambushed a Russian fleet sent from the Baltic to relieve Russian forces in the Far East, and its decisive success was arguably the clearest victory ever achieved in a battle between fleets of armored ships. Subsequent engagements involving fleets of steam-powered battleships, most notably the main German and British fleets at the Battle of Jutland on 31 May 1916, produced outcomes that failed to fulfill the expectations of the proponents of battleship warfare. Despite naval treaties designed to slow the process, battleship moderniza-tion and construction continued on a large scale after World War I, lead-ing to the largest and most heavily armed versions of this type – the ultimate examples being the Japanese battleships *Yamato* and *Musashi*, each of which displaced 65,000 tons and carried nine 18-inch guns.

Between 1855 and 1955 approximately 650 battleships were built by those maritime nations that could afford them (Woodward, 1982). These vessels varied considerably in their armor and armament, but all of them were true capital ships that served as centerpieces for their fleets. Of these vessels, only 16 were sunk unequivocally as the result of ship-to-ship fleet actions at sea. The remainder succumbed to a wide variety of mishaps, including mines, torpedoes, internal explosions, gunfire from shore bat-teries, aerial bombing, and scuttling (data from Woodward, 1982: 143–46). None of these outcomes was seriously envisioned by the naval planners who ordered these ships built. It is in this context that we can appreciate the maritime historian Robert O'Connell's (1991: 3) comment that

> The battleship concept was an exercise in tunnel vision. In fact, the possible applications of technology to naval warfare were far broader than those defined by the simple interaction of big guns, armor plate, and steam propulsion, so in wartime the fate of the battleship would be that of tactical underachiever and victim. Nonetheless, the dominant element of virtually all the world's navies resisted this reality with all of their strength.

What can underwater archaeology contribute to an explanation for the consistent misapplication of new technologies to naval tactics in the history of the modern battleship? Maritime archaeologists have been slow to turn their attention to this issue. The sample of armored, steam-powered warships recorded archaeologically is significantly smaller than for their wooden counterparts, and further work will be needed to produce representative examples of every phase of the history of the battleship. The examples studied so far, however, have produced results that point clearly to the complexity of this history. Four of the best archaeological examples of the development of the battleship span a period of almost eighty years – two shipwrecks from the 1860s, one from the 1870s, and another from the 1940s. While we are far from achieving a complete archaeological understanding of this period in naval technology, the cases of the USS *Monitor*, the HMS *Vixen*, the HMVS *Cerberus*, and the USS *Utah* provide insights into the sociocultural history of battleship technology and tactics.

The Archaeology of Tactical Indecision

Many Americans still believe that the USS *Monitor*, famous for its historic battle with the Confederate ironclad *Merrimac* (CSS *Virginia*) in 1862 during the American Civil War, was the first ironclad warship. Similarly, many people in England claim HMS *Warrior*, launched in 1860, as the first of this type. Each of these ships was innovative and presented important technological features in the development of the modern battleship, but neither was the first. Credit for the initiative in ironclad warship development rests with the French (Baxter, 1933: 92–115; Toudouze et al., 1939). The French artillerist Henri-Joseph Paixhans conducted experiments with guns firing explosive shells and forecast their destructive effects upon wooden-walled warships in 1821. His experiments led him to conclude in a pamphlet in 1825 that iron armor at least 18–20 centimeters thick would be required to withstand the effects of his shell-firing guns, and in 1827 his guns were first introduced into military service by the French (Baxter, 1933: 26). The results were closely watched and discussed by naval planners in other nations, but it was the French who led the way in adopting iron armor for warships.

In the light of continuing experiments during the Crimean War, the French Ministry of Marine ordered the construction of ten iron-armored floating batteries that could be used against fortified positions on shore. This was seen as a way of offsetting the advantages that land-based coast defenses then enjoyed by making it possible to use big shell-firing guns against wooden warships. After experiments of their own, the British agreed to join in building five of these vessels, with the aim of having the complete force ready by 1855. Despite delays in producing the necessary iron armor and the loss of one British vessel due to a dockyard fire

(*Illustrated London News*, 12 May 1855), the five French floating batteries arrived in the Black Sea in time to play a key role in the successful bombardment of the Russian fort at Kinburn (*Illustrated London News*, 3, 10, and 17 November 1855; *Illustrated Times*, 27 October 1855; Bent and Nicholson, 1857). Their armor effectively protected them against Russian shell fire and proved its value to such an extent that in 1856 the *directeur du matériel*, Dupuy de Lôme, ordered the construction of an iron-armored frigate of 5,620 tons displacement, the *Gloire* (Fig. 57).

Despite superficial resemblances to the *Napoléon*, a 92-gun wooden ship of the line with steam propulsion and a single screw propeller launched in 1850 (Lambert, 1984: 37), the *Gloire* was not merely a cut-down version of an earlier wooden line-of-battle ship (Baxter, 1933: 98; *Illustrated London News*, 9 March 1861). It was a wooden-hulled ship with combined sail and steam propulsion using a single screw propeller, but its armor afforded it decisive superiority over such earlier ships. Plans were quickly made to build twenty-five more seagoing ironclads for the French navy, and with the support of Napoleon III this program got under way immediately. The British quickly approved plans for a larger, all-iron-hulled seagoing warship, the *Warrior* (Fig. 58), which was launched in December 1860 (Brownlee, 1985, 1987; Wells, 1987; Lambert, 1987). By August 1861 Britain had ordered fifteen seagoing ironclads and suspended further

Fig 57. Early depiction of the world's first true ironclad warship, the *Gloire*, launched in 1859. The appearance of this armored frigate (frégate cuirassée) initiated a major naval arms race between France and England.

Fig 58. *H.M.S. Warrior* undergoing restoration in 1986 in Hartlepool, England. This ship was England's immediate response to the *Gloire*, and it was launched in 1860. Shown here is the ship's original all-iron hull, before the addition of much in the way of reconstructed elements such as masts, rigging, engines, and guns.

construction of large wooden warships except for those with iron armor (Baxter, 1933: 140). A modern arms race enlisting the full energies of the Industrial Revolution had begun.

The earliest seagoing ironclad ships had the same external appearance as their wooden predecessors and carried full complements of sail. This was necessary because of the inefficiency of early steam engines, which were used mainly to move the ships in and out of port, in calm conditions, and in battle. Most of their guns were also arrayed along the ship's sides in the familiar broadside pattern, since the masts and rigging effectively blocked an all-around field of fire. Iron hull construction provided greater strength than wood, so, not surprisingly, many of these early ironclads were larger than their predecessors. Iron hulls stood up better to the vibrations and strain produced by the ship's engine, especially around the stern near the screw propeller, and to the shock of firing the larger guns that were coming into use at sea.

The concept of installing a rotating, armored gun turret on a raft was first proposed in detail by the British officer-inventor Commander

Cowper Phipps Coles in 1855 (Baxter, 1933: 185–86), but it was the Swedish-American inventor John Ericsson who independently developed and built the first operational turreted ironclad, the *Monitor*. After this ship's engagement with the *Merrimac*, at least thirty-one more such ships (called "monitors"), including four double-turreted ones, were built in the United States from the Civil War into the 1870s. The Russians started construction on seventeen monitors in 1863 and had a squadron of ten Ericsson-type vessels (Fig. 59) operating in the Baltic before the end of the American Civil War (Gardiner, 1979: 172; Alopaeus, 1984: 52–53). From 1865 to 1867 the Swedes built three monitors, naming the first of the series the *John Ericsson*, followed by another of a similar type in 1871. Norway acquired four Ericsson-type monitors from 1866 to 1872. Even Britain, which showed little interest initially in monitor-type ships, built four turreted monitors between 1870 and 1872, mainly for use as coast-defense ships in Britain's overseas colonies. One of these ironclads, the H.M.V.S. *Cerberus*, was sent to Australia, where it served as the flagship of the navy operated by the state of Victoria until it was scuttled for use as a breakwater in Port Phillip Bay, near Melbourne, in 1926.

Fig 59. Fleet of Russian Ericsson-type monitors at the South Harbor, Helsinki, Finland, sometime during the late 1860s. Their resemblance to Federal monitors of the American Civil War is almost uncanny and shows how quickly other nations adopted this type of ironclad warship. Courtesy of the Helsinki City Museum.

All of these early monitors were intended for use in sheltered waters; their low freeboard and near-neutral buoyancy made them unseaworthy. Several monitor-type ironclads made epic long-distance sea voyages, but such voyages received attention mainly because they were exceptional. In heavy seas it could be a harrowing experience to serve aboard one of these vessels, and the *Monitor* itself was lost in bad conditions off Cape Hatteras, North Carolina, on 31 December 1862 (Miller, 1978: 53–84).

It is possible to see a continuous evolution from the original monitors through larger though still monitor-like turret ships such as the *Devastation* and *Thunderer*, often cited as the first mastless, seagoing turret ships (Gardiner, 1979: 23), and larger turreted ships such as the *Dreadnought* of 1875, the Victoria and Trafalgar classes of 1890–91, and the Royal Sovereign class of 1892–94. A thorough review of ironclad ships, however, reveals a more complex history reflecting not only technical improvements in guns and ship construction but also tactical indecision and failure. The encounter between the *Monitor* and the *Merrimac* in 1862 was neither the starting point for the ironclad warship nor the defining moment for the development of the modern battleship. For example, repeated attempts were made by the British to employ Coles-type turrets aboard monitor-like ironclads, that combined sail and steam propulsion with a low freeboard. Coles' efforts to advance this design approach during the 1860s resulted in a variety of iron clads ranging from the small *Huascar*, a single-turreted ship operated successfully by the Peruvian Navy and later by the Chileans (Somervell and Maber, 1986; Wood and Somervell, 1986), to the much larger HMS *Captain*, which capsized in a squall off Cape Finisterre, Spain, in 1870 with the loss of Commander Coles and almost five hundred officers and men (Hawkey, 1963). The sinking of the *Captain* made it clear that the combination of sails and heavy turrets with a low freeboard was dangerously unstable, and no further ironclad ships of this type were built.

Throughout the 1860s there was uncertainty about how to make the best tactical use of steam and iron technology. One of the most hotly debated and inherently contradictory approaches was ramming.

Seeking a tactical solution for the use of new steam and iron technologies in sea battles, naval planners looked backwards to the Graeco-Roman practice of ramming with oared galleys. Strong advocacy for ramming appeared in the writings of the British admiral George Rose Sartorius at the time of the Crimean War, and during the 1860s the British commander Philip H. Colomb and the Russian admiral Gregorie Boutakov advocated similar tactics (Sandler, 1979: 118–33). After the *Warrior*, ironclad warships sprouted reinforced bows that projected underwater. Ramming proved successful in battle only under exceptional conditions. In perhaps the best-known such instance, the ramming by the *Merrimac* of the Union wooden sailing sloop *Cumberland*, the victim was anchored under calm conditions in the sheltered waters of Hampton Roads. After driving the ram into the *Cumberland*'s hull, the *Merrimac* drew back, tearing its ram away and leaving it embedded in the side of the *Cumberland* (Fig. 60). All ramming encounters between ships during the Civil War occurred in confined waters where the victim's opportunities for escape were constrained by the shoreline and not in the open-sea fleet actions envisioned by the ramming advocates. The only encounter that even came close to their expectations was the Battle of Lissa between Italian and Austrian fleets in the Adriatic Sea in 1866 (Lewis, 1883; Clowes, 1902),

Fig 60. In this contemporary drawing, the casemated ironclad *Merrimac* (Confederate ship *Virginia*) is shown ramming and sinking the Federal sloop *Cumberland* on 8 March 1862 at Hampton Roads, Virginia.

which involved repeated ramming by both sides and culminated in the ramming and sinking of the Italian ironclad flagship *Re d'Italia* by the Austrian ram *Erzherzog Ferdinand Max*. This sinking occurred after the Italian captain had his crews removed from the ship's guns, thinking that he would have to repel boarders as the ships drew closer, making the *Re d'Italia* a sitting duck. After this battle, naval officers often referred to the "lesson from Lissa" to support the efficacy of ramming, but, as the naval historian Stanley Sandler (1979: 150) points out, the real lesson was that it was only a unique combination of circumstances that had allowed the *Ferdinand Max* to succeed at it. The realities of ramming in the American Civil War and at Lissa were ignored in favor of the theory, despite evidence to the contrary, until the launching of the *Dreadnought* in 1906.

Underwater archaeology provides a reality check on the design and use of the early ironclads and the later development of the armored battleship. The lesson that shipwrecks offer is like the "real" lesson from Lissa – namely, that the history of armored capital ships must be understood by confronting and explaining the totality of the evidence available rather than by relying upon evidence selected to support a particular point of view.

Shipwrecks of the Monitors

In August 1973 a systematic search by researchers from Duke University and the North Carolina Department of Cultural Resources located the wreck of the *Monitor* in 67 meters of water at Cape Hatteras, North Carolina. The ship's hull was found resting inverted on the seabed, partially covering the turret, which was also upside down (Fig. 61a–b). In 1975 the shipwreck site was declared the United States' first National Marine Sanctuary, and a series of expeditions followed that produced a photomosaic of the wreck site and recovered objects from the wreck including the ship's anchor and lantern. The 1985 and 1987 research was directed primarily at gathering information for use in managing the site, although some innovative recording techniques were also developed as the work proceeded. For example, computer modeling and imaging was used, based on a combination of accoustic and photographic recording, to generate three-dimensional images of the wreck, with particular attention to controlling for ambiguities and uncertainties associated with underwater remote sensing (Stewart, 1991).

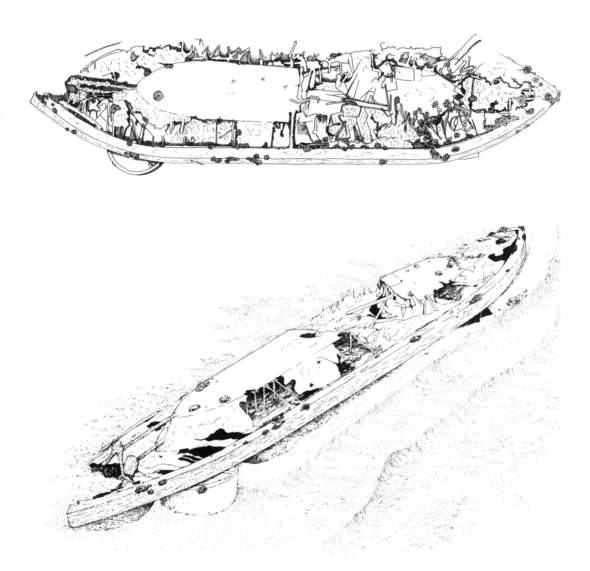

Fig 61a. Plan view of the *U.S.S. Monitor* wreck. Fig 61b. Elevation drawing of the *Monitor* wreck. Both views show the badly corroded condition of the bottom plating and the way in which the hull rests upside down and partially covers the turret, also upside down. Published with permission of NOAA.

The most important results so far have been to identify and measure the effects of corrosion and other postdepositional processes, especially as they related to the general instability of the ship's structure and to the deterioration of specific components of the ship. For example, it was found that the port armor belt had lost at least 2 meters of its length at the stern, at least half since 1983 (Arnold, et al., 1991: 11). The skeg (an assembly outside the hull used to support the rudder), propeller, and propeller shaft, became detached from the hull and had sagged measurably since 1983. Iron plates that formed the bulkheads along the inside of the stern armor belt had collapsed, thus accelerating corrosion of the iron-armor belt from the inside as well as the exterior. Especially alarming are bulges that have appeared along the bottom of the armor belt. These may have resulted from weaknesses produced by manufacturing stresses at the time of the ship's construction, mainly due to the original foundry's inability to maintain uniform temperatures when rolling iron plate (Arnold, et. al., 1991: 11). In short, the 1987 survey found evidence of serious and rapid corrosion in the ship's structure.

Similar problems were encountered in the lower hull, where many portions have collapsed, and in the engineering spaces underneath. Since the *Monitor*'s hull rests upside down, partially propped up by the turret, debris from the lower hull and machinery within the ship is now resting on the ship's deck, in an unstable situation. Deck plates and debris now cover portions of the turret that are visible beyond the armor belt, whereas in 1985 the side-scan sonar images showed this area to be relatively clear. A hole in the main deck near the midships bulkhead has increased in size since 1983. This and other changes are exposing additional structure to oxygenation and further corrosion, accelerating the process of deterioration and collapse.

There are signs that some of this accelerated postdepositional damage may be due to human activities. Certain areas of the ship showed signs of rapid and recent corrosion that resulted from the removal of marine growth (which generally protects the underlying metal against corrosion), especially in the midships area (Arnold, et. al., 1991: 13). Bent frames and dislocated deck plates in the area forward of the midships indicated mechanical stresses that were probably due to grappling or snagging of the stern end of the armor belt from the surface. This would also help to account for the damage to the skeg. From 1973 to 1983 the observed changes due to corrosion were slow but have increased since 1983 due to removal of protective marine encrustation. These findings raise serious management questions, especially about how to protect the shipwreck against unauthorized encroachment.

The overall prognosis for the *Monitor* shipwreck site is not good. Increasing rates of deterioration and change at the site suggest that the structure is weakening more rapidly now than was seen earlier. This raises the likelihood of structural collapse, especially in the unsupported stern area of the wreck that rests upon the turret. In the light of these findings, NOAA is being urged to conduct periodic on-site examinations with a low-cost ROV and to consider the recovery of portable artifacts and perhaps even the turret (Arnold, et. al., 1991: 15). Cathodic protection through the use of sacrificial anodes at key locations within the wreck has also been recommended to slow the rate of corrosion, although further testing is needed before this can be done effectively (Hamilton, 1981; Arnold, et. al., 1991: 21–33). The archaeology of the U.S.S. *Monitor* is an ongoing effort to manage and preserve the site and should be viewed as a work in progress.

The ship contained many unique features besides its famous turret and overall raftlike shape and was widely regarded as a landmark in the history of mechanized warfare. For example, because the engineering spaces and living quarters were located below the waterline, it was necessary to provide forced-draft ventilation (Mindell, 1995: 247–48) and toilets that could be flushed against the water pressure – both important technological firsts. Questions such as how the *Monitor*'s system of ventilation compared with the belowdecks ventilation of other ironclads and the method of steering the ship, using an armored cupola near the bow (probably the ship's most vulnerable point in battle), compared with other responses to the problem of steering ironclads under fire must await the appearance of more complete archaeological information.

The HMVS *Cerberus*, laid down in 1867 and completed in 1870, was one of the first examples of what came to be known as the "breastwork monitor." It had the low freeboard and flat decks of the American monitors but also possessed a central superstructure that contained fore- and aft-turret of Coles design. Each circular armored turret contained two 10-inch rifled muzzle-loading guns and could be rotated to bear on a target without having to turn the ship. A full three-masted sailing rig was provided for the *Cerberus*'s five-month cruise to Australia despite the recent loss of the *Captain* while under sail. Temporary built-up sides along the hull were added to give at least limited protection. Although vulnerable to capsizing in the same way as the *Captain*, the *Cerberus* never rolled more than 15 degrees during heavy weather and survived the voyage (Parkes, 1957: 168–69). After it arrived at Melbourne in 1871 its masts were replaced with two light poles and the built-up sides were removed as well. The *Cerberus* never went to sea again, and its subsequent operations were limited to the sheltered waters of Port Phillip Bay and Melbourne Harbor. It joined the Royal Australian Navy when it was formed in 1910 and was renamed HMAS *Platypus*, serving as a submarine depot ship until 1924 (Herd, 1986: 12).

The *Cerberus* was then declared obsolete and sold for scrap in 1924, with some of the breastwork plating being purchased by the Victorian Railways. The engines, boilers, and portions of the superstructure including the remaining pole mast were removed as well. In 1926 the ship was scuttled in 4.6 meters of water as a breakwater near the entrance to the Sandringham Yacht Club on Port Phillip Bay, and the anchor from the foredeck was placed at the entrance to the Club. Wave action has since produced corrosion and physical damage along the seaward side of the hull. By 1993 the hull plating along the seaward side was corroded completely through. The iron frames were severely corroded as well and were showing signs of imminent collapse from the weight of the massive armor belt and turrets.

The hull survives to its full, original 69-meter length and 14-meter beam, probably because of the great strength of the armor belt along the ship's sides. In 1993 the hull was still intact and rested upright and level on the sandbank where it was originally scuttled, with the deck, armored breastwork, conning tower, and two Coles turrets (each complete with its guns) visible above the surface and preserved as well (Fig. 62). The teakwood deck and many deck features were in surprisingly good condition. Fittings for the steering gear were still visible, and the framing and decks of the belowdecks compartments were relatively intact except for a large opening in the midships area decks where the engines had been removed.

The ship's vertical armor was 15–20 centimeters thick along the sides of the hull, 20–23 centimeters thick for the breastwork structure, and

Fig 62. Interior of one of the Coles turrets aboard the wreck of *H.M.V.S. Cerberus*, showing two 18-ton rifled muzzle-loading guns inside.

23–25 centimeters thick for the Coles turrets. All of this armor was reinforced with teakwood backing 23–28 centimeters thick. Horizontal armor was 3.8 centimeters thick on the upper deck and 2.5 centimeters thick on the breastwork deck, and the upper deck was covered with a further 25.4 centimeters of teakwood (Cahill et al., 1983). The combined use of iron armor plate and thick layers of teak was a widespread practice in the construction of British ironclads from the *Warrior* into the 1870s. One commentator said of the *Cerberus* and its sister ship, the *Magdala*, that with their combination of big turreted guns and slow trial speed (9.75 knots) "they might be said to resemble full-armed knights riding on donkeys, easy to avoid but bad to close with" (Ballard, 1980: 219).

The ship's guns, like the combination of iron armor and teakwood, were characteristic of those in use on Royal Navy ships and in coast defenses throughout the British Empire from the 1860s onward. They weighed 16,363 kilograms each and were closely similar to preserved examples of this type of weapon that can be seen today in, for example, Bermuda and Halifax. The *Cerberus*, however, contains the only extant examples of this type of gun on their original mountings within Coles turrets. Maritime archaeologists may therefore find it worthwhile to conduct a detailed comparison of the Ericsson turret aboard the *Monitor* and the Coles turrets aboard the *Cerberus*.

The superficial resemblances of the *Monitor*'s turret to those of Coles's design and the fact that they appeared almost simultaneously have sometimes prompted questions about whether this important technological innovation was independently invented or copied. As was noted by the maritime historian James Phinney Baxter III (1933: 233), the Union Navy Department proposed the construction of twenty ironclads on 29 November 1861, all to be armored wooden ships with two Coles turrets each. Coles had been receiving wide attention from the press since he started promoting his turret design in 1860 (*Illustrated London News*, 19 April 1862). Supporting Ericsson's claim for priority, however, was the proposal for an "impregnable battery and revolving cupola" that he presented to Napoleon III in 1854, which included drawings and a model of a single domed turret mounted upon a raftlike hull that clearly anticipated the *Monitor* (Baxter, 1933: 254; Miller, 1978: 12–13). Ericsson's design was one of six different plans for turreted ironclads submitted to the Navy Department in September 1861, and it differed significantly from Coles's in one important way – the gun carriages were attached directly to the sides of the turret, which rode on rollers upon which it rotated. This meant that the mass of the armored turret absorbed the full shock of the guns' firing and recoil, whereas the Coles turret was based upon a turntable, which was thought to be less well suited to withstand recoil. One disadvantage of Ericsson's turret, however, was the tendency for leakage to occur through the gap where the turret rested upon its rollers. This happened twice during the *Monitor*'s voyage from New York to Hampton Roads and nearly led to the loss of the ship, although the problem was later attributed to the captain's having jacked up the turret and stuffed oakum around the base, contrary to Ericsson's instructions (Miller, 1978: 37).

The historical chronology surrounding the design and adoption of the Ericsson and Coles turrets suggests that these were neither independent inventions nor cases of diffusion but inventions linked by common circumstances of technological and military history. Each inventor was seeking the same advantages in the context of the available technology.

The comparative archaeology of the *Monitor* and the *Cerberus* offers an opportunity to measure the degrees of similarity and differentiation produced under parallel conditions of technological development and intense competitive pressure.

As we have seen, the *Cerberus* was deployed as a coast-defense monitor in Port Phillip Bay and Melbourne Harbor. During its career within these confined waters, a special U-shaped breakwater of loose rocks was constructed near the center of the narrow entrance to the bay. This area is relatively shallow, with strong currents sweeping in and out of the deeper waters outside the bay. The breakwater was designed to enclose the *Cerberus*, providing protection against waves and currents and affording a stable position from which the ship's guns could control the approaches and entrance to the bay. It would also have protected the ship against attempts at ramming and mining. This breakwater was sited with overlapping and continuous fields of fire from the guns of coastal defenses like Fort Gellibrand along the shore of Port Phillip Bay (Lovell, A., and Associates Pty. Ltd., 1993). In short, the *Cerberus* became increasingly integrated into an evolving defensive system.

The Archaeology of Ramming

Tactical indecision by the Union Navy Department at the time the *Monitor* was ordered was reflected by the simultaneous order of two other, very different ironclad warships, the *Galena* and the *New Ironsides*. Both were wooden, broadside-battery, combination sail-and-steam vessels with iron cladding. The *Galena* proved vulnerable to shell fire during an action against Confederate shore batteries at Drewry's Bluff, near Richmond, Virginia, and was deemed a failure. The *New Ironsides*, however, was a strongly armored ship of 3,486 tons with 18 heavy guns. The ship saw combat in support of combined (amphibious) operations against Confederate shore installations and coast defenses. Although built to serve in a manner comparable to the *Gloire* and *Warrior*, the *New Ironsides* achieved its successes in an arena more like that of the original floating batteries at Kinburn during the Crimean War. Neither *Galena* nor the *New Ironsides* played any role against Confederate ships at sea during the Civil War.

Ironclad rams were also being built for use at sea with fleet units during the 1860s, especially by the British. Three ships, *Vixen*, *Viper*, and *Waterwitch*, were laid down in 1865–66 and completed in 1866–67.

Although related in design, they were different and reflected different technologies. The *Vixen* and *Viper* were both twin-screwed (the first in the Royal Navy), combination sail-and-steam vessels. The *Waterwitch* represented a more radical approach to this tactical philosophy that employed hydraulic turbine propulsion to enable the ship to ram forward and *backward* by reversing its hydraulic jets instead of turning the ship (*Engineering*, 26 October and 2 November 1866). This unique vessel had a ram bow and stern for this purpose, but it proved to be slow and difficult to maneuver and failed to perform up to expectations. All three ships were iron-framed and iron-hulled, and each had iron armor backed by teak (similar to the *Warrior* and the *Cerberus*), but the *Vixen* had an additional heavy outer cladding of teakwood covering the entire hull.

All three ships performed poorly in their 1867 trials (*The Engineer*, 23 August 1867; Murray, 1874: 184–89). With top speeds of just over 9 knots, these were the slowest ironclads in the Royal Navy at that time. Experience with the *Vixen* during a winter gale in the Irish Channel in 1867 showed that the ship was unseaworthy, and this, combined with bunkerage for only twelve days' continuous steaming, meant that the *Vixen* and its sister ships were poorly suited to sustained fleet operations at sea with larger and faster ships of that period like the *Warrior*, the *Achilles*, and the *Minotaur* (Gould, 1991: 143). Not surprisingly, the *Vixen* and the *Viper* were deemed unfit for fleet operations at sea and were towed to Bermuda in 1868, where they remained as coast-defense vessels for the rest of their careers. The *Waterwitch* stayed in English waters, saw little if any active service, and was retired early.

The *Vixen* was scuttled as a blockship in the narrow Chubb Cut Channel near Daniel's Head on Bermuda, probably in 1896, in connection with a proposed defensive battery at Daniel's Head (Gould, 1991: 144). This event, along with efforts at modernizing Bermuda's coast defenses – such as the iron armor, painted camouflage, and 12.5-inch rifled muzzle-loaded (RML) guns at Fort Cunningham overlooking The Narrows (the main entrance channel into Bermuda) at Bermuda's east end (Gould, Harris, and Triggs, 1991, 1992), an electric telegraph linking at least eleven installations by 1866–67 (Major-General "X", 1888), and a variety of other improvements including electric "submarine mining," "defense electric lights" (searchlights), and preset ranges and arcs of fire to various buoyed locations in The Narrows (unpublished plans and maps of

Fort Cunningham, 1893–1905, Bemuda Archives) – all point to an increasingly organized defensive system comparable to what was taking place at the approaches to Melbourne, Victoria, at about the same time. The removal of the masts and rigging from both the *Vixen* and the *Viper* at the Dockyard in 1873 indicated a total commitment at that time to their role as coast-defense vessels.

The archaeology of the *Vixen* contributes to our understanding of its defense function. A nondestructive archaeological survey was conducted by Earthwatch volunteers and students from Brown University, with support from the Bermuda Maritime Museum, in 1986–88. The shipwreck site was mapped (Fig. 63) and photographed in detail, including the ship's interior structure. The results of this survey were compared with plan drawings and documents of the *Viper* and the *Vixen* at the National Maritime Museum, Greenwich, and at the Public Record Office, Kew. These comparisons revealed differences between the plans and the wreck. The ship's engines, propellers, and other machinery as well as portable artifacts had been removed in the Dockyard prior to scuttling, so the research concentrated on structural remains. Among other things, the study of the *Vixen* shows how much can be learned from the archaeology of a relatively recent shipwreck even after it has been stripped and damaged.

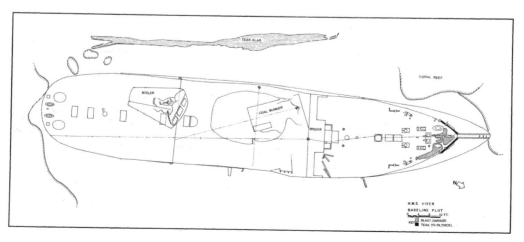

Fig 63. Trilateration plan of wreck of composite ironclad ship *H.M.S. Vixen*, Daniels Head, Bermuda. Note the two oval-shaped openings near the stern for vertical trunks to house the twin screws while the ship was under sail.

The structural investigation of the *Vixen* revealed that the ship was primarily a ram. Its principal weapon was a bow structure that projected under water and was massively reinforced inside the hull. Although the *Vixen* was listed in Royal Navy publications with its sister ships as an "armoured gunboat," its guns were puny and poorly protected. The ship was originally armed with two 7-inch rifled muzzle-loaders and two 20-pounder breech-loaded guns on the exposed main deck, none of which were shielded by the ship's ironclad armor. No guns were found at the wreck site, but a single 7-inch rifled muzzle-loader gun was encountered on display in a public park in St. George's. Since the only 7-inch rifled muzzle-loaders ever reported in Bermuda were the four on board the *Vixen* and the *Viper*, this gun probably came from one of these ships.

As shown in the elevation drawings (Fig. 64), the main armor belt shielded the ship's engines and midships machinery, and secondary armor belts extended along the waterline fore and aft. The forward armor belts on either side converged to join the massive vertical iron bow slab that formed the core of the ram. The ram was further supported by a vertical iron slab that extended back along the ship's centerline and was attached directly to the keel. This latter item did not appear on the ship's plans, nor did four heavy longitudinal frames bracing the hull against the fore- and aft-ends of the main armor belt. These unique reinforcing structures are most easily explained as supports for the ship's hull and machinery against the anticipated shock of ramming. The *Vixen* was seriously overbuilt, even by the general standards of early ironclad ship construction.

The need to shift back and forth from sail to steam propulsion led to the adoption of lifting screws in late wooden naval ships powered by steam and sail and by early British ironclads like the *Warrior*. The lifting screw required a vertical trunk in the stern to hold it while cruising under sail. The *Vixen*, the *Viper*, and the slightly later twin-screwed armored corvette *Penelope* all shared the unusual feature of two vertical trunks and a double-sterned shape under water to accommodate their twin lifting screws. The slow speed and excessive fuel consumption of all three of these vessels can be attributed, in part, to the cavitation created by the large concave spaces beneath the stern. The design of the stern was criticized at the time of the construction and trials of these ships (Symonds, 1866), and this kind of engineering for twin-screwed Royal Navy warships was never repeated.

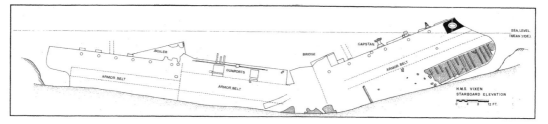

Fig 64. Elevation drawings of the *Vixen*, providing a dramatic view of how the ship broke and settled into the Chubb Cut Channel after scuttling charges were set off in 1896. Further blast damage is visible near the bow.

Twin-screw propulsion, combined with twin rudders, was intended to provide exceptional maneuverability under steam, suitable for ramming. The *Vixen* could turn 180 degrees within a radius of 314 meters to starboard with the port engine full ahead and starboard engine astern and within 480 meters to port with starboard engine ahead and port engine astern. The asymmetry of the ship's turning radius was probably due to the torque effect of having both screws turning in the same direction. These turning radii were much tighter than that of larger, seagoing ironclads like the *Warrior* (which could complete a 180-degree turn within a radius of 2,379 meters, eight times that of the *Vixen*), although the larger vessels were faster by about 5 knots. A hypothetical ramming encounter at sea between the *Vixen* and the *Warrior* (Fig. 65) illustrates the difficulties of ramming as a tactic. Despite their superior turning abilities, the *Vixen* and the *Viper* would have needed to close within one-third of a nautical mile of the *Warrior* head-on in order to have any chance of ramming. Given the *Warrior's* superior speed, its officers and men would have to have been extraordinarily inattentive to allow a ship like the *Vixen* to get that close. There was no way that clever tactics could overcome such difficulties, and with this case in mind it is easy to see why ramming never achieved its hoped-for success in battle at sea following the advent of steam and iron.

Other unique features of sail-and-steam warships of the 1850s and 1860s were the use of telescoping funnels that could be lowered and a low and lightly constructed bridge, both intended to reduce interference with the sails while cruising under sail. Routine sailing and new tasks such as raising and lowering the screw propellers and funnel were perfomed manually. It

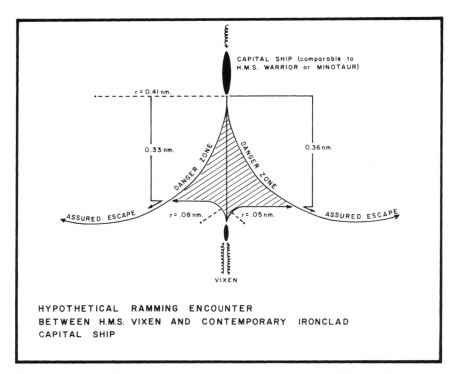

CAPITAL SHIP (comparable to H.M.S. WARRIOR or MINOTAUR)

r = 0.41 nm.

0.33 nm.

DANGER ZONE

DANGER ZONE

0.36 nm.

ASSURED ESCAPE

r = .08 nm.

r = .05 nm.

ASSURED ESCAPE

VIXEN

HYPOTHETICAL RAMMING ENCOUNTER BETWEEN H.M.S. VIXEN AND CONTEMPORARY IRONCLAD CAPITAL SHIP

Fig 65. Hypothetical ramming encounter at sea between *H.M.S. Vixen* and *H.M.S. Warrior*, based on known performance of the ships. This diagram illustrates the difficulty any ship trying to ram another in the open sea would encounter.

has been suggested that this was because seamen had to be kept busy. This view was widely held at the time and is echoed by maritime historian Walter Brownlee (1987: 133):

> The Royal Navy was so convinced of the benefit to be derived from putting its Jack tars through hardship that it refused to include any steam-operated mechanical aids on the new ship.

But there is another, more parsimonious explanation that should be considered. Steam operating manuals (King, 1879: 85–86; Lyon and Hinds, 1915: 312–15) pointed out the dangers of unequal expansion and contraction when a boiler is heated at a rate exceeding its natural draft, with water-tube boilers requiring at least two hours when raising steam. While the exact amount of time varied with each type of engine, several hours were always required to get up steam from a cold start. This was not always practical when a quick response was needed, for example, to haul anchor or raise sail. For combination sail-and-steam warships it was often better to have crewmen available at a moment's notice to perform such tasks.

The twin trunks for the lifting screws, the twin sternposts for rudder attachment (and associated twin stern concavities), and the low and lightly constructed bridge were all documented in the archaeological survey of the *Vixen*. The manually operated capstan on the ship's foredeck (Fig. 66) was of special interest, indicating as it did that even the heaviest tasks, such as raising and lowering the ship's anchors, were performed manually and not steam-assisted in any way. As we have seen, the merchant ships of this period, especially the large iron "windjammers," presented a mirror image of this pattern. Merchant vessels probably needed steam as quickly as warships, but it was easier to keep a small "donkey" boiler heated at all times. Ironclad steam-and-sail warships presented an extreme example of

Fig 66. Manually operated capstan on foredeck of *H.M.S. Vixen*. The use of hand-operated deck machinery like this provides a contrast to the steam-powered deck machinery found on commercial ships of this period (see Fig. 47).

labor-intensive manning, while iron merchant sailing vessels were chronically undermanned in order to cut operating costs.

In the absence of detailed figures, we can provisionally accept Lubbock's (1927: 62) estimate of crews of 18–20 men for a 2,000-ton iron barque of the late 1870s, which was a significant change from the wooden Blackwall Frigates (passenger and cargo vessels despite their military-sounding name) of the 1850s, which ranged in size from 1,000 to 1,600 tons (Lubbock, 1992; MacGregor, 1993: 30–31) and were manned by around 60 men. Thus in the span of twenty-five–thirty years we see a fourfold increase in tons per man in commercial sailing vessels. By contrast, the *Warrior* displaced 9,137 tons and had a crew of 707, with a tons-per-man ratio of 13:1. The *Gloire* displaced 5,630 tons and had a crew of 570, with a tons-per-man ratio of 10:1. The *Vixen* and the *Viper* displaced approximately 1,230 tons each with a crew complement of 80–83 men, producing a tons-per-man ratio of 15:1. These combination sail-and-steam warships had what amounted to two crews – one to sail the ship and another to tend the machinery. By 1870 the workload for each crewman aboard a commercial iron sailing ship of about 2,000 tons was almost ten times that of his counterpart aboard a combination sail-and-steam warship. In the case of wooden warships with combined sail-and-steam propulsion, figures for forty-one British vessels built or converted between 1848 and 1861 presented even lower tons-per-man ratios than the ironclads, ranging from 5 to 9:1 (data from Lambert, 1984: 122–40).

Figures available for the *Monitor*, the *Cerberus*, and other monitors are complicated by the fact that these ships rarely operated at sea. They required smaller crews in their coast-defense role, when they remained at anchor or dockside much of the time, than when they were en route to a new location. These ships also relied upon steam-powered auxiliary machinery more than their combination sail-and-steam contemporaries. This was especially true for heavy tasks like rotating the turrets but also included powering the ventilators and operating capstans to raise and lower anchors. The *Cerberus* and the *Magdala* each displaced 3,344 tons and had ships' companies that varied from thirty-seven while operating close to shore in a coast-defense mode to seventy-seven while at sea, for a tons-per-man ratio of from 43 to 90:1 depending upon the circumstances. The *Monitor*, with a displacement tonnage of 987 and a complement of sixty-two officers and crew, had a tons-per-man ratio of 16:1, which was closer to that of the combination sail-and-steam warships of the period.

To varying degrees, ironclad warships, like their wooden predecessors, included individuals counted as part of the ship's company but not directly involved with running the ship who had virtually no counterpart in the commercial sailing vessels of that period. The presence of gunners, doctor and purser, marines, and others contributed to the lower overall tons-per-man ratios of ironclad warships when compared with large, contemporary iron commercial sailing ships and should be taken into account in comparisons of commercial and naval vessels in this regard.

The Lessons of the Ironclads

The shipwrecks of the *Monitor*, the *Cerberus*, and the *Vixen* reveal different degrees of tactical indecision about the use of the new technologies of iron and steam. The low-freeboard, raftlike hulls of the monitors were poorly suited to operations at sea, yet each ship was called upon to make long ocean voyages. Neither the *Monitor* nor the *Cerberus*, however, was expected to fight at sea. The *Vixen*, by contrast, was intended for use at sea with the main battle fleet. Despite the presence of guns, the wreck reveals a primary function as a ram. By redeploying the *Vixen* and the *Viper* to the sheltered waters of Bermuda, the Admiralty made a rational decision that recognized the limitations of these ships both at sea and in battle. There they were available at the Royal Navy Dockyard to proceed to The Narrows and ram possible attackers while under the protection of the big guns of nearby shore defenses such as Fort Cunningham, Fort St. Catherine, Fort George, and Forts Albert and Victoria (Harris, 1997: 147–82). In short, while generally intended for decisive battles at sea, either through the use of gunnery or ramming (or, in some cases, *both*, though never in a manner explained well by naval tacticians), the *Monitor*, the *Cerberus*, and the *Vixen* all operated close to shore, with both the *Cerberus* and the *Vixen* serving as coast-defense vessels in conjunction with adjacent shore batteries. Here we see that new technologies of iron and steam originally meant for warfare at sea wound up functioning quite differently.

All of these three ships were built of wrought iron, as were most of their guns. This technology has virtually disappeared today, but in the late-nineteenth century it was a major industry. True steel production increased dramatically after the invention of the Bessemer converter in 1850, the open-hearth furnace in 1860, and further improvements in the 1870s, and steel replaced wrought iron everywhere in the 1880s. The industrial-scale wrought-iron technology needed to produce slabs of armor and rifled muzzle-loading guns has no modern counterpart. Despite its apparent industrial scale of production, wrought iron remained essentially a craft-based enterprise that required special, individualized skills and immense amounts of labor (Abell, 1981: 147). Lumps of wrought iron were hand-formed by "puddlers" and drawn by hand using large numbers of workmen (*Illustrated London News*, 14 September 1861) through rollers to produce the 11.4-centimeter-thick armor plate used on the *Vixen*. Riveting was done by hand with sledgehammers; in an 1860s shipyard it took five workmen to drive a rivet (Abell, 1981: 137). In other words, the construction of ironclads was as labor-intensive as their operation. A vivid account of this labor-intensity can be found in Charles Dickens's essay "Chatham Dockyard," which describes the construction of HMS *Achilles*, a large combination sail-and-steam ironclad launched in 1863. Fortunately, many of the products of wrought-iron technology have been preserved in the archaeological record and can be evaluated in relation to published manuals and other documents.

Remembering Pearl Harbor – But How?

At the opposite end of the continuum from the early ironclads, maritime archaeologists have explored and documented the warships sunk at Pearl Harbor by the Japanese on 7 December 1941. Archaeologists from the U.S. National Park Service, together with U.S Navy divers, recorded a variety of shipwreck materials in a series of nondestructive surveys conducted from 1983 to 1988. In the public imagination, pride of place belongs to the USS *Arizona*, which sustained the worst battle damage of any U.S. ship at Pearl Harbor as well as the largest loss of life (1,177 officers and men) in U.S. Navy history. Remains of some of the dead were recovered after the attack, but 1,102 men remain entombed in the ship. Today the *Arizona* is graced with a memorial cantilevered over and across the wreck, enabling visitors to view some of the ship's structure. The dead aboard the ship are classified as "lost at sea," and the Park Service now administers the *Arizona* Memorial as a war graves site.

In its archaeological survey of the Pearl Harbor wrecks, the Park Service's Submerged Cultural Resources Unit concentrated primarily on the archaeological documentation of the *Arizona* shipwreck. The *Arizona* epitomized the U.S. "battleship navy" that evolved during the 1920s and 1930s. The ship's keel was laid in 1914, and the *Arizona* was commissioned in 1916. It was 185 meters long and displaced 31,400 tons. It was heavily armed for that period, with a primary armament of twelve 14-inch guns and twenty-two 5-inch guns along with a variety of smaller guns and two submerged torpedo tubes. The ship's career was punctuated by peacetime service in the North Atlantic and the Caribbean. Like other battleships of that period, it underwent periodic overhauls and modifications, especially in 1929, when its earlier cage masts were replaced with tripod masts and it was provided with improved antiaircraft guns, armor, and "blisters" on the outer hull to protect it against torpedoes. At that time the ship also received new engines and boilers. The work was completed in 1931, and the ship was once again placed in commission as a fully modernized battleship. These efforts at modernization affected other U.S. battleships as well and should be viewed in the context of efforts to evade the limitations imposed by a series of international naval treaties and conferences during the interwar years. Prevented from building new or bigger battleships, nations turned to upgrading existing ships.

The *Arizona* was transferred to Hawaiian waters in 1940 in response to growing tensions with Japan. The ship was at sea until 6 December 1941, when it returned to Pearl Harbor and docked at the battleship moorings on the east side of Ford Island, and it was sunk there the following day. Throughout its history, the *Arizona* served in its designed role as a big-gun capital ship with a fleet of similar ships as the U.S. Navy's primary force in the Pacific. Improvements were made to the ship's antiaircraft defenses between 1939 and 1941, but these did not alter its character as a battleship designed to fight other large ships at sea. After the Japanese attack on Pearl Harbor, however, U.S. battle fleets based on battleships were replaced in the Pacific by aircraft-carrier task groups.

The most persistent of the myths that have grown up about the loss of the *Arizona* at Pearl Harbor is the idea that the ship was destroyed by a Japanese bomb dropped directly down its funnel (Lenihan and Murphy, 1989: 95). Japanese Petty Officer Noburo Kanai was credited with having dropped the fatal bomb (Prange, 1981: 513), which reportedly penetrated and exploded near turret number 2 (well back from the ship's bow and forward of the bridge). One of the most important findings of the underwater archaeology team was evidence of massive blast damage near the bow. The twist and scatter patterns of the hull plating indicated that the blast occurred deep within the ship, with its main force directed upward and outward – consistent with a magazine explosion forward of the foremost gun turret. Side elevations of the ship's hull show that the force of this explosion caused the entire forward turret to slump 6–8.5 meters below the deck line. There were no indications of comparable damage near the number 2 turret or at the midships area close to the funnel location, so the myth is not supported by the archaeological evidence.

The ship reportedly received further bomb hits as it sank, but these were hard to confirm because of the extensive salvage efforts conducted by the U.S. Navy during World War II. The ship's entire superstructure was removed and deposited on shore, obscuring any superficial damage. All of the ship's 14-inch guns were removed except for the pair in the forward, number 1, turret. The guns from the aft turrets were placed in shore batteries on Oahu. This effort at recycling was cut short by the war's end, and the batteries never became fully operational. The archaeology of the *Arizona* provided useful information about the proximate causes of the ship's loss, and it presents a kind of snapshot of a classic prewar battleship of the kind still viewed by many U.S. Navy officers as the centerpiece of the U.S. fleet at the time of the attack.

The *Arizona*, like several other battleships sunk at Pearl Harbor, was a late example of several dreadnoughts approved for construction by the U.S. Navy before World War I. These ships took their name from the *Dreadnought*, a radically new capital ship built for the Royal Navy and launched in 1906. This ship displaced 17,900 tons and was built in record time. It carried a main armament of ten 12-inch guns, was heavily armored, and could achieve a maximum speed of 20.9 knots with its steam turbine engines (Roberts, 1992). The *Dreadnought* rendered previous battleships obsolete and led to rapid imitation by other naval powers as they scrambled to build their own battleships to match its performance.

The *Dreadnought* never saw combat against other capital ships during World War I, but it did succeed in ramming and sinking a German U-boat in 1915. The *Dreadnought* and its successors lacked the sharply projecting, pointed ram bow of earlier battleships, suggesting that big guns rather than ramming were envisioned (at last) as the ship's definitive weapons – another break with tradition. Yet the *Dreadnought's* bow projected forward underwater in a manner superficially similar to earlier rams on warships. This design served to lighten the bow and provided greater lift and efficiency as the ship moved through the water. Thus the *Dreadnought's* sinking of a U-boat by ramming was ironic, since its bow shape was never intended for ramming.

The USS *Utah* was sunk by two aerial torpedoes at its moorings on the west site of Ford Island, Pearl Harbor (Hyde, 1982: 23). Fifty-eight officers and men are estimated to have been lost when it rolled over and sank upside down. The Japanese attackers had been alerted to the fact that *Utah* was no longer in service as a front-line battleship and were under orders to concentrate on more modern vessels. In their eagerness and inexperience, however, some of the torpedo bomber pilots attacked the ship anyway, sinking it at almost the same time as the *Arizona*.

Built in 1909, the *Utah* was one of the earliest dreadnoughts. It was larger than the *Dreadnought*, 159 meters long and displacing 21,825 tons. It originally had five gun turrets with two 12-inch guns each, along with sixteen 15-inch guns and other, smaller weapons. With a maximum speed of about 20 knots, it was formidable for a first-generation dreadnought, but by the time of the attack at Pearl Harbor it was one of the oldest ships in the fleet. Following service in the North Atlantic during and after World War I, it had been reclassified as an auxiliary ship in 1931. In 1932 it was converted into a sophisticated radio-controlled target ship that could perform battle maneuvers using remote control. The ship's 12-inch guns were removed, although the turrets were left in place (Fig. 67a). Gunnery exercises were conducted against targets towed by the *Utah*, while dive and horizontal bombers attacked the ship directly with practice bombs. In 1935 the *Utah* was once again converted, this time to an antiaircraft training ship. This conversion included installation of coordinated fire control for 50-caliber and 1.1-inch antiaircraft guns and in 1940 was modified to include twenty-five 5-inch guns as well. Further additions were made to the ship's antiaircraft armament in the summer of 1941 (Fig. 67b), including newly designed 20-mm weapons (Martinez, 1989: 42). The effective use of coordinated fire control to focus and direct antiaircraft fire using guns of different sizes was an advanced technique that anticipated the principal role of the battleship during World War II more fully than did the

Fig 67a. Aerial view of the *U.S.S. Utah* following the ship's conversion to a radio-controlled target ship. Fig 67b. Detail showing the installation of anti-aircraft guns shortly before the Pearl Harbor attack. Published with permission of the National Park Service.

big guns aboard *Arizona* and the other battleships sunk at Pearl Harbor. By the time the *Utah* returned to the Pacific Fleet in September 1941, it was probably the most advanced and heavily armed anti-aircraft ship in the world.

One can only speculate on what effect the anti-aircraft weapons aboard the *Utah* would have had on the Japanese attack if they had been manned and ready. Like so many others at Pearl Harbor, the ship was caught unprepared during a weekend break in port following training exercises. Documentary sources indicate that at the time of the attack the ship's anti-aircraft machine guns were stored below decks, with the ammunition secured in the magazines (Lenihan and Murphy, 1989: 107). The *Utah*, along with the *Arizona*, was one of the first ships sunk during the attack, so its antiaircraft defenses never had a chance to prove themselves. During World War II salvage attempts were made that left the ship resting on its port side at a 38-degree angle in its present position. In 1972 a small pier and memorial were constructed on the adjacent shore of Ford Island, but unlike the *Arizona* Memorial it is administered by the Navy and is open to the public only by special arrangement.

Like that of the *Arizona*, most of the *Utah*'s superstructure was removed during salvage operations in World War II. Much more of the ship's hull and decks is visible above water (Fig. 68), however, and, like the *Arizona*, the *Utah* wreck was surveyed and documented in detail by Park Service and Navy diver teams in 1983–88 (Lenihan and Murphy, 1989: 98–108). The ship's hull was virtually complete (Fig. 69). Even the limited portion exposed above the surface of the water presented a contrast between its original construction and later modifications. The shape of the hull up to the deckline revealed the ship's dreadnought ancestry, with a recessed bay originally constructed in 1909 as a casemate for some of the ship's secondary armament. Additional casemates were recorded under water. The bow also resembled that of the original *Dreadnought* of 1906, and, like the *Dreadnought*'s, its ramlike appearance was only superficial.

Above the deckline, however, considerable evidence remains of the late modifications to the ship in its final role as an antiaircraft vessel. A 5-inch gun was found mounted but without an enclosing shield on the top of the number 1 turret, while near the stern two similar guns were found mounted on top of the aft turrets, one of which still retained its enclosing shield. Two circles of bolts were visible above water on the deck, indicating

Fig 68. Above-water view of the wreck of the *U.S.S. Utah*, Pearl Harbor, Oahu.

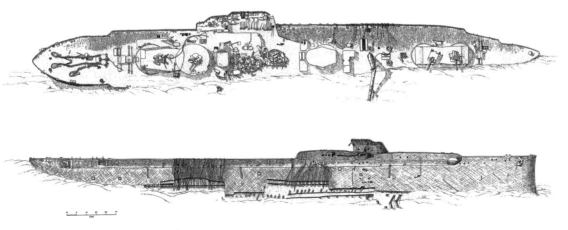

Fig 69. Plan drawing and elevation of *U.S.S. Utah* wreck. Published with permission of the National Park Service.

machine-gun positions. Mounts for smaller antiaircraft weapons were also recognizable on the deck areas amidships, one of which contained a 1.1-inch four-barreled gun that was undergoing evaluation at the time of the attack. One of the archaeological surprises of the survey was that so much of the *Utah*'s armament remained intact despite obvious indications of salvage following the ship's sinking. Other oddities included cement on portions of the deck, probably used to patch damage from practice bombs. Parts of the steel superstructure were visibly corroded where the wakes of passing boats that have created a broad wet-dry zone, and the remains of salvage attempts are visible in the form of cables draped over the wreck and patches on the hull near the stern.

Battleship Archaeology

The archaeological remains of the *Arizona* and the *Utah* present a Pompeii-like set of associations that indicate divergent pathways in the evolution of the battleship late in its life history. The results of the archaeological survey of the *Arizona* provided evidence of a renewed committment by U.S. battleship admirals to fleets of big-gun capital ships during the interwar years despite international agreements intended to limit the growth of such fleets. Visible modifications such as the base for one of the tripod masts showed that improvements to this ship were intended to maintain and enhance its role as a dreadnought. The ship retained its 14-inch guns throughout its history, and two are still present on the wreck. By contrast, the wreck of the *Utah* abounds with evidence for modifications leading to a new use for the battleship as an antiaircraft vessel. This, in fact, proved to be one of the primary roles of the battleship in World War II, especially when the need arose later in the war to ward off Japanese kamikaze attacks. For much of the war, U.S. battleships, heavily armed in a manner comparable to the *Utah*, served as antiaircraft platforms to escort carriers (O'Connell, 1991: 317). They were effective in this role, although other, cheaper types of ships could have accomplished this mission. This was not a role ever envisioned for the battleship, although it provided a limited ex post facto justification for building and maintaining these costly ships. It seems fair to say on archaeological grounds that the *Utah* represented a role that proved to be more important in World War II than that of the *Arizona* and other battleships of its type.

The divergence of roles evidenced by the archaeology of the Pearl Harbor wrecks was presaged by similar divergences among the early ironclads. Some, like the pure steam-powered, turreted gun-bearing armored

ship, had a long run, while some, like the sail-and-steam-powered turreted ships, did not. Others, like the broadside-battery steam-and-sail ironclad and the ram, were iterations of the new technologies of steam and
iron that persisted longer at sea than they deserved to. Like the dreadnoughts, rams were chronic underachievers. As is apparent from the
archaeological examination of the *Vixen*, engineering anomalies suggest
confusion and indecision on the part of naval planners and designers trying to decide how best to use new technologies spawned by the Industrial
Revolution.

11 · The Archaeology of Maritime Infrastructure

Ships of all times and places operate within an infrastructure of harbors, canals, shipyards, coastal defenses, ports, docks, and specialized cargo handling and processing facilities that is as important as the ships themselves. The exploration and recording of these kinds of structures has been an important part of underwater archaeology for almost a century. The French engineer Gaston Jondet pioneered the archaeological study of submerged port facilities at Pharos, near Alexandria, in the early 1900s, and André Poidebard, a French Jesuit priest and scholar, carried out similar research at Tyre in 1934–36. Poidebard's studies influenced later research and introduced the concept of the *proto-harbor*, applying it specifically to the pre-Roman ports of the Levantine coast (Frost, 1972: 97). The coastline of the eastern Mediterranean, including that of modern Syria and Israel, lacks good natural harbors and is exposed to the full force of Mediterranean winds and waves. This stretch of coastline was close to important centers of land commerce in the ancient world, so there were powerful economic incentives for the development of trading ports along this coast from the Bronze Age on.

The idea of the proto-harbor was that the earliest ports along this coast would not have been built up in their entirety but instead would have depended on the presence of natural reefs, rock outcrops, and offshore islands that could be modified by flattening and shaping to provide good anchorages by extensive rock cutting. Rocks removed from such cuttings would have been used to build walls and quays as needed, mainly to supplement or fill in natural formations. Archaeological examples of this technique abound, with the island of Arwad, surveyed by the English maritime archaeologist Honor Frost in 1963–64, being an especially well documented case.

Frost (1972b) expanded the concept of the proto-harbor in the eastern Mediterranean to explain the volume of pre-Roman trade between Turkey and Egypt, as evidenced by the spacing of major harbors along the coast. These rock-cut harbors required islands large enough to be habitable, and three of these – Arwad, Tyre, and Pharos – were studied in detail. This system of three major harbors was supported by minor ports such as Byblos, Sidon, and Athlit, which also had rock-cut anchorages. For coast-hugging merchantmen, a system of harbors along this difficult coast was essential for the conduct of trade, and, as Frost (1972b: 97) points out, this is still true to some degree today. Aerial survey and photography, land surveying, and underwater survey methods were all used by Frost and her associates to record these pre-Roman harbors and anchorages. Along with trade goods found in land excavations and shipwreck remains, these ports provided a further indication of the extent and patterning of maritime commerce by the Phoenicians and their contemporaries. It is in the Roman era, however, that we encounter the first truly large-scale port facilities, with the Levantine coast providing perhaps the most dramatic example.

Ancient Caesarea Maritima

Prior to the Romans, the port of Caesarea was probably an example of the sort of minor anchorage described by Frost. It lies along a particularly bleak stretch of the Levantine coast. A Hellenistic settlement, fortifications and some limited pre-Roman harbor facilities have been identified archae-ologically at this site (Raban, 1989), and Roman-era chroniclers such as Josephus pointed out the dangerously exposed conditions of this stretch of coastline (Oleson and Branton, 1992: 50). The only type of stone locally available for building was a soft sandstone that was poorly suited to mon-umental construction of any kind. Therefore, in more ways than one this locality might seem to have been an unpromising place for what was one of the greatest artificial harbors of the ancient world.

It was these difficulties, however, that determined Caesarea's monu-mental scale. Once the decision was taken by Herod, the Roman gover-nor of the region, to proceed with its construction in 22 B.C., massive efforts were required to overcome a host of practical problems brought about by the exposed nature of the site and its distance from Italy. The Classical archaeologist and historian Robert Hohlfelder (1992) has reviewed the geopolitical factors that affected Herod's decision, emphasizing his desire to create a harbor that might replace Alexandria as Rome's principal entrepôt in the eastern Mediterranean. The Israeli archaeologist Avner Raban, one of the principals in the Caesarea Ancient Harbor Excavation Project, has further suggested that, by constructing a year-round port and providing an anchorage from which merchantmen could sail earlier than from any other Levantine port, Herod sought to monopolize maritime trade in the eastern Mediterranean (1992: 74).

Although the great harbor initiated by Herod continued in use until the the third century A.D., it never displaced the port of Alexandria. As Hohlfelder (1992: 77) points out:

> The harbour complex was too grand, too costly to maintain, and too overbuilt for the needs of the provincial capital in Palestine. Roman Caesarea required only an all-weather harbour: it did not need warehouses, towers, and support facilities on the very breakwaters . . . Nor did it need the sophisticated engineering that had permitted Herod to extend his city out into the sea.

The Romano-Jewish historian Josephus described the harbor at Caesarea in his history of the Jewish Wars (Thackeray, 1927). His account was written approximately 80 years after the harbor was built, so he did not witness its construction. Nevertheless, Josephus described three columns on each side flanking the harbor's entrance, with a massive statue atop each one, along with other grand public buildings. While ample evidence exists today of the harbor's breakwaters, Josephus's description stated that their foundations were made entirely of stone blocks, most of them measuring 15 meters long, 3 meters wide, and 2.7 meters thick.

As underwater archaeologists have found, however, the key element in the construction of the artificial harbor at Caesarea, as in other Roman harbors, was the use of hydraulic concrete. This technology appeared by at least the second century B.C. at the Roman port of Cosa and characteristically employed pozzolana, a form of volcanic sand from the vicinity of Puteoli near Mt. Vesuvius in Italy, mixed with lime, clay, metallic salts, and a fine aggregate of sand and crushed stone (Brandon, 1996). Hydraulic concrete required wooden forms to mold it into the desired shape.

Although volcanic sands from other regions closer to Palestine would probably have worked as well (Oleson and Branton, 1992: 58), the Roman engineers at Caesarea requisitioned hundreds of shiploads of pozzolana from Italy. Chemical analyses of samples of the volcanic components of concrete from the Caesarea breakwaters and seventeen sites and source regions revealed that the powdery volcanic ash in the Caesarea concrete probably came from the environs of Mount Vesuvius (Oleson and Branton, 1992: 60). It appears that Roman engineers at Caesarea never deviated from their original formula for hydraulic concrete, even when adequate sources were available nearby. Other building materials, such as marble, were shipped from Italy as well, making the logistics of the construction of the harbor at Caesarea exceptional.

The Roman architect and chronicler Vitruvius described the use of hydraulic concrete and the construction of large breakwaters in a series of much-quoted texts (Granger, 1934). These texts mentioned several important details, such as the use of double-walled wooden frameworks for forms in which to pour the concrete (for non-pozzolana concrete, however), but were vague on other points such as the ways in which these forms were moved and positioned on the seabed. Much of the archaeological analysis, therefore, focused on this issue. Unlike Vitruvius's texts, the archaeologists took into account the practical difficulties involved in this type of construction, and they addressed limitations imposed by the conditions under which these building efforts took place.

The Roman harbor at Caesarea consisted of two massive breakwaters that enclosed the principal anchorage and an inner harbor complex for smaller craft. The breakwaters were connected to natural headlands at a settlement of pre-Roman origin known as Straton's Tower. This earlier construction may have been a proto-harbor at Caesarea prior to the appearance of Roman engineering on a large scale. Some of the concrete blocks examined underwater by the Caesarea project's divers showed the impressions of simple boxlike wooden forms supported by horizontal beams in a manner comparable to those described by Vitruvius (Oleson and Branton, 1992: 65) and seen at other ancient Roman harbors (Brandon, 1996). In 1982, however, evidence was found in a location designated as Area K of wooden forms of a type not previously seen or described, and further archaeological work concentrated on this mode of construction.

The northern breakwater projected 240 meters west from the shore. It was the better-preserved of the two breakwaters, and at its seaward end there was a massive heap of jumbled blocks of local sandstone thought to have been used for the Roman pier head. Several of these blocks had square sockets made of lead, which were probably used with iron clamps to connect and stabilize the blocks in their original position to form a solid face for the channel entrance. In addition, a concrete block 15 meters long, 11.5 meters wide, and 2 meters high was found at the northwestern tip of the northern breakwater. Together with the stone blocks, this concrete block protected the the most exposed end of the breakwater against the southwesterly storms that are a major hazard to navigation along this coast. There were archaeological indications of a desilting system using sluices along the southern breakwater to draw away up to about 10,000 cubic meters of sand and mud each year. The project archaeologists interpreted this as an adaptation to local conditions rather than general Roman engineering practice (Oleson and Branton, 1992: 55). The two breakwaters were built up from a series of lattice-like structures of wooden forms within huge, rectangular caissons. Concrete was poured into each interior cell once the caissons were submerged in place at their intended locations to provide the necessary mass to withstand wave action. Discussion continues among archaeologists about how this feat was accomplished. The likeliest explanation involves the use of double outer walls for each rectangular structure. These were prefabricated on shore and made watertight so they could be floated into position. This type of construction was especially evident in Area K, where the outer walls of the caisson forms resembled contemporary Roman ship construction methods (shell-first, with mortise-and-tenon joinery). These floating structures were, in effect, one-way barges that were maneuvered into position by boats and sunk in place (Brandon, 1996: 34–39).

The double-walled outer hull of each of these bargelike wooden structures was watertight, but the interior cells were open. By admitting water into the outer hull, the entire structure could be settled in place on the seabed. Then the hydraulic concrete was poured into the interior spaces, with the concrete resting directly in contact with the seabed. This scenario provides a parsimonious answer to two key questions about the construction of the breakwaters: how the wooden forms were fabricated and moved to the precise locations where they came to rest and how the base

304 · The archaeology and social history of ships

of each concrete structure was firmly affixed to the seabed. Another technical question addressed by the archaeologists at Caesarea concerned the actual pouring of the concrete. It is clear from chemical analysis that this was done in layers, with an initial half-meter layer of hydraulic pozzolana concrete at the bottom of each caisson followed by a second layer of non-hydraulic concrete and a final layer of the hydraulic variety. Perhaps this layered method resulted from temporary shortages of pozzolana stocks at the building site during the construction (Brandon, 1996: 40).

The total length of the two breakwaters was over 800 meters, providing a roomy outer harbor that was fully protected from winds and waves. The construction methods as well as the logistics of transporting materials such as pozzolana indicate that this was an extremely labor-intensive effort. The work as Caesarea was on a scale comparable to the huge floating concrete caissons ("Mulberries") that were fabricated in England and towed across the English Channel to form an artificial harbor following the invasion of Normandy during World War II. In the case of Caesarea, however, it was all done without the benefit of modern machinery. It is no exaggeration to suggest, as Hohlfelder (1996) does, that the harbor was the centerpiece of Herod's city and the key to both its success as a port and to its eventual failure as a result of maintenance requirements that exceeded its productive capacity.

Not surprisingly, an important Roman-era shipwreck was found near Caesarea, along the shore outside the harbor area. It appears to have been relatively large – comparable in size to the Madrague de Giens ship – with a minimum length of 34 meters and a beamy hull about 10 meters wide as estimated from limited amounts of wooden structure including double-layered hull planking and stringers. It was heavily framed and may have been constructed frame-first. Estimates based upon admittedly uncertain evidence suggest a date for the ship's loss of sometime during the first century A.D. – that is, early in the history of the harbor (Fitzgerald, 1994). No unambiguous evidence indicates that this ship was directly involved with the construction history of the Caesarea harbor, but it seems likely that it was. At least one scholar (Raban, 1992: 74) has argued that it was a bulk carrier used for the transport of building materials from Italy, but no remains of the ship's cargo were found at the wreck site.

The monumental scale of the harbor was as much a mark of Imperial Rome's maritime commerce as the great Alexandrian grain ships described in texts and the largest Roman-era shipwrecks. The details of its construction are better-known through underwater archaeology than from historical texts. Josephus's claim that the breakwaters' foundations were made of massive dressed stones was not supported, and there has been no evidence so far of the great statues that he reported. In the case of Vitruvius, none of his instructions for the use of caissons and hydraulic concrete could have accurately predicted what archaeologists would find in the Area K breakwater. Instead of confirming the historical accounts, underwater archaeologists at Caesarea encountered evidence of construction practices that were measurably different from information provided in the texts. These findings have expanded our understanding and provided a detailed appreciation for ancient Roman techniques of harbor construction under extreme conditions. Another example of how underwater archaeology can expand our knowledge of maritime infrastructure can be found in the wreck of H.M. Floating Dock, *Bermuda*.

The Naval Dockyard and Floating Dock, *Bermuda*

The Dockyard on Ireland Island at Bermuda's West End was intended to provide a base for the Royal Navy to control maritime activity along the east coast of North America following the American Revolution (Wilkinson, 1973). Major construction began there, however, only after the arrival of the first convict ship, the *Antelope*, in 1824. Experience during the War of 1812, when persistent easterly winds had kept a Royal Navy force bottled up inside the Bermuda anchorage for several weeks, led the Admiralty to question its utility as a port. It was only with the advent of steam that it became possible to traverse The Narrows even in unfavorable winds, and the development of a dockyard there could be seriously envisioned.

The construction of the dockyard was monumental in scale. Local supplies of hard limestone were quickly exhausted in an effort to build the facing for the Commissioner's House, a grand multistoried structure with a prefabricated iron framework shipped in numbered pieces from England. Softer local limestone, supplemented by granite and other hard stone imported from England, was then used to complete the work, which was supervised by the Royal Corps of Engineers and by Royal Marines. While convicts were building the Commissioner's House, they were simultaneously engaged in a more expedient form of construction, much of which is now partially submerged. Hard limestone from a quarry at Moresby Plain on Ireland Island was transported by barge to a series of stone-rubble embayments adjacent to the Commissioner's House. These structures were shown as natural reefs on a hydrographic survey chart produced by the H.M.S. *Thunder* survey of 1843–45 and were mapped in detail by underwater archaeologists in 1986–88 (Gould, 1990b). Side by side at the dockyard and dated to the same period, there is evidence of elaborate, preplanned construction – often well documented like the Commissioner's House – associated with ad hoc structures like the semi-submerged stone barge embayments that became known through the process of archaeological recording.

During the initial period of construction, Royal Navy ships were careened at dockside whenever it was necessary to make repairs or to clean marine growth off the underwater portions of the ship's hull. This process involved removal of loose equipment, such as guns, from the ship, and then by tilting the ship, first on one side and then on the other, using winches on shore with ropes attached to the ship's mast. With the arrival of ironclads and other ships that were too large to be careened, the Admiralty recognized that Bermuda's usefulness as a base depended on having a dry dock for this type of servicing. Parliamentary debates in 1862 called for a dry dock in Bermuda, but surveys indicated that a conventional dry dock would not be practical because seawater flowed freely with the tides through the porous limestone bedrock. A radical solution to this problem was suggested in the form of a scale model for a new type of floating dock, which was presented to Parliament in 1866 by Lord Paget. A patent for the Bermuda floating dock was published by James Campbell in 1868. This model (now at the Science Museum, South Kensington, London) represented the largest floating dock ever built up to that time and the first one ever made entirely of wrought iron (Gould and Souza, 1996: 6). Unlike earlier floating docks built in Britain, this one was to be fully constructed and then towed to the location of intended use. Until then, the practice had been to ship the components to the intended dockyard for final assembly on site. The most visible feature that set the Bermuda floating dock apart from others was its U-shaped cross-section (Fig. 70). Contemporary engineering journals (*Engineering*, 10 October 1866: 294) made much of the fact that the chambers in the floating dock

GENERALIZED RECONSTRUCTION OF H.M. FLOATING DOCK "BERMUDA"

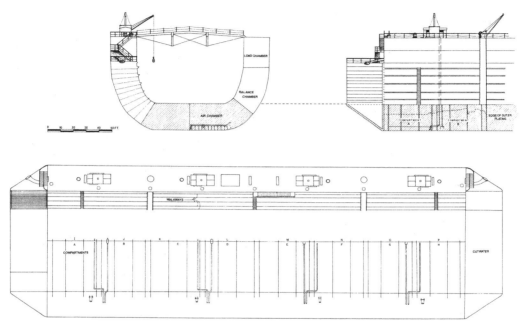

Fig 70. Scale drawing of H.M. Floating Dock, *Bermuda*. The hatched area shows how much of the original structure remains at the wreck site at Spanish Point, Bermuda. Drawn by George Montgomery.

Bermuda could be differentially filled and emptied to provide a self-careening capability (Fig. 71). Not only was the floating dock expected to lift and service ships up to about 10,000 tons displacement but also it had itself to be careened to clean marine growth off its hull and to service and clear its underwater intake valves and drain. Its size of 8,340 tons displacement made it impossible to careen by more conventional methods.

Construction of the floating dock began at the Campbell and Johnstone shipyard on the Thames in 1866. The work was watched closely by the British and Bermudian press and by leading engineering journals, which reported that up to one thousand four hundred workmen were needed at one time during construction. As a result of this public scrutiny, the failed first attempt to launch the floating dock on 2 September 1868 was widely noted, but on 13 September the launch was successful (Fig. 72). The floating dock then wintered submerged near Sheerness until the following

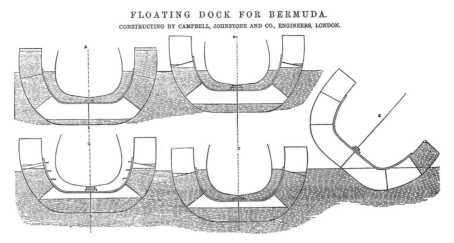

FLOATING DOCK FOR BERMUDA.
CONSTRUCTING BY CAMPBELL, JOHNSTONE AND CO., ENGINEERS, LONDON.

Fig 71. Contemporary engineering drawings showing the Bermuda Floating Dock in cross-section with various chambers filled and emptied for raising, lowering, and careening the Dock.

June, when it was made ready for the trip to Bermuda. Two of the Royal Navy's largest steam-and-sail ironclads, *Agincourt* and *Northumberland*, took the dock in tow to Madeira. From Madeira to Bermuda the tow was taken over by the ironclads *Warrior, Terrible,* and *Black Prince*.

The tow from England to Bermuda occurred without incident. A journal kept by an anonymous officer (One of Those on Board, 1870) recorded engineering details that were designed specifically for the floating dock's voyage, including a midships rudder (not very successful), a sail set inside the U-shaped hull to take advantage of following winds, and iron-plated cutwaters around the submerged ends of the dock to reduce drag. The tow covered a total distance of 3,985 nautical miles at an average speed of 4.8 knots and on two occasions exceeding 6 knots. When the floating dock arrived at The Narrows on 28 July 1869, the large ironclads towing it were too long to pass through the channel and had to remain outside. The steam tug *Spitfire*, two small twin-screwed ironclads, *Vixen and Viper,* and a twin-screwed dispatch boat, *Lapwing*, completed the tow to the dockyard. (The much-reproduced chromo-lithograph of 1869 showing the *Warrior* resting inside the floating dock in Bermuda with the dock in an elevated position [*Engineering*, 4 June 1869] is imaginative but historically inaccurate [Gould, 1990c].)

Fig 72. Contemporary drawing of the successful launch of the Floating Dock, *Bermuda*, in England on 13 September 1868. In addition to showing the shape and size of this object, the illustration reveals the penchant of Victorian-era artists for portraying engineering triumphs of gargantuan size with people shown like ants.

Public interest in the Floating Dock declined after its arrival at the Dockyard, perhaps because it performed so well that its activities were perceived as routine and no longer newsworthy. Like the outer harbor at Caesarea Maritima, the floating dock was the centerpiece of the dockyard operations in Bermuda.

The floating dock effectively performed its functions at the dockyard for thirty-seven years. Its efficiency was occasionally noted when ships in excess of 6,000 tons were lifted and serviced using its full capabilities. The servicing of HMS *Challenger* during its oceanographic survey of Bermuda in 1873 was also an occasion for publicity and photographs. There is no accurate tally of the lifts accomplished by the floating dock in the course of its career, but seventy-eight lifts were recorded by dockyard officials and by a dockyard worker, D. B. B. Barritt, from 1869 until 1906 (*Bermuda Royal Gazette*, 15 December 1874; unpublished diary of D. B. B. Barritt, 1891–1910) and the total was certainly much higher. Even after a new steel floating dock went into service in 1905, the old dock lifted at least one more ship, HMS *Pallas*, in 1906. Although dislodged from its moorings by hurricanes and damaged by minor dockyard accidents, its activities were never seriously interrupted.

The final disposal of the floating dock is poorly understood. According to one account, it broke loose in a storm while being towed from the dockyard by German ship breakers. Another story is that the Germans were too slow in scrapping it and dockyard authorities towed it to Spanish Point and beached it there for them to complete the work (Arnell, 1979: 48; Willock, 1988: 55; Downing and Harris, 1984). The Barritt diaries, however, indicate that it was sold for scrap in 1906 and in January 1907 a party of German workmen arrived at the dockyard and began dismantling it. By November the bright metals (copper, bronze, and brass), teak, and some accessible iron plating had been removed from it, and in March 1908 tugs hauled what remained to a small cove at Spanish Point, directly opposite the dockyard across the sound. A marine surveyor's report for 11 April 1908 indicated that the floating dock was secured with hawsers at Spanish Point attached to anchors embedded in the ground. The agent and manager in charge of the dock had explained to the surveyors that he had feared it would sink inside the dockyard while it was being scrapped and had therefore recommended moving it to the shallow waters of Spanish Point before undertaking further salvage. During the tow the floating dock struck the dockyard breakwater, damaging its port side, and it was further damaged by storms at Spanish Point. The surveyors concluded that further efforts at salvage were impractical and issued a certificate of abandonment on 18 April 1908.

Photographs taken at Spanish Point in 1914 (Bermuda Archives) showed the remains of the floating dock during the salvage process, which, according to an elderly eyewitness interviewed in 1980, continued for two years (*Bermuda Royal Gazette*, 21 October 1980). These photographs revealed that approximately one-third of the floating dock's structure remained more or less intact at that time, in particular the bottom chambers and centerline bulkhead as well the side plating and frames curving upward from the turn of the bilge. One picture, viewing the wreck from the landward end, showed the framework of one of the cutwaters, although with the outer plating removed. Another, at the seaward end, showed the plating being removed and placed on a barge. In this picture, the outer plating on the seaward cutwater was still in place, so the photograph must have been taken at an earlier stage in the salvage process. In this same picture the floating dock's two caissons, originally inserted at each of the open, U-shaped ends of the dock when it was in use, could be seen resting on their sides in the water off to the right side of the main body of the wreck.

The floating dock originally contained sixteen watertight compartments, eight on each side of the longitudinal centerline bulkhead, separated from each other by watertight double bulkheads and divided by two bulkheads that were not watertight. Apart from its use in raising and lowering the dock, this dense compartmentalization added strength to a structure that was already strong by virtue of its heavy iron plating and closely spaced rivets. Viewed end-on, the compartments were originally divided into three sets of chambers. The lowest, termed air chambers, were arranged symmetrically on either side of the centerline bulkhead. The air chambers had the largest volume of all the chambers within the floating dock and were the primary devices for lifting and lowering it ("Rules for Working the Floating Dock," n.d., Bermuda Maritime Museum). Above the air chambers on both sides were balance chambers, which served as the primary devices for controlling side-to-side tilt or heel, and above these were the load chambers, which stood above the water to the dock's full height. Special instructions cautioned that opening the valves to the balance chambers when there was water in the load chambers would cause the floating dock to heel over quickly and uncontrolled. Apart from the ability to careen itself, this tilting feature allowed the dock to accommodate off-center and unbalanced loads and therefore to service more than one ship at a time even if they were of different sizes and weights. Photographs taken sometime late in the floating dock's career show two small ships inside the dock (Photos 1/109 and 1/111, Bermuda Archives).

Intermittent research was conducted on the floating dock from 1986 to 1991 by trained volunteers sponsored by Earthwatch and the Bermuda Maritime Museum. This initial work was followed by nondestructive site recording and documentation in 1992–93, this time aided by the Bermuda Sub-Aqua Club and Maritime Archaeological and Historical Society (MAHS) of Washington, D.C. These studies resulted in a detailed trilateration map of the wreck, including the caissons and all elements of attached structure (Gould and Souza, 1996). The site plan (Fig. 73) shows that 89.5 meters of continuous, attached iron structure remains of the

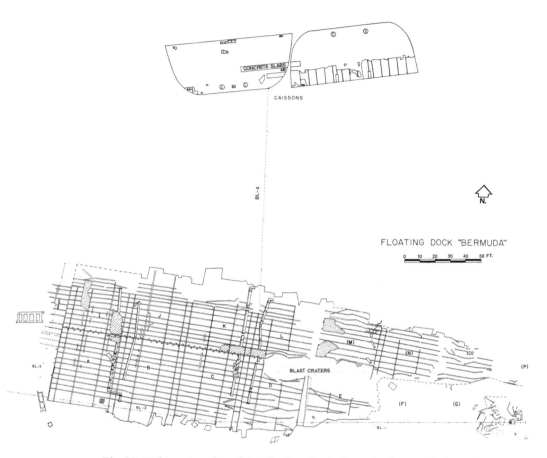

Fig 73. Trilateration plan of the Floating Dock, *Bermuda*, along with the caissons.

floating dock's original 115.6-meter length as measured along the center-line. Additional elements of structure extend a further 8.2 meters to the east before disappearing below the present siltline, but these frames and pieces of plating are badly twisted and may no longer be attached to the main body of the wreck. The beam dimensions of the Floating Dock's structure survive to a maximum of 34.6 meters of continuously connected frames and plates out of its original 37.6-meter width.

Visible on the site plan is a cratered area along the midsection of the wreck from compartments labeled L and D eastward. Because the frames and longitudinal stringers around the cratered area are all bent outward from it, this seems to be the principal center of the blast damage caused by dynamiting, probably during the 1950s or early 1960s, when there were attempts to remove the rusting remains of the floating dock for both aesthetic and practical reasons. Additional blast damage is visible in the form of V-shaped fractures extending vertically from the tops of nearly all the bulkheads on both sides of the midsection of the wreck along with large pieces of iron plating, especially on the north side, that were separated from their frames but are still attached to each other and to the main structure. Loose pieces of plating and bent frames scattered around the wreck are also attributed to blast effects. In order to measure the extent of blast damage, surviving longitudinal stringers on the inside of the outer hull of the wreck were examined for bends, breaks, or twists and were enumerated by compartment in relation to whole and unbent stringers. In all, 136 longitudinal stringers and stringer fragments were identified, 75 of which were bent or broken, and most of the broken ones occurred adjacent to the crater area at the landward end of the wreck. These figures apply only to preserved elements of structure and not to portions that are missing completely and so are relative, as opposed to absolute, measures of blast damage.

The seaward end of the wreck is exposed to strong wave action whenever storms come from the southwest, and considerable erosion of wrought-iron plating above the low-tide mark is evident. The double bulkhead at this end was photographed in 1986, when a large part of the structure was visible high above the water. During the 1992 field season a series of southwest storms battered the wreck, and the upper part of the bulkhead was bent by the force of the waves. Weakened by corrosion at the intertidal zone of the wreck, the plates and bulkheads at the seaward end are now deteriorating rapidly and likely to collapse. The midsection of the wreck is the best-preserved part and here the massive longitudinal bulkhead along the centerline survives to its full height along with substantial lengths of pipe and most of the outer hull plating. What we see today represents about one-sixth of the original structure, with only portions of the bottom and adjacent turn of the hull preserved.

The compartments shown in the site plan are all remnants of the original air chambers used to lift and lower the dock. No trace of the balance or load chambers remains today. Three rows of pipes were found extending across the width of the wreck through the centerline bulkhead.

None of the machinery originally associated with these pipes is present, however, so their operation remains obscure. There is one well-preserved grate (Feature M), still attached to the outer hull plating of air chamber A, which was used for the intake and expulsion of water from the chamber to the sea. Other bits and pieces of various items scattered throughout the wreck site hint at its original fittings and hardware. A possible ladder (F-5) and nearby length of chain (F-6) as well as a robust rectangular, box-like structure (F-3, a chain locker?) were associated with the landward end of the wreck.

The two caissons resting on their sides to the north of the main body of the wreck are the best-preserved elements at the site. Each caisson originally weighed about 400 tons. When the floating dock was in use, these caissons were positioned vertically at each end to contain and expel water when it was lifted. When not in use or when removed to allow a ship to move in or out, they were moored next to the dock as pontoons. The end-to-end positioning of the caissons, which has remained undisturbed since 1914, suggests that they were placed that way intentionally, perhaps for use as an impromptu pier.

Unlike the main body of the floating dock, the caissons show no obvious signs of blast damage or salvage apart from the removal of bronze, copper, and brass fittings. The internal structure of each caisson consisted of X-shaped supporting frames across each compartment. Both caissons contained relatively well-preserved machinery consisting of valves and valve trunks. Two circular openings along the bottom edge of each caisson were connected to valves in iron casings, and each valve in turn was connected to a solid iron shaft that extended vertically from the teakwood top deck of each caisson, where it was encased by a rectangular iron trunk at the point where it met the underside of the caisson deck. Gears and handles for these shafts are no longer present (except for those inside the iron casings), but their original presence and location can be inferred. During operations the caissons stood upright, and the two valves at the bottom of them were rotated using handles on the top deck to admit or expel water, adjusting the water level inside the floating dock when a ship was settled on blocks for servicing. The original caisson machinery is well enough preserved to allow archaeologists to relate the operating procedures presented in the instruction manual to the mechanisms used to carry them out, thus providing information beyond what the written sources contain.

The mere fact that the dock and its caissons are preserved at all after being subjected to repeated destructive processes since arriving at Spanish Point in 1908 is testimony to the robust nature of Victorian-era engineering and construction. Its builders and the Admiralty intended the floating dock to operate in a remote part of the empire where dependability and self-sufficiency were important for its success.

Infrastructure and Empire in Maritime History

Historical and archaeological evidence shows that the Bermuda floating dock was a unique, one-off technological development designed to operate under special conditions imposed by Bermudian geography. It should not be viewed as a stage within a linear progression in floating dock technology but was more a response to local conditions. The great concrete breakwaters of the Roman port of Caesarea and the Bermuda floating dock represented extreme examples of monumental infrastructure during the peaks of their respective empires. Despite the existence of standardized manuals for their construction and use, these structures showed unique characteristics which underwater archaeology was able to reveal. These monumental structures embodied the dominant technologies of their period, namely hydraulic concrete and wrought iron, yet each was so unusual when examined in detail that it would be hard to claim that either one was typical of harbor or dockyard construction in a more general sense. They do, however, provide a baseline against which to compare with the findings of underwater archaeologists in other locations, such as the recent discoveries in the submerged harbor of ancient Alexandria (Empereur, 1999).

12 · The Future of Underwater Archaeology

The most serious challenge to underwater archaeology today is counteracting the effects of treasure hunting. These effects are both direct and indirect. The direct ones have to do with the destruction of submerged archaeological sites, and the indirect ones arise from the confusion created by the appropriation of the techniques of underwater archaeology for profit instead of preservation.

Peter Benchley (1989: 74) celebrates the joys of finding and taking objects from shipwrecks in Bermuda as follows:

> Have you ever lain on the bottom in a sand hole, surrounded by ancient timbers, let some sea water trickle past your mouthpiece and tasted something wondrous and exotic and suddenly realized that what you were tasting was 300-year old cedar? It is a taste so rich, so redolent of yore, that you can imagine yourself standing on the quarterdeck, can feel the roll of the sea beneath your feet, can hear the slap of canvas and the thunder of cannon . . .

However romantically phrased, the approach advocated by Benchley and others is entrepreneurial, aimed at increasing the sale value of artifacts recovered from shipwrecks whenever possible. Behar (1986) and Wilkinson (1991) warn investors to regard treasure-hunting schemes as high-risk ventures with little likelihood of profit, pointing to a tendency for otherwise rational people to make irrational decisions when it comes to investments of this kind. The best litmus test for distinguishing treasure hunting from archaeology is what happens to the materials after they are recovered. Treasure hunters often sell off valuable items and transfer the burden of conservation and storage of more ordinary materials such as ships' timbers and cannonballs to museums. Breaking up collections in this way violates the principle of association that is the basis of all archaeological science. Treasure hunters regard shipwrecks as lodes of valuables to be mined, and their aim is to make as much profit as possible as quickly as possible, which usually means using destructive methods such as blasting and scouring the wreck site. For example, the use of stern-mounted, hinged and angled pipes called "mailboxes" by the Florida treasure hunter Mel Fisher in his search for the *Atocha* enabled him to focus the propeller wash of his boat directly down at the seabed (Fig. 74a–b). In the shallow waters off the Florida Keys, this blasting technique quickly cratered the seabed and blew away timbers and other vulnerable materials but left dense, compact substances such as gold and silver bars intact and exposed. This approach has much in common with the concept of salvage, in which shipwrecks and their contents are recovered and "returned to commerce." The methods are similar, although the materials recovered by salvors do not always qualify as treasure. In both cases the profit motive is uppermost. Salvors, like treasure hunters, tend to concentrate their investment and efforts on the recovery of high-value items (for example, phosphor-bronze ship propellers, priority and sumptuary cargoes, and specialized ship fittings) in the absence of gold and silver.

In the case of treasure hunting, there is a growing tendency to appropriate archaeology as a means of enhancing the monetary value of the finds. For example, Spanish doubloons and eight-real silver coins from Mexico (known as pieces-of-eight) have a basic monetary value derived from the current price of the constituent metal. To increase the price of such coins beyond this level, treasure hunters may create "sea stories" about the shipwreck and thereby promote a bogus historical association that will attract buyers. It can be profitable for treasure-hunting firms to create archaeological dramas on the seabed – nowadays recorded on video – to create the impression that the historical associations of the wreck site are being faithfully recorded. Treasure hunting might be viewed as a victimless crime were it not for the public's interest in the remains of its past. Like endangered species, archaeological sites, once demolished by treasure hunters or relic collectors, are gone forever.

Fig 74a–b. Treasure-hunter Mel Fisher's boat and his stern-mounted "mailboxes" (blasters) at Key West, Florida. These devices are hinged over the stern and can be positioned to focus the propwash straight down to the seabed. They can crater the seabed to depths of around 8 meters.

The Demolition of the DeBraak

The story of the *DeBraak* is one of those rare examples of a detailed account of treasure hunting by someone other than a treasure hunter. Archaeologists rarely, if ever, write about treasure-hunting episodes in detail, mainly because they do not have complete access to the materials from such wrecks and are rarely in a position to give a full account of what happened. Statements by the treasure hunters themselves cannot be trusted, since they exist mainly to support the sale of artifacts they have recovered.

The HMS *DeBraak* was a British warship that sank while escorting a Spanish merchant ship near the mouth of the Delaware River in May 1798. The ship's log and journals were also lost, but rumors persisted that it had been carrying Spanish coins and other treasure (Brodeur, 1988). Encouraged by such rumors, salvage efforts were undertaken with grappling hooks and vague compass bearings in the 1930s, and in 1984 treasure hunters led by the commercial diver and entrepreneur Harvey Harrington mounted a campaign using a magnetometer and side-scan sonar. Promising indications including an anchor and a cannon as well as gold and silver coins quickly led to a falling-out among the original partners and the formation of two separate salvage companies to exploit the wreck. This dispute, in turn, complicated the salvors' efforts to gain a license from the state of Delaware to work the wreck, but eventually Harrington's company, Sub-Sal, prevailed. The publicity blitz that followed was intended to attract investors with estimates of booty of up to $500 million. Salvage operations quickly produced almost two hundred artifacts that further fueled the publicity campaign. In their haste to obtain coins and other valuables, Harrington and his associates dredged up the ship's galley and dozens of human skeletons, which were dumped back into the water without being recorded. Meanwhile the finds were announced with headlines such as the *New York Times*'s "18TH-CENTURY WRECK YIELDS GOLD RING AND TROVE OF COINS" (Brodeur, 1988: 45).

At this point Harrington's earlier partners reasserted their claim before the U.S. District Court in Wilmington. Harrington had previously recovered the ship's bell, coins, and other items in violation of the licensing agreement, and now he ordered these items replaced on the seabed and "rediscovered" them on 10 October 1984 for the state's benefit (Brodeur,

1988: 46). By November the salvage efforts had lost momentum, and in 1985 Harrington was effectively bought out. A new company continued the search for treasure with a team of fourteen divers using a shipboard air lift and a modified gold-mining sluice. This system was unwieldy and led to delays, but about three thousand seven hundred artifacts were recovered. The take included only fifty-seven coins – far less than was needed to pay the $837,000 that had been invested in this second phase of the *DeBraak* project.

Harrington now began to explore alternative ways to recover the treasure and hired an underwater archaeologist, David Beard, from East Carolina University, who, with a team of three Sub-Sal divers, videotaped and surveyed the wreck in anticipation of another round of salvage. These efforts led to a proposal to place the wreck on a cradle and move it to provide access to portable artifacts and other loose items that were believed to have fallen from it and settled in the silt underneath. A barge crane was used to move a nearly 21-meter section of the *DeBraak*'s hull after dislodging it with high-pressure water jets and hoisting it in a sling. The hull was placed on a specially designed steel cradle to be lifted to the surface at a controlled rate of 45.7 centimeters per minute to minimize damage. With the media present and a storm bearing down, however, the salvors lifted the *DeBraak* more quickly, and soon afterward it was discovered that as much as 22.7 cubic meters of silt within the hull had been washed away in the process. David Beard called this an "archaeological disaster" (Brodeur, 1988: 54).

The lift was followed by salvage of the underlying silts using a barge-mounted bucket crane and a gravel screener. Any pretense at archaeology was abandoned at this point, with artifacts of all kinds, along with human remains, being dredged up in large amounts. Despite the removal and sluicing of thousands of cubic meters of silt, few coins were found. With operating costs of $70,000 per week, the salvors were losing their gamble to recover marketable treasure, and they closed down the project in November 1985. Curators at the Delaware Division of Historical and Cultural Affairs continued to inventory, conserve, and house the roughly twenty thousand artifacts, plant remains, and other items recovered. The archaeological value of this material has yet to be determined, since most of it was not collected under controlled conditions or recorded in accordance with accepted archaeological standards.

The history of the *DeBraak* venture reveals some important aspects of the conduct of treasure hunting. Every step of the project depended upon the sale of whatever was found. The press was manipulated to lure investors into supporting the project. Adversarial relationships developed between rival claimants and the state government, resulting in prolonged litigation. The treasure hunters spent at least as much time talking to lawyers and in court as they did on site. The treasure hunters were willing to relocate items associated with the wreck to suit their purposes. "Salting" the site was acceptable behavior. Advanced technologies were used to locate and extract the materials from sites, but components of the shipwreck that were poor candidates for sale were destroyed. Archaeologists were co-opted and even hired, presumably in part to increase the appearance of legitimacy. The courts and government officials took ambiguous positions, sometimes offering tacit support for the treasure hunters. No firm concept of the public interest emerged until after the damage had been done. The image of angst-stricken archaeologists wringing their hands after the fact is also familiar in such cases. Finally, the gambler's instinct guided the effort throughout. L. John Davidson, a real-estate entrepreneur who took over from Harrington in 1985, is quoted as saying, "I realized that I had become involved in a gigantic crapshoot" (Brodeur, 1988: 52). All of these features were at odds with good archaeological science and the preservation and care of submerged cultural resources.

The Spoils of the *Geldermalsen*

The case of the *Geldermalsen*, a Dutch East India Company ship that sank in 1752 near Indonesia, highlights what often happens to the artifacts obtained through treasure hunting. The ceramic specialist George L. Miller (1987) has reviewed how over one hundred and fifty thousand Chinese porcelain pieces and other valuables were mined from the wreck site in 1985 by Capt. Michael Hatcher, a British treasure hunter based in Singapore. Hatcher made no pretense at archaeology on the *Geldermalsen*. Although the wreck contained excellent associations, with the porcelains still in their original crates, no effort was made to record these associations or to preserve any part of the wreck site. The artifacts recovered were dubbed "The Nanking Cargo" for marketing purposes and were sold at auction by Christie's Amsterdam in April 1986.

The role of Christie's Amsterdam here was at least as important as Hatcher's. Treasure hunting is market-driven, and Christie's Amsterdam advertised itself as a clearing house for "shipwreck sales" (*Auction News from Christie's*, April 1986). Without ready buyers and the market provided by Christie's and other similar outlets treasure hunters would have little or no financial incentive for their activities. Christie's Amsterdam was particularly aggressive in its promotion of the *Geldermalsen* porcelains. In addition to fears that this flood of Chinese porcelains would depress their prices, there was concern that they were simply mass-produced tableware intended for sale to the European middle classes. Faced with the task of boosting the sale value of these objects in order to make a profit, the auction house broke up the collection and parceled it out to suppliers for interior decorators. Bloomingdale's, a trendsetter in this field, purchased more than 3,000 pieces, advertising them as "a rare opportunity to bring museum-quality artifacts into your home" (*Boston Globe*, 21 November 1986). Instead of the anticipated $4.5 million, the collection brought in $16 million, with many pieces earning ten to fifteen times the catalogue value.

An apparent anomaly in the marketing of the collection noted by Miller was Christie's reluctance to identify its source by name. At first glance one might think that such an attribution, with its historic associations with the Dutch East India Company, could only have served to enhance the value of the objects from the wreck. And, indeed, two bronze cannons from the wreck with Dutch East India Company markings were shown in a supplement to the catalogue and sold at auction along with an illustration of the ship's bell dated 1747 in this same publication. Miller points out, however, that when the Dutch East India Company went bankrupt in 1798, its ownership was transferred to the Batavian Republic, which became the Kingdom of the Netherlands in 1813, and thus the Dutch government claimed ownership of all the company's wrecks. Title to a wreck, which derives from continuous ownership or a traceable record of ownership transfer, must of course be weighed against *access*, and the possibility that the *Geldermalsen* wreck site lay within Indonesian territorial waters had resulted in a lawsuit by the Indonesian government against Christie's claiming that the wreck was illegally excavated. The case of the *Geldermalsen*, however, illustrates how such claims are possible on the basis of the principle of access as well as title. In cases before the fact — that is, before salvors, treasure hunters, or archaeologists approach a wreck site —

the principle of access is generally more important, since governments usually have effective means of controlling access.

Business as Usual?

Treasure hunting extends from seemingly innocent efforts to remove souvenirs such as brass plates and bronze portholes from a wreck to display on a shelf or mantelpiece to high-tech operations in deep water using modern remote-sensing techniques and ROVs from well-equipped mother ships. Objects of all kinds recovered from wrecks are displayed and marketed in "shipwreck fairs." Pervading all these activities is the assumption that these are "found" objects that may be taken and kept or sold by anyone who finds them. On land such activities are usually viewed as theft; why is this not the case underwater?

Increasingly, in fact, the same standards of law and behavior are being applied equally to submerged antiquities and to buried antiquities on land. This trend has been slow and halting, but there is visible movement. A significant step in the United States was the Abandoned Shipwreck Act of 1987. The importance of this law is largely symbolic, since except for national parks and sanctuaries, it delegates the details of coverage and enforcement to the individual states. It does, however, represent the first recognition by the U.S. government of a public interest in preserving submerged cultural resources, especially shipwrecks. It departs from the earlier Law of Wreck and Salvage (Marvin, 1858), which encouraged and rewarded salvage efforts, in acknowledging that 'historic shipwrecks that contain both historic information and tangible artifacts are subject to salvage operations, with resultant loss of historical information and artifacts to the public' (Report to Accompany Public Law 100–298, *Abandoned Shipwreck Act of 1987*, 14 March 1988: 2). However, it addresses only matters of title and remains silent about access. Not surprisingly, it has led to a patchwork of legislation in the various states. Arkansas and Texas, for example, have well-designed programs that have brought uniformity to the management of archaeological resources both on land and underwater. Florida and other states along the East Coast, in contrast, have either no programs at all or programs that continue to split the take with salvagers and treasure hunters (as Delaware did in the case of the *DeBraak*). In 1989, eighteen of the thirty states with laws regarding shipwrecks still permitted the commercial recovery of shipwrecks, and one, Washington, allowed the finder to keep 90 percent of the wreck's value (Giesecke, 1989: 101).

Another, somewhat unexpected problem is the reluctance of the federal courts to give up any of their traditional admiralty jurisdiction (Pelkofer, 1996: 64). In the case of the wreck of the *Brother Jonathan*, a 1,360-ton, double side-wheeled paddle steamer reported carrying a military payroll that struck a reef off Point St. George, northwestern California, in 1865, the state of California was unable to convince a federal district judge that the shipwreck had been definitely abandoned. His consequent voiding of the state's claim opened the door to further claims by the salvagers, contradicting the provisions of the Abandoned Shipwreck Act of 1987 and leading to an appeal by the state that is being heard by the U.S. Supreme Court (Greenhouse, 1997).

The federal court's narrow definition of abandonment is currently invoked by treasure hunters who purchase interests in vessels by locating an insurer of the wreck and offering it a percentage of the value of items recovered (Pelkofer, 1996: 65). They are encouraged to use this approach because the federal courts will allow challenges to claims of title by individual states, despite the provisions of the law. In the case of the *Brother Jonathan*, the Federal District Court and the U.S. Court of Appeals for the Ninth Circuit effectively overruled the act by dismissing the statute that the United States claims title to any abandoned shipwreck and can transfer such title to individual states.

A cynic might say that, despite the act, the situation is one of business-as-usual in many states. As public awareness grows, however, there are signs that treasure hunters in U.S. waters are finding it harder to carry on as they did before. Treasure-hunting activities have declined since the mid-1980s (Giesecke, 1989: 101), and creative approaches have been developed to involve the public in shipwreck and maritime preservation. Even enforcement has turned in a new direction. To see how times are changing, one need only compare the federal court decision in Florida in 1981 in favor of the treasure-hunter Mel Fisher's claim to ownership of the *Atocha* and five other wrecks in state waters with the recent federal court decision in Florida against the company founded by Fisher, Salvors Inc., for causing environmental damage at shipwreck sites within the Florida Keys National Marine Sanctuary (*New York Times*, 3 August 1997). The enforcement process in this case was indirect, but it does reflect a new willingness to pursue such cases – a "sea change" in attitudes toward submerged antiquities in the United States. One impetus behind the Abandoned Shipwreck Act of 1987 was a concern on the part of the Congress to limit the damage done by treasure hunters using advanced technologies – a reaction to entrepreneurial excess that was at last recognized as damaging to the public interest in shipwrecks as a historical and recreational resource.

An Alternative Solution from Australia

More coherent and proactive steps taken by other nations can serve as models for the protection of shipwrecks and other submerged cultural resources. There is a growing appreciation for the nonmarket value of historic shipwrecks and an increased willingness to regard them in the same way as environmental and natural resources (Kaoru and Hoagland, 1994). Nowhere is this appreciation more evident than in Australia, where a Historic Shipwrecks Act was first enacted in 1976 in the state of Western Australia and the Australian Territories and has since been extended to the waters of all of the Australian mainland states (Henderson, Lyon, and MacLeod, 1983).

Arguably the most historically significant shipwreck currently being excavated by underwater archaeologists in Australia is the HMS *Pandora*, the ship sent from England to Tahiti in 1790 to search for and capture mutineers from the crew of HMS *Bounty*. While most of the *Bounty* mutineers had already fled to Pitcairn Island, fourteen men who had remained behind on Tahiti were captured and imprisoned in a specially constructed brig aboard the ship (referred to as the "*Pandora*'s Box") for transport back to England. On 28 August 1791 the ship ran aground on a portion of Australia's Great Barrier Reef near the eastern approach to the Torres Strait. It struck hard and sank in 30–33 meters of water. Four mutineers were drowned along with thirty-one of the ship's company. Captain Edward Edwards had had the prisoners handcuffed and leg-ironed as the ship was sinking and given orders to shoot any who attempted to escape. After the captain had abandoned the ship, the bosun's mate had allowed the mutineers to swim free, and ten had joined the survivors. Together with the captain and other surviving members of the ship's company, they eventually made their way to Batavia and arrived in England in June 1792

(Henderson, Lyon, and MacLeod, 1983: 30). After its loss, the exact location of the *Pandora* was forgotten.

The wreck of the *Pandora* was finally located in November 1976 by the British documentary-filmmaker John Heyer and the naturalist Steve Domm, who were later joined on site by Ben Cropp. Their search was aided by an aerial magnetometer survey conducted by a Royal Australian Air Force "Neptune" patrol plane (Gesner, 1991). A magnetometer "hit" led the searchers to a cluster of objects on the seabed that included cannons, a large Admiralty-pattern anchor (a good clue for dating and identifying the wreck), pieces of copper hull sheathing, and ceramic items. Among these finds was a collection of rudder fittings resting on top of the reef, suggesting that the ship had lost all or part of its rudder before it sank in deeper water (Gesner, 1991: 28). Later investigation confirmed the identification of the wreck as that of the *Pandora* when a rudder pintle found on top of the reef was cleaned and found to bear the mark of the Broad Arrow (which identified it as the property of the crown) and the inscription "FORBES," a well-known eighteenth-century English foundry and supplier of bronze ship fittings to the Royal Navy.

An archaeological survey conducted by Graeme Henderson (Henderson, 1980; Clark and Jeffery, 1984) quickly confirmed the wreck's historical significance and led to the application of the Historic Shipwrecks Act to protect the site. In 1981 a no-entry zone of 500 meters around the site was established, with entry requiring a permit from the Federal Minister for Arts, Tourism, and Territories or the Director of the Queensland Museum (Gesner, 1991: 31). Furthermore, a $10,000 reward was paid to the finders for reporting the find and leaving the materials on the site. Efforts are under way to increase the bounties paid to divers when they report new finds (Henderson, Lyon, and MacLeod, 1983: 31) and to permit the finders to participate in further work at the site under archaeological supervision. The incentives provided by the act have already had positive results.

Since the initial survey, several archaeological field programs have been carried out on the *Pandora*. The 1986 field season, for example, produced human skeletal remains, navigation instruments, a flintlock pistol, hourglasses, and ceramics – a total of 786 portable artifacts. The most intriguing finds from this season, however, were Polynesian artifacts that were being transported back to England as curiosities when the ship was wrecked. These items, which included three ornately decorated war clubs, assorted fishing lures and hooks, and a stone poi pounder, afforded anthropologists a unique opportunity to study a well-documented and dated ethnographic collection from an early phase of European contact with traditional cultures in the South Pacific. Work at the *Pandora* site, with increasing emphasis on details of the ship's construction, is continuing under the leadership of the maritime archaeologist Peter Gesner at the Queensland Museum. There are plans to place these materials on public exhibition at the Queensland Museum following completion of the basic research and conservation.

The case of the *Pandora* highlights the positive effects of well-designed legislation for preserving important culture-historical resources that might otherwise be lost to treasure hunters or relic collectors. In international waters, however, shipwrecks remain open to plunder and destruction despite a strongly worded UNESCO Convention on Cultural Property that is widely recognized and accepted by museum organizations and archaeological societies. The obvious problem is that treasure hunters, their auction houses, and their customers can disregard these organizations and the UNESCO Convention with impunity, since these bodies lack enforcement powers. The advanced technologies of underwater location and recovery that initially threatened shipwrecks and antiquities in shallow water are now being extended to the ocean depths (Carrell, 1996: 75). So far, the high cost of deepwater shipwreck recovery has limited the number and extent of these efforts, but that situation can be expected to change. It remains to be seen who will get there first with these new technologies – the treasure hunters or the archaeologists.

Underwater Archaeology in the Twenty-First Century

We have seen how the scope of underwater archaeology has broadened and how it has become better-controlled and more analytical. We have also witnessed an increasing interest in applying the results of underwater archaeology to broader questions of social history and social science. Rapid advances in marine technology are being matched by increased awareness of the postdepositional factors affecting submerged sites. These accomplishments serve as a basis for exploring the characteristics of the cultures that produced shipwrecks and the remains of maritime infrastructure.

Underwater archaeology as a scholarly enterprise is taking its place as good archaeological science and is achieving a more convincing integration of the physical study of site remains and conclusions about past human behavior.

These changes should not, however, be viewed as simple advances in archaeological science. Just as the archaeological study of ships presents a complicated picture of branchings, variable rates of change, dead ends, and unexpected outcomes, so does the development of the discipline itself. While technical improvements abound, they produce ironies and contradictions that make the long-term outlook for the discipline problematic. The same advanced technologies that support better work in underwater archaeology also provide new entrepreneurial opportunities for treasure hunters as they move their efforts farther offshore. The underwater archaeologist Toni Carrell (1996) has cast this dilemma in almost Darwinian terms, suggesting that underwater archaeologists must either adapt to these new conditions with better efforts at public education and awareness and more effective involvement with the legal system or risk becoming extinct. She points out that treasure hunters increasingly mimic the methods of underwater archaeology in order to achieve their goals. Aided by the media and by high-profile marketing, they offer the public spectacle instead of science, and Carrell suggests that this may be what the public wants. The problem for underwater archaeologists will be to decide how much to accommodate such public demands in order to gain support. As she notes (1996: 75), today's treasure hunters are cultivating a new image. Dressed in business suits instead of cutoffs and Hawaiian prints, toting briefcases instead of sacks of doubloons, the new breed talk of "sustainable recovery" of "commercially viable shipwrecks" using "cutting-edge technology" that will result in "tourism enhancement" and "edutainment products." In short, there is no guarantee that better archaeological science underwater will produce more and better-quality underwater archaeology. The very improvements we have seen in underwater archaeology could conceivably lead to its demise as treasure hunters appropriate new subsea technologies to exploit (and, as a consequence, destroy) potentially profitable sites.

Scholars sometimes have difficulty engaging the public, especially through media presentations controlled by reporters, publicists, and other figures who may be more interested in a good story or in encouraging celebrity than in accuracy. Underwater archaeologists have, however, often presented their findings effectively, especially on television. Excellent underwater and maritime documentaries appear on public television as well as in a variety of BBC productions. Programs such as those on *La Trinidad Valencera* and the PBS production "The Navigators" are fascinating accounts based upon solid research. They demonstrate that it is possible to present a good story in underwater archaeology and maritime history without compromising good scholarship and serve as models for this kind of media activity. The trouble is that the treasure hunters enjoy at least as much media exposure and are completely uninhibited in their efforts to capture public attention. Media executives endorse such efforts by pointing out that the press is obliged to present all sides of an issue. True though this is, it also serves the interests of the press by providing the kind of copy that sells well. High-minded evocations of freedom of the press should not be allowed to obscure the essentially self-serving manner in which the media encourage treasure hunters to present their case. In a sense, everyone is an expert when it comes to the study of human behavior, past or present, and without the benefit of archaeological training it is difficult for most readers and TV viewers to judge the accuracy or legitimacy of the treasure hunters' claims. No untrained person would presume to offer expert opinions in fields like molecular biology or quantum physics, but archaeology seems to attract such unqualified opinions. It will never be easy for underwater archaeologists to challenge the treasure hunters effectively in an arena where the public is encouraged to form opinions based upon a superficial exposure to their field of expertise.

The publicity generated by treasure hunters can have ripple effects that extend to other domains. During our underwater archaeology program on the wreck of the *Vixen* in Bermuda, the site was visited each day by a large glass-bottomed tour boat. The bow of the wreck was above water, and some of the wreckage could be viewed in the shallow parts of the site. It was our practice to recall our divers whenever this boat appeared to avoid safety problems in the water, and they would assemble on the surface near the *Vixen*'s bow. Sound carries across water, and we could hear the tour guide each day telling the tourists about the wreck. One day we heard that the *Vixen* was a World War I troop transport that had been torpedoed by a German U-boat (see also Benchley, 1989: 75), with the loss of two hundred soldiers and sailors. On another day we were told that it was a passenger liner that had struck the reef and sunk with a locker full of gold bullion later recovered by the Bermudian treasure hunter Teddy Tucker. On yet another occasion it was a private yacht damaged in a hurricane and towed to its present location, where it sank. The tour operator seemed to be dreaming up a new sea story about the *Vixen* every time he left Hamilton harbor for the wreck site. This was harmless enough, of course, and one might even say it was just good fun – exactly the sort of entertainment that treasure hunters provide the public on demand.

With this kind of activity in mind, underwater archaeologists are often tempted to simplify their presentations to avoid being too technical. By contrast, the treasure hunters take great pains to look and sound like archaeologists by employing as much technical razzle-dazzle as possible and by inventing historical scenarios for their finds. The publicity war between underwater archaeology and treasure hunting is structured by the protagonists' operating at cross-purposes to gain legitimacy and support. It is small wonder that the public is often confused about the differences between them.

Alternative Pasts and Special-Interest Politics

Underwater archaeology requires greater political awareness now than ever before. Shipwreck studies often involve present-day interest groups, and seeking the support or approval of such groups can involve the archaeologist in politically charged rivalries, especially when the results of archaeological research are used to claim territory or cultural property. With such high stakes, underwater archaeologists can expect to see their results appropriated by groups whose goals may be totally contrary to their own. Land archaeologists are currently engaged in ongoing debates about whether to embrace or reject special-interest archaeology.

Historically, there is a compelling case to be made that archaeology has served as a tool for controlling and manipulating non-Western cultures, especially in the context of colonial and neocolonial domination. The Canadian archaeologist Bruce Trigger (1989: 110–47) describes what he terms the "imperial synthesis" of archaeology as an extension of European colonialism, especially during the late nineteenth century. Indigenous groups such as Native Americans and Australian Aborigines, for example, were marginalized and relegated to an inferior status by cultural stereotyping through the use of archaeological creations like the Mound Builder myth in North America and quasi-legal notions about Aborigines' lack of connection to their land in Australia. In the case of the Aborigines, nomadic movement was common and was accurately reflected in the archaeological record in many parts of Australia, but this in no way indicated that the Aborigines lacked structured relationships to their lands (a concept of ownership that is now termed "native title") equivalent to possession based upon agriculture. These were simply convenient myths to help rationalize the seizure of native lands.

Some archaeologists have embraced political awareness as a major goal of the discipline. The British archaeologist Ian Hodder (1986) points to the existence of "alternative archaeologies" by various groups defined in terms of ethnic, nationalist, or feminist interests. Each of these groups has a version of the past that is intended to situate and support its role within the dominant society. Hodder interprets archaeology as an exercise in political control, using ideology as a tool. His view of alternative archaeologies extends even to such groups as the Biblical creationists and the amateurs who use metal detectors and even occult means to locate and interpret sites. This willingness to embrace any kind of archaeological interpretation as legitimate if it provides meaning for the group in question has more to do with freedom of expression than it does with scientific scholarship. Its main purpose is to bolster the identity of such groups in the face of dominant economic and cultural forces, and in most cases it is explicitly antiscientific. Science, from this perspective, is a mechanism of cultural dominance – something to be used to exclude alternative views of the past and to subjugate groups that adhere to those views.

This position is understandable as extreme cultural relativism, an extension of anthropology's long-standing tradition of studying non-Western societies in a manner that attempts to minimize ethnocentric bias. Relativism usually involves a degree of participant observation – that is, living with and participating in the activities of the people being studied, often encouraging close personal relationships. It also requires a disciplined understanding of the insider's point of view, which means learning the language and comprehending indigenous categories of thought and experience as fully as possible. Anthropologists habitually avoid judging other societies by the standards of their own. It is not surprising, therefore, that many of them should have come to view Western science as judgmental in that it presents a framework for evaluating behavior in non-Western contexts that is external to those contexts.

For contemporary neo-Marxists like Hodder ideology drives human history, whereas Marx fully appreciated the importance of ideology but accorded prime-mover status to the material relations of production. Both forms of Marxism are, however, profoundly ethnocentric. Historically they are the product of social and economic conditions in mid-to-late-nineteenth-century England, when the Industrial Revolution reached extremes of mass production and mass consumption with consequences for overseas imperial exploitation and the treatment of workers in factories and mills, aboard ships, and in similar situations. Marx addressed these conditions directly, and the social and economic relations he examined belonged exclusively to mercantile-capitalist Western societies and, by extension, to societies enmeshed in the web of colonial exploitation they generated. Non-Western societies that somehow eluded this exploitation did not fit well into this theory; the traditional kula of the Trobriand Islanders, for example, lacked any kind of mercantile-capitalist base and was structured along wholly different lines. There may, of course, have been non-Western societies that evolved their own mercantile-capitalist types of social order independently of the West, but projection of Marxist materialism onto the preindustrial and non-Western past risks the fallacy of affirming the consequent. The social order of past societies needs to be understood in the context of their own places and times. The apparent applicability of Marxist theories to non-Western colonial expansion masks important differences among nonindustrial and even nonmarket societies that found their own ways to exploit their neighbors as well as minorities within them. Marx notwithstanding, these past societies were not part of any linear sequence of evolutionary stages leading to the present global social order.

While Marxist theory is ethnocentric, there are grounds for thinking that science is not. Of course, science is a culturally constructed body of knowledge derived specifically from Western cultural and historical sources. Undeniably, too, it has been used to dominate. However, the cultural relativism that suggests to some that Western-derived science is no better than any other system of knowledge is itself the product of Western science. Archaeological science is neither to be feared because of its rigor nor disdained as ethnocentric or hegemonic. It continues to be the key to credibility in all branches of archaeology. Documentary evidence needs to be compared with and tested against the results of archaeological science. Such a testing process inevitably leads to a choice, among alternative ideas of the past, of the explanation that best accounts for the available evidence.

Archaeological theorists such as Michael Shanks and Christopher Tilley (1988) regard choosing a past as a political and moral act rather than a scholarly effort, viewing choice based upon scientific criteria as a way of appropriating the past that denies such ideas to "a multitude of pasts which cannot answer for themselves" (Shanks and Tilley, 1988: 136). This point of view essentially denies that there is a knowable past of any kind. About the only point on which they and I can agree is that R. G. Collingwood (1946) was right when he said that the past is truly over. Archaeologists and historians must construct ideas about the past, but I am arguing here that some ideas are better than others. Archaeologists should not be timid about applying the standards of science when making such choices. The goal of archaeology, as of all historical sciences, is to achieve progressively better − though necessarily imperfect − approximations of the past by choosing the best ideas in relation to the available evidence. Not all "pasts" are equally valid, despite the appeal they may have for special groups or individuals. Belief is one thing; scholarly acceptance is quite another, and it will rest on good archaeological science.

For underwater archaeologists, this problem of alternative pasts is critical, since it directly affects the preservation of the archaeological record. Embracing the sea stories made up by treasure hunters would be disastrous, because it would ensure the destruction of the submerged cultural resources upon which the discipline depends and which will be available to the public in the future. Such acceptance would undermine the credibility of underwater archaeology as a historical science. How far each underwater archaeologist will need to go to deal effectively with the threat of treasure hunting remains an individual decision. The future of underwater archaeology may well depend as much upon its practioners' willingness to engage and oppose the treasure hunters and their "phoney baloney" alternative pasts as upon further improvements in technique and theory.

References cited

Abandoned Shipwreck Act of 1987 1988 Report to accompany Public Law 100–298.

Abell, W. 1981 *The Shipwright's Trade*, London: Conway Maritime Press.

Alopaeus, H. 1984 Suomenlinnan vedenlaiset esteet (Suomenlinna's underwater fortifications), *Narinkka*, Helsinki: Helsinki City Museum Yearbook, pp. 18–58.

Ammerman, A. J., C. Matessi, and L. L. Cavalli-Sforza 1978 Some new approaches to the study of the obsidian trade in the Mediterranean and adjacent areas, in I. Hodder (ed.) *The Spatial Organisation of Culture*, Pittsburgh: University of Pittsburgh Press, pp. 179–196.

Arnell, J. 1979 *The Bermuda Maritime Museum and the Royal Naval Dockyard, Bermuda: Official Guide*, Bermuda.

Arnold, B. 1974 La barque gallo-romaine de la baie de Bevaix, Lake Neuchâtel, Switzerland, *International Journal of Nautical Archaeology and Underwater Exploration* 4: 123–126.

Arnold, J. B., III and R. Weddle 1978 *The Nautical Archaeology of Padre Island*, New York: Academic Press.

Arnold, J. B., III., G. M. Fleshman, D. B. Hill, C. E. Peterson, W. K. Stewart, S. R. Gegg, and G. P. Watts, Jr. (eds.) 1991 *The 1987 Expedition to the Monitor Marine Sanctuary: Data Analysis and Final Report*, Washington, DC: National Oceanic and Atmospheric Administration.

Ballard, G. A. 1980 *The Black Battlefleet*, Annapolis: Naval Institute Press.

Ballard, R. D. 1987 *The Discovery of the Titanic*, New York: Madison Press.

Bass, G. F. 1966 *Archaeology Under Water*, New York: Praeger.

Bass, G. F. (ed.) 1967 *Cape Gelidonya: A Bronze Age Shipwreck*, Philadelphia: Transactions of the American Philosophical Society 57.

Bass, G. F. 1982a Conclusions, in G. F. Bass and F. H. van Doorninck, Jr. (eds.) *Yassi Ada. A Seventh-Century Byzantine Shipwreck*, College Station: Texas A & M University Press, pp. 311–320.

Bass, G. F. 1982b The pottery, in G. F. Bass and F. H. van Doorninck, Jr. (eds.) *Yassi Ada: A Seventh-Century Byzantine Shipwreck*, College Station: Texas A & M University Press, pp. 155–188.

Bass, G. F. 1983 A plea for historical particularism in nautical archaeology, in R. A. Gould (ed.) *Shipwreck Anthropology*, Albuquerque: University of New Mexico Press, pp. 91–104.

Bass, G. F. 1986 A Bronze Age shipwreck at Ulu Burun (Kaş): 1984 campaign, *American Journal of Archaeology* 90: 269–296.

Bass, G. F. and F. H. van Doorninck, Jr. 1971 A fourth-century shipwreck at Yassi Ada, *American Journal of Archaeology* 21: 27–37.

Bass, G. F., D. A. Frey, and C Pulak 1984 A Late Bronze Age ship at Kaş, Turkey, *International Journal of Nautical Archaeology and Underwater Exploration* 13: 271–279.

Bauer, K. J. 1988 *A Maritime History of the United States*, Columbia: University of South Carolina Press.

Bax, A. and C. J. M. Martin 1974 A Dutch East Indiaman lost on the Out Skerries, Shetland, in 1771, *International Journal of Nautical Archaeology and Underwater Exploration* 3: 81–90.

Baxter, J. P., III. 1933 *The Introduction of the Ironclad Warship*, Cambridge: Harvard University Press.

Bearss, E. C. 1980 *Hardluck Ironclad*, Baton Rouge: Louisiana State University Press.

Bednarick, R. G. 1998 *An experiment in Pleistocene seafaring, International Journal of Nautical Archaeology and Underwater Exploration* 27: 139–149

Behar, R. 1986 Play Loot-O, *Forbes*, June: 146–149.

Bell, O. 1925 Escambia clay, *Florida on the Gulf*, November: 25–30.

Bellico, R. H. 1992 *Sails and Steam in the Mountains*, Fleischmanns, NY: Purple Mountain Press.

Benchley, P. 1989 A diver's map of Bermuda: here there be treasures, *New York Times Magazine*, 12 March: 70–75.

Bender, B. 1978 Gatherer hunter to farmer: A social perspective, *World Archaeology* 10: 204–222.

Bent, Lt. Col. (R. E.) and Maj. Nicholson (R. E.) 1857 Journal of the operations of the expedition to Kinburn in October, 1855, *Professional Papers of the Corps of Royal Engineers* 6: 130–139.

Binford, L. R. 1968 Post-Pleistocene adaptations, in S. R. and L. R. Binford (eds.), *New Perspectives in Archaeology*, Chicago: Aldine, pp. 313–341.

Birdsell, J. B. 1977 The recalibration of a paradigm for the first peopling of Greater Australia, in J. Allen, J. Golson, and R. Jones (eds.) *Sunda and Sahul*, New York: Academic Press, pp. 113–167.

Blake, W. and J. Green 1986 A mid-XVI century Portuguese wreck in the Seychelles, *International Journal of Nautical Archaeology and Underwater Exploration* 15: 1–23.

Boczar, M. L. 1866 The craft in use at the rivergate of Dunajec, *Mariner's Mirror* 52: 211–222

Bonino. M. 1978 Lateen-rigged medieval ships: New evidence from wrecks in the Po Delta (Italy) and notes on pictorial and other documents, *International Journal of Nautical Archaeology and Underwater Exploration* 7: 9–28.

Braidwood, R. J. and B. Howe 1960 *Prehistoric Investigations in Iraqi Kurdistan*, Chicago: Oriental Institute.

Brandon, C. 1996 Cements, concrete, and settling barges at Sebastos: Comparisons with other Roman harbor examples and the descriptions of Vitruvius, in A. Raban and K. G. Holmes (eds.) *Caesarea Maritima*, Leiden: E. J. Brill, pp. 25–49.

Braudel, F. 1972 *The Mediterranean and the Mediterranean World in the Age of Philip II*, Vol. 1, New York: Harper and Row.

Brodeur, P. 1988 The treasure of the *De Braak*, *New Yorker*, 15 August: 33–60.

Brønsted, J. 1960 *The Vikings*, Harmondsworth: Penguin Books.

Brownlee, W. 1985 *Warrior, The First Modern Battleship*, Cambridge: Cambridge University Press.

Brownlee, W. 1987 *H.M.S. Warrior*, *Scientific American* 257: 130–136.

Butlin, N. G. 1993 *Economics and the Dreamtime*, Cambridge: Cambridge University Press.

Cahill, D., D. Carroll, R. Davenport, S. McKenzie, and D. McPherson (eds.) 1983 *The Cerberus* (compiled documents and plans), Melbourne: Maritime Archaeology Association of Victoria.

Carpenter, J. and I. D. MacLeod 1993 Conservation of corroded iron cannon and the influence of degradation on treatment times, *10th Triennial Meeting, ICOM Committee for Conservation*, Washington, DC, pp. 759–766.

Carrell, T. L. 1996 Mutate, migrate, adapt, or die, *Common Ground* 1: 72–75.

Casson, L. 1971 *Ships and Seamanship in the Ancient World*, Princeton: Princeton University Press.

Casson, L. 1991 *The Ancient Mariners*, Princeton: Princeton University Press.

Casson, L. and J. R. Steffy (eds.) 1991 *The Athlit Ram*, College Station: Texas A & M University Press.

Catling, H. W. 1964 *Cypriot Bronzework in the Mycenean World*, Oxford: Oxford University Press.

Cederlund, C. O. 1983 *The Old Wrecks of the Baltic Sea*, BAR 186, Oxford.

Chapelle, H. I. 1967 *The Search for Speed under Sail, 1700–1855*, New York: Norton.

Childe, V. G. 1936 *Man Makes Himself*, London: Watts.

Christensen, A. E. 1996 Proto-Viking, Viking and Norse craft, in A. E. Christensen (ed.), *The Earliest Ships*, London: Conway Maritime Press, pp. 72–88.

Cipolla, C. 1965 *Guns, Sails, and Empires*, New York: Barnes and Noble.

Clark, D. 1974 Contributions to the later prehistory of Kodiak Island, Alaska, *Archaeological Survey of Canada, Paper No. 20*, Ottawa.

Clark, J. G. D. 1952 *Prehistoric Europe: The Economic Basis*, London: Methuen.

Clark, J. G. D. 1954 *Excavations at Star Carr*, Cambridge: Cambridge University Press.

Clark, P. and B. Jeffery 1984 Surveying the *Pandora*: the methodology and techniques used on the 1983 *H.M.S. Pandora* survey, *Bulletin of the Australian Institute for Maritime Archaeology* 8: 17–23.

Clowes, W. L. L. 1894 The ram in action and accident, *Journal of the Royal United Service Institution* 38: 223–233.

Clowes, W. L. L. 1902 The naval campaign of Lissa, 1866, in *Four Modern Naval Campaigns*, London: Unit Library, pp. 1–71.

Coates, J. F. 1989 The trireme sails again, *Scientific American* 260: 96–103.

Collingwood, R. G. 1946 *The Idea of History*, Oxford: Oxford University Press.

Collins, H. B. 1937 *Archaeology of St. Lawrence Island, Alaska*, Smithsonian Miscellaneous Collections Vol. 96, Washington, DC.

Conlin, D. 1994 The Loggerhead Reef Ship Trap: Maritime Formation Processes on DRTO-036 and Beyond, MA. thesis, Brown University, Providence, RI.

Cornewall-Jones, R. J. 1898 *The British Merchant Service*, London: Sampson Low, Marston and Co.

Crumlin-Pedersen, O. 1967 Parallel to Dunajec craft, *Mariner's Mirror* 53: 31.

Crumlin-Pedersen, O. 1972 Skin or wood? A study of the origin of the Scandinavian plankboat, in O. Hasslof (ed.) *Ships and Shipyards, Sailors and Fishermen*, Copenhagen: pp. 208–234.

Crumlin-Pedersen, O. 1991 Ship types and sizes, A.D. 800–1400, in O. Crumlin-Pedersen (ed.) *Aspects of Maritime Scandinavia*, Roskilde: Viking Ship Museum, pp. 41–54.

Dalton, G. 1975 Karl Polanyi's analysis of long-distance trade and his wider paradigm, in J. A. Sabloff and C. C. Lamberg-Karlovsky (eds.) *Ancient Civilization and Trade*, Albuquerque: University of New Mexico Press, pp. 63–132.

Darby, H. C. 1962 The clearing of the woodland in Europe, in W. L. Thomas, Jr. (ed.) *Man's Role in Changing the Face of the Earth*, Chicago: University of Chicago Press, pp. 183–216.

Deetz, J. 1967 *Invitation to Archaeology*, New York: Doubleday.

Deetz, J. 1977 *In Small Things Forgotten*, New York: Doubleday.

De Laguna, F. 1956 Chugach prehistory: The archaeology of Prince William Sound, Alaska, *University of Washington Publications in Anthropology* 13, Seattle.

Desmond, C. 1919 *Wooden Ship-Building*, New York: Rudder Publishing.

Dixon, J. E., J. R. Cann, and C. Renfrew 1968 Obsidian and the origins of trade, *Scientific American* 218: 38–46.

Downing, J. and E. C. Harris 1984 Bermuda's floating docks, *The Bermudian* 55: 19–21.

Doyère, C. 1895 *Mécanique du Navire*, Paris: Challamel.

Dreijer, M. 1986 *The History of the Åland People*, Mariehamn: Almqvist and Wiksell.

Dunnell, R. C. and W. S. Dancey 1983 The siteless survey: A regional scale data collection strategy, in M. B. Schiffer (ed.) *Advances in Archaeological Method and Theory, Vol. 6*, New York: Academic Press, pp. 267–287.

Edwards, R. 1972 *Aboriginal Bark Canoes of the Murray Valley*, Adelaide: Rigby.

Ellmers, D. 1994 The cog as cargo carrier, in R. W. Unger (ed.) *Cogs, Caravels and Galleons*, London: Conway Maritime Press, pp. 29–46.

Ellsworth, L. F. 1974 Raiford and Abercrombie: Pensacola's premier antebellum manufacturer, *Florida Historical Quarterly* 52: 247–260.

Empereur, J. 1999 Diving on a sunken city, *Archaeology*, March/April: 36–46.

Evans, A. C. 1994 *The Sutton Hoo Ship Burial*, London: British Museum Press.

Fallon, N. 1978 *The Armada in Ireland*, Middletown, CT: Wesleyan University Press.

Farb, R. M. 1985 *Shipwrecks: Diving the Graveyard of the Atlantic*, Birmingham, AL: Menasha Ridge Press.

Fenwick, V. 1978 *Graveney Boat*, BAR 53, Oxford.

Fernández-Armesto, F. 1989 *The Spanish Armada*, Oxford: Oxford University Press.

Finney, B. R. 1977 Voyaging canoes and the settlement of Polynesia, *Science* 196: 1277–1285.

Finney, B. R. 1985 Anomalous westerlies, El Niño, and the colonization of Polynesia, *American Anthropologist* 87: 9–26.

Finney, B. R. 1988 Voyaging against the direction of the trades: A report of an experimental canoe voyage from Samoa to Tahiti, *American Anthropologist* 90: 401–405.

Firth, R. 1983 Magnitudes and values in kula exchange, in J. W. and E. R. Leach (eds.) *The Kula*, Cambridge: Cambridge University Press, pp. 89–102.

Fitzgerald, M. A. 1994 The ship, in J. P. Oleson, M. A. Fitzgerald, A. Sherwood, and S. E. Sidebotham (eds.) *The Harbours of Caesarea, Vol. 2*, BAR 594, Oxford, pp. VI.E.2-VI.N.

Flannery, K. V. 1967 Culture history vs. culture process: A debate in American archaeology, *Scientific American* 217: 119–122.

Flexner, J. T. 1944 *Steamboats Come True*, Boston: Little, Brown and Co.

Flick, C. 1975 Muntz Metal and ships' bottoms: The industrial career of G. F. Muntz, *Transactions of the Birmingham and Warwickshire Archaeological Society* 87: 71–84.

Foley, V. and W. Soedel 1981 Ancient oared warships, *Scientific American* 244: 148–163.

Ford, J. A. 1959 Eskimo prehistory in the vicinity of Pt. Barrow, Alaska, *Anthropological Papers of the American Museum of Natural History, Vol. 47 (1)*, New York.

Franzén, A 1961 *The Warship Vasa*, Stockholm: Norstedts.

Frost, H. 1972a The discovery of a Punic ship, *International Journal of Nautical Archaeology and Underwater Exploration* 1: 113–164.

Frost, H. 1972b Ancient harbours and anchorages in the eastern Mediterranean, in UNESCO (ed.) *Underwater Archaeology: A Nascent Discipline*, Paris: United Nations, pp. 95–114.

Frost, H. 1973 First season of excavation on the Punic wreck in Sicily, *International Journal of Nautical Archaeology and Underwater Exploration* 2: 33–49.

Frump, R. and T. Dwyer 1983 Death ships, *Philadelphia Inquirer*, 1–3 May.

Gardiner, R. (ed.) 1979 *All the World's Fighting Ships, 1860–1905*, London: Conway Maritime Press.

Gentry, R. C. 1984 Hurricanes in South Florida, in P. J. Gleason (ed.) *Environments in South Florida II*, Coral Gables: Miami Geological Society.

Gesner, P. 1991 *Pandora: An Archaeological Perspective*, Brisbane: Queensland Museum.

Giddings, J. L. 1964 *The Archaeology of Cape Denbigh*, Providence: Brown University Press.

Giesecke, A. G. 1989 Abandoned Shipwreck Act – Business as usual?, *Sea Technology*, April: 101.

Gladwin, T. 1970 *East is a Big Bird*, Cambridge: Harvard University Press.

Glasgow, T., Jr. 1964 The shape of the ships that defeated the Spanish Armada, *Mariner's Mirror* 50: 177–187.

Glassie, H. 1968 *Pattern in the Material Folk Culture of the Eastern United States*, Philadelphia: University of Pennsylvania Press.

Gould, R. A. 1988 The *U.S.S. Monitor* Project research design, in W. B. Cogar (ed.) *Naval History: The Seventh Symposium of the U.S. Naval Academy*, Wilmington: Scholarly Resources, Inc., pp. 83–88.

Gould, R. A. 1990a *Recovering the Past*, Albuquerque: University of New Mexico Press.

Gould, R. A. 1990b Underwater construction at the Royal Naval Dockyard, Bermuda, *Bermuda Journal of Archaeology and Maritime History* 2: 71–86.

Gould, R. A. 1990c The case of the "two Gibraltars" in nautical history, in T. L. Carrell (ed.) *Underwater Archaeology Proceedings from the Society for Historical Archaeology Conference*, Society for Historical Archaeology, pp. 21–26.

Gould, R. A. 1991 The archaeology of *HMS Vixen*, an early ironclad ram in Bermuda, *International Journal of Nautical Archaeology and Underwater Exploration* 20: 141–153.

Gould, R. A. 1995 The Bird Key wreck, Dry Tortugas National Park, Florida, *Bulletin of the Australian Institute for Maritime Archaeology* 19: 7–16.

Gould, R. A. and D. Conlin 1999 Archaeology of the "Barrel Wreck," Loggerhead Key, Dry Tortugas National Park, *International Journal of Nautical Archaeology and Underwater Exploration* 28: 207–228.

Gould, R. A., E. C. Harris, and J. R. Triggs 1991 The 1991 archaeological field season at Fort Cunningham, Bermuda, *Bermuda Journal of Archaeology and Maritime History* 3: 65–83.

Gould, R. A., E. C. Harris, and J. R. Triggs 1992 The 1992 archaeological field season at Fort Cunningham, Bermuda, *Bermuda Journal of Archaeology and Maritime History* 4: 21–57.

Gould, R. A. and D. J. Souza 1996 History and archaeology of HM Floating Dock, *Bermuda, International Journal of Nautical Archaeology and Underwater Exploration* 25: 4–20.

Granger, F. 1934 *Vitruvius on Architecture, Books I–IV*, Cambridge: Harvard University Press.

Green, C. 1963 *Sutton Hoo*, New York: Barnes and Noble.

Green, J. N. 1975 The VOC ship *Batavia* wrecked in 1629 on the Houtman Abrolhos, Western Australia, *International Journal of Nautical Archaeology and Underwater Exploration* 4: 43–63.

Green, J. N. 1983a The Song Dynasty shipwreck at Quanzhou, Fujian Province, People's Republic of China, *International Journal of Nautical Archaeology and Underwater Exploration* 12: 253–261.

Green, J. N. 1983b The Shinan excavation, Korea: An interim report on the hull structure, *International Journal of Nautical Archaeology and Underwater Exploration* 12: 293–301.

Green, J. N. 1989 *The AVOC Retourship Batavia Wrecked in Western Australia, 1629*, BAR 489, Oxford.

Green, J. N. 1990 *Maritime Archaeology: A Technical Handbook*, London: Academic Press.

Green, J. N. 1996 Arabia to China – The oriental tradition, in A. E. Christensen (ed.) *The Earliest Ships*, London: Conway Maritime Press, pp. 89–109.

Green, J. N. and R. Harper 1983 The excavation of the Pattaya Wreck site and survey of three other sites, Thailand, 1982, *Australian Institute for Maritime Archaeology Special Publication No. 1*, Fremantle.

Green, J. N. and V. Intakosi 1983 The Pattaya wreck excavation, Thailand: An interim report, *International Journal of Nautical Archaeology and Underwater Exploration* 12: 3–14.

Green, J. N. and Z. G. Kim 1989 The Shinan and Wando sites, Korea: Further information, *International Journal of Nautical Archaeology and Underwater Exploration* 18: 33–41.

Green, J. N. and R. Parthesius 1989 *Batavia* and a modern replica, *Bulletin of the Australian Institute for Maritime Archaeology* 13: 33–34.

Greenhill, B. 1993 The iron and steel sailing ship, in R. Gardiner (ed.) *Sail's Last Century*, London: Conway Maritime Press, pp. 74–97.

Greenhill, B. and A. Giffard 1988 *The British Assault on Finland: 1854–1855*, London: Conway Maritime Press.

Greenhill, B. and J. Morrison 1995 *The Archaeology of Boats and Ships*, Annapolis: Naval Institute Press.

Greenhouse, L. 1997 Supreme Court hears test of "treasure law," *New York Times*, 2 December.

Guilmartin, J.F., Jr. 1988 Early modern naval ordnance and European penetration of the Caribbean: The operational dimension, *International Journal of Nautical Archaeology and Underwater Exploration* 17: 35–53.

Gurcke, K. 1987 *Bricks and Brickmaking: A Handbook for Historical Archaeology*, Moscow, Idaho.

Haddon, A. C. and J. Hornell 1975 *Canoes of Oceania*, Honolulu: B. P. Bishop Museum.

Håfors, B. 1985 The preservation of the *Wasa*, in C. O. Cederlund (ed.) *Postmedieval Boat and Ship Archaeology*, BAR 256, Oxford, pp. 15–18.

Haldane, C. W. 1986 Archaeobotanical remains from four shipwrecks off Turkey's southern shore, paper presented at Fifth OPTIMA Conference, Istanbul.

Hamilton, D. 1981 Conservation of the *U.S.S. Monitor* plate, in D. B. Hill (ed.) Hull plate sample analysis and preservation, *U.S.S. Monitor Technical Report*, Raleigh, NC: North Carolina Division of Archives and History, pp. 52–66.

Hamilton, D. 1996 *Basic Methods of Conserving Underwater Archaeological Material Culture*, Washington, DC: U.S. Department of Defense Legacy Resource Management Program.

Harris, E. C. 1997 *Bermuda Forts: 1612–1957*, Somerset: Bermuda Maritime Press.

Hawkey, A. 1963 *H.M.S. Captain*, London: G. Bell and Sons.

Henderson, G. 1976 *James Matthews* excavation, summer 1974: An interim report, *International Journal of Nautical Archaeology and Underwater Exploration* 5: 245–251.

Henderson, G. 1984 Finds from *H.M.S. Pandora*, *International Journal of Nautical Archaeology and Underwater Exploration* 9: 237–243.

Henderson, G. 1986 *Maritime Archaeology in Australia*, Nedlands: University of Western Australia Press.

Henderson, G., D. Lyon, and I. MacLeod 1983 *H.M.S. Pandora*: Lost and found, *Archaeology* 36: 29–35.

Hennessy, J. B and J. du Plat Taylor 1967 The pottery, in G. F. Bass (ed.) *Cape Gelidonya: A Bronze Age Shipwreck*, Philadelphia: Transactions of the American Philosophical Society 57, pp. 126–130.

Herd, R. J. 1986 *H.M.V.S. Cerberus*: Battleship to breakwater, *Sandringham Historical Series* 3: 1–24.

Heyerdahl, T. 1950 *Kon Tiki*, New York: Simon and Schuster.

Hobsbawm, E. J. 1969 *Industry and Empire*, Harmondsworth: Penguin Books.

Hoffman, P., K. Choi, and Y. Kim 1991 The 14th-century Shinan ship: Progress in conservation, *International Journal of Nautical Archaeology and Underwater Exploration* 20: 59–64.

Hohlfelder, R. L. 1992 The changing fortunes of Caesarea's harbours in the Roman period, in R. L. Vann (ed.) *Caesarea Papers*, Ann Arbor: Journal of Roman Archaeology Supplementary Series No. 5, pp. 75–78.

Hole, F., K. V. Flannery, and J. A. Neely 1969 *Prehistory and Human Ecology of the Deh Luran Plain*, Ann Arbor: University of Michigan Museum of Anthropology.

Hornell, J. 1970 *Water Transport*, Cambridge: Cambridge University Press.

Hyde, A. P. 1982 Pearl Harbor, then and now, *After the Battle* 38: 53 pp.

Irwin, G. J. 1983 Chieftainship, kula, and trade in Massim prehistory, in J. W. and E. R. Leach (eds.) *The Kula*, Cambridge: Cambridge University Press, pp. 29–72.

Irwin, G. J. 1989 Against, across and down the wind: A case for the systematic exploration of the remote Pacific Islands, *Journal of the Polynesian Society* 98: 167–206.

Irwin, G. J. 1992 *The Prehistoric Exploration and Colonisation of the Pacific*, Cambridge: Cambridge University Press.

Irwin, G. J., S. H. Bickler, and P. Quirke 1990 Voyaging by canoe and computer: Experiments in the settlement of the Pacific, *Antiquity* 64: 34–50.

Johnstone, P. 1980 *The Sea-Craft of Prehistory*, Cambridge: Harvard University Press

Jones, G. 1989 *A History of the Vikings*, Oxford: Oxford University Press.

Jones, R. and B. Meehan 1977 Floating bark and hollow trunks, *Hemisphere* 21: 16–21.

Kaoru, Y. and P. Hoagland 1994 The value of historic shipwrecks: Conflicts and Management, *Coastal Management* 22: 195–213.

Katzev, M. L. 1974 Last harbor for the oldest ship, *National Geographic* 146: 618–625.

Katzev, M. L. 1982 Iron objects, in G. F. Bass and F. H. van Doorninck, Jr. (eds.) *Yassi Ada: A Seventh-Century Byzantine Shipwreck*, College Station: Texas A & M University Press, pp. 231–265.

Keegan, J. 1989 *The Price of Admiralty*, New York: Viking.

Keith, D. H. and C. J. Buys 1981 New light on medieval Chinese seagoing ship construction, *International Journal of Nautical Archaeology and Underwater Exploration* 10: 119–132.

Keith, D. H., J. A. Duff, S. R. James, T. J. Oertling, and J. J. Simmons 1984 The Molasses Reef wreck, Turks and Caicos Islands, B.W.I.: A preliminary report, *International Journal of Nautical Archaeology and Underwater Exploration* 13: 45–63.

Kemp, P. (ed.) 1976 *The Oxford Companion to Ships and the Sea*, London: Oxford University Press.

Kennedy, P. M. 1976 *The Rise and Fall of British Naval Mastery*, London: Ashfield Press.

King, W. H. 1879 *Lessons and Practical Notes on Steam, The Steam Engine, Propellers, etc.*, New York: Van Nostrand.

Kirsch, P. 1990 *The Galleon*, London: Conway Maritime Press.

Kivikoski, E. 1967 *Finland*, London: Thames and Hudson.

Knapp, A. B. 1993 Thalassocracies in Bronze Age eastern Mediterranean trade: Making and breaking a myth, *World Archaeology* 24: 332–347.

Knuth, E. 1952 An outline of the archaeology of Peary Land, *Arctic* 5: 17–33.

Konstam, R. A. 1988 16th century naval tactics and gunnery, *International Journal of Nautical Archaeology and Underwater Exploration* 17: 17–23.

Kvarning, L. A. 1985 The planning of a new museum for the *Wasa*, in C. O. Cederlund (ed.) *Postmedieval Boat and Ship Archaeology*, BAR 256, Oxford, pp. 27–37.

Lambert, A. 1984 *Battleships in Transition*, London: Conway Maritime Press.

Lambert, A. 1987 *Warrior: The World's First Ironclad Then and Now*, London: Conway Maritime Press.

Lampert, R. J. 1981 The great Kartan mystery, *Terra Australis* 5, Canberra: Australian National University.

Langille, R. 1998 *U.S.S. Constellation* restoration, *Maritime Archaeological and Historical Society (MAHS) News* 10: 1–3.

Laughton, J. K. (ed.) 1895 *State Papers Relating to the Defeat of the Spanish Armada*, 2 vols., London: Navy Research Society.

Lavery, B. (ed.) 1981 *Deane's Doctrine of Naval Architecture, 1670*, London: Conway Maritime Press.

Lavery, B. 1988 *The Susan Constant, 1605*, London: Conway Maritime Press.

Leach, E. R. 1983 The kula: An alternative view, in J. W. and E. R. Leach (eds.) *The Kula*, Cambridge: Cambridge University Press, pp. 529–538.

Leach, J. W. 1983 Introduction, in J. W. and E. R. Leach (eds.) *The Kula*, Cambridge: Cambridge University Press, pp. 1–26.

Leach, J. W. and E. R. Leach (eds.) 1983 *The Kula*, Cambridge: Cambridge University Press.

Lenihan, D. J. (ed.) 1987 *Shipwrecks of Isle Royale National Park*, Duluth: Lake Superior Port Cities, Inc.

Lenihan, D. J. (ed.) 1989 *U.S.S. Arizona Memorial and Pearl Harbor National Historic Landmark*, Santa Fe: National Park Service.

Lenihan, D. J. and L. E. Murphy 1989 Archaeological record, in D. J. Lenihan (ed.) *U.S.S. Arizona Memorial and Pearl Harbor National Historic Landmark*, Santa Fe: National Park Service, pp. 75–115.

Levathes, L. 1994 *When China Ruled the Seas*. Oxford: Oxford University Press.

Levison, M., R. G. Ward, and J. W. Wright 1973 *The Settlement of Polynesia: A Computer Simulation*, Minneapolis: University of Minnesota Press.

Lewis, A. R. and T. J. Runyan 1990 *European Naval and Maritime History, 300–1500*, Bloomington: University of Indiana Press.

Lewis, J. F. 1883 The attack on Lissa, 1866, *Professional Papers of the Corps of Royal Engineers* 9: 197–207.

Lewis, M. 1960 *Armada Guns*, London: Allen and Unwin.

Lipke, P. 1984 *The Royal Ship of Cheops*, BAR 225, Oxford.

Lolos, Y. G. 1993 Late Cypro-Mycenean seafaring: New evidence from sites in the Saronic and Argolic Gulfs, paper presented at symposium, *Cyprus and the Sea*, Nicosia: 25–26 September.

Lovell, A. and Associates Pty., Ltd. 1993 *Fort Gellibrand, Williamstown*, Melbourne: Department of Defense Conservation Management Plan.

Lubbock, B. 1922 *The Blackwall Frigates*, Glasgow: Brown, Son and Ferguson.

Lubbock, B. 1927 *The Last of the Windjammers*, Vol. 1, Glasgow: Brown, Son and Ferguson.

Lubbock, B. 1987 *The Down Easters*, New York: Dover Publications.

Lyon, Lt. Cmdr. F. and Lt. Cmdr. A. W. Hinds 1915 *Marine and Naval Boilers*, Annapolis: U.S. Naval Institute.

MacCutcheon, E. M. 1989 World War II development and expansion (1942–1945), in R. W. King (ed.), *Naval Engineering and American Seapower*, Baltimore: Nautical and Aviation Publishing Company of America, pp. 207–255.

MacGregor, D. R. 1993 The wooden sailing ship: Over 300 tons, in B. Greenhill (ed.) *Sail's Last Century*, London: Conway Maritime Press, pp. 20–41.

MacLeod, I. D., N. A. North, and C. J. Beagle 1986 The excavation, analysis and conservation of shipwreck sites, in *Preventive Measures during Excavation and Site Protection*, Rome: International Centre for the Study and the Restoration of Cultural Property, pp. 113–131.

Maddin, R., T. S. Wheeler, and J. D. Muhly 1977 Tin in the ancient Near East: Old questions and new finds, *Expedition* 19: 41–47.

Major-General "X" 1888 Bermuda, our oldest colony, *Illustrated Naval and Military Magazine* 9: 191–200.

Malinowski, B. 1922 *Argonauts of the Western Pacific*, London: Routledge.

Marsden, P. 1966 *A Roman Ship from Blackfriars*, London: Guildhall Museum.

Marsden, P. 1976 Boat of the Roman period found at Bruges, Belgium in 1899 and related types, *International Journal of Nautical Archaeology and Underwater Exploration* 5: 23–55.

Marsden, P. 1977 Celtic boats of Europe, in S. McGrail (ed.) *Sources and Techniques in Boat Archaeology*, BAR 29, Oxford, pp. 281–288.

Martin, C. J. M. 1972 *El Gran Grifón*: An Armada wreck on Fair Isle, *International Journal of Nautical Archaeology and Underwater Exploration* 1: 59–71.

Martin, C. J. M. 1973 The Spanish Armada expedition, 1968–70, in D. J. Blackman (ed.) *Marine Archaeology*, London: Archon Books, pp. 439–461.

Martin, C. J. M. 1975 *Full Fathom Five*, New York: Viking.

Martin, C. J. M. 1978 The *Dartmouth*, a British frigate wrecked off Mull, 1690, 5, the ship, *International Journal of Nautical Archaeology and Underwater Exploration* 7: 29–58.

Martin, C. J .M. 1979 *La Trinidad Valencera*: An Armada invasion transport lost off Donegal, *International Journal of Nautical Archaology and Underwater Exploration* 8: 13–38.

Martin, C. J. M. and G. Parker 1988 *The Spanish Armada*, New York: Norton.

Martinez, D. A. 1989 Historical record, in D. J. Lenihan (ed.) *U.S.S. Arizona Memorial and Pearl Harbor National Historic Landmark*, Santa Fe: National Park Service, pp. 13–73.

Marvin, W. 1858 *A Treatise on the Law of Wreck and Salvage*, Boston: Little, Brown and Company.

Mattingly, G. 1959 *The Armada*, Boston: Houghton Mifflin.

McCarthy, M. 1988 *S. S. Xantho*: The pre-disturbance assessment, excavation and management of an iron steam shipwreck off the coast of Western Australia, *International Journal of Nautical Archaeology and Underwater Exploration* 17: 339–347.

McCarthy, M. 1989a The *S. S. Xantho* project: Management and conservation, in I. MacLeod (ed.) *Conservation of Wood and Metal*, Fremantle: Western Australian Museum, pp. 9–12.

McCarthy, M. 1989b The excavation continues . . . in the laboratory, *Bulletin of the Australian Institute for Conservation of Cultural Materials* 15: 21–26.

McGhee, R. 1974 Beluga hunters: An archaeological reconstruction of the history and culture of the Mackenzie Delta Kittegaryumiut, *Newfoundland Social and Economic Studies No. 13*, Toronto: Memorial University of Newfoundland.

McGowan, A. 1980 *The Ship: The Century before Steam*, London: HMSO.

McGowan, A. 1981 *The Ship: Tiller and Whipstaff*, London: HMSO.

McGrail, S. 1975 The Brigg "raft" re-excavated, *Lincolnshire History and Archaeology* 10: 5–13.

McGrail, S. 1978 *Logboats of England and Wales*, BAR 51, Oxford.

McGrail, S. 1981 *The Ship: Rafts, Boats, and Ships*, London: HMSO.

McGrail, S. 1983 *Ancient Boats*, Aylesbury: Shire Publications.

McGrail, S. 1998 *Ancient Boats in North-West Europe*, London: Longman.

McGrath, H. T., Jr. 1981 The eventual preservation and stabilization of the *U.S.S. Cairo*, *International Journal of Nautical Archaeology and Underwater Exploration* 10: 79–94.

McKusick, M. B. 1960 Aboriginal canoes in the West Indies, *Yale University Publications in Anthropology No. 63*, New Haven.

McNeill, W. H. 1982 *The Pursuit of Power*, Chicago: University of Chicago Press.

McPhee, J. 1990 *Looking for a Ship*, New York: Farrar Straus Giroux.

Millas, J. C. 1968 *Hurricanes of the Caribbean and Adjacent Regions, 1492–1800*, Miami: Academy of the Arts and Sciences of the Americas.

Miller, E. M. 1978 *U.S.S. Monitor: The Ship that Launched a Modern Navy*, Annapolis: Leeward Publications.

Miller, G. L. 1987 The second destruction of the *Geldermalsen*, *American Neptune* 47: 275–281.

Mindell, D. A. 1995 "The clangor of that blacksmith's fray": Technology, war, and experience aboard the *U.S.S. Monitor*, *Technology and Culture* 36: 242–270.

Morrison, I. A. 1980 Man-made islands in Scottish lochs, in K. Muckelroy (ed.) *Archaeology Under Water*, New York: McGraw-Hill, pp. 156–161.

Morrison, J. S. and J. F. Coates 1986 *The Athenian Trireme*, Cambridge University Press.

Mostert, N. 1974 *Supership*, New York: Knopf.

Muckelroy, K. 1978 *Maritime Archaeology*, Cambridge: Cambridge University Press.

Muckelroy, K. 1980a Prologue, in K. Muckelroy (ed.) *Archaeology Under Water*, New York: McGraw-Hill, pp. 6–11.

Muckelroy, K. 1980b Early cross-Channel shipping, in K. Muckelroy (ed.) *Archaeology Under Water*, New York: McGraw-Hill, pp. 62–67.

Murphy, L. E. 1981 Shipwrecks as a data base for human behavioral studies, in R. A. Gould (ed.) *Shipwreck Anthropology*, Albuquerque: University of New Mexico Press, pp. 65–89.

Murphy, L. E. 1993a Fort Jefferson National Monument archaeological record, in L. E. Murphy (ed.) *Dry Tortugas National Park*, Santa Fe: National Park Service, pp. 201–243.

Murphy, L. E. 1993b Windjammer Site (FOJE 003), in L. E. Murphy (ed.) *Dry Tortugas National Park*, Santa Fe: National Park Service, pp. 245–272.

Murphy, L. E. and R. W. Jonsson 1993a Environmental factors affecting vessel casualties and site preservation, in L. E. Murphy (ed.) *Dry Tortugas National Park*, Santa Fe: National Park Service, pp. 97–109.

Murphy, L. E. and R. W. Jonsson 1993b Fort Jefferson National Monument documented maritime casualties, in L. E. Murphy (ed.) *Dry Tortugas National Park*, Santa Fe: National Park Service, pp. 143–163.

Murphy, L. E. and T. G. Smith 1995 Submerged in the past, *Geo Info Systems*, October: 26–33.

Murray, R. 1874 *A Treatise on Marine Engines and Steam Vessels*, London: Lockwood and Co.

Nance, J. D. 1983 Regional sampling in archaeological survey: The statistical perspective, in M. B. Schiffer (ed.) *Advances in Archaeological Method and Theory, Vol. 6*, New York: Academic Press, pp. 289–356.

Needham, J. W. 1970 *Clerks and Craftsmen in China and the West*, Cambridge: Cambridge University Press.

Needham, J. W. 1971 *Science and Civilisation in China*, Vol. 4, Part 3, Cambridge: Cambridge University Press.

O'Connell, R. L. 1991 *Sacred Vessels*, Oxford: Oxford University Press.

Oertling, T. J. 1989a The Molasses Reef wreck hull analysis: Final report, *International Journal of Nautical Archaeology and Underwater Exploration* 18: 229–243.

Oertling, T. J. 1989b The Highborn Cay wreck: The 1986 field season, *International Journal of Nautical Archaeology and Underwater Exploration* 18: 244–253.

Oleson, J. P. and G. Branton 1992 The technology of King Herod's harbour, in R. L. Vann (ed.) *Caesarea Papers*, Ann Arbor: Journal of Roman Archaeology Supplementary Series No. 5, pp. 49–67.

One of Those on Board 1870 *Narrative of the Voyage of HM Floating Dock Bermuda from England to Bermuda*, London.

Paasch, Capt. H. 1890 *Illustrated Marine Encyclopedia*, Watford, UK: Argus Books.

Parker, A. 1980 Roman wrecks in the western Mediterranean, in K. Muckelroy (ed.) *Archaeology Under Water*, New York: McGraw-Hill, pp. 50–61.

Parkes, O. 1957 *British Battleships*, Annapolis: Naval Institute Press.

Pastor, X. 1992 *The Ships of Christopher Columbus*, London: Conway Maritime Press.

Pearson, C. 1987 *Conservation of Maritime Archaeological Objects*, London: Butterworth.

Pelkofer, P. 1996 A question of abandonment, *Common Ground* 1: 64–65.

Penderleith, H. J. and A. E. A. Werner 1971 *The Conservation of Antiquities and Works of Art*, London: Oxford University Press.

Penn, G. 1955 *Up Funnel, Down Screw!*, London: Hollis and Carter.

Phillips, C. R. 1994 The caravel and the galleon, in R. W. Unger (ed.), *Cogs, Caravels and Galleons*, London: Conway Maritime Press, pp. 91–114.

Playford, P. 1996 *Carpet of Silver: The Wreck of the Zuytdorp*, Nedlands: University of Western Australia Press.

Prange, G. W. 1981 *At Dawn We Slept*, Harmondsworth: Penguin Books.

Pryor, J. H. 1994 The Mediterranean round ship, in R. W. Unger (ed.), *Cogs, Caravels and Galleons*, London: Conway Maritime Press, pp. 59–76.

Pulak, C. 1988 The Bronze Age shipwreck at Ulu Burun, Turkey: 1985 campaign, *American Journal of Archaeology* 92: 1–37.

Raban, A. (ed.) 1989 *The Harbours of Caesarea Maritime, Vol. 1*, BAR 491, Oxford.

Raban, A. 1992 Two harbours for two entities?, in R. L. Vann (ed.) *Caesarea Papers*, Ann Arbor: Journal of Roman Archaeology Supplementary Series No. 5, pp. 68–74.

Redknap, M. 1984 *The Cattewater Wreck*, BAR 131, Oxford.

Redknap, M. 1985 *The Cattewater* wreck: A contribution to 16th Century maritime archaeology, in C. O. Cederlund (ed.) *Postmedieval Boat and Ship Archaeology*, BAR 256, Oxford, pp. 39–47.

Reed, R. 1978 *Combined Operations in the Civil War*, Annapolis: Naval Institute Press.

Renfrew, C. 1967 Cycladic metallurgy and the Aegean Early Bronze Age, *American Journal of Archaeology* 71: 1–16.

Renfrew, C. 1975 Trade as action at a distance, in J. A. Sabloff and C. C. Lamberg-Karlovsky (eds.) *Ancient Civilizations and Trade*, Albuquerque: University of New Mexico Press, pp. 1–59.

Renfrew, C. 1977 Alternative models for exchange and spatial distribution, in T. K. Earle and J. E. Ericson (eds.) *Exchange Systems in Prehistory*, New York: Academic Press, pp. 71–90.

Renfrew, C. and P. Bahn 1991 *Archaeology: Theories, Methods and Practice*, London: Thames and Hudson.

Renfrew, C., J. R. Cann, and J. E. Dixon 1965 Obsidian in the Aegean, *Annual of the British School of Archaeology at Athens* 60: 225–247.

Renfrew, C. and J. E. Dixon 1976 Obsidan in western Asia: A review, in G. Sieveking, I. H. Longworth, and K. E. Wilson (eds.) *Problems in Economic and Social Archaeology*, London: Duckworth, pp. 137–150.

Roberts, J. 1992 *The Battleship Dreadnought*, London: Conway Maritime Press.

Roberts, O. T. P. 1994 Descendants of Viking boats, in R. W. Unger (ed.) *Cogs, Caravels and Galleons*, London: Conway Maritime Press, pp. 11–28.

Robinson, W. S. 1981 Marine gribbles, shipworms, and wood piddocks, *International Journal of Nautical Archaeology and Underwater Exploration* 10: 12–14.

Rodger, N. A. M. 1986 *The Wooden World*, Glasgow: Collins.

Ronen, A. 1983 Late Quaternary sea levels inferred from coastal stratigraphy and archaeology in Israel, in P. M. Masters and N. C. Fleming (eds.) *Quaternary Coastline and Marine Archaeology*, New York: Academic Press, pp. 121–134.

Ropp, T. 1987 *The Development of a Modern Navy: French Naval Policy 1871–1904*, Annapolis: Naval Institute Press.

Rowland, M. J. 1995 Indigenous watercraft use in Australia: The "big picture" and small experiments on the Queensland coast, *Bulletin of the Australian Institute for Maritime Archaeology* 19: 5–18.

Rule, M. 1982 *The Mary Rose*, London: Conway Maritime Press.

Runyan, T. J. 1994 The cog as warship, in R. W. Unger (ed.) *Cogs, Caravels and Galleons*, London: Conway Maritime Press, pp. 47–58.

Sabloff, J. A. and W. L. Rathje 1975 The rise of a Maya merchant class, *Scientific American* 233: 73–82.

Sams, G. K. 1982 The weighing implements, in G. F. Bass and F. H. van Doorninck, Jr. (eds.) *Yassi Ada: A Seventh-Century Byzantine Shipwreck*, College Station: Texas A & M University Press, pp. 202–230.

Sandler, S. 1979 *The Emergence of the Modern Capital Ship*, Newark: University of Delaware Press.

Schiffer, M. B. 1987 *Formation Processes of the Archaeological Record*, Albuquerque: University of New Mexico Press.

Schiffer, M. B., T. E. Downing, and M. McCarthy 1981 Waste not, want not: An ethnoarchaeological study of reuse in Tucson, Arizona, in R. A. Gould and M. B. Schiffer (eds.) *Modern Material Culture: The Archaeology of Us*, New York: Academic Press, pp. 67–86.

Shanks, M. and C. Tilley 1988 *Social Theory and Archaeology*, Albuquerque: University of New Mexico Press.

Sharp, A. 1957 *Ancient Voyagers in the Pacific*, Harmondsworth: Penguin Books.

Sherratt, A. and S. Sherratt 1991 From luxuries to commodities: The nature of Mediterranean Bronze Age trading systems, in N. H. Gale (ed.) *Bronze Age Trade in the Mediterranean*, Oxford, pp. 351–384.

Sieveking, G. de G. 1954 Recent archaeological discoveries in Malaysia (1952–3), *Journal, Malayan Branch of the Royal Asiatic Society* 27: 224–233.

Simmons, J. J., III. 1988 Wrought-iron ordnance: Revealing discoveries from the New World, *International Journal of Nautical Archaeology and Underwater Exploration* 17: 25–34.

Simmons, J. J., III. 1993 A closer look at wrought-iron swivel guns: A case study, *Bermuda Maritime Museum Quarterly*, 6: 25–28.

Sinoto, Y. H. 1983 The Huahine excavation: Discovery of an ancient Polynesian canoe, *Archaeology*, March/April: 10–15.

Sinoto, Y. H. 1988 A waterlogged site on Huahine Island, French Polynesia, in B. A. Purdy (ed.) *Wet Site Archaeology*, Caldwell, NJ: Telford Press, pp. 113–130.

Smith, R. C. 1993 *Vanguard of Empire*, Oxford: Oxford University Press.

Somervell, P. and J. Maber 1986 The ironclad turret ship Huascar, *Warship* 37: 2–11.

South, S. 1979 Historic site content, structure, and function, *American Antiquity* 44: 213–237.

Souza, D. 1998 *The Persistence of Sail in the Age of Steam*, New York: Plenum.

Steffy, J. R. 1982a The reconstruction of the eleventh century Serçe Liman vessel: A preliminary report, *International Journal of Nautical Archaeology and Underwater Exploration* 11: 13–34.

Steffy, J. R. 1982b Reconstructing the hull, in G. F. Bass and F. H. van Doorninck, Jr. (eds.) *Yassi Ada: A Seventh-Century Byzantine Shipwreck*, College Station: Texas A & M University Press, pp. 65–86.

Steffy, J. R. 1985 The Kyrenia Ship: An interim report on its hull construction, *American Journal of Archaeology* 89: 71–101.

Steffy, J. R. 1994 *Wooden Ship Building and the Interpretation of Shipwrecks*, College Station: Texas A & M University Press.

Stenuit, R. 1972 *Treasures of the Armada*, London: Dutton.

Stewart, W. K. 1991 Multisensor visualization for underwater archaeology, *IEEE Computer Graphics and Applications*, March: 13–18.

Still, W., Jr. 1971 *Iron Afloat: The Story of the Confederate Armorclads*, Nashville: Vanderbilt University Press.

Sturges, W. 1993 Dry Tortugas oceanography, in L. E. Murphy (ed.) *Dry Tortugas National Park*, Santa Fe: National Park Service, pp. 27–49.

Svensson, B. O. 1988 *Pommern*, Mariehamn: Åland Nautical Club.

Swiny, H. W. and M. L. Katzev 1973 The Kyrenia shipwreck: A fourth century B.C. merchant ship, in D. J. Blackman (ed.) *Marine Archaeology*, London: Archon Books, pp. 339–359.

Symonds, Capt. T. E. 1866 On the present and future of the twin-screw system – its application to ships with broadside batteries and their construction, *The Engineer*, 13 April: 265–267.

Thackeray, J. 1927 *Josephus II, The Jewish War Books I–III*, Cambridge: Harvard University Press.

Throckmorton, P. 1964 *The Lost Ships*, Boston: Little, Brown, and Company.

Thucydides 1951 *The Peloponnesian War*, New York: Random House.

Tomalin, D., J. Cross, and D. Motkin 1988 An Alberghetti bronze minion and carriage from Yarmouth Roads, Isle of Wight, *International Journal of Nautical Archaeology and Underwater Exploration* 17: 75–86.

Toudouze, G. G., Ch. de la Roncière, J. Tramond, C. Rondeleux, C. Dollfus, and R. Lestonnat 1939 *Histoire de la Marine*, Paris: L'Ilustration.

Trigger, B. G. 1980 *Gordon Childe: Revolutions in Archaeology*, London: Thames and Hudson.

Trigger, B. G. 1990 *A History of Archaeological Thought*, Cambridge: Cambridge University Press.

Tuck, J. A. and R. Grenier 1981 A 16th-Century Basque whaling station in Labrador, *Scientific American* 245: 180–187.

Ucelli, G. 1950 *Le Navi de Nemi*, Rome: La Libreria dello Stato.

Unger, R. W. 1980 *The Ship in the Medieval Economy, 600–1600*, Montreal: McGill-Queens University Press.

U.S. Life Saving Service 1885–1909 *Annual Report of the Operations of the United States Life Saving Service*, Washington, DC: Government Printing Office.

van Doorninck, F. H., Jr. 1967 The seventh-century ship at Yassi Ada; Some contributions to the history of naval architecture, Ph.D. thesis, University of Pennsylvania.

van Doorninck, F. H., Jr. 1982a The hull remains, in G. F. Bass and F. H. van Doorninck, Jr. (eds.) *Yassi Ada: A Seventh-Century Byzantine Shipwreck*, College Station: Texas A & M University Press, pp. 32–64.

van Doorninck, F. H., Jr. 1982b The galley, in G. F. Bass and F. H. van Doorninck, Jr. (eds.) *Yassi Ada: A Seventh-Century Byzantine Shipwreck*, College Station: Texas A & M University Press, pp. 87–120.

Ville, S. 1993 The transition to iron and steel construction, in B. Greenhill (ed.) *Sail's Last Century*, London: Conway Maritime Press, pp. 52–73.

Waddell, P. J. A. 1986 The disassembly of a 16th century galleon, *International Journal of Nautical Archaeology and Underwater Exploration* 15: 137–148.

Wade, W. C. 1986 *The Titanic*, New York: Penguin.

Watts, G. P., Jr. 1985 Deep-water archaeological investigations and site-testing in the *Monitor* National Marine Sanctuary, *Journal of Field Archaeology* 12: 315–332.

Watts, G. P., Jr. 1988 Bermuda in the American Civil War: A reconnaissance investigation of archival and submerged cultural resources, *International Journal of Nautical Archaeology and Underwater Exploration* 17: 159–171.

Watts, G. P., Jr. 1989 Runners of the Union blockade, *Archaeology* 42: 32–39.

Watts, G. P., Jr. 1993 A decade of shipwreck research in Bermuda, *Bermuda Journal of Archaeology and Maritime History* 5: 12–57.

Weigand, P. C., G. Harbottle, and E. V. Sayre 1977 Turquoise sources and source analysis: Mesoamerica and the the Southwestern U.S.A., in T. K. Earle and J. E. Ericson (eds.) *Exchange Systems in Prehistory*, New York: Academic Press, pp. 15–34.

Weiner, A. 1976 *Women of Value, Men of Renown: New Perspectives in Trobriand Exchange*, Austin: University of Texas Press.

Wells, J. 1987 *The Immortal Warrior*, Emsworth, Hampshire: Kenneth Mason.

Wen Wu Editorial Committee 1975 Song Dynasty ship excavated near Quanzhou Harbor, *Wen Wu* 10: 1–34 (French summary by Salmon and Lombard).

Weslowsky, A. B. 1994 Review of *Archaeology, History, and Custer's Last Battle*, in *Journal of Field Archaeology* 21: 253–256.

Whittier, B. 1987 *Paddle Wheel Steamers and their Giant Engines*, Duxbury, MA: Seamaster.

Wilkinson, F. 1991 Doubloon or nothin', *Forbes*, March: 59–63.

Wilkinson, H. C. 1973 *Bermuda from Sail to Steam*, Oxford: Oxford University Press.

Willock, R. 1988 *Bulwark of Empire*, Somerset: Bermuda Maritime Press.

Wilson, D. M. 1966 Medieval boat from Kentmere, Westmorland, *Medieval Archaeology* 10: 81–88.

Wise, S. R. 1988 *Lifeline of the Confederacy*, Columbia: University of South Carolina Press.

Wood, G. and P. Somervell 1986 The ironclad turret ship *Huascar*, Part II, *Warship* 38: 86–94.

Woodward, D. 1982 *Sunk! How the Great Battleships were Lost*, London: Allen and Unwin.

Worcester, G. R. G. 1971 *The Junks and Sampans of the Yangtze*, Annapolis: Naval Institute Press.

Wright, E. V. 1976 *The North Ferriby Boats*, Greenwich: National Maritime Museum Monograph 23.

General index

Ship and site index